DRIGO GORDILLO MICHAEL PHILBRICK **WES GRAY** MEB FABER **POR**

SAMUEL LEE LEIGH DROGEN F

NSBERRY STEVEN GERMANI **CHARLES GRANT** PETER MLADINA CHRIS BRIGHTMAN

JON SEED MORGAN HOUS

VITALI KALESNIK **JOSEPH SHIM** ELROY DIMSON MIKE STAUNTON **MORGAN HOUS**

PAUL MARSH MORGAN HOUS

RRY RITHOLTZ **STEVE SJUGGERUD** NILS JENSON **TAVI COSTA** KEVIN SMITH

CULLEN ROCHE RU

NNEL **ADAM LUDWIN** TOM MCCLELLAN **CHARLIE BILELLO** STAN ALTSHULLER **ROB ARNOTT** NO

BECK **VITALI KALESNIK** ASWATH DAMODARAN **COREY HOFFSTEIN** JEREMY SCHWARTZ **NORBER**

LING ED EASTERLING **RICK FRIEDMAN** ANNA CHETOUKHINA **CHRIS MEREDITH** DAN RASMUSSEN

BER JONATHAN CLEMENTS **JOHN MAULDIN** TODD TRESIDDER **MICHAEL KITCES** JIM O'SHAUGHN

USTY GUINN BEN HUNT **EHREN STANHOPE** LARRY SWEDROE **ANDREAS CLENOW** ADAM BUTLE

THE BEST
INVESTMENT WRITING
VOLUME 2

Also by Meb Faber

*The Ivy Portfolio: How to Invest Like the Top
Endowments and Avoid Bear Markets*

Shareholder Yield: A Better Approach to Dividend Investing

*Global Value: How to Spot Bubbles, Avoid Market
Crashes, and Earn Big Returns in the Stock Market*

*Global Asset Allocation: A Survey of the World's
Top Asset Allocation Strategies*

Invest with the House: Hacking the Top Hedge Funds

*The Best Investment Writing – Volume 1: Selected
Writing From Leading Investors and Authors*

THE BEST INVESTMENT WRITING

Selected Writing From Leading Investors and Authors

VOLUME 2

Edited by
Meb Faber

Hh

HARRIMAN HOUSE LTD
18 College Street
Petersfield
Hampshire
GU31 4AD
GREAT BRITAIN
Tel: +44 (0)1730 233870
Email: enquiries@harriman-house.com
Website: www.harriman-house.com

First published in Great Britain in 2018

Hardback ISBN: 978-0-85719-673-6
eBook ISBN: 978-0-85719-674-3

British Library Cataloguing in Publication Data
A CIP catalogue record for this book can be obtained from the British Library.

Contents

INVESTMENT PORTFOLIOS, STRATEGIES & EDGES

PRICING& VALUATION

Contents

FREE EBOOK EDITION

Every owner of a physical copy of this edition of

The Best Investment Writing – Volume 2

can download the eBook for free direct from us at Harriman House,
in a format that can be read on any eReader, tablet or smartphone.

Simply head to:

ebooks.harriman-house.com/bestinvestwriting2

to get your free eBook now.

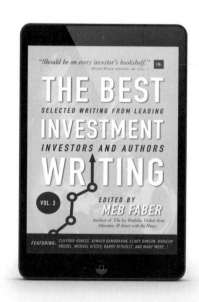

Introduction

—

MEB FABER

The signal in the noise...

While most of the public is not familiar with the term, if you're reading this book, there's a fair chance you are.

The phrase has its roots in the scientific and engineering communities, the etymology referring to the signal-to-noise ratio, which is a measure that compares the level of a desired signal to the level of ambient background noise. If the noise is too loud, the signal itself is lost.

Over the years, the term has become more popular within the investment community. It can refer to market trading signals – think stochastics, trend lines, or relative strength indicators – but it has also come to take on more metaphorical significance: the truth distinguished from the surrounding fluff.

Of course, there's a challenge. How does one accurately know what's the signal, and what's the noise?

Yahoo Finance is a popular website that provides investment information. Among the stock quotes and financial data, there's a tab called "Conversations." Here, any internet user logged into his or her Yahoo account can post a comment or opinion about a respective stock. I just clicked on the first stock I saw on Yahoo's website – J.C. Penney – and looked under the Conversations tab. At the time of this writing, there are 16,254 posts.

They cover the entire spectrum, ranging from seemingly-logically-sound reasons to buy J.C. Penney's stock immediately... to seemingly-logically-sound reasons to dump every share you own. But what's what? Which of these posts is the signal and which is the noise?

In my introduction to the first volume of *The Best Investment Writing* series, I highlighted this challenge. There are myriad investment "experts" out there, screaming their opinions at us with utmost certainty. Of course, many times, these opinions represent diametrically opposite perspectives, leaving the average retail investor baffled as to the right direction.

As serious investors, we need a better way. *The Best Investment Writing Volumes 1 & 2* represent our efforts to address this need. You're holding a collection of essays written over the last few months by some of the brightest, most successful figures in investing. Collectively, they manage hundreds of billions of dollars, are the most respected thought leaders of the investment universe, and are dedicated to improved investment market performance for their clients and themselves.

You're holding, quite literally, a volume of wisdom that comes from decades of market experience. It reflects countless hours of study and research, scores of historical back-tests, market hypotheses that played out as hoped, turning into massive wins, and calculated wagers that went all wrong, resulting in brutal losses. Simply put, it's market-tested wisdom that can help improve your own investing results.

Friends, I'm proud to bring you *The Best Investment Writing – Volume 2* – the signal distinguished from the noise. I hope you enjoy and benefit from it every bit as much as I have.

Good investing,

Meb

Meb Faber is donating to charity his author royalties from the sales of this book.

With thanks

I'd like to give a special shout out to Jeff Remsburg at Cambria Investment Management for all of the work he has put into making this book a reality, including helping me to compile the articles and pull everything together. Cheers, Jeff.—Meb.

MARKET CONDITIONS, RISK & RETURNS

The Evolution of Equity Markets

ELROY DIMSON, PAUL MARSH AND MIKE STAUNTON

To understand risk and return, we must examine long periods of history. This is because asset returns, and especially equity returns, are very volatile. In the *Global Investment Returns Yearbook 2018*, we document the financial market history of the 20th and 21st century to date. The core of the *Yearbook* is a long-run study covering the annual returns since 1900 from all the main asset categories in 23 countries and three regions, including a worldwide index. The unrivalled quality and breadth of the underlying dataset makes the *Yearbook* the global authority on the long-run performance of stocks, bonds, bills, inflation and currencies. Our new publication extends and brings up to date the key findings from our Princeton University Press book, *Triumph of the Optimists*.

The global database that underpins the *Yearbook* contains annual returns on stocks, bonds, bills, inflation, and currencies for 23 countries from 1900 to 2017 inclusive. The countries comprise the United States and Canada, ten countries from what is now the euro currency area (Austria, Belgium, Finland, France, Germany, Ireland, Italy, the Netherlands, Portugal, and Spain), six non-Eurozone markets in Europe (Denmark, Norway, Russia, Sweden, Switzerland, and the United Kingdom), four Asia-Pacific markets (Australia, China, Japan, and New Zealand) and one African market (South Africa). Together, at the start of 2018, these countries make up 91% of the investable universe for a global investor, based on free-float market capitalizations.

Our database also includes three regional indexes for equities and bonds denominated in a common currency, here taken as US dollars. These are a 23-country World index, a 22-country World ex-USA index and a

16-country Europe index. The equity indexes are weighted by each country's market capitalization, while the bond indexes are weighted by GDP.

All 23 countries experienced market closures at some point, mostly during wartime. In almost all cases, it is possible to bridge these voids and construct a returns history that reflects the experience of investors over the non-trading period. For 21 countries, we therefore have a complete 118-year history of investment returns, for which the *Yearbook* presents summary statistics and cross-country analysis, as well as detailed information on each individual market.

Russia and China, however, are exceptions since their markets were interrupted by long periods of communist rule. The expropriation of Russian assets after 1917 and Chinese assets after 1949 could be regarded as wealth redistribution, rather than wealth loss, but investors would not warm to this view. For these countries we have returns for the pre-communist era, and then for the period since these markets reopened in the early 1990s. We assume that shareholders and domestic bondholders in Russia and China suffered total wipeouts in 1917 and 1949, respectively, and we then re-include these countries in the World and regional index after their markets re-opened in the early 1990s and once reliable market indexes were initiated.

Our index series all commence in 1900, and this common start date aids international comparisons. Data availability and quality dictated this choice of start date, and for practical purposes, 1900 was the earliest plausible start date for a comparative international database with broad coverage.

Figure 1 shows the relative sizes of world equity markets at our starting date of end-1899 (upper panel), and how they had changed by end-2017 (lower panel). The lower panel shows that the US market dominates its closest rival and today accounts for over 51% of total world equity market value. Japan (8.6%) is in second place, ahead of the UK (6.1%) in third place. France, Germany, China, Canada and Switzerland each represent around 3% of the global market. Australia occupies ninth position with 2.4%.

In Figure 1, nine of the Yearbook countries – each representing 2% or more of world market capitalization – are shown separately, with 14 smaller markets grouped together as "Smaller Yearbook." The remaining area of the lower pie chart, labelled "Not in Yearbook," represents countries, comprising 9.3% of world capitalization, for which our data does not go all the way back to 1900. Mostly, they are emerging markets. Note that the lower panel of Figure 1 is based on the free-float market capitalizations of the countries in the FTSE All-World index, which spans the investable universe for a global investor. Emerging markets represent a higher proportion of the world total when measured using full-float weights, when investability criteria are relaxed, or if indexes are GDP-weighted.

The upper panel of Figure 1 shows the equivalent breakdown at the end-1899 start of the database. The chart shows that at the start of the 20th century, the UK equity market was the largest in the world, accounting for a quarter of world capitalization, and dominating even the US market (15%). Germany (13%) ranked in third place, followed by France, Russia, and Austria-Hungary. Non-Yearbook countries are again labelled "Not in Yearbook." In total, the dataset covers almost 98% of the global equity market at the start of 1900. By the end of 2017, our 23 countries still represented some 91% of the investable universe.

The volatile investment performance of individual countries raise two important questions. The first relates to survivorship bias. Investors in some countries were lucky, but others suffered financial disaster. If countries in the latter group are omitted, there is a danger of overstating worldwide equity returns. In 2013, we therefore added Russia and China to our database – the two best known cases of markets that failed to survive. China was a small market at the beginning of the 20th century, and even in the 1940s, but Russia accounted for some 6% of world market capitalization at end-1899.

Figure 1: Relative sizes of world stock markets, end-1899 versus end-2017

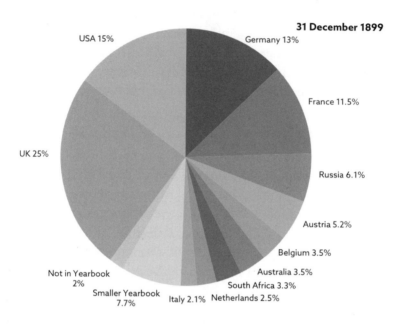

Source: E. Dimson, P. Marsh and M. Staunton, *DMS database* (2018).

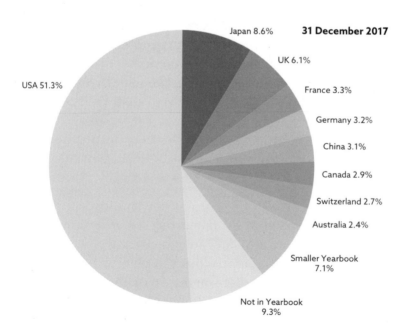

Source: FTSE Analytics, FTSE All-World Index Series (December 2017).

The second and opposite source of bias, namely success bias, is even more serious. In 2013 we also added Austria-Hungary, which had a 5% weighting in the end-1899 world index. While Austria-Hungary was not a total investment disaster, it was the worst-performing equity market and the second worst-performing bond market of our 21 countries with continuous investment histories. Adding Austria – as well as China and Russia – to our database and to the world index was important in eliminating non-survivorship and "unsuccess" bias. In 2014, we added another "unsuccessful" market, Portugal, to our dataset.

Figure 2 shows the evolution of global equity market share for key countries over the last 118 years. Early in the 20th century, the US equity market overtook the UK and has since then been the world's dominant stock market, although at the end of the 1980s Japan was very briefly the world's largest market. At its peak, at start-1990, Japan accounted for almost 45% of the world index, compared with around 30% for the USA. Subsequently, Japan's weighting fell to just 8%, reflecting its poor relative stock market performance since then. In contrast, the US has regained its dominance and today comprises 51% of total world capitalization.

The USA is by far the world's best-documented capital market. Prior to assembly of our database, the evidence cited on long-run asset returns was almost invariably taken from US markets and was typically treated as being universally applicable. Yet organized trading in marketable securities began in Amsterdam in 1602 and London in 1698 but did not commence in New York until 1792. Since then, the US share of the global stock market has risen from zero to 51%. This reflects the superior performance of the US economy, a large volume of IPOs, and the substantial returns from US stocks. No other market can rival this long-term accomplishment. But this makes it dangerous to generalize from US asset returns since they exhibit success bias. That is why we focus on global investment returns.

How should you respond to the fluctuating fortunes of markets from around the world? You may choose to be a country-picker, tilting your portfolio strongly towards countries that you think will outperform over the short and medium term. But you may make the wrong call: market timing can be dangerous. The safer option is to hold a globally diversified equity portfolio. That is the most important lesson we learn from our detailed study of financial market history.

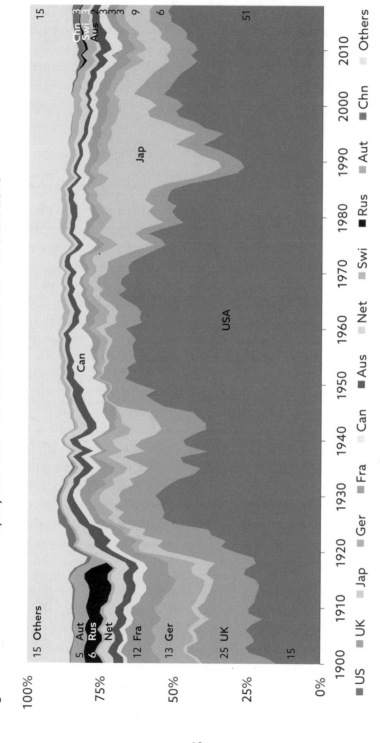

Figure 2: The evolution of equity markets over time from end-1899 to start-2018

Source: Elroy Dimson, Paul Marsh and Mike Staunton, *Global Investment Returns Yearbook 2018* (Credit Suisse Research Institute, 2018).

ABOUT ELROY DIMSON, PAUL MARSH AND MIKE STAUNTON

Elroy Dimson, Paul Marsh, and Mike Staunton jointly wrote the influential investment book, *Triumph of the Optimists*, published by Princeton University Press. They have authored the *Global Investment Returns Yearbook* annually since 2000. They distribute the *Yearbook*'s underlying dataset through Morningstar Inc. The authors also edit and produce the Risk Measurement Service, which London Business School has published since 1979. They each hold a PhD in Finance from London Business School.

Elroy Dimson is Chairman of the Centre for Endowment Asset Management at Cambridge Judge Business School, Emeritus Professor of Finance at London Business School, and Chairman of the Academic Advisory Board and Policy Board of FTSE Russell. He previously served London Business School in a variety of senior positions, and the Norwegian Government Pension Fund Global as Chairman of the Strategy Council.

He has published in *Journal of Finance, Journal of Financial Economics, Review of Financial Studies, Journal of Business,* Journal of Portfolio *Management, Financial Analysts Journal,* and other journals.

Paul Marsh is Emeritus Professor of Finance at London Business School. Within London Business School he has been Chair of the Finance area, Deputy Principal, Faculty Dean, an elected Governor and Dean of the Finance Programmes, including the Masters in Finance. He has advised on several public enquiries; was previously Chairman of Aberforth Smaller Companies Trust, and a nonexecutive director of M&G Group and Majedie Investments; and has acted as a consultant to a wide range of financial institutions and companies.

Dr Marsh has published articles in *Journal of Business, Journal of Finance, Journal of Financial Economics, Journal of Portfolio Management, Harvard Business Review,* and other journals. With Elroy Dimson, he co-designed the FTSE 100-Share Index and the Numis Smaller Companies Index, produced since 1987 at London Business School.

Mike Staunton is Director of the London Share Price Database, a research resource of London Business School, where he produces the London Business School Risk Measurement Service. He has taught at universities in the United Kingdom, Hong Kong and Switzerland. Dr Staunton is co-author with Mary Jackson of *Advanced Modelling in Finance Using Excel and VBA*, published by Wiley and writes a regular column for *Wilmott* magazine.

He has had articles published in *Journal of Banking & Finance*, *Financial Analysts Journal*, *Journal of the Operations Research Society*, *Journal of Portfolio Management*, and *Quantitative Finance*.

The Reasonable Formation of Unreasonable Things

An explanation of market bubbles that doesn't blame greed or incompetence, and a strategy to protect yourself from their inevitability.

―――――――

MORGAN HOUSEL

The majority of your lifetime investment returns will be determined by decisions that take place during a small minority of the time.

Most of those periods come when everything you thought you knew about investing is thrown out the window.

How you invested from 1990 to 1998 wasn't all that important. The choices you made from 1999 to 2001 shaped the rest of your investing career.

What you did from September 2008 to March 2009 likely had more impact on your lifetime investment returns than what happened cumulatively from 2002 to 2007, or from 2009 to 2017.

The pilot's famous answer when asked about his job—"Hours of boredom punctuated by brief moments of terror"—applies perfectly to investing. The brief moments of terror are the rise and fall of bubbles.

But there's a problem.

Bubbles are not like cancer, where a biopsy gives us a clear warning and diagnosis. They are more like the rise and fall of a political party, where the outcome is known in hindsight but the cause and blame are never settled on.

Competition for returns is fierce, and someone has to own every asset at every point in time. Which means the idea of bubbles will always be controversial in real time, and in hindsight we're more apt to blame than learn.

After suffering from financial bubbles for hundreds of years, we still don't have a good definition of what they are, let alone an understanding of why they happen. Without an easy and logical answer, most bubble commentary shifts to the comfort of attacking others (the Fed, banks, Congress) and, worse, assuming they're one-off accidents.

This is unfortunate, given how much impact they have on our investment results. As a rule of thumb, the more indignant you are, the harder it is to understand what's happening.

I've always considered it a cop-out to blame bubbles on greed and incompetence alone. This report will argue three points:

1. Bubbles are not anomalies or mistakes. They are an unavoidable feature of markets where investors with different goals compete on the same field. They would occur even if everyone was a financial saint.

2. Bubbles have less to do with rising valuations and more to do with shrinking time horizons among people playing a different game than you are.

3. Protecting yourself as an investor is mostly a function of understanding and acting upon your own time horizon, accepting that other people's goals are different than your own.

To make these points, we first have to understand the philosophies of a wild-haired economist named Hyman Minsky, who figured out decades ago that all financial markets are utterly incapable of sitting still.

1. The Inevitability of Insanity Among Sane People

The 1960s were a period of scientific optimism. In the previous 50 years the world had gone from horse and buggy to a man on the moon, and from bloodletting to organ transplants.

This caused a push among economists to try to eradicate the scourge of recessions. If we could launch intercontinental ballistic missiles, surely we could prevent two quarters of negative GDP growth.

Hyman Minsky, who spent most of his career at Washington University in St. Louis, was fascinated in the boom and bust nature of economies. He also thought the idea of eradicating recessions was nonsense, and always would be.

Minsky's seminal theory was called the financial instability hypothesis.

The paper itself wasn't heavy on math and formulas. It briefly explained the origin of financial crises that happen in the absence of an outside shock, like a war.

The instability hypothesis basically goes like this:

- When an economy is stable, people get optimistic.

- When people get optimistic, they go into ever increasing amounts of debt.

- When they pile on debt, the economy becomes unstable.

Minsky's big idea was that *stability is destabilizing*. A lack of recessions plants the seeds of the next recession. Which is why we can never get rid of them.

"Over periods of prolonged prosperity, the economy transits from financial relations that make for a stable system to financial relations that make for an unstable system," he wrote.

A growing belief that things will be OK pushes us, like a law of physics, toward something not going OK.

This applies to investments too.

To wrap your head around the inevitability of the financial instability hypothesis, you have to take it to its extreme.

Imagine a world where bear markets are somehow outlawed. Market stability is all but assured.

What would you do?

You would buy as many risky assets as you possibly could. You'd bid their valuation up to the point that their return prospects equaled other non-volatile assets, like FDIC-insured bank accounts.

That would be the *smart, rational* thing to do. Everyone would do it. And the seeds of breakdown would, at that moment, start to sprout.

The higher valuations become, the more sensitive markets are to being caught off guard from life's inevitable ability to surprise the hell out of you in ways you never imagined.

There are six inevitabilities that will always be present in any social gathering:

1. Incomplete information.

2. Uncertainty.

3. Randomness.

4. Chance.

5. Unfortunate timing.

6. Poor incentives.

With assets priced high and no room for error, the world would be hanging on by a thread, snipped at the first sniff of anything less than perfection.

The irony is that when markets are guaranteed not to crash—or, more realistically, when people think that's the case—they are far more likely to crash. The mere idea of stability causes a *smart and rational* movement toward bidding asset prices up high enough to cause instability.

Think of it this way. There are two states that financial markets can be in:

1. Knowing there will be an eventual decline.

2. Thinking there won't be an eventual decline, in which there will be one soon.

If Minsky were alive today, I imagine he'd describe investing like this:

1. If markets never crashed, they wouldn't be risky.

2. If they weren't risky, they would get really expensive.

3. When they're really expensive, they crash.

The important thing is realizing that crashes are not a mistake, or a bug. They don't (necessarily) indicate that politicians failed, the Fed screwed up, that companies are greedy, or that investors are short-sighted.

They would happen if everyone was a well-behaved financial saint. Because if assets didn't crash they wouldn't offer a big return. And since we want big returns we push them toward occasional crashes.

Constant and guaranteed volatility, like a law of physics.

2. When Reasonable Insanity Gets Out of Hand

There is a distinct difference between volatility and things getting completely out of hand.

Stocks fell 19% in the summer of 2011, and quickly recovered. That's volatility. The Nasdaq fell 80% after 2000, and didn't recover for a decade. That's something else.

But the fact that markets spread from volatile to utterly out of control—like a bubble—makes sense. *Rational sense.* It makes so much sense that we should expect it to keep happening.

One of the biggest flaws to come out of academic finance is the idea that assets have one rational price in a world where investors have different goals and time horizons.

Ask yourself: How much should you have paid for Yahoo! stock in 1999? The answer depends on who "you" are.

If you have a 30-year time horizon, the smart price to pay was a sober analysis of Yahoo!'s discounted cash flows over the subsequent 30 years.

If you have a ten-year time horizon, it's some analysis about the industry's potential over the next decade and whether management could execute on its vision.

If you have a one-year time horizon, it's an analysis of current product sales cycles and whether we'll have a bear market.

If you're a daytrader, the smart price to pay is "who the hell cares?," because you're just trying to squeeze a few basis points out of whatever happens between now and lunchtime, which can be accomplished at any price.

When investors have different goals and time horizons—and they do in every asset class—prices that look ridiculous for one person make sense to another, because the factors worth paying attention to are totally different.

People can look at Yahoo! stock in 1999 and say "This is crazy! A zillion times revenue! This valuation makes no sense!"

But many investors who owned Yahoo! stock in 1999 had time horizons so short that it made sense for *them* to pay a ridiculous price.

A daytrader could accomplish what they need whether Yahoo! was at $5 a share or $500 a share, as long as it moved in the right direction. Which it did, for years.

Money chases returns. Bubbles form when the momentum of short-term returns attracts enough money that the makeup of investors shifts from mostly long term to mostly short term.

That process feeds on itself. As traders push up short-term returns, they attract more traders. Before long—and it really doesn't take long—the dominant price-setters with the most authority are those with ever-shortening time horizons.

Bubbles aren't so much about valuations rising. That's just a symptom of something else: Time horizons shrinking. This might seem like subtle point, but it explains a lot about why the mere existence of bubbles confuses so many smart investors.

Valuations during the dot-com bubble made no sense if you were a long-term investor. But most participants were not long-term investors.

People say the bubble was rooted in irrational optimism about the future. Really? One of the most common headlines of that era was announcing record trading volume. Investors—particularly the ones setting prices—were not thinking about the next 20 years. The average mutual fund had 120% annual turnover in 1999, meaning they were, at most, thinking about the next eight months.

So were the individual investors who bought these funds. Maggie Mahar wrote in her book *Bull!*:

> "By the mid-nineties, the press had replaced annual scorecards with reports that appeared every three months. The change spurred investors to chase performance, rushing to buy the funds at the top of the charts, just when they were most expensive."

This was also the era of day trading, short-term option contracts, and up-to-the minute market commentary. Not the kind of thing you'd associate with investors excited about the prospects of the generation.

Same for the housing bubble.

It's hard to justify paying $700,000 for a two-bedroom Miami track home to raise your family in for the next 20 years. But it makes perfect sense if you plan on flipping it in a few months into a liquid market with price momentum. Which is exactly what many people were doing during the bubble.

Do you think people who own a property for just a few months before re-selling it care about long-term price-to-rent ratios? Of course not. It isn't relevant to their game.

You can say a lot about these investors.

You can call them speculators. You can call them irresponsible. You can shake your head at their willingness to take huge risks.

But I don't think you can call all of them irrational.

Bubbles aren't so much about people irrationally participating in long-term investing. They're about people somewhat rationally moving toward short-term trading to capture momentum that had been feeding on itself. What do you expect people to do when momentum creates a big short-term return potential? Sit and watch patiently? Never. That's what Minsky proved. And the short-term traders that flood in operate in an area where the rules governing long-term investing—particularly around valuation—are ignored, because they're irrelevant to the game being played.

Which makes bubbles more rational than they are often portrayed. It's why we'll always have them.

It's also why they're so dangerous.

3. Wandering to the Wrong Side of the Tracks

The dot-com bubble reduced household wealth by $6.2 trillion. The housing bubble cut away more than $8 trillion.

It's hard to say something so destructive "makes rational sense."

19

The disconnect between bubbles happening for rational reasons and doing huge societal harm comes down to people with different objectives thinking they're playing the same game.

Imagine a group of accountant buddies who want to play a friendly game of flag football. They find a field at a local park to play. There's even a group of players at the field who want to join them. They're 300-pound NFL players, suited up and ready to smash anyone in their way.

A coach in this situation would step in and say, "Whoa, guys, no. I know you're both playing football, but your goals are so different that you have to play on different fields."

The problem is that there's one field in investment markets, where the accountants have to play with the Raiders.

Think about the daytrader in 1999 whose marginal trade helped push Yahoo! stock to $430 a share. This trade made sense, because he thought shares would probably go to $431 by closing, when he'd sell.

Now think of the grocery store worker who was saving for her retirement 40 years down the road. If she wanted to invest in Yahoo! that day, $430 per share is the price she has to pay, because there's only one market price. And it's a price that, if taken, materially reduced her chance of retiring.

These two people rarely even know that each other exist. They're playing completely different games. But they're on the same field, running toward each other. When their paths collide, someone gets hurt.

Bubbles do damage when long-term investors mistakenly take their cues from short-term traders.

It's hard to grasp that other investors have different goals than we do, because an anchor of psychology is not realizing that rational people can see the world through a different lens than your own. When momentum entices short-term investors, and short-term investors dominate market pricing and activity, the long-term investor is at risk of seeing rising prices as a signal of long-term worth. Rising prices persuade all investors in ways the best marketers envy. They are a drug that can turn value-conscious investors into dewey-eyed optimists, detached from their own reality by the actions of someone playing a different game than they are.

Few things matter more in investing than understanding your own time horizon and not being persuaded by the price actions caused by people with different time horizons.

No matter what kind of investor you are, the key to success is not participating in a game other than the one you intended to play. And you can only do that if you make an effort to identify what games the people surrounding you are playing, separating them from your own. It is the only way I know of to have a reasonable shot at not getting sucked into bubbles in the first place.

This requires:

- Sizing up the value of news, commentary, and analysis based on whether it aligns with your own goals and time horizon, rather than its analytical merits alone.

- Paying extraordinary attention to things like volume and asset turnover in your industry, understanding that it reflects the marginal investor's time horizon, and tells you what game current prices are keeping score of.

The latter is particular important because of how bubbles play out.

All games eventually end, and the rational move toward short-term trading potential that defines bubbles eventually becomes tapped out, as Minsky wrote decades ago.

It's at these moments—when there's a transition from one game to the next—that bubbles do the most damage.

If you view the plunge in asset prices that marks the end of bubbles as an indication that everything you thought you knew about long-term investing is wrong, you end up using the end of someone else's game as an excuse to never again play your own. Like a passenger who questions whether it's safe to get on a plane because he sees hundreds of people eagerly getting off the previous flight.

It is the most devastating trick investors play on themselves.

Realizing that the rise and fall of bubbles does not negate the effectiveness of diversified long-term investing is one of the most powerful understandings an investor can have. And one of the hardest things an investor can do is maintain conviction on a long-term strategy when there's a changing of the guard between one game and the next.

These moments have outsized influence on your lifetime returns, because extreme high or low valuations magnify the impact of investment decisions. The exponential nature of compounding means that the decisions you make when assets are in a state of chaos are magnitudes more important than the ones you make when they're tranquil. This is why periods when markets are transitioning from one game to the next—perhaps 1% or 2% of your time as an investor—are so important.

Investing is seven parts emotional, three parts analytical. The emotional rollercoaster of bubbles will always be something even the smartest investors struggle with.

But a lot of the emotions—excitement, greed, fear, and frustration—stem from not knowing what bubbles are or why they're happening. Breaking the process down into two points:

1. Volatility has to happen for any asset to have decent long-term returns, and;

2. Sometimes that volatility gets out of hand when people with short time horizons become the dominant investors, pricing assets in ways that make no sense to long-term investors,

… is the strongest shield I know of to maintain a level head through the inevitable chaos.

Originally published June 2017;
www.collaborativefund.com/uploads/Collaborative%20Fund%20Bubbles.pdf.

ABOUT MORGAN HOUSEL

Morgan Housel is a partner at The Collaborative Fund.

He is a two-time winner of the Best in Business award from the Society of American Business Editors and Writers and a two-time finalist for the Gerald Loeb Award for Distinguished Business and Financial Journalism. He was selected by the *Columbia Journalism Review* for the

Best Business Writing 2012 anthology. In 2013 he was a finalist for the Scripps Howard Award.

@morganhousel

An Expert's Guide to Calling a Market Top

The landscape is filled with pundits
predicting the demise of the bull market.
Here's how to get in on the action.

———

BARRY RITHOLTZ

Everyone and members of his and her close family seem ready to call a market top.

You've heard the arguments and any number of permutations time and again: This bull market is geriatric, it's mainly a few overrated tech behemoths that account for all the gains, valuations are stretched and are too far ahead of fundamentals. So you figure if the clueless pundits can do it, why can't you? If you're in the money management business, you'd look like a star if you got this one right. So go ahead and give it a shot.

Well, we're here to help. And you do need help, since all the major market players have their top calls ready to go. But with the following step-by-step guide, we can make sure that your top call gets all due recognition and stands out from the pack. This is a can't-lose proposition:

No. 1. **Pick a bogeyman**: This is your first step to making a top call. Find whatever it is that will precipitate the next collapse, and home in on it. Tweet about it and write 5,000-word screeds explaining why this spells doom. The specific bogeyman isn't all that important—just so long as you have one. Some good starter examples are: the Federal Reserve (or zero interest rates or quantitative easing), the national debt, hyperinflation, or the collapse of the dollar. Or how about New York Stock Exchange margin debt or that robots will take away everyone's job? Mix and match these or be creative and invent a few of your own.

No. 2. **Cite household-name authority figures**: You may be little known, but there are lots of better-known folks out there who feel the way you do, or at least some of what they've said can be massaged to seem like they support your argument. As we learned with the Milgram experiment, people tend to place greater weight on the opinions of authority figures (this is true regardless of its actual content). Your best bets are to cite legendary investors and billionaires. Or try a self-help guru, the more famous, the better.

No. 3. **Always be confident**: The degree of confidence in your manner and voice is the key to getting a television audience to believe you. This, as we have noted before, is because the expert who prattles on without any hint of doubt is more likely to be believed by TV viewers.[1] Remember to avoid nuance, caveats or hedging. These only undermine the sense of authority you want to convey. Hint: Try not to read anything that challenges your viewpoint. It just makes the pose that much harder to maintain.

No. 4. **Pay attention to non-financial events**: Season your market calls with a helping of news drawn from the headlines (there's no penalty for not reading the stories). They are invariably compressed and potentially misleading, but referring to them lends a sense of urgency and timeliness to your forecast.

No. 5. **Pick a favored asset class**: Gold is always a good one, but it has been beaten to death by top-callers. You are better off with something that doesn't have a daily quoted price, the more exotic the better. Farmland is good too—think Argentina or New Zealand.

No. 6. **Charts, plenty of charts**: Once you have your bogeyman and your preferred asset class, fire up Google and collect as many charts as you can. Never mind selection bias; you want to overwhelm your challengers with as many tangentially related charts as humanly possible. Charts make you strong; lots of them make debunking difficult.

---

[1]   Also, the more self-confident an expert appears, the worse his or her track record is likely to be. Forecasters who get one single big outlier correct are more likely to underperform the rest of the time.

No. 7. **Claim vindication early and often**: Volatility is your friend. Use each move down as an opportunity to remind people of your call; toy with readers by asking questions: "Is this the beginning of the end?" You know when it just feels right. Be careful not to overplay your hand too soon; otherwise the reversal will kill you.

No. 8. **Don't forget the esoteric technical indicators**: The less followed, the more obscure and spurious the better. The Hindenburg Omen, death cross, VIX and Fibonacci are favorites. If you feel creative, data mine the CRSP US Stock Databases and make your own.

No. 9. **Ignore contradictory data**: This is important for two reasons. The first is simply that you don't want to present this as a debate, as that tends to confuse your followers. Instead, present this as a fait accompli. And more importantly, you always want to project an air of self-assuredness. Never acknowledge any doubt. TV viewers pick that up right away. If that happens, you're done.

No. 10. **Don't manage money**: This is important to all top-callers. If you manage capital for clients, your top call will raise all sorts of issues with them. You certainly can't be long the markets after your top call. Remember what the great Barton Biggs, Morgan Stanley's former strategist, said: "Bullish and wrong and clients are angry; bearish and wrong and they fire you."

These 10 bullet points should help every top-caller to make his or her mark. Best of luck!

Originally published July 7, 2017; bloom.bg/2r1tJwf.

Originally published on BloombergView.com

Bloomberg View copyright © 2017 Bloomberg LP

www.bloomberg.com/view/articles/2017-07-07/an-expert-s-guide-to-calling-a-market-top

---

ABOUT BARRY RITHOLTZ

Barry L. Ritholtz is the co-founder and chief investment officer of Ritholtz Wealth Management. Launched in 2013, RWM is a financial planning and asset management firm, with $850 million in assets. The firm offers a variety of services to the investing public, including LiftOff—a low cost online-only investment site.

Ritholtz is a frequent commentator on many financial topics. He was named one of the '15 Most Important Economic Journalists' in the United States, and has been called one of The 25 Most Dangerous People in Financial Media. He writes a daily column for Bloomberg View and a twice monthly column on Personal Finance and Investing for *The Washington Post*. Ritholtz is the creator and host of *Masters in Business*, a popular podcast on Bloomberg Radio.

Beyond his commentary and published articles, Mr. Ritholtz also authors *The Big Picture*—a leading financial weblog, generating several million page views per month. In 2008–09, Ritholtz wrote the book *Bailout Nation*, published by Wiley in 2009; the updated paperback was released in 2010.

Mr. Ritholtz performed his graduate studies at Yeshiva University's Benjamin N. Cardozo School of Law in New York. His undergraduate work was at Stony Brook University, where on a Regents Scholarship, he focused on Mathematics and Physics, graduating with a Bachelor Arts & Sciences degree in Political Science.

@ritholtz

Why $1 Trillion Will Soon Flow Into China

STEVE SJUGGERUD

This, my friend, is one of the greatest opportunities I have ever seen...

I never imagined I would see a day where NOBODY was invested in the world's second-largest economy and second-largest stock market. But that's where we are in early 2018.

Nobody owns locally traded Chinese stocks. But that will change in the coming years. And it's created a huge investment opportunity.

One trillion dollars—or more—should flow into Chinese stocks and bonds in the next five to seven years.

You see, fund managers will soon be forced to "rebalance" their portfolios to include more Chinese positions. It's a long story, but a powerful one, and the result is a lot more money in China.

The specifics of what's going on include a little-known, technical decision. Nobody is talking about it. But the story is simple at its core...

China is the world's second-largest stock market. It's larger than every other stock market in the world, except the U.S. But right now, *China's stock market is not included in world stock market indexes.*

That is crazy, when you think about it...

How can you have a complete, legitimate, world stock market index if you leave out the world's second-largest stock market?

Apple's iPhone operating system is the world's second-largest by market share (behind Google's Android). Would it be right to completely ignore the iPhone when talking about the global mobile-phone market?

That's what's happening with China right now.

It's clearly a wrong that needs to be righted.

As this story unfolds, it will cause a lot of money—as much as $1 trillion—to ultimately flow into China's stock market. We want to make sure we have our money there first.

The only question is when this wrong will be righted... But we actually already know the details.

The process began with a major decision in June 2017. Money will begin pouring in starting in 2018... and for years to come.

Before I explain the exact details of what's going on, you need to understand the incredible transformation that has occurred in China over the last 20 years.

This transformation, as much as anything, is why investing in China is a smart idea for the next few years at least.

Let me explain...

The Greatest Transformation I've Ever Seen

"No pictures! No pictures!" our guide screamed.

"Settle down, buddy," I thought... I didn't even have a camera.

It was 1996, and I was entering the doors of China's Shanghai Stock Exchange.

At first, I thought the guide was trying to protect state secrets. After going through the doors, my opinion changed...

"What a dump!" I thought. China wasn't protecting state secrets—it was protecting itself from embarrassment!

I had been to plenty of stock exchanges (back when people actually traded on them). And Shanghai's stock exchange in 1996 was the most embarrassing one I had ever seen.

It didn't feel like you were entering a stock exchange. It felt like you were entering a decrepit old hotel in New York City. You could tell it had been a special place a century ago. But those days were long gone. Nobody had cared for it in a very long time.

It turns out, that was exactly the case. The Shanghai Stock Exchange was located in what was formerly the Astor House Hotel. Only now, it was a youth hostel. For $10 to $20 a night, you could sleep in a cot—right next to stock exchange rooms.

It was dark. It was dingy. And it had the enthusiasm of a public library.

The few traders who were around (wearing little red vests) were typically asleep—faces down on their desks.

"No pictures" was the right policy.

I also visited China's other stock market exchange, the Shenzhen Stock Exchange, in 1996.

"No pictures!" my guide yelled. Yes, I knew the drill.

The Shenzhen Stock Exchange was a dramatic improvement. It was in a large building actually designed to be a stock exchange. It had a large, fancy quotation board inside and hundreds of computers at tiny, individual desks.

But it was dead. There were a couple of guys in red vests—once again, asleep over their keyboards—and that was about it.

Back then, if you'd told me that China's stock market (made up of the Shanghai and Shenzhen stock exchanges) would be the world's second-largest stock market less than 20 years later, I wouldn't have believed you.

The most optimistic China-lover couldn't have imagined it. The starting point for China almost 20 years ago was nothing.

The transformation from 1996 to now is the greatest I have ever seen.

The stock markets have grown at an unbelievable, exponential rate. The new buildings for the Shanghai and Shenzhen stock exchanges are cutting-edge architectural designs—and they're landmarks in each city.

I visited the new Shanghai stock exchange in 2016. Today, it's completely modern. It's also nearly empty, but that's because most trading is done electronically. It's nothing like what I saw 20 years prior

China's stock market has come a long way in 20 years. Farther than I could have ever imagined. It's truly the most incredible transformation I've seen in my lifetime.

That's another major reason why a major shift of money into Chinese stocks is about to take place.

The vote has already happened. And the flow of up to $1 trillion will begin into China's stock market in 2018.

Here are the exact details why...

How Fund Managers *Really* Operate

You might not believe me when I tell you this...

But most fund managers are wimps.

They aren't driven by making the most money for their investors. And they aren't driven by being the absolute best in their field.

What drives them? The desire to keep their easy jobs.

Most folks have no idea that this is how investment management really works. But fund managers are truly incentivized to not screw up. Think about it...

If a fund manager makes a crazy bet, there are two possible outcomes:

1. The bet works out, and investors see a slightly higher-than-normal return.

2. The bet doesn't work, and the manager underperforms because he took unnecessary risk.

In the first scenario, the manager might get a pat on the back, or a larger-than-normal year-end bonus. But if he's wrong, in the second scenario, there's only one outcome...

He gets fired.

In short, fund managers keep their jobs not by performing well... but by not performing poorly in their bosses' eyes.

How do their bosses measure their performance? Against a benchmark index.

To keep his job, the typical fund manager doesn't deviate his holdings much from his benchmark index. If the stocks you hold don't deviate from the stocks in your benchmark index, then you will never dramatically underperform—and you won't lose your job.

I don't blame these fund managers. But they're wimps. They make decisions with the sole intent of not getting fired.

Today, we have a way to take advantage of the simple fact that we know what these fund managers will do next. This is an unbelievable opportunity—one that I never thought I would see in my lifetime.

In short, the world's second-largest economy is NOT included in global benchmark indexes. But that's changing in 2018. And it means $1 trillion will flow into this market soon.

This won't happen overnight. But it WILL happen. We know it. And we want to get our money there first.

Here are the details...

Why $1 Trillion Will Flow Into Chinese Stocks

One trillion dollars will flow into Chinese stocks in the coming years.

That might sound crazy. But it's not crazy at all.

First, let's cover a few facts...

China is the world's second-largest economy today. It's second only to the U.S.

Country	GDP
United States	$19 trillion
China	$12 trillion
Japan	$5 trillion
Germany	$3 trillion
U.K.	$3 trillion

China also has the second-largest stock market in the world. China's stock market—especially the stocks trading in China's currency—is worth roughly $12 trillion in market value. That's around 8% of global market cap. And again, that's second only to the U.S. But China does NOT show up in global stock market indexes.

Country	GDP	MSCI World Stock Market Index Percentage
United States	$19 trillion	59%
China	$12 trillion	???
Japan	$5 trillion	9%
Germany	$3 trillion	4%
U.K.	$3 trillion	7%

This makes no sense.

How could China be the world's second-largest economy, and have the world's second-largest stock market, but NOT be included in global stock market indexes?

This is a wrong that has to be righted... And the process has already started with the MSCI Emerging Markets Index.

You see, the world's leading provider of benchmark indexes is MSCI. About $9.5 trillion is benchmarked to MSCI indexes. And $1.7 trillion of that is benchmarked to MSCI's Emerging Markets Index. Remember those wimpy fund managers we talked about? They mostly just try to match these indexes.

Right now, in early 2018, **stocks trading in China are not part of the MSCI Emerging Markets Index.**

They make up 0% of it. That's crazy.

China's stock market—stocks trading in China's currency—is worth $12 trillion in market value. It makes no sense that these Chinese stocks are NOT part of the major emerging markets index.

Chinese stocks should be THE MAJOR PART of an index of emerging market stocks... Instead, they make up 0%. This is nuts...

Stocks trading in China make up roughly 8% of the world's stock market value—and NOBODY OWNS THEM. You don't. I don't. And no major investors do, either.

This is about to change. MSCI announced a plan to include Chinese A-shares in June 2017. And when it goes into effect, it will force a flood of money into stocks trading in China—ultimately $1 trillion, as index providers like MSCI start to include local Chinese stocks (called "A-shares") in their indexes.

Now, before you object, MSCI actually DOES include something it calls "China" in its emerging markets index... But for the most part, these are not actually shares trading in China. They are typically businesses trading in Hong Kong.

MSCI is moving toward having more actual Chinese companies in its China indexes. It has already started…

It plans to begin including these stocks in 2018. Here are the details of their likely roadmap…

The MSCI Road Map for Chinese Stocks

MSCI announced its intentions to begin including Chinese A-shares in June 2017. It also laid out its road map for China's new place in the MSCI Emerging Markets Index.

In early 2018, Chinese A-shares had a 0% weighting in the index. But MSCI expects that to increase to a massive 40% weighting by the time the change is complete. Here's how it'll happen…

The first step is a baby step, with Chinese A-shares taking only 5% of their long-term weighting. This is likely what we'll see with the first inclusion in June 2018. Take a look at these numbers from MSCI...

China A-shares: Initial Weighting

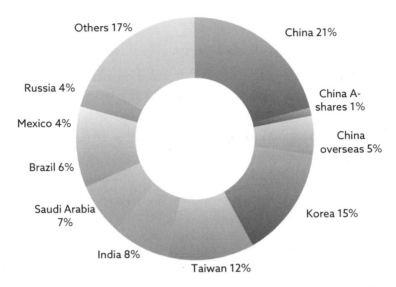

But again, this is just the start. Over the next few years, MSCI will continue to allocate more and more to China's A-share market. Eventually, the weightings will look like this:

China A-shares: Long-term Weighting

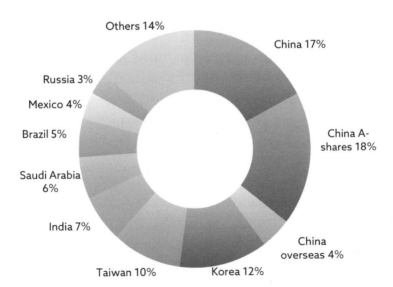

Let's think about the numbers for a second...

Remember, currently $1.7 trillion is benchmarked to the MSCI Emerging Markets Index. Over the next few years, Chinese A-shares will go from a 0% weighting to an 18% weighting.

A move of 18% of $1.7 trillion means more than $300 billion will be forced into China's A-share market in the coming years. And this is only one index...

Fund company Vanguard wanted to "get a jump" on MSCI—so it added a 5% allocation to Chinese A-shares in 2015 in its emerging markets fund... The fund is around $50 billion—so that 5% allocation forced roughly $2.5 billion into Chinese A-shares.

Just imagine what will happen *when thousands of fund managers* put money into China in the next few years...

Keep in mind that money will not necessarily flow into China because it's the right thing to do, but because index funds HAVE to move that money into China. And because wimpy fund managers will simply follow their benchmark index and try to protect their jobs.

MSCI has $9.5 trillion benchmarked to its indexes. But it's not the only game in town... MSCI's biggest competitor is FTSE... And FTSE has already added a 5% China component to its emerging markets indexes in anticipation of the day when China-related stocks make up more than 40% of the major emerging markets indexes.

In short, a lot of money is going to flow into Chinese stocks in the next five to ten years as fund managers feel forced to follow the indexes and increase their purchases of Chinese stocks.

What's also interesting is what happened after MSCI made its June 2017 announcement. It began a global shift of acceptance towards investing in China...

China Goes Mainstream

MSCI's landmark decision was actually small. It set us on the right track, but it will prove inconsequential compared with what's to come.

MSCI chose to include local Chinese A-shares in a single emerging markets index. That means a few hundred billion dollars will flow into

Chinese stocks in the coming years. And including Chinese A-shares in other indexes will likely move that number over $1 trillion eventually.

But this is just the trickle that breaks open the flood gates.

What MSCI's decision really did was make it "OK" to move money into China. It told large investors that buying China isn't foolish... It's the first step to becoming a mainstream idea.

Before MSCI's decision the major investment banks had barely written about this big idea. And they'd just started getting bullish (or at least less bearish) on China.

That changed quickly after MSCI announced its plan to include Chinese A-shares. Wall Street quickly scrambled to get up to speed on Chinese stocks.

Immediately after MSCI's announcement, Reuters reported that a few major investment firms are finally opening up to the idea of owning China. According to the article...

> Global fund managers are ramping up their presence in China, aiming to be well ahead of next June's inclusion of mainland-listed stocks into MSCI's benchmark index.
>
> Wells Fargo Asset Management, Neuberger Berman, Fidelity International and Robeco are among fund houses sharpening their stock-picking skills in mainland "A" shares and hiring staff in China to get a first-mover advantage.

Why the sudden change? Why were those shops suddenly interested in Chinese A-shares?

It's not because they now love the idea of owning Chinese stocks. It's not because they see it as a bullet-proof investment.

They're moving in for one reason: They have to!

These firms have to move into China now that MSCI has made its landmark announcement. They can either adapt or fall behind their competitors.

Private investment-management firm Neuberger Berman plans to relocate its Chinese equity research shop from Hong Kong to mainland China, according to Reuters. And 20-plus global managers have set up investment subsidiaries in China—including Fidelity, Vanguard, and Allianz.

These folks are behind the curve. They haven't focused on China. At least not well enough. But they must now.

Hundreds of billions of dollars must flow into China's stock market starting in 2018. But more importantly, MSCI made it OK to own China.

I wouldn't go as far as to say China is "hot" in the investment community. But folks are starting to realize that China isn't going away. And Wall Street is taking it seriously now.

Again, this is one of the biggest, most obvious opportunities I've seen in my career. It's a major long-term theme. But we know the end result.

Over the next five to seven years as much as $1 trillion will eventually move into Chinese A-shares. And that alone makes Chinese stocks a smart long-term investment now.

Originally published November 2017.

ABOUT STEVE SJUGGERUD

Dr. Steve Sjuggerud is the editor of *True Wealth*, an investment advisory specializing in safe, alternative investments overlooked by Wall Street.

Throughout his career, Steve has addressed hundreds of financial conferences in the U.S. and around the world, including at the New York Stock Exchange. He has also appeared in the media, including Bloomberg, Fox Business News, the *Wall Street Journal*, and *Forbes*.

Steve holds a doctorate in finance and has worked as a stockbroker, vice president of a $50 million global mutual fund, and a hedge-fund manager.

@DSjuggerud

Crescat Capital Quarterly Investor Letter
Q3 2017

KEVIN C. SMITH, OTAVIO COSTA
AND NILS JENSON

U S large cap stocks are the most overvalued in history, higher than prior speculative mania market peaks in 1929 and 2000. We prove it conclusively across six comprehensive dimensions:

1. Price to Sales

2. Price to Book

3. Enterprise Value to Sales

4. Enterprise Value to EBITDA

5. Price to Earnings

6. Enterprise Value to Free Cash Flow

Brutal bear markets and recessions have historically followed from record valuations like we have today, and this time will almost certainly be no different. Not even positive macro factors like low interest rates, low inflation, or recently improving earnings growth can justify today's extreme valuation levels. As we show herein, that was the same backdrop that we had in 1929, the setup to the biggest market crash in history and the Great Depression. Optimism over "new-era" technologies are not justification for high multiples today; they are hallmarks of market tops. Artificial intelligence and crypto-currencies feature prominently in current investor enthusiasm, a climate akin to the tech bubble peak. Also, excitement over new pro-business and pro-economic growth policies coming from Washington are poor grounds to rationalize today's valuations. Again, this is a hallmark of a market top. History has proven that market plunges routinely follow first-year Republican presidents where ebullience over business-friendly government policy runs rampant and only sets the market up for failure. Witness the market meltdowns that followed Hoover (1929), Eisenhower (1953), Nixon (1969), Reagan (1981), and Bush (2001) in their first years. Any real economic boost from Republican tax cuts is already more than priced into the market.

There are many catalysts that are likely to send stocks into a bear market in the near term. A likely bursting of the China credit bubble is first and foremost among them. Our data and analysis show that China today is the biggest credit bubble of any country in history. We believe its bursting will be globally contagious for equities, real estate, and credit markets. The US and China bubbles are part of a larger, global debt-to-GDP bubble, which is also historic in scale, and the product of excessive, lingering central bank easy monetary policies in the wake of the now long-passed 2008 Global Financial Crisis. These policies failed to resolve the debt-to-GDP imbalances that preceded the last crisis. Now, easy money policies have created even bigger debt-to-GDP imbalances and asset bubbles that will precipitate the next one.

We are in the very late stages of a global economic and business expansion cycle with investor sentiment reflecting record optimism typical at market peaks, a sign of capitulation at the end of a bull market.

Proof of the Most Overvalued US Stock Market in History

Below, we show that the median price-to-sales ratio for the S&P 500 today is the highest ever by a wide margin, more than 60% greater than the tech bubble peak.

Highest Valuations Ever Based on Price to Sales

Source: Bloomberg/Crescat

The median price-to-book value for the S&P 500 is also at the highest valuation ever.

Highest Valuations Ever Based on Price to Book

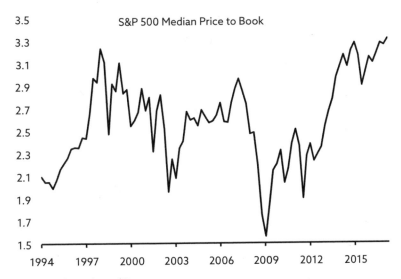

Source: Bloomberg/Crescat

Adding to risk in the markets today, we show that S&P 500 companies are more leveraged than ever before.

S&P 500 Leverage at All-Time Highs

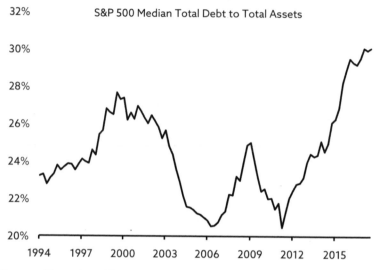

Source: Bloomberg/Crescat

We also show that corporate leverage for the whole US economy, not just the S&P 500, is at all-time highs relative to GDP.

Broad US Corporate Leverage is the Highest Ever Relative to GDP

Source: Bloomberg/Crescat

Now that we have looked at leverage, we look at enterprise value (EV), the market value of a firm that incorporates net corporate leverage to get the total value of a company's capital structure. Based on the median EV-to-sales multiples for the S&P 500, the market is at record valuation levels.

Highest Valuations Ever Based on Enterprise Value to Sales

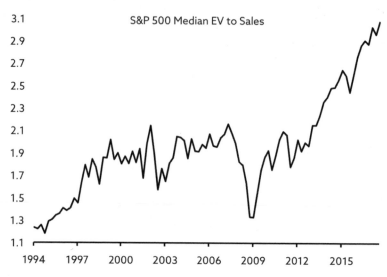

Source: Bloomberg/Crescat

EBITDA (earnings before interest, taxes, depreciation, and amortization) is a popular valuation measure among investment bankers. We show below that based on median EV to EBITDA, the S&P 500 is at its highest-ever valuation.

Highest Valuations Ever Based on Enterprise Value to EBITDA

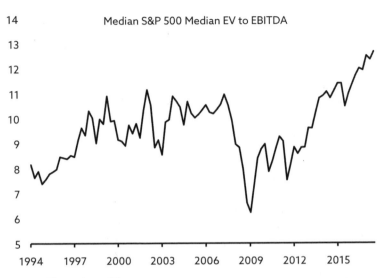

Source: Bloomberg/Crescat

Bear with us now as we dig into the necessary nuances of the price-to-earnings (P/E) ratio. It is critical to use cyclical smoothing to accurately gauge market valuations in their current and historical context when using P/E.

Yale economics professor, Robert Shiller, received a Nobel Prize in 2013 for proving this fact so we hope you will believe it. The problem with just looking at trailing 12-month P/E ratios to determine valuation is that it produces sometimes-false readings due to large cyclical swings in earnings at peaks and valleys of the business cycle. For example, in the middle of the recession in 2001, P/Es looked artificially high due to a broad earnings plunge. P/Es can also look artificially low at the peak of a short-term business cycle, which can produce what is known as a "value trap", such as in 2007 during the US housing bubble and such as we believe is the case today in China, Australia, and Canada.

Shiller showed a method for cyclically-adjusting P/Es using a ten-year moving average of real earnings in the denominator of the P/E. Shiller's Cyclically-Adjusted P/E, called CAPE multiples, have been better predictors of future full-business-cycle stock market returns than raw 12-month trailing P/Es. Shiller showed that markets with historically high CAPEs lead to low long-term returns for long-only index investors. Shiller CAPEs are fantastic, but they can be improved by including an adjustment for corporate profit margins which makes them even better predictors of future stock price performance and therefore even better measures of cyclically-adjusted P/E for valuation purposes. Below we show Shiller's CAPE prior to adjusting for the cyclicality of profit margins.

Shiller Cyclically-Adjusted P/Es Show Market Near All-Time High Valuations but P/Es at All-Time Highs Today when Slight Flaw in CAPE's is Corrected

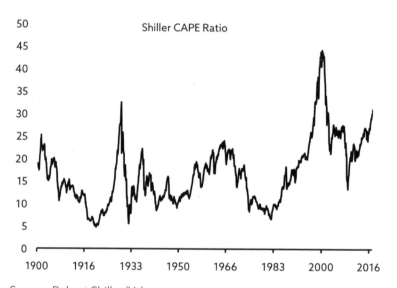

Source: Robert Shiller/Yale

The Shiller CAPE of 31 today is in the same vicinity as it was at its peak in 1929, which it reached before the market crashed and sent the economy into the Great Depression. In Shiller's view, the 1999 Shiller CAPE sets the record for the highest ever P/E at 44. That fact that Shiller's CAPEs do not reconcile more precisely with our four prior valuation measures points to a slight flaw in CAPE.

Shiller's CAPEs simply need an adjustment for profit margins because margins are a key element of earnings cyclicality. We can understand this by looking at median S&P 500 profit margins in the next chart. For example, even though profit margins were cyclically and historically high during the tech bubble, they are even higher today. In the same spirit of

Shiller's attempt to cyclically adjust earnings to determine a useful P/E, CAPEs need to be adjusted for cyclical swings in profit margins.

Today Profit Margins are at All-Time Unsustainable Highs – Note Surge in Profit Margins at the End of Business Cycle Before Bear Markets

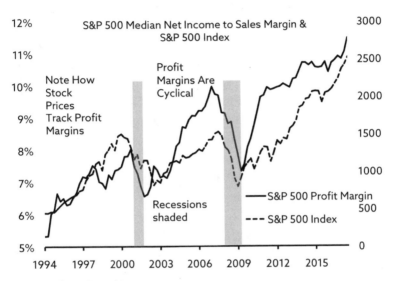

Source: Bloomberg/Crescat

When we multiply Shiller CAPEs by a cyclical adjustment factor for profit margins (ten-year trailing profit margins divided by long-term profit margin), we get a margin-adjusted CAPE that is not only theoretically valid but empirically valid as it proves to be an even better predictor of future returns than Shiller's CAPE! Credit goes to John P. Hussman, Ph.D. for the idea and method to adjust Shiller CAPEs for swings in profit margins.

At the time of writing, margin-adjusted CAPE shows that today's P/E ratio for comparative historical purposes is 43, the highest ever! The 1999 peak P/E was 41 and the 1929 P/E was 40. Once again, we can see that today we have the highest valuation multiples ever for US stocks, higher than 1929 and higher than 1999 and 2000!

Note also that the market is so overvalued today that margin-adjusted CAPE is predicting **negative average returns** for the **next 12 years**! This should prove terrible news for buy-and-hold index fund investors fully invested today. Index investing has never been more popular and crowded. The biggest part of the future possible 12-year negative returns for the market should come within just the next one to three years, the first part of the typical bear market which often includes a crash. We are not perma-bears for the long-term, we are cyclical bears for the next one to three years.

We need just one more valuation metric to thoroughly prove our case that the stock market today is the most over-valued market ever. We have saved the best for last, enterprise value to free cash flow. It is critical to perform Shiller/Hussman-style cyclical smoothing. We use three-year smoothing for real FCF and margins. This is sufficient enough time to iron out outlier cyclical years given that we are working with a more limited 22-year look-back (compared to Shiller's 100+ years) for reliable free cash flow data. This period is long enough for statistical significance because it includes three business cycles. We propose that three-year smoothing is better than ten-year anyway for active investors trying to time short-term business cycles. Shiller and Hussman seem to be focused on very long-term cycles. We also exclude banks from our universe where free cash flow and EV are less relevant. The result as we show below is that median cyclically-adjusted EV to FCF for non-banks in the S&P 500 today is at an insanely-high 41 times!

Median EV to Free Cash Flow Multiples are Highest Ever When adjusted for Cyclicality

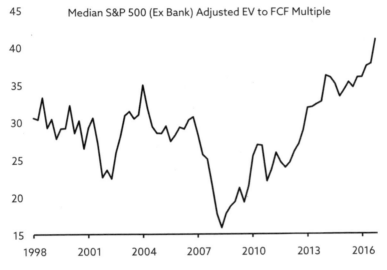

Source: Bloomberg/Crescat

So, we have obtained the same result for every valuation multiple that we have studied. With each and in combination, we have proven that the US stock market is at all-time high valuations. We have shown it across six completely different measures that consider the totality of the corporate income statement, balance sheet, and cash flow statement.

Macro Factors

Undeterred bulls will say, OK you might have a point about record valuations today, but aren't they justified due to low interest rates, low inflation, low unemployment, and recently improving earnings growth? No. They are not! Our empirical analysis of stock market and economic history strongly proves otherwise, as we will show next.

Below, we plot ten-year yields with Shiller CAPE ratios going back to 1900 along with today's margin-adjusted CAPE. We do not have margin-adjusted data going that far back, so we are using CAPE which is still highly useful. The regression line shows that there is indeed a relationship between higher multiples and lower interest rates, but with a huge deviation. The problem is that we are already at the extreme end of the deviation for the current level of interest rates. As we show below, both today's CAPE and margin-adjusted CAPE are at the highest multiples ever for the current level of interest rates. In other words, a more than 50% stock market correction would be justified just to get today's margin adjusted-CAPE back to its average multiple for the 2% interest rate zone on the 10-Year Treasury Note.

P/E Multiple Simply Too High Even in Low Interest Rate Environment

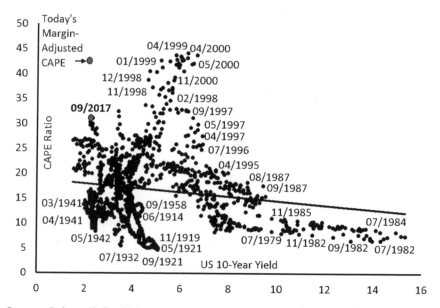

Source: Robert Shiller/Yale

What about inflation? Aren't inflation conditions just perfect today with a very low but still-positive inflation rate? As we show below with data going back to 1914, P/E multiples do indeed tend to be higher under low positive inflation, but today's multiples are again among the highest P/Es ever for the current 2% headline CPI level. Again, there is a huge variation, suggesting that we could see a 50% decline in stock prices just to get back to mean historical P/E multiples for this level of inflation. And that is just the mean. As one can see, P/E levels have gone well below the mean to mid-single-digit level even in a low, positive inflation environment.

Note also from our chart below that if we move in either direction, toward deflation or inflation to any significant degree, P/E multiples shrink **dramatically**, i.e., stock prices crash when starting from record high multiple environments like today.

P/E Multiples Mean Revert Over Time; Inflation and Deflation Shrink P/Es; P/Es Too High Today Even for Low Positive Inflation with Average Growth

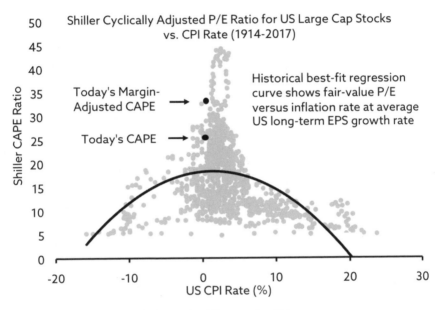

Source: Robert Shiller/Yale/Bureau of Economics/Crescat

But what about earnings growth? Isn't it really starting to pick up now and doesn't that justify high multiples today? It is true that earnings growth has been picking up recently, but it is very typical for earnings growth to pick up when it is late in the business cycle before topping out and falling off a cliff. It did that in 1928–9, in 1999–2000, and in 2006–7. Below, using the Shiller data, we show how closely the earnings growth pattern in the last seven years matches that of the Roaring Twenties!

Recent S&P 500 EPS Growth Resembles 1929 Pattern – Growth is Not Sustainable Late in a Business Cycle; Does Not Justify Record P/E Multiples

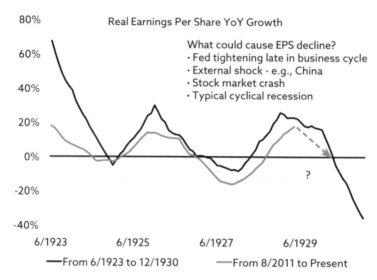

Source: Robert Shiller/Yale

What about the Goldilocks zone that we are in now for simultaneous low inflation and low unemployment? It's an ideal spot on the Phillips Curve, isn't it? Doesn't that justify extended valuation multiples today? Based on history, no. The problem is that there is a natural boom-and-bust business cycle. Our long-term Phillips Curve analysis below going back to 1900 shows that inflation and unemployment tends to stray wildly with the business cycle. Downturns in the business cycle are often deflationary and lead to high unemployment, but there can be inflationary routs too.

US Economy Does Not Stay in Phillip's Curve Goldilocks Zone Forever: Unemployment & Inflation Stray Wildly with Business Cycle

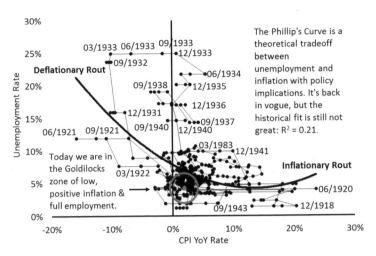

Source: BEA/BLS/NBER/Crescat

Imagine the perfect economy: full employment, low interest rates, low inflation, strong corporate earnings growth. Perhaps that would be the market that could legitimately sustain a high valuation multiple. Irving Fisher, the most well-known economist of his time, thought so. He declared just nine days before the stock market crash of 1929 that stock prices had "reached what looks like a permanently high plateau." The chart below shows the remarkable similarities between 1929 and today.

Think of the Perfect Economy: Full Employment, Low Inflation, Strong Earnings Growth, Low Interest Rates. Add High Valuations. Only Happened Twice in History

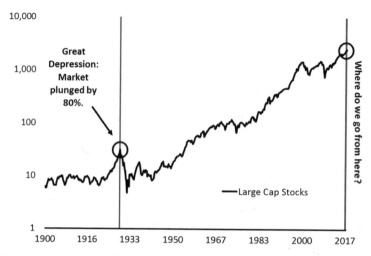

Source: Bloomberg/Crescat/Robert Shiller/Yale/Bureau of Economics

Inflation Versus Deflation

What is a bigger risk today in the US and globally as we go into the next business cycle downturn—inflation or deflation? It is indeed a paradox. Given the record debt-GDP levels, aging population, China credit bubble, housing bubbles in Australia and Canada, and the Federal Reserve tightening, the biggest risk in the short-term is deflation, which is typical when asset bubbles burst. We started to see deflation emerge in the Global Financial Crisis until central banks came to the rescue with massive quantitative easing, but not before a market crash. Similarly, we started to see deflation emerge in China in 2015 before policymakers there ramped up money and credit growth even further to make global asset bubbles in stocks, real estate, and credit even bigger today relative to underlying world GDP. The paradox is that once a true deflationary spiral gets going, central banks are forced to resort to extraordinary inflationary money printing or quantitative easing to counter it. In the face of truly massive QE, at a certain tipping point, the mindset of the world should ultimately shift to a lack of confidence in central bankers' ability to contain inflation. Only then does inflation become a self-fulfilling prophesy as investors start ratcheting up their inflation expectations. Rising inflation expectations never happened in the wake of the last crisis. Instead, the response of investors to QE was to build bigger asset bubbles. What will it take to change the mindset? Probably a bigger crisis and certainly a bigger central bank response. At that point, it is not only inflation but very possibly hyperinflation that becomes the end game. We see hyperinflation as a likely outcome to emerge first and foremost in China, but not before a deflationary crisis emerges first.

The Catalysts

The tightening of credit by the Fed in our view is the main catalyst that will burst global asset bubbles including the credit bubble in China. The chart below illustrates how the end of a US business cycle works. Whenever the Federal Reserve starts a campaign of tightening credit conditions in earnest, late in the business cycle, to temper an overheating stock market, economy, and/or inflation by raising interests, it is soon the kiss of death for the stock market and ultimately the economy. Today, it is also the kiss of death for China that has been pegging its currency to the dollar. Recently, the Fed has been raising rates at the highest rate of change ever very late in the business cycle. It is also beginning a long-term campaign to reduce its balance sheet, a quantitative tightening. We are in the ninth year of an expansion. The longest economic expansion ever in the US lasted only into its tenth year, but the stock market topped out in the ninth year, March 2000. That was the peak of the tech bubble. Asset bubbles tend to top out first, then business fundamentals turn down, then the recession is declared, usually well after it already started, at which point past GDP reports get revised downward.

When Fed Hikes Rates Too Late in Business Cycle – It's Kiss of Death for Market and Economy

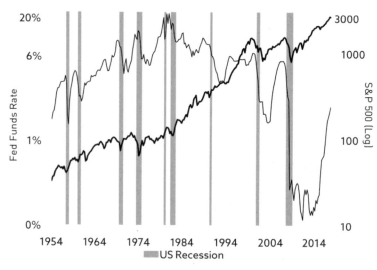

Source: Bloomberg

There are many good indicators of contrary bullish sentiment that we could point to today to further serve as confirming indicators that we are very near a major market top. One is the Investors Intelligence Survey from Yardini Research, Inc., which in late 2017 showed record net bulls versus bears.

And at the same time, a Merrill Lynch Fund Manager Survey found a record number of Fund Manager Survey participants taking higher than normal risk.

Nothing epitomizes the speculative mania in the global financial markets today better than Bitcoin. The novel crypto-token has appreciated **720-fold** in the last five years! That's **12 times** more than tulip bulbs during the Dutch mania of the 1600s!

The problem with Bitcoin is that it is easily replicated to dilute its value by any number of competing crypto-currencies. This is not the problem with gold of course. Gold has been true money that has stored value in all countries for thousands of years. However, gold and silver are significantly undervalued compared to fiat money today as we showed in our Q2 2017 letter. Gold will almost certainly prove its mettle over both fiat money and Bitcoin in the coming Bitcoin bust that should go hand in hand with the coming global asset bubble meltdown.

Originally published November 18, 2017; www.crescat.net/crescat-capital-quarterly-investor-letter-q3-2017.

ABOUT KEVIN C. SMITH, OTAVIO COSTA AND NILS JENSON

Kevin C. Smith is the owner, founder, and CEO of Crescat Capital. He manages the investment team. He has twenty-one years of portfolio management experience and has been the primary portfolio manager of Crescat's investment strategies since the firm's inception. He is the architect of Crescat's quant models. Prior to Crescat, he worked as an investment executive at Kidder Peabody. He holds an MBA from the University of Chicago, Booth School of Business with a specialization in finance and concentration in statistics. He earned an undergraduate degree in economics from Stanford University. He holds the Chartered Financial Analyst designation.

Otavio Costa works on the Crescat investment team as a research analyst with a focus on global macro themes, foreign markets, and currencies. "Tavi" is a native of São Paulo, Brazil and is fluent in Portuguese, Spanish, and English. Before joining Crescat, Tavi worked with the underwriting of financial products and in international business at Braservice, a large logistics company in Brazil. Tavi graduated cum laude from Lindenwood University in St. Louis with a B.A. degree in Business Administration with an emphasis in finance and a minor in Spanish. He played NCAA Division 1 tennis for Liberty University. He is a Level-2 CFA candidate.

Nils Jenson serves on the investment team where he focuses on the energy and materials sectors. Nils' specialized economics background and quantitative skills help Crescat to identify and capitalize on important sector trends. Prior to joining Crescat, Nils worked in natural resource policy for Senator Mark Udall. Nils holds an MS in Mineral and Energy Economics from the Colorado School of Mines and an MA in Economics from the University of Colorado. He also earned a BA in Economics from the University of Denver.

Tackling Myths in Investing:
Bonds Lose Value if Rates Rise

———

CULLEN ROCHE

If there's one thing we all seem to understand about bonds it's that bond prices fall when interest rates rise. So, the natural thinking in a low rate environment is, "rates can't go much lower so that means bond prices will fall if they rise." It seems like such a naturally negative asymmetric bet that it scares a lot of people from owning bonds today. There's only one problem with this thinking—it's not necessarily right! The correct statement is, if interest rates rise then bonds prices fall in *the short-term.*

Importantly, there's a pretty good historical precedent for today's bond market and a rising rate environment—the 1940s. In the early '40s, ten-year interest rates had fallen to about 2% in the wake of the Great Depression. Bond investors were essentially pricing in a permanent stagnation (sound familiar?). But rates slowly ticked higher and higher until we got to the crazy high rates of the '70s. But you didn't lose money holding a 10-year T-Bond during this 40-year rise in rates. In fact, you did quite well in nominal terms:

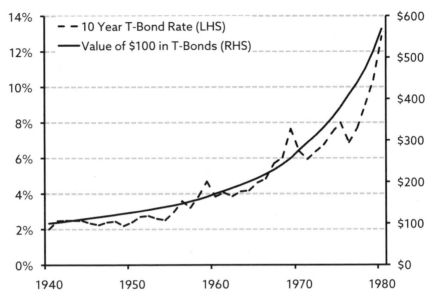

Source: Orcam Group.

The story is a bit different in real terms. When adjusted for inflation bonds barely break even over this same 40-year period:

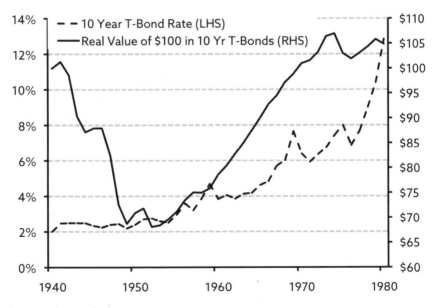

Source: Orcam Group.

Although you experienced several real losing ten-year periods during this 40-year period, you didn't lose money in nominal terms during any ten-year period across this rising rate environment. In other words, if held to maturity you did quite well in nominal terms even if you lost money in real terms. And that's exactly what we should expect since bonds typically don't beat the rate of inflation anyhow.

Historical back-tests can be unreliable and we shouldn't let them influence our thinking too much. So let's look at this from a more operational perspective. Take, for instance, the case of an individual five-year US government bond with a face value of $1,000 paying 2% per year. If interest rates rise by 1% every year that bond still pays you 2% every year plus you get your principal upon maturity. Here's how the total return of that bond looks over the course of your five years:

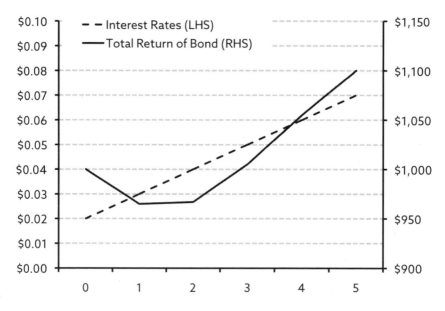

Source: Orcam Group.

If you held on for five years you didn't lose money despite the fact that interest rates rose. In fact, you lost some principal in the first two years and then made up for it as the bond reached maturity. This is slightly more complex in the case of a bond fund which is essentially a constant maturity bond, but the same general principles apply.[1] But let's take a closer look at a constant maturity bond since more and more investors own bond funds these days.

To understand the returns on bond funds in a rising rate environment we have to understand what's called bond convexity. Bond convexity is a measure of the non-linear relationship between bond prices and interest rate changes. Without getting too deep into the weeds, we should recognize something about bonds—as interest rates rise bond duration declines (bond duration is the bond's price sensitivity to interest rate changes, so a 1% rise in rates will result in a 5% loss for a bond with a duration of 5). In English, that basically means that a 1% rise in interest rates has a bigger impact on long-maturity, low-interest rate bonds than it does on long-maturity, high-interest rate bonds. Let's look at an example here for more clarity.

Let's say you buy a seven-year constant maturity bond portfolio yielding 2% in year one.[2] Each year interest rates rise by 1% until they reach 15% like they did in 1981. Remember, this is a crazy extreme example, but useful for illustrative purposes. The image below shows interest rates (the dashed line) rising from 2% to 15% in increments of 1% per year. The solid line shows the cumulative price (yield plus price change due to interest rate increase) of the seven-year bond portfolio.

[1] A lot of people argue that individual bonds are safer than bond funds, however, this isn't exactly accurate. Individual bonds expose you to significantly more individual entity risk and as I've shown here, a constant maturity bond fund is just as safe as an individual bond when it's held for the right holding period. Unfortunately, the liquidity of bond funds often lures the investor into treating this long-term instrument as a short-term instrument. In fact, I'd argue that the ability to see your daily price fluctuations in bond funds significantly increases the behaviorally-induced risk of short-termism in bonds.

[2] I used a seven-year constant maturity bond because that's pretty close to the Barclays Aggregate Bond Index. Of course, if you own a longer duration bond portfolio these numbers will not look nearly as friendly. I also assumed you were buying and holding this portfolio which is not realistic given that many investors will be contributing or reinvesting interest payments.

Seven-Year Constant Maturity Bond Price in Rising 1% Interest Rate Environment

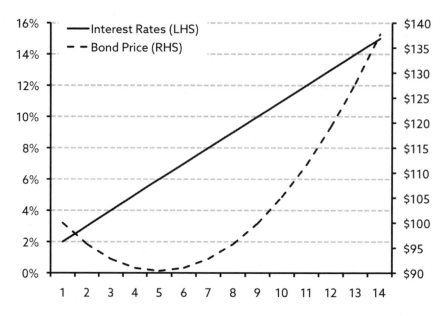

Source: Orcam Group.

Year 1	−4.23%
Year 2	−3.00%
Year 3	−1.79%
Year 4	−0.58%
Year 5	0.61%
Year 6	1.79%
Year 7	2.97%
Year 8	4.13%
Year 9	5.29%
Year 10	6.44%
Year 11	7.58%
Year 12	8.71%
Year 13	8.98%

What happens here is really important because the constant maturity bond portfolio gets dinged pretty bad at first. I've shown the annual price changes in the table. Because the bond is more sensitive to rising rates when rates are low, the 1% increase in rates has a big impact upfront, but then it actually has a positive impact as rates rise. In other words, as rates rise a medium duration constant maturity bond portfolio does not necessarily fall in price. It actually rises in price because the higher interest rate more than offsets the impact of the price decline. This should seem obvious to everyone, but it's not what we tend to think of when we hear that rising interest rates mean falling bond prices.

The point of this exercise is to put the risk of bonds in the right perspective. Yes, if rates rise sharply you'll almost certainly lose purchasing power in your bonds, however, you will also earn a nominal return better than cash if held to maturity.[3] But we should also remember that an aggregate bond portfolio with a constant maturity of about seven years will not necessarily experience traumatic losses. In fact, even in our *worst-case scenario*, the seven-year bond only declines by a total amount of 9.6% at its low point.[4] Over the course of our entire 14 years that constant maturity bond portfolio actually generated 2.85% per year. Not bad for a worst-case scenario!

And this brings us to the primary problem with bond investing and asset allocation in general—most people don't apply the right maturity and/or duration to their portfolios. Most of us suffer from a horrid case of short-termism. As I like to say, asset allocation is all about asset and liability mismatch. We have short-term cash flow liabilities that we try to match to longer-term assets. Most people want high returns today from instruments that are not designed to provide us with immediate returns. This results in a misuse of the instrument, as a bond (and even a stock to some degree) is designed to pay its cash flows over certain periods of time. If you're not prepared to potentially hold the instrument for most or all of its maturity then your risk of permanent loss increases substantially.

The key lesson here is simple—rising rates don't necessarily mean you will lose money in bonds. While you might lose money in real terms if rates rise, your probability of losing money in nominal terms is fairly low if you hold the instrument for its proper time horizon. In either case (rising rates or continued low rates), buying the appropriate bonds in a

---

3   "Cash" in this example is a 0% note and not a Treasury Bill or other risk-free short-term interest bearing note.

4   Some people might argue that this is a good argument in favor of holding individual bonds, however, I would disagree and argue that this is not a flaw in bond funds, but rather a misunderstanding of how they reflect an investor's goals. The individual bond holder would have to repurchase new individual bonds every year in order to maintain the same constant maturity portfolio. This would result in greater single entity risk, higher costs and lower average returns. It should also be noted that the seven-year individual bond purchaser only holds a seven-year bond for a brief instant in time. After all, as time goes on that bond slowly becomes a six-year bond, five-year bond, four-year bond, etc.

diversified portfolio is still a perfectly suitable approach for the investor who constructs their portfolio properly and within the scope of their risk profile.

Originally published February 17, 2017; www.pragcap.com/the-biggest-myths-in-investing-part-5-bonds-lose-value-if-rates-rise.

ABOUT CULLEN ROCHE

Mr. Cullen Roche is the Founder of Orcam Financial Group, LLC a financial services firm offering fee-only financial advisory services. He has over a decade of experience in the financial services industry working with some of the biggest firms in finance as well as founding his own firms.

Prior to establishing Orcam, Mr. Roche founded his own investment partnership in 2005 after working at Merrill Lynch Global Wealth Management where he worked on a team overseeing $500MM+ in assets under management. Over the next seven years he guided the partnership to average annual returns of 14.5% with a Sharpe Ratio of 1.21 and no negative full year returns during one of the most turbulent periods in stock market history.

He is the author of the popular book *Pragmatic Capitalism: What Every Investor Needs to Know About Money and Finance* as well as *Understanding the Modern Monetary System*, one of the top 10 all-time most downloaded research papers on the SSRN network. He is the long-time #1 economics writer on the popular financial website Seeking Alpha, was named one of the 'Top Wall Street Economists, Experts and Opinion Leaders' of 2011 by Wall Street Economists and was named one of the '101 Best Finance People' and "one of the most influential economic thinkers today" by *Business Insider*. In 2015 Mr. Roche was named one of the '40 Under 40' most influential people in finance by *InvestmentNews*. He is regularly cited in the *Wall Street Journal*, on CNBC and in the *Financial Times*.

Mr. Roche is an alumnus of Georgetown University.

@cullenroche

Mind the Gap

Global Investor Returns Show the Costs
of Bad Timing Around the World

———

RUSSEL KINNEL

The struggle is real. The average investor has lagged behind the average fund for the past ten years. The reason is that, in aggregate, investors' timing is not very good. Over the ten years ended 2016, the average U.S. investor in diversified equity funds enjoyed a 4.36% return, even though the average diversified equity fund returned 5.15%. That's a fair amount to give up. In fixed income, the gap was nearly as large, and that's painful because the returns are much smaller. In bondland, we found the average investor received a 2.99% return, versus 3.72% for the average bond fund.

Combining all funds, we come up with a return for the average fund of 4.33% compared with a 3.96% return for the average investor.

This is why I always take time out to warn you to "Mind the Gap." Saving enough money and selecting the right investments are crucial to your success. But timing is another vital piece that investors tend to forget.

Inside the Data

To calculate fund investor returns, we adjust the official returns by using monthly flows in and out of the fund. Thus, we calculate a rate of return generated by a fund's investors. As with an internal rate of return calculation, investor return is the constant monthly rate of return that makes the beginning assets equal to the ending assets, with all monthly cash flows accounted for.

In order to roll up that data, we asset-weight investor returns so that we arrive at the average investor return for an asset group. We then compare that with the average fund to see whether investors timed their investments well. To add a new wrinkle, I compared these numbers with asset-weighted total returns based on funds' asset sizes at the beginning of the time period in order to judge whether investors made wise changes over the subsequent ten years, or whether they should have stood pat.

You can find Morningstar Investor Return data for a fund on its Morningstar.com page by selecting the Performance tab. As you look, it is worth thinking about the investor return on its own as well as the gap with total returns. The investor return is essentially the aggregate investor's bottom line. Even if the gap is significant, as long as the investor return is good, you know they did OK. If you see a big gap, it's worth considering why that gap happened and whether it might be an issue for you.

All single-fund investor returns come with the caveat that there is a fair amount of randomness in them that is beyond the fund manager's control. Two funds doing the same thing might have different investor returns just because they are in different sales channels or had different launch dates. Some factors are more within the fund company's control than others, such as how a fund is positioned, the soundness of the strategy, and how volatile a fund is. All of these things play key roles in how well investors use a fund.

What if Everyone Left Their Funds Alone?

Hmmmm. That might be a good idea. When I asset-weight returns using assets from ten years ago, I get better results than from either investor returns or a straight average of returns. For example, the typical diversified equity fund investor would have had a return of 5.31%, topping the 5.15% average fund return and the 4.36% average investor return. For bond funds, the hands-off return was 4.30%, compared with 2.99% for the average investor return and 3.72% for the average fund return.

Even allocation funds lagged the hands-off portfolio: They enjoyed 4.31% returns compared with 4.298% for asset-weighted results at the beginning of the period and 3.87% for the average fund. Why did investors get it right in allocation? Because of 401(k)s and target-date funds. Investing in a 401(k) means you invest every paycheck, and that's even better than standing pat because you are buying low during sell-offs—provided you don't panic and give up in a sell-off. As the results show, most investors were able to stick to their plans.

Factors in Investor Returns

We sliced and diced the fund universe based on some factors to see if there was a link with investor returns. Expense ratios had the strongest link. The gap grew for each successive quintile of fund expense ratios in equities, and investor returns steadily declined, too. For example, the cheapest quintile (at the start of the ten years) in diversified equity returned 4.59% compared with 1.78% for the priciest. That means investor returns were much worse in higher-cost funds even if you were to add fees back in. In that same group, the returns gap grew from 1.24% to 2.57% for the priciest funds.

In bonds, the gap was steady across fee groups, though investor returns were higher for cheaper funds. Specifically, cheap funds had investor returns of 3.14% compared with 2.34% for pricey funds. However, the data understate the impact of fees because many high-cost funds were liquidated over the ten-year period we studied and their returns did not make it into the final data. Bond funds in the cheapest quintile were twice as likely to survive as those in the priciest and eight times as likely to survive and outperform their peer group. Thus, the gap issue is hidden by the fact that the high-cost failures were wiped out.

We also tested standard deviation, Morningstar Risk rating, and manager tenure. The results were mixed. Equity funds with lower standard deviation and risk rating had modestly better investor returns than those that were more volatile. However, those factors didn't really move the needle for bonds or allocation funds. In addition, manager tenure showed no link at all with investor returns.

Global Perspective

We've expanded our look at investor returns to some key markets around the world. In general, the gaps and behavior patterns were not so different from what we saw in the U.S. However, in most cases we were limited to five years' worth of data. Those figures probably understate the gap because markets have generally trended up and because the gap compounds over time. You can see the gap around the globe in this map. We also published a white paper on global investor returns, "Mind the Gap: Global Investor Returns Show the Costs of Bad Timing Around the World."[1]

Investor Return Gaps Around the World

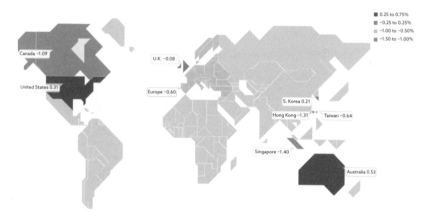

Source: Morningstar Inc. Data as of December 31, 2016.

Strong Results for Automatic Investment Plans

In South Korea, investors had particularly good timing in fixed-income funds. In Australia, superannuation funds enjoyed positive gaps. In the U.S., allocation funds had positive gaps. The link across these markets was automatic investment plans. In the U.S., target-date funds have consistently had positive gaps because U.S. investors contribute to their 401(k) savings with every paycheck. In South Korea, general savings plans feature automatic monthly investments, though they are not the only means of investing in funds. These relatively simple plans work wonders at keeping investors on track and preventing them from unwise market-timing moves. Seeing this work in three different investment cultures is a strong endorsement for the practice worldwide.

[1] corporate1.morningstar.com/ResearchArticle.aspx?documentId=810671

Ten-Year Investor Returns in the U.S.

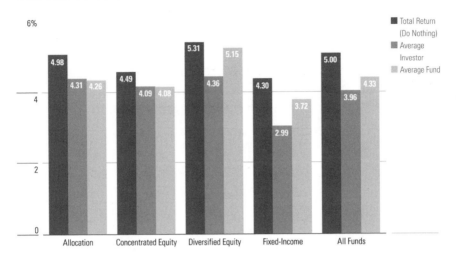

Source: Morningstar Inc. Data as of December 31, 2016.

This is a structure that many regulators around the world are considering as a way to encourage retirement savings. The most recent example is the launch of the Default Investment Strategy on April 1, 2017, by Hong Kong's Mandatory Provident Fund Schemes Authority. The evidence suggests the idea has merit for its ability to help investors realize the potential of retirement plans. It combines some of the strengths of defined benefit with defined contribution by making low-cost diversified investments the default option.

Originally published 30 May 2017; www.morningstar.com/articles/810470/mind-the-gap-global-investor-returns-show-the-cost.html.

ABOUT RUSSEL KINNEL

Russel Kinnel is director of manager research for Morningstar.

@RussKinnel

A Letter to Jamie Dimon

And anyone else still struggling to understand cryptocurrencies

———

ADAM LUDWIN

Dear Jamie,

My name is Adam Ludwin and I run a company called Chain. I have been working in and around the cryptocurrency market for several years.

As I write this, you've said a few things about Bitcoin—questioning its worth, value and existence—in a short space of time.

It's easy to believe cryptocurrencies have no inherent value. Or that governments will crush them.

It's also becoming fashionable to believe the opposite: that they will disrupt banks, governments, and Silicon Valley giants once and for all.

Neither extreme is true.

The reality is nuanced and important. Which is why I've decided to write you this briefing note. I hope it helps you appreciate cryptocurrencies more deeply.

Let me start by stating that I believe:

- The market for cryptocurrencies is overheated and irrationally exuberant

- There are a lot of poseurs creating them, and some scammers, too

- There are a lot of conflicts of interest, self-serving hype, and obfuscation

- Very few people in the media understand what's going on

- Very few people in finance understand what's going on

- Very few people in technology understand what's going on

- Very few people in academia or government understand what's going on

- Very few people *buying cryptocurrencies* understand what's going on

- It's very possible *I* don't understand what's going on

Also:

- Banks and governments aren't going away

- Traditional software isn't going away

In short: there's a lot of noise. But there is also signal. To find it, we need to start by *defining* cryptocurrency.

Without a working definition we are lost. Most people arguing about cryptocurrencies are talking past each other because they don't stop to ask the other side what they think cryptocurrencies are *for*.

Here's my definition: cryptocurrencies are a *new asset class* that enable *decentralized applications*.

If this is true, your point of view on cryptocurrencies has very little to do with what you think about them in comparison to traditional currencies or securities, and everything to do with your opinion of *decentralized applications and their value relative to current software models*.

Don't have an opinion on decentralized applications? Then you can't possibly have one on cryptocurrencies yet, so read on.

And since this isn't about cryptocurrencies vs. fiat currencies let's stop using the word *currency*. It's a head fake. It has way too much baggage and I notice that when you talk about Bitcoin in public you keep comparing it to the dollar, euro, and yen. That comparison won't help you understand what's going on. In fact, it's getting in the way. So for the rest of this note, I will refer to cryptocurrencies as *crypto assets*.

So, to repeat: crypto assets are a *new asset class* that enable decentralized applications.

And like every other asset class, they exist as a mechanism to *allocate resources to a specific form of organization*. Despite the myopic focus on trading crypto assets recently, they don't exist solely to be traded. That is, in principle at least, they don't exist for their own sake.

To understand what I mean, think about other asset classes and what form of organization they serve:

- Corporate equities *serve* companies

- Government bonds *serve* nations, states, municipalities

- Mortgages *serve* property owners

And now:

- Crypto assets *serve* decentralized applications

Decentralized applications are a *new form of organization* and a *new form of software*. They're a new model for creating, financing, and operating software services in a way that is decentralized top-to-bottom. That doesn't make them *better* or *worse* than existing software models or the corporate entities that create them. As we'll see later, there are major trade-offs. What we can say is simply that they are *radically* different from software as we know it today and *radically* different from the forms of organization we are used to.

How different? Imagine the following: you grew up in a rainforest and I brought you a cactus and told you it was a tree. How would you react? You'd probably laugh and say it's not a tree because there's no point in a tree being a stumpy water tank covered in armor—after all, water is abundant here in the rainforest! This, roughly, is the reaction of many people working in Silicon Valley to decentralized applications.

But I digress. I owe you an important explanation:

What is a decentralized application?

A decentralized application is a way to create a service that no single entity operates.

We'll come to the question of *whether that's useful* in a moment. But first, you need to understand how they work.

Let's go back to the birth of this idea.

It's November 2008. The nadir of the financial crisis.

An anonymous person publishes a paper explaining how to make electronic payments without a trusted central party like Chase or PayPal or the Federal Reserve. It's the first *decentralized application* of this kind ever proposed.

It's a decentralized application *for payments*.

The paper is titled "Bitcoin."[1]

How does it work? How is it possible to send an electronic payment without a designated party who will track and update everyone's balances? If I hand you a dollar that's one thing. But data is not a bearer instrument. Data needs intermediation and validation to be trusted.

The paper proposes a solution: form a peer-to-peer network. Make it public. Announce your transaction to everyone. In your announcement, point to the specific funds on the network you want to spend. Cryptographically sign your announcement with the same software key that is linked to those funds so we know they're yours.

It almost works. We need one more thing: a way to make sure that if you broadcast two competing announcements (that is, if you try to spend the same funds twice) that only one of your attempts counts.

Bad solution: designate a party to timestamp the transactions and only include the transaction that came first. We're back to square one. We have a trusted intermediary.

Breakthrough solution: let entities compete to be the "timestamper!" We can't avoid the need for one, but we can avoid designating one in advance or using the same one for every batch of transactions.

"Let entities compete." Sounds like a market economy. What's missing? A reward for winning. An incentive. An asset.

Let's call that asset Bitcoin. Let's call the entities competing for the right to timestamp the latest batch of announced transactions "miners." Let's make sure anyone can join this contest at any time by making the code and network open.

---

[1]   bitcoin.org/bitcoin.pdf

Now we need an actual contest. The paper proposes one. On your mark, get set: find a random number generated by the network! The number is really, really hard to find. So hard that the only way to find it is to use tons of processing power and burn through electricity. It's a computing version of what Veruca Salt made her dad and his poor factory workers do in Willy Wonka. A brute force search for a golden ticket (or in this case, a golden number).

Why the elaborate and expensive competition to do something as simple as timestamp transactions for the network? So that we can be sure the competitors have incurred a *real financial cost*. That way, if they win the race to find the random number and become the designated timestamper for a given batch of transactions, they won't use that power for evil (like censoring transactions). Instead, they will meticulously scan each pending transaction, eliminate any attempts by users to spend the same funds twice, ensure all rules are followed, and broadcast the validated batch to the rest of the network.

Because if they do indeed follow the rules, the network is programmed to reward them…

… with newly minted Bitcoin, plus the transaction fees, denominated in Bitcoin, paid by the senders. (See why they are called *miners* and not *timestampers*, now?)

In other words, miners follow the rules because it is in their economic self-interest to do the right thing.

You know, like Adam Smith said:

> It is not from the benevolence of the butcher, the brewer or the baker, that we expect our dinner, but from their regard to their own self interest.

Crypto assets: the invisible hand… of the internet.

Bitcoin is capitalism, distilled. You should love it!

And since these miners have debts to pay (mostly electricity bills), they will likely sell their newly earned Bitcoins on the open market in exchange for whatever real currency they need to satisfy their liabilities. Anything left is profit. The Bitcoin is now in circulation. People who need it can buy it. And so can people who just want to speculate on it. (More on the people who "need it" vs. those who are speculating later.)

Eureka! We have killed two birds with one stone: the financial reward that substitutes our need for a trusted central party with a marketplace of competing yet honest timestampers *is the same asset* that ends up in circulation for use as a *digital bearer instrument* in an electronic payments network that has no central party (it's circular, I know).

Now that you understand Bitcoin, let's generalize this to decentralized applications as a whole.

In general, a decentralized application allows you to do something you can already do today (like payments) but without a trusted central party.

Here's another example: a decentralized application called Filecoin enables users to store files on a peer-to-peer network of computers instead of in centralized file storage services like Dropbox or Amazon S3. Its crypto asset, also called Filecoin, incentivizes entities to share excess hard drive space with the network.

Digital file storage is not new. Neither is electronic payments. What's new is that they can be operated *without a company*. A new form of organization.

One more example.

Warning: this one is a bit confusing because it's *meta*.

There's a decentralized application called Ethereum that is a *decentralized application for launching decentralized applications*. I am sure by now you have heard of "initial coin offerings" (ICOs) and "tokens." Most of these are issued on top of Ethereum. Instead of building a decentralized application from scratch the way Bitcoin was, you can build one on top of Ethereum much more easily because a) the network already exists and b) it's not designed for a *specific* application but rather as a platform to build applications that can execute arbitrary code. It is "featureless."

Ethereum's protocol incentivizes entities to contribute *computing resources* to the network. Doing so earns these entities Ether, the crypto asset of Ethereum. This makes Ethereum a new kind of computing platform for this new class of software (decentralized apps). It's not cloud computing because Ethereum itself is decentralized (like *aether*, get it?). That's why its founder, Vitalik Buterin, refers to Ethereum as a "world computer."

To summarize, in just the last few years the world has invented a way to create software services that have no central operator. These services are called decentralized applications and they are enabled with crypto assets that incentivize entities on the internet to contribute resources—processing, storage, computing—necessary for the service to function.

It's worth pausing to acknowledge that this is kind of *miraculous*. With just the internet, an open protocol, and a new kind of asset, we can instantiate networks that dynamically assemble the resources necessary to provide many kinds of services.

And there are a lot of people who think this model is the *future of all software*, the thing that will finally challenge the FANG stocks and venture capital to boot.

But I'm not one of them. Because there's a problem.

It's not at all clear yet that decentralized applications are actually useful to most people relative to traditional software.

Simply put, you cannot argue that for *everyone* Bitcoin is *better* than PayPal or Chase. Or that for everyone Filecoin is *better* than Dropbox or iCloud. Or that for *everyone* Ethereum is *better* than Amazon EC2 or Azure.

In fact, on almost every dimension, decentralized services are *worse than their centralized counterparts*:

- They are slower
- They are more expensive
- They are less scalable
- They have worse user experiences
- They have volatile and uncertain governance

And no, this isn't just because they are new. This won't fundamentally change with bigger blocks, lightning networks, sharding, forks, self-amending ledgers, or any other technical solutions.

That's because there are structural trade-offs that result directly from the primary design goal of these services, beneath which all other goals must be subordinated in order for them to be relevant: *decentralization*.

Remember that "elaborate and expensive competition" I described? Well, it comes at the cost of throughput. Remember how users need to "cryptographically sign" their transaction announcements? Well, those private keys need to be held onto much more securely than a typical password (passwords can be recovered). Remember how "no single entity operates" these networks? The flip side is that there is no good way to make decisions or govern them.

Sure, you can make decentralized applications more efficient and user friendly by, for example, centralizing users' cryptographic signing keys (i.e., control of their coins) with a trusted entity. But then we're mostly back to square one and would be better off using a service that is centralized.

Thus, Bitcoin, for example, isn't best described as "Decentralized PayPal." It's more honest to say it's an extremely inefficient electronic payments network, *but in exchange we get decentralization.*

Bottom line: centralized applications beat the pants off decentralized applications on virtually every dimension.

EXCEPT FOR ONE DIMENSION.

And not only are decentralized applications better at this one thing, *they are the only way we can achieve it.*

What am I referring to?

Censorship resistance.

This is where we come to the elusive signal in the noise.

Censorship resistance means that access to decentralized applications is open and unfettered. Transactions on these services are *unstoppable.*

More concretely, nothing can stop me from sending Bitcoin to anyone I please. Nothing can stop me from executing code on Ethereum. Nothing can stop me from storing files on Filecoin. As long as I have an internet connection and pay the network's transaction fee, denominated in its crypto asset, I am free to do what I want.

(If Bitcoin is capitalism distilled, it's also a kind of freedom distilled. Which is why libertarians can get a bit obsessed.)

And for readers who are crypto enthusiasts and don't want to take my word for it, will you at least listen to Adam Back and Charlie Lee?

> Ability to make payments you otherwise could not is the killer app
> [Adam Black, bit.ly/2G2BZ4c]

> It's about uncensorable payments, not PayPal 2.0
> [Charlie Lee, bit.ly/2Ibivwn]

So while we can't say "for everyone Bitcoin is better than Visa," it is possible that *for some cohort of users* Bitcoin truly is the only way to make a payment.

More generally, we can ask:

For whom is this the right trade-off?

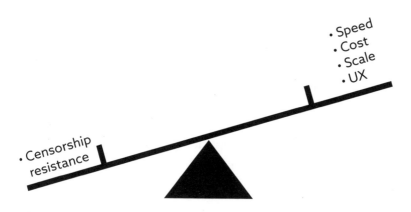

Who needs censorship resistance so much that they are willing to trade away the speed, cost, scalability, and experience benefits of centralized services?

To be clear, I'm not saying you have to make this trade-off *in order to buy/speculate on crypto assets*. I am saying that in order for decentralized applications themselves to have utility to some cohort, that cohort must be optimizing for censorship resistance.

So, who are these people?

While there is not a lot of good data, actual *users* of decentralized applications seem to fall into two categories:

1. People who are off the grid: that is, in countries where access to competently operated traditional services is limited (for any number of reasons) but where internet is not

2. People who *want to be* off the grid: that is, people who don't want their transactions censored or known

With that framework in mind we can ask:

• For whom is Bitcoin the best/only way to make a payment?

• For whom is Filecoin the best/only way to store a file?

• For whom is Ethereum the best/only way to compute code?

These are the questions that get at the heart of the value proposition of the technology.

So far, most decentralized applications have very little use relative to traditional services. Bitcoin, for example, has fewer mainstream merchants accepting it as a payment option in the U.S. today than in 2014. And for all the talk of Bitcoin's value as a payments system in developing countries or emerging markets like China, it is traditional software (i.e., apps) like AliPay and Paytm that are actually driving sweeping change in these places.

At the same time, use of Bitcoin on the dark web and for ransomware is evident, even if it is hard to get good data.

But aren't people using Bitcoin as a "store of value?" Sure, which is just another way of saying people are investing in Bitcoin with a longish time horizon. But remember I'm not talking about investing in the crypto asset yet. I'm talking about whether there are people who find a *decentralized application for payments* (which is enabled by that asset) useful. Real estate is only a good store of value *in the long run* if people live and work in the buildings. The same is true of decentralized applications.

What should we make of Ethereum evaluated through the "censorship resistance" lens? After all, it seems to be getting a ton of use by developers. Since Ethereum is a *developer platform for decentralized applications*, does that mean it is *developers* who have been censored or blocked somehow? In a way, yes. Developers and start-ups who wish to build financial products do not have open and unfettered access to the world's financial infrastructure. While Ethereum doesn't provide access to that infrastructure, it does provide a different infrastructure that can be used to, for example, create and execute a financial contract.

Since Ethereum is a platform, its value is ultimately a function of the value of the applications built on top. In other words, we can ask if Ethereum is useful by simply asking if anything that has been built on Ethereum is useful. For example, do we need censorship resistant prediction markets? Censorship resistant meme playing cards? Censorship resistant versions of YouTube or Twitter?

While it's early, if none of the 730+ decentralized apps built on Ethereum so far seem useful, that may be telling.[2] Even in year one of the web we had chat rooms, email, cat photos, and sports scores. What are the equivalent killer applications on Ethereum today?

So where does this leave us?

Given how different they are from the app models we know and love, will anyone *ever really use* decentralized applications? Will they become a critical part of the economy? It's hard to predict because it depends in part on the technology's evolution, but far more on society's reaction to it.

For example: until relatively recently, encrypted messaging was only used by hackers, spies, and paranoids. That didn't seem to be changing. Until it did. Post-Snowden and post-Trump, everyone from Silicon Valley to the Acela corridor seems to be on either Signal or Telegram. WhatsApp is end-to-end encrypted. The press solicit tips through SecureDrop. Yes, the technology got a little better and easier to use. But it is mainly changes in society that are driving adoption.

In other words, we grew up in the rainforest, but sometimes things change and it helps to know how to adapt to other environments.

And this is the basic argument that the smart money is making on crypto assets and decentralized applications: that it's simply too early to say anything. That it is a profound change. That, should one or more of these decentralized applications actually become an integral part of the world,

---

[2] www.stateofthedapps.com

their underlying crypto assets will be extremely valuable. So, might as well start placing bets now and see how it goes. Don't get to hung up on whether we see the killer apps yet.

That's not a bad argument and I tend to agree.

I would summarize the argument as: in the long-run, a crypto asset's value is driven by use of the decentralized application it enables. While it's early, the high valuations are justified because even if the probability of mass adoption is small, the impact would be very large, so might as well go along for the ride and see what happens.

But how do we explain the recent mania?

Bitcoin is up 5x in a year, Ethereum is up 30x. The total market cap of all cryptocurrencies is ~$175B, up from $12B just a year ago. Why?

As in every mania in history, it is currently rational to be irrational.

To understand what's going on, let's look at the buyer and seller mentality right now, starting with the buyers.

If you invested early in Bitcoin or Ethereum, you are sitting on a windfall. It feels like you are playing with "house money," a well-known psychological effect.[3] You feel smart and willing to risk more than you otherwise would if it was "your money." Might as well diversify a bit and parlay your gains into the next crypto asset, or two, or three.

If you *didn't* invest, the fear-of-missing-out continues to build until the "screw it" moment when you buy in. Maybe you read about Bitcoin, didn't understand it, and followed Warren Buffett's (good) advice not to invest in things you don't understand. Some of your friends made money but you still ignored it. Then you read about Ethereum, which you *really* didn't understand, also passed on buying, and later found out that your friends are planning to retire because they did. The lesson seems to be *anti-Buffett*: only invest in things you *don't understand*. This is causing people to check their judgement at the door when the latest all-time high finally convinces them to jump into the market.

And that is not good.

---

[3] bit.ly/2rAVUlA

Because there will be sellers to fill the demand, especially the demand coming from people who have decided they will never understand this stuff so will just place bets on things that *sound complex and impressive.*

Let's think about these sellers. And by sellers, I don't mean people selling their holdings of existing crypto assets. I mean new issuers. Teams launching new crypto assets.

The basic model is to pre-sell some percentage of the crypto assets the proposed network will generate as a way to fund the development of the decentralized application before it launches. The project founders tend to hold on to some percentage of these assets. Which means that raising money for a project this way is a) non-dilutive as it is not equity and b) not debt, so you never have to pay anyone back. This is basically free money. It's never been this good for entrepreneurs, even in the '90s dot-com boom. Which makes it incredibly tempting to try and shoe-horn every project that *could perhaps* justify an "initial coin offering" to go for it, even if they aren't actually building a *decentralized* application. After all, an ICO lets you exit before you even launch.

And there is a pervasive narrative out there that supports entrepreneurs looking to create new crypto assets. The idea is that by selling assets to users before your network launches, you create "evangelists" who will be early users and promoters you wouldn't otherwise have if there were no financial incentive to participate in your community.

The problem with this line of thinking is that it conflates early *investors* with early *users.* The overlap between people who buy your crypto asset and people who actually want to use the service you are building is likely very, very small, especially during market manias like this one. It creates a false sense of "product-market fit." Yes, people are buying your crypto asset. But that's because the "market" are people who want to get rich and the "product" you are selling is a "way to get rich."

But "this is fine."

Everyone's making money. For now.

It's currently rational to be irrational.

As long as that blue line keeps going up.

At the same time, I wouldn't bet against crypto assets.

Consider the following. The total market cap of crypto assets has been increasing by an *order of magnitude* every few years. Where will they be in 2022? It's certain that many (most?) of the crypto assets launching today won't make it. But neither did most of the ones that were launched back in the 2013/4 boom (when they were referred to as "alt coins"). Though an important alt coin from 2014 did stick around and drove the most recent boom to new heights by being the platform to power all the others: Ethereum.

2008	2011	2013	2017	2022
0 Mkt Cap	0.1 bn Mkt Cap	10 bn Mkt Cap	100 bn Mkt Cap	??? Mkt Cap

So, Jamie, what's the bottom line?

Allow me to summarize.

- Cryptocurrencies (which I prefer to call crypto assets) are a new asset class that enable decentralized applications

- Decentralized applications enable services we already have today, like payments, storage, or computing, but without a central operator of those services

- This software model is useful to people who need censorship resistance which tend to be people that are either off the grid or who want to be off the grid

- Most everyone else is better off using normal applications because they are 10x better on every other dimension, at least for now

- Society's embrace or rejection of new technology is hard to predict (think about encrypted messaging)

- In the long-run, the value of a crypto asset will rise and fall in proportion to the use of the decentralized application it enables

- In the short-run, there will be extreme volatility as FOMO competes with FUD, confusion competes with understanding, and greed competes with fear (on both the buyer side and the issuer side)

- Most people buying into crypto assets have checked their judgement at the door

- Many sellers of new crypto assets aren't actually building decentralized applications but are instead shoe-horning an ICO into their service because of the market mania; that doesn't mean decentralized applications are bad, it just means people are capitalizing on the confusion and are probably themselves confused

- Don't bet against crypto assets in the long-run: as we approach the ten-year anniversary of the Bitcoin paper it is clear that they aren't going anywhere and that decentralized applications may very well find an important place alongside all the other forms of organization we have come to take for granted.

Best, Adam

PS. You may have noticed that I didn't use the word "blockchain" in this note. The word now tends to confuse more than enlighten.

PPS. There is another, related market I didn't talk about: cryptographic ledgers for the enterprise. My perspective on that can be found in my article, "Introducing Sequence." blog.chain.com/introducing-sequence-e14ff70b730

Originally published October 16, 2017; https://blog.chain.com/a-letter-to-jamie-dimon-de89d417cb80.

ABOUT ADAM LUDWIN

Adam Ludwin is the Chief Executive Officer at Chain (www.chain.com).

@adamludwin

Running Out of Workers

TOM MCCLELLAN

By now you have already heard that the U.S. unemployment rate is down to 4.1%, as of the October 2017 data. But that is only one way to measure what is happening in the labor market. This week, I want to explore some other ways to depict how many people are working, versus some other measures.

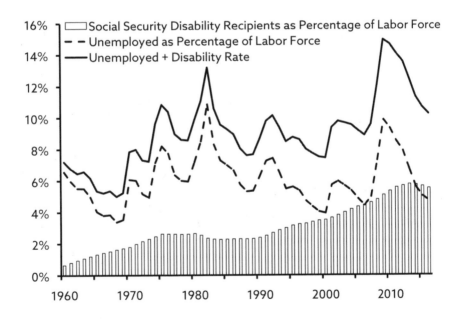

The chart above compares the headline unemployment rate (year-end values) to another plot which factors in disabled workers. At the end of 2016, the percentage of the labor force who were unemployed was 5.0%.

That is slightly different from the "unemployment rate", because the Labor Department factors out labor force members who have become discouraged and given up looking for a job.

Also shown in that chart is the number of disability payment recipients as a percentage of the labor force. In 2015 and 2016, disabled persons exceeded unemployed ones for the first time ever. It is true that the percentage who are receiving disability payments has been declining slightly for those two years, but this is a pretty high level, historically speaking.

If we add the unemployed and the disability recipients together, then we get the top plot in that chart, showing that together they comprise 10.2% of the labor force. That is a pretty high percentage, meaning that only 89.8% of the working age people who could be working actually are.

It gets worse when we consider that the workers have to support not only themselves and their families, but also those disabled workers who are receiving Social Security Disability payments and those receiving unemployment insurance payments. On top of that, the workers also have to support Social Security Retirement recipients, and the numbers of them are growing:

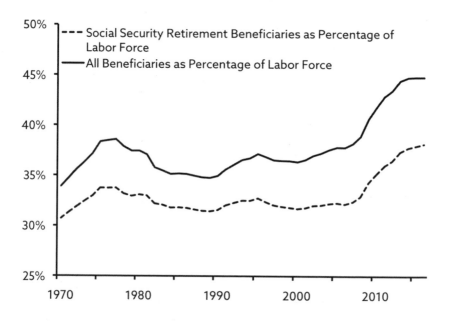

As recently as 2007, Social Security Retirement recipients were just 32% of the labor force. Now that number is up to 38.2%, as Baby Boomers (those born 1946–64) are starting to retire. The tail end of the Baby Boom, those born in 1964, are just 53 years old now, and so there a lot more Boomers coming who have yet to reach retirement age.

In that chart, I also show a plot reflecting the percentage if we include retirement beneficiaries, dependents, survivors, and disability recipients. That number is up to 44.8%!

Putting that last statistic in another way, we are getting down close to only two workers per recipient of any type of Social Security benefit payment:

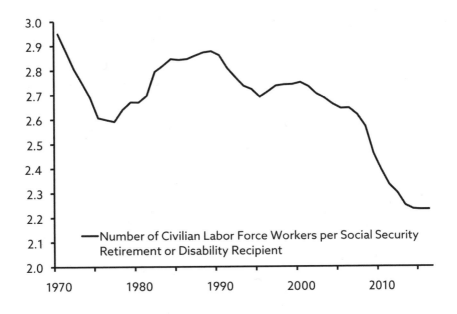

Looking ahead, these numbers do not appear likely to get any better. Here is the age demographic profile from the 2010 Census:

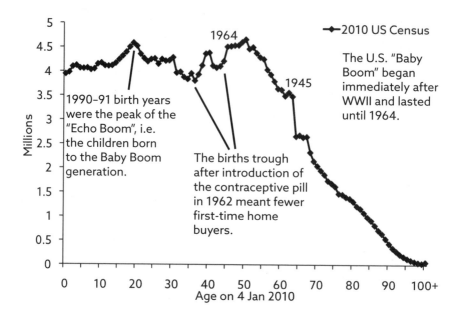

We are just now hitting the fat part of the Baby Boom in terms of people reaching retirement age. Those people all think that they have "paid in", and thus should be entitled to collect what is owed to them. But the "Social Security Lockbox" is a myth. There is no pile of money waiting to be paid out. Instead, we have a pay as you go system, with the money going out as payments simply being the money that is coming in from current workers. At some point, if this trend continues, we won't have enough workers to support all of the beneficiaries, especially if we have another economic slowdown like 2008–09.

For FY2017, according to data from the Treasury Department, the federal government brought in $1.162 trillion for "social insurance and retirement receipts", including unemployment insurance, and paid out $1.001 trillion.[1] That's a $161 billion surplus in that area, which is really good, but understand that revenues are up because more people are working and therefore paying into that FICA deduction on your pay stub. If unemployment rises, those revenues will not be as good.

---

[1]   www.fiscal.treasury.gov/fsreports/rpt/mthTreasStmt/mts0917.pdf

The alarming point, however, is that payouts are growing rapidly. In 2013, the Social Security Administration outlays were $867 billion. To be at $1.001 trillion four years later is a 3.6% annualized growth rate in payouts. And those payouts are up 37.6% from FY2009. So unless we can grow the size of GDP and the payments into Social Security taxes faster than the growth rate of the payouts, we are pretty soon going to be digging a hole in the form of payouts faster than it can be filled in by current workers.

So if you are a Boomer approaching retirement, be sure to think of your children and grandchildren, because they are going to be the ones picking up the tab for the retirement promises made by the Congresses that we have elected.

Originally published November 24, 2017; www.mcoscillator.com/learning_center/weekly_chart/running_out_of_workers.

ABOUT TOM MCCLELLAN

Tom McClellan is a graduate of the US Military Academy at West Point where he studied aerospace engineering, and he served as an Army helicopter pilot for 11 years. He began his own study of market technical analysis while still in the Army, and discovered ways to expand the use of his parents' indicators to forecast future market turning points. Tom views the movements of prices in the financial market through the eyes of an engineer, which allows him to focus on what the data really say rather than interpreting events according to the same "conventional wisdom" used by other analysts.

In 1993, Tom left the Army to join his father Sherman in pursuing a new career doing this type of analysis. Tom and Sherman spent the next two years refining their analysis techniques and laying groundwork.

In April 1995 they launched their newsletter, The McClellan Market Report, an eight-page report covering the stock, bond, and gold markets, which is published twice a month. They utilize the unique indicators they have developed to present their view of the market's structure as well as their forecasts for future trend direction and the timing of turning points. A Daily Edition was added in February 1998 to give subscribers daily updates on their indicators and also provide market position indications for stocks, bonds and gold. Their subscribers range from individual investors to professional fund managers. Tom serves as editor of both publications, and runs the newsletter business from its location in Lakewood, WA.

@McClellanOsc

10,000 Hours or 10 Minutes

What Does It Take to Be a
"World-Class" Investor?

CHARLIE BILELLO

"The 10,000-hours rule says that if you look at any kind of cognitively complex field, from playing chess to being a neurosurgeon, we see this incredibly consistent pattern that you cannot be good at that unless you practice for 10,000 hours, which is roughly 10 years, if you think about four hours a day."

— Malcolm Gladwell

10,000 hours of "deliberate practice." That is the key to achieving "world-class" expertise in any field. So said Malcolm Gladwell in his best-selling book, *Outliers: The Story of Success.*

The Beatles and Bill Gates, according to Gladwell, had this much in common before hitting it big: more than 10,000 hours perfecting their craft.

The saying "practice makes perfect" resonates with us all. We are taught that the more we work at something, the harder we try, the better we become. And very often, this is true, up to a point.

If we run more, we become faster. If we lift more weights, we become stronger. If we do more math problems, we become better at math. If we practice the piano longer, we sound better.

But all disciplines are not created equal. "Deliberate practice" has been found to be most effective in explaining the variance of performance in games, music and sports.[1] These are fixed, stable systems where the rules don't change. In less stable fields, deliberate practice is a much poorer predictor of success.[2] Randomness and serendipity play a much greater role in these fields than we *want* to believe.

Which is why what I'm going to say next may not sit well with many, especially if you do this for a living.

The 10,000 hour rule does not apply to trading/investing.

Why not?

Because trading/investing is not tennis or chess; it is at the complete opposite end of the spectrum. Tennis and chess are games with fixed rules; investing is a game where the rules (markets, probabilities) are always changing. As Michael Burry of *The Big Short* fame once said: "no school could teach someone to become a great investor."[3] For if there was such a school "it'd be the most popular school in the world, with an impossibly high tuition."

There can be no standardized path to excellence in a field that is so heavily dictated by chance. Whether you believe the markets are perfectly efficient and follow a purely random walk or not (I do not),[4] we know that luck trumps skill in investment outcomes. Let me say that one more time: luck trumps skill in investment outcomes.[5]

This is most glaringly true in the short run but also can be true in the long run (if a million people flip a coin or pick a stock, someone will likely land on heads or pick a winner 20 straight times).

As such, the successes of the "market wizards" of years past are hard to decipher. They were certainly "outliers" in terms of their performance, but we cannot definitively tell whether that performance was the result of skill or luck. There is no simple test that can delineate between the two. Even if we concluded that there was some skill involved,[6] doing x, y,

---

[1]   journals.sagepub.com/doi/abs/10.1177/0956797614535810
[2]   bit.ly/2wEaA9J
[3]   bit.ly/2IsHiiS
[4]   papers.ssrn.com/sol3/papers.cfm?abstract_id=2741701
[5]   bit.ly/2I47JMh
[6]   unc.live/2IynLxG

and z because a "market wizard" did x, y, and z in the past is a guarantee of nothing.

For no amount of practice, "deliberate" or otherwise, would be sufficient to achieve their "world-class" or "mastery" status because the environment they operated in no longer exists. It was ephemeral. If the wizards themselves were faced with the task of repeating their prior successes, they too would fail—Warren Buffett would not be the next Warren Buffett if he had to start over again today. Paul Tudor Jones would not be the next Paul Tudor Jones. Stanley Druckenmiller would not be the next Stanley Druckenmiller.

Different markets. Different environments. Different outcomes.

But you can do much worse than trying to emulate the market wizards of the past. What many so-called "professional" investors consider "practice" is nothing of the sort. They spend their entire careers reading the news, watching financial TV, trading stocks on rumors and tips, and practicing old wives' tales and myths. They can spend 50,000 hours during a career engaging in such activities and have achieved "mastery" of ... nothing.

In *Thinking, Fast and Slow*, Daniel Kahneman relates a story on the "illusion of financial skill." He and Richard Thaler were given a vast amount of performance data on a group of 25 wealth advisers over an eight-year period. The advisers were compensated in large part based on their investment performance and all "felt they were competent professionals doing a serious job."

Their finding: there was no evidence whatsoever of persistent stock-picking skill—"the results resembled what you would expect from a dice-rolling contest." And yet the company was "rewarding luck as if it were skill." When Kahneman/Thaler presented their findings, the firm went on just as before, learning nothing at all from the experience. "I have done very well for the firm and no one can take that away from me," said one adviser.

This should not be all-that surprising, for as Kahneman noted, "facts that challenge such basic assumptions—and thereby threaten people's livelihood and self-esteem—are simply not absorbed."

The experience of these advisers was by no means unique. As Kahneman goes into detail explaining: "professional investors, including fund managers, fail a basic test of skill: persistent achievement." The best performing fund managers over the standard three-year evaluation periods often become the worst and vice versa.[7] Study after study show a lack of persistence in performance and to the contrary, evidence of mean reversion.[8]

Herein lies the dilemma. What is the average investor to do if spending 10,000 hours or more "practicing" will not *necessarily* make you perform better?

They can start by spending just ten minutes learning of the importance of controlling costs, diversification and asset allocation.[9] If they do this and nothing else they will beat most of the so-called "pros" as a jack of all trades and a master of nothing. In a field where the outcome is driven more by luck than by skill, being a master of nothing (diversifying and protecting yourself from the unknowable future) yields the highest probability of success.

How can this be? Doesn't more effort/practice/trading equal better outcomes? No, not necessarily.

Doing less actually tends to lead to higher returns.[10] Not for everyone (there will always be outliers, skillful or otherwise), but for most.

It is one of the unique paradoxes of this business that more "practice," more "trading," more "opining" on markets can actually lead to poorer results. This is so because we are dealing with an unstable system where "deliberate practice" is nearly impossible. What do you practice if the future will look nothing like the past?

This is so antithetical to our way of thinking that doing nothing is probably the most difficult thing you can do, so difficult that you can become "world-class" simply by sitting on your hands. Which is why I firmly believe that there is such a thing as an investment professional. It's just not anything close to what we tend to think it is (an overly confident, brash personality making extreme forecasts and firing away trades all

---

[7] papers.ssrn.com/sol3/papers.cfm?abstract_id=2732060
[8] www.vanguard.com/bogle_site/lib/sp19980129.html
[9] advisors.vanguard.com/iwe/pdf/ICRPC.pdf
[10] bit.ly/1VZMp7a

day). Being an investment professional is more akin to being a 1st grade teacher and a psychologist: educating your clients on the same simple concepts over and over again while helping to control their emotions. This is true regardless of where you are in the active-passive spectrum.[11]

If you are a fiduciary and are going to spend 10,000 hours doing something, shut off the TV and spend your time doing this:

- Helping your clients understand what they own and why they own it.[12]

- Helping your clients control their fear of missing out and their impulse to panic and sell (fear of drawdowns/losses).

There is no harder task in this business than protecting investors from themselves. After more than 10,000 hours into my journey, of this one thing I am sure.

Originally published, January 1, 2017; pensionpartners.com/10000-hours-or-10-minutes-what-does-it-take-to-be-a-world-class-investor.

ABOUT CHARLIE BILELLO

Charlie Bilello is the Director of Research at Pension Partners, LLC, an investment advisor that manages mutual funds and separate accounts. He is the co-author of four award-winning research papers on market anomalies and investing. Charlie is responsible for strategy development, investment research and communicating the firm's investment themes and portfolio positioning to clients. Prior to joining Pension Partners, he was the Managing Member of Momentum Global Advisors and previously held positions as a Credit, Equity and Hedge Fund Analyst at billion dollar alternative investment firms.

Charlie holds a J.D. and M.B.A. in Finance and Accounting from Fordham University and a B.A. in Economics from Binghamton

---

[11] pensionpartners.com/the-passive-investor-test
[12] pensionpartners.com/the-3-most-important-questions-in-investing

University. He is a Chartered Market Technician (CMT) and also holds the Certified Public Accountant (CPA) certificate.

In 2017, Charlie was named the StockTwits Person of the Year. He has been named by Business Insider and MarketWatch as one of the top people to follow on Twitter (@CharlieBilello) and his research has been featured in *Barron's*, Bloomberg, and the *Wall Street Journal*.

Forecasting Factor and Smart Beta Returns

(Hint: History Is Worse than Useless)

ROB ARNOTT, NOAH BECK
AND VITALI KALESNIK

Key Points

1. Using past performance to forecast future performance is likely to disappoint. We find that a factor's most recent five-year performance is negatively correlated with its subsequent five-year performance.

2. By significantly extending the period of past performance used to forecast future performance, we can improve predictive ability, but the forecasts are still negatively correlated with subsequent performance: *the forecast is still essentially useless!*

3. Using relative valuations, we forecast the five-year expected alphas for a broad universe of smart beta strategies as a tool for managing expectations about current portfolios and constructing new portfolios positioned for future outperformance. These forecasts will be updated regularly and available on our website.

* * *

In a series of articles we published in 2016,[1] we show that relative valuations predict subsequent returns for both factors and smart beta

---

[1] "How Can 'Smart Beta' Go Horribly Wrong?" by Arnott et al. (February 2016); "To Win with 'Smart Beta' Ask If the Price Is Right" by Arnott, Beck, and Kalesnik (June 2016); and "Timing 'Smart Beta' Strategies? Of Course! Buy Low, Sell High!" by Arnott, Beck, and Kalesnik (September 2016).

strategies in exactly the same way price matters in stock selection and asset allocation. To many, one surprising revelation in that series is that a number of "smart beta" strategies are expensive today relative to their historical valuations. The fact they are expensive has two uncomfortable implications. The first is that the past success of a smart beta strategy— often only a simulated past performance—is partly a consequence of "revaluation alpha" arising because many of these strategies enjoy a tailwind as they become more expensive. We, as investors, extrapolate that part of the historical alpha at our peril. The second implication is that any mean reversion toward the smart beta strategy's historical normal relative valuation could transform lofty historical alpha into negative future alpha. As with asset allocation and stock selection, relative valuations can predict the long-term future returns of strategies and factors—not precisely, nor with any meaningful short-term timing efficacy, but well enough to add material value. These findings are robust to variations in valuation metrics, geographies, and time periods used for estimation.

Two assumptions widely supported in the finance literature form the basis for how most investors forecast factor alpha and smart beta strategy alpha. We believe both, although strongly entrenched in investors' thinking, are wrong. The two assumptions we take issue with are that past performance of factor tilts and smart beta strategies is the best estimate of their future performance, and that factors and smart beta strategies have constant risk premia (value-add) over time.

Common sense tells us that current yield begets future return. Nowhere is this more intuitive than in the bond market. Investors fully understand that the average 30-year past return of long bonds, currently north of 7%, tells us nothing about the future return of long bonds. The current yield, around 3%, is far more predictive. In the equity market, at least since the 1980s, we know that the cyclically adjusted price-to-earnings (CAPE) ratio, as demonstrated by Robert Shiller, and the dividend yield are both good predictors of long-term subsequent returns.

If relative valuation, and the implication it has for mean reversion, is useful for stock selection and for asset allocation, why would it *not* matter in choosing factor tilts and equity strategies? The widespread promotion by the quant community of products based on past performance—*often backtests and simulations*—has contributed, and still does contribute, to investors' costly bad habit of performance chasing. The innocent-looking assumption of "past is prologue" conveniently encourages investors and asset managers to pick strategies with high past performance and to presume the past alpha will persist in the future.

In our 2016 smart beta series we offer evidence that relative valuations are important in the world of factors and smart beta strategies. We show that variations in valuation levels predict subsequent returns and that this relationship is robust across geographies, strategies, forecast periods, and our choice of valuation metrics. Our research tells us that investors who (too often) select strategies based on wonderful past performance are likely to have disappointing performance going forward. For many, mean reversion toward historical valuation norms dashes their hopes of achieving the returns of the recent past.

These conclusions are, of course, just qualitative. To make them practical, we need to quantify the effects we observe. In this article we do precisely that. We measure the richness of selected factors based on their relative valuations versus their respective historical norms and calculate their implied alphas. We also call attention to the real-world "haircuts" on the implied alphas—implementation shortfall, trading costs, and manager fees—which don't show up in paper portfolios and simulations.

Why Valuations Matter

We can easily see the link between valuation and subsequent performance on a scatterplot created using these two variables. The two scatterplots in Figure 1 are from Arnott, Beck, and Kalesnik (2016a) and are examples of the historical distributions of valuation ratios and subsequent five-year returns for a long–short *factor*, the classic Fama–French definition of value, and for a smart beta *strategy* (the low volatility index), as of March 31, 2016. In June 2016, we identified the former as the cheapest factor, relative to its history, and the latter as the most expensive strategy, relative to its history.

The value factor consists of a long value portfolio and a short growth portfolio. We measure performance and relative valuation by comparing the value portfolio relative to the growth portfolio. For the low-volatility index we measure performance and relative valuation by comparing the low-volatility portfolio with the cap-weighted stock market. The dotted line shows the average relationship between valuations and subsequent five-year performance. Both scatterplots show negative slope: richer valuations generally imply lower subsequent returns, while cheaper valuations imply higher subsequent returns. We use the same method for other factors and smart beta strategies. For most strategies and factors across multiple geographic regions the relationship is both statistically and economically significant.

Figure 1. Relative Valuations Forecast Subsequent Returns, United States Jan 1967–Mar 2016

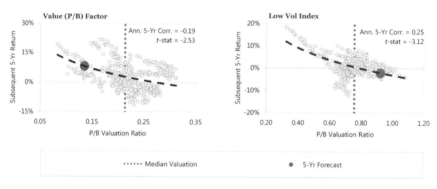

Source: Research Affiliates, LLC, using CRSP/Compustat. All *t*-statistics are Newey–West adjusted.
Note: Each dot in the scatterplots represents a month from January 1967 to March 2011.

Comparing Alpha-Forecasting Models

Many investors expect the alpha of a strategy to be its historical alpha, so much so that this assumption itself is an example of an alpha-forecasting model. One of the cornerstones of any investment process is an estimate of forward-looking return. We argue that a good alpha-forecasting model, whether for a strategy or a factor tilt, should have three key attributes:

1. Forecasts should correlate with subsequent alphas.

2. Forecasts should be paired with a measure of the likely accuracy of the forecast. A standard statistical way to measure the accuracy of a forecast is mean squared error, a measure of how reality has differed from past forecasts.

3. Forecasts should provide realistic estimates of expected returns.

These criteria provide useful metrics for us to compare different alpha-forecasting models. We select six models for comparison. One model assumes an efficient market: no factors or strategies have any alpha. Two of the models use only past performance and ignore valuations, and four of the models are based on valuation levels relative to historical norms.

Model 0. Zero factor alpha. In an early version of the efficient market hypothesis—the capital asset pricing model, or CAPM—researchers argued that an asset's return was solely determined by its exposure to the market risk factor. Similarly, Model 0 assumes the risk-adjusted alpha of a factor tilt or smart beta strategy is approximately zero. We measure the mean squared error relative to an expected alpha of zero.

Model 1. Recent past return (most recent five years). This model uses the most recent five-year performance of a factor or strategy to forecast its future return. Because our research tells us that investors who select strategies based on wonderful past performance are likely buying stocks with high valuations, we expect this model will favor the strategies that are currently expensive and have low future expected returns.

Model 2. Long-term historical past return (inception to date). Long-term historical factor returns are perhaps the most widely accepted way to estimate factor premiums (expected returns), both in the literature and in the practitioner community. Doing so requires that we extrapolate historical alpha to make the forecast: what has worked in the past is deemed likely to work in the future. Averaging performance over a very long period of time should *theoretically* mitigate vulnerability to end-point richness.[2] By using multiple decades of history (versus a short five-year span as Model 1 does), we would expect this model to perform relatively well in differentiating well-performing factors from less-well-performing ones.

Model 3. Valuation dependent (overfit to data). This model is a simple and intuitive valuation-dependent model, as illustrated by the log-linear

---

[2]   As we show in Arnott et al. (2016), even a half-century (1950–1999) is too short to correctly gauge the stock-versus-bond risk premium. With most simulated histories for factors and smart beta strategies spanning only a quarter-century (sometimes much less), we should not expect past results to accurately predict future performance.

line of best fit in Figure 1.[3] At each point in time, we calibrate the model only to the historically observed data available at that time; no look-ahead information is in the model calibration. This model encourages us to buy what's become cheap (performed badly in the past), rather than chasing what's become newly expensive (has performed exceptionally well).

Model 4. Valuation dependent (shrunk parameters). A model calibrated using past results may be overfitted, and as a result provide exaggerated forecasts that are either too good or too bad to be true. Parameter shrinkage is a common way to reduce model overfitting to rein in extreme forecasts. (Appendix A provides more information on how we modify the parameters estimated in Model 4 to less extreme values.)

Model 5. Valuation dependent (shrunk parameters with variance reduction). Model 5 further shrinks Model 4 by dividing its output by two. The output of this model is perfectly correlated with the output of Model 4, with the forecast having exactly two times lower variability.

Model 6. Linear model (look-ahead calibration). Model 6 allows look-ahead bias. With our log-linear valuation model we estimate using the full sample. Of course, this model will deliver past "forecasts" that are implausibly good because no one has clairvoyant powers! Nevertheless, it provides a useful benchmark—a model that, by definition, has perfect fit to the data—against which we can compare our other models. How close can we come to this impossible ideal?

For our model comparison we use the same eight factors in the US market as we use in our previously published research. (The description of our factor construction methodology is available in Appendix B.) We use the first 24 years of data (Jan 1967–Dec 1990) in the initial model calibration, encompassing several valuation cycles, and use the remaining data (Jan 1991–Oct 2011) to run the model comparison. These data end

---

[3]   Referring to the scatterplots in Figure 1, the log-linear line of best fit can serve as a simple alpha-forecasting model. For instance, the blue dot on the value factor scatterplot suggests that prior to March 2016 the valuation level of 0.14—meaning the value portfolio was 14% as expensive as the growth portfolio measured by price-to-book ratio, and lower than the historical norm of 21% relative valuation—would have delivered an average annualized alpha of 8.1% over the next five years.

in 2011 because we are forecasting subsequent five-year performance; an end date in October allowed us to conduct our model comparison analysis in November and December. We report the comparison results in Table 1. Model 0 and Model 2 are our base cases. We need to beat a static zero-alpha assumption (Model 0) in order to even argue for the use of dynamic models in alpha forecasting. And we need to beat Model 2 to demonstrate the usefulness of a valuation-based forecasting model.

Assuming that future alpha is best estimated by the past five years of performance, Model 1 provides the least accurate forecast of alpha (i.e., based on mean squared error (MSE), it performs the worst of all six models). Further compounding its poor predictive ability, its forecasts are *negatively* correlated with subsequent factor performance. Focusing on recent performance—the way many investors choose their strategies and managers—is not only inadequate, it leads us in the wrong direction.

Model 2, which uses a much longer period of past performance to forecast future performance, provides a significant improvement in accuracy over Model 1, as reflected by a much smaller MSE. Still, as with Model 1, its forecasts are negatively correlated with subsequent performance, and its forecast accuracy is worse than the zero-factor-alpha Model 0.

The key takeaway in the comparison of Models 1 and 2 is that a very long history of returns, covering at least several decades, may provide a more accurate forecast of a factor's or smart beta strategy's return than a short-term history, *but the forecast is still essentially useless.* Selecting strategies or factors based on past performance, regardless of the length of the sample, will not help investors earn a superior return and is actually more likely to hurt them. The negative correlations of the forecasts of both Models 1 and 2 with subsequent factor returns imply that factors with great past performance are likely overpriced and are likely to perform poorly in the future.[4]

---

[4] We acknowledge that the result we obtained is based on a sample of factors that were selected based on their current popularity, such that their popularity is primarily a function of their high historical performance. Using a long sample of past returns may still be helpful in identifying the expected outperformance of factors or strategies. We would also argue that a measure of structural alpha, which adjusts past performance for the changes in valuations, would be more suitable for this task.

Table 1. Alpha-Forecasting Model Comparison (Test period 20 years, Jan 1991–Oct 2011; Initial calibration period 24 years, Jan 1967–Dec 1990)

Model #	0	1	2	3	4	5	6	
Model Description	Zero Factor Alpha	Past Return (Most Recent 5 Years)	Past Return (Inception to Date)	Valuation Dependent (Overfit to Data)	Valuation Dependent (Shrunk Parameters)	Valuation Dependent (Shrunk Parameters with Variance Reduction)	Valuation Dependent (Look-ahead Calibration)	Average Standard Deviation of Realized 5-Year Alpha
Standard Deviation of Alpha Forecast	0.0%	5.4%	0.6%	3.7%	2.3%	1.1%	3.0%	5.5%
Average Mean Squared Error (MSE)	0.346%	0.784%	0.418%	0.372%	0.315%	0.298%	0.253%	
Average MSE vs. Model 2	0.83	1.88	1.00	0.89	0.75	0.71	0.61	
t-stat of Difference in MSE vs. Model 2	-7.11***	6.93***	n/a	-2.98***	-8.14***	-13.90***	-11.01***	
Average MSE vs. Model 0	1.00	2.27	1.21	1.08	0.91	0.86	0.73	
t-stat of Difference in MSE vs. Model 0	n/a	9.22***	7.23***	1.67*	-1.90*	-5.10***	-5.44***	
Correlation of Forecast with Subsequent Return	n/a	-0.18	-0.39	0.37	0.36	0.36	0.54	
t-stat of Correlation	n/a	-1.48	-2.85	3.77	3.57	3.57	8.05	

Source: Research Affiliates, LLC, using CRSP/Compustat and Worldscope/Datastream data.

Note: A more detailed analysis of the comparison between Model 4 and Model 5 is provided in endnote 5.

Valuation-dependent Models 3–6 all have positive correlations between their forecasts and subsequent returns, and all beat Model 0 in this regard; the correlation is undefined for Model 0 because its forecasts are always constant. Models 4–6 beat Model 0 in forecast accuracy, with all having a lower MSE than Model 0.

Model 6, which is fit to the full half-century data sample, provides the best forecast of expected return because, of course, it's hard to beat clairvoyance! The improvement in forecasting error of 39% for Model 6 compared to Model 2 shows how much, *at best*, a valuation-based model can reduce the error term. Model 3, a linear model that does not use any look-ahead information in its calibration, reduces the error term by 11% compared to Model 2—nice, but not impressive—and its errors are a bit larger than the naïve assumption that all alphas are zero.

Model 4, which does not use look-ahead information in its calibration, reduces the error term by 25% versus Model 2, roughly two-thirds as good as clairvoyance! All four models that forecast using valuations (Models

3–6) are able to substantially improve forecast accuracy compared to Models 1 and 2, which use only past returns.[5]

Model 4 shrinks parameter estimates away from extreme values, mitigating the risk of overfitting the data. It also provides a more realistic out-of-sample alpha forecast compared with Model 5. We therefore apply it in the next section (while cheerfully acknowledging it could likely be further improved) to investigate what current valuations are telling us about the alpha forecasts for factors and smart beta strategies. Readers who are more interested in the current forecasts of Model 5, which is also a very good model, merely need to cut these forecasts in half.

Factor and Smart Beta Strategy Alpha Forecasts

Using Model 4, we calculate the alpha forecasts over the next five-year horizon for a number of factors and smart beta strategies.[6]

[5] A comparison of Models 4 and 5 shows that reducing the model forecast variability increases the accuracy of the forecasts (decreases MSE). For Model 4, the improvement in MSE is statistically significant only at the 10% confidence level, and for Model 5 the improvement is significant at more than a 1% confidence level. If we examine the variability of the alpha forecasts by comparing it to the realized alpha variability (both measured as standard deviation), we observe that Model 4's forecasted alpha variability is closer to actual variability, indicating that Model 4 forecasts a more realistic level of magnitude compared to Model 5. Models 4 and 5 are both adequate expected returns models useful for different purposes. Model 5's more muted output could make it a better candidate for use in portfolio optimization where higher amplitudes of inputs could lead an optimizer to create extreme portfolios. Model 4's unmuted output is more useful for investors interested in the level of potential excess returns—how positive or how negative—they might experience going forward.

[6] Expected returns forecast models come with multiple sources of uncertainty. The expected returns model we use estimates higher expected returns when the strategy or factor is valued below its historical norm, and vice versa. Cheap strategies can continue to get cheaper, however, resulting in poor returns when our model projects high returns. Expensive strategies can continue to get more expensive, resulting in high returns when our model projects poor returns. The choice of an expected returns model is also a source of uncertainty. Model parameters were estimated using a finite amount of data and are therefore subject to estimation error. Model specification choices, such as when and

Factors

We find that almost all popular factors in the US, developed, and emerging markets have shown strong historical returns. This outcome is utterly unsurprising: the road to popularity for a factor or a strategy is high past performance. The only popular factors with negative (but insignificant) past performance are illiquidity and low beta in the developed markets, and size in the emerging markets.

Figure 2, Panel A, plots the historical excess return and historical volatility, and Panel B the five-year expected return and expected volatility, at year-end 2016 for a number of common factors in the US market, constructed as long–short portfolios. We provide the same data for the developed and emerging markets in Appendix C. (The results can also be found in tabular form later in the article in Table 2, Panel A.) The alpha forecasts are plotted against the projected volatilities, which are estimated as an extrapolation of recent past volatility.[7]

The volatilities of the factor portfolios are a measure of the volatility of a long–short portfolio; in other words, these volatilities measure the volatility of the return *difference* between the long and short portfolios. Take, for example, the low beta factor in the United States, which has a volatility second only to the momentum factor. Does this mean that low beta stocks have high volatility? No. The factor portfolio that goes long in low beta stocks and short in high beta stocks carries with it a substantial negative net beta, which contributes to the volatility of the factor.[8]

---

how to shrink parameter estimates, could result in different expected returns outputs than are generated by the model used here.

[7]   For volatility forecasts we estimate past volatility using the full sample of returns with higher weight given to more recent data. The weights on squared deviations from the mean (for the standard deviation computation) follow an exponential decay process with a half-life of 5 years, so that the most recent data point has twice the weight in the volatility estimate as 5 years ago, which has twice the weight as 10 years ago, and so on. The 5-year half-life was chosen to match the 5-year expectation period of equity portfolios. The exponential decay-weighted volatility estimates function as an approximation of current volatility, which is our best estimate for forward-looking volatility. Expected tracking error of smart beta strategies is computed in the same way.

[8]   Our low beta factor is dollar neutral, but not beta neutral, unlike the popular leveraged betting-against-beta (BAB) factor (Frazzini and Pedersen,

Figure 2. Risk and Return Characteristics for US Factors

Panel A. Historical Returns, Jul 1968–Dec 2016

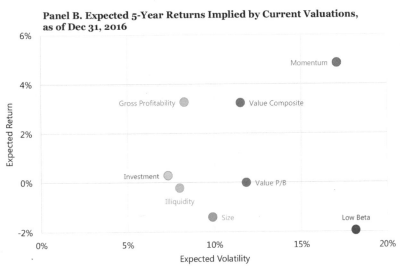

Panel B. Expected 5-Year Returns Implied by Current Valuations, as of Dec 31, 2016

Source: Research Affiliates, LLC, using CRSP/Compustat and Worldscope/Datastream data.

2014), which is beta neutral but not dollar neutral. Whereas the BAB factor is appropriate for use in factor regressions, it is difficult and expensive to replicate. Our dollar-neutral factor is appropriate for comparison with typical low beta strategies that do not employ leverage.

The volatility of the low beta factor in this long-short framework therefore suggests that a long-only low beta investor should expect large tracking error with respect to the market, even if the portfolio is much less risky than the market. Momentum also typically leads to high tracking error, while the investment factor leads to low tracking error. Viewing projected alpha and relative risk together gives us an insight into the likely information ratios currently available in these factors.

Factors with negative forecasted alpha. Forecasted alphas for low beta factors are negative in all markets. Having experienced a strong bull market from 2000 through early 2016, and even after a large pullback over the second half of 2016, low beta factors are still quite expensive relative to their historical valuation norms. We hesitate to speculate if this is due to the rising popularity of the factor driving the relative valuation higher or the soaring valuation driving the rising popularity. As anyone in the social sciences knows, correlation is not causation. Either way, the data suggest we should not expect low beta strategies to add much value to investor portfolios until their valuations are more consistent with their past norms.

We also hesitate to dismiss the low beta factor solely because of its relative valuation. Diversification and the quest for return are both important goals. Even at current valuation levels, low volatility can serve an important role in both reducing and diversifying risk. A sensible response is to rely on the low beta factor less than we might have in the past.

Alpha forecasts for the size factor (small cap versus large cap) are negative in all markets. Put another way, the size factor in all regions is expensive relative to its own historical average. In the United States this relationship has flipped from a year ago: the Russell 2000 Index beat the Russell 1000 Index by over 1,000 bps in the second half of 2016. This huge move takes the size factor (in the United States) from somewhat cheap a year ago to neutral now. Size has lower long-term historical performance compared to other factors in most regions, so modest overvaluation (outside the United States) is enough to drive our alpha forecasts negative. Other factors with less attractive projected alphas are illiquidity in the US market and gross profitability in the developed markets, both forecast to have close to zero expected return over the next five years.

Factors with positive forecasted alphas. Value outperformed handily in 2016, but not enough to erase the relative cheapness of the strategy in most markets, especially in the emerging markets. Increasing valuation dispersion around the globe has opened up many great opportunities for the patient value investor, the mirror image—tumbling popularity, tumbling relative valuations, and tumbling historical returns—of the picture painted by low beta.

We look at value two ways. The first, a composite, is one of the factors with the highest projected expected returns across all regions. The composite is constructed using four valuation metrics, each measuring the relative valuation multiples of the long portfolio (value) relative to the short portfolio (growth): Price to book value (P/B), price to five-year average earnings (P/E), price to five-year average sales (P/S), and price to five-year average dividends (P/D).

The second value factor we construct is based on P/B, the classic measure most favored in academe. Unlike the value composite, it has close to zero projected return. The lower forecasted return may be associated with the big gap in profitability observed among companies today versus in the past. A strategy favoring high B/P companies may favor less profitable companies, increasing investor exposure to "value traps"—those companies that look cheap on their way to zero!

After a lousy second half of 2016, momentum has flipped from overpriced to underpriced. Is this because momentum underperformed so drastically that it's now cheap? No. Its composition changed. A year ago, the FANGs (Facebook, Amazon, Netflix, and Google) had great momentum—the momentum factor was signaling "buy." Value stocks are handily outpacing growth now, and value has the momentum. It turns out that, although for most factors relative valuation plays out slowly over a number of years, valuation is a pretty good short-term predictor for momentum performance. Across all markets, we expect momentum to deliver respectable future performance slightly above historical norms. The "signal" changes pretty rapidly from year to year (and sometimes even from month to month).

Finally, we are projecting good performance for gross profitability in the US market over the next five years, a switch from last spring. Quality's disappointing performance in the second half of 2016 sowed the seeds for this turn in relative attractiveness.

Our return forecasts are all before trading costs and fees. In the real world, these anticipated costs should be subtracted from return forecasts to reflect the investor's true expected return. In the case of momentum, trading costs can dwarf fees.

Smart Beta Strategies

In addition to factors, which are theoretical difficult-to-replicate long–short portfolios, we estimate the expected risk–return characteristics for a selection of the more-popular smart beta strategies. The list of strategies and the description of their methodologies is available in Appendix B. In order to produce forecasts we replicate the strategies using the published methodologies of the underlying indices. Any replication exercise is subject to deviation from the original due to differences in databases, rebalancing dates, interpretations of the written methodologies, omitted details in the methodology description, and so forth; our replication is no exception.[9] The results of the replicated exercise, albeit imprecise, should be informative of the underlying strategies.[10]

---

[9] The data sources (CRSP, Compustat, Worldscope, Datastream, and Bloomberg) used to construct and evaluate portfolios may contain multiple errors. These errors may bias performance (up or down) of certain strategies or factors compared to what an actual investor would have been able to achieve in the real market. Further, the simulation results ignore management fees, costs of shorting, and other potentially very important elements that may make the live portfolio outcome different from the theoretically simulated portfolio.

[10] Risks associated with individual equity factors are also borne by investments that tilt their holdings toward these factors. Investing in factors can subject investors to unique risks that include, but are not limited to, the following: Momentum strategies invest in recent winners that tend to continue outperforming, however, when the market changes direction, momentum investors are subject to a quick burst of severe underperformance known as a momentum crash. Low beta or low-volatility strategies have lower absolute risk than the market, but typically come at the cost of higher relative risk. Low-vol strategies tend to have higher tracking error, which represents the risk that the strategy deviates from the market for extended periods of time. Value strategies often have prolonged periods of underperformance, sometimes followed by quick bursts of outperformance. Value investors who reduce their

The results for the smart beta strategies yield a number of interesting observations, some of which are quite similar to our observations about factors. Like popular factors, all popular strategies in all regions (with the exception of small cap in emerging markets) have positive historical returns. Again, this should not be surprising because these strategies would not be popular without strong historical returns! Note many of the strategies are simulated backtests for most of the historical test span. Accordingly, as with factors, the high historical returns for long-only investment strategies should be adjusted downward for selection bias.

The historical and expected alphas for the smart beta strategies, as well as their respective tracking errors, implied by current US valuation levels are shown in the scatterplots in Figure 3. Appendix D presents the same data for the developed and emerging markets. (The data are also provided in tabular form later in the article in Table 2, Panel B.)

Smart beta strategies with negative forecasted alphas. Like our findings regarding the low beta factor, we project that the low beta and low-volatility strategies will underperform their respective benchmarks across all regions. Even after some pretty disappointing results during the second half of 2016, these strategies still trade at premium valuations. This doesn't mean that investors should avoid them altogether! They will reduce portfolio volatility and are complementary to many other strategies.

---

value exposure following periods of value underperformance run the risk of mistiming their exposure and missing out on the periods when the value factor recovers. The profitability factor often invests in more expensive companies: high corporate profits can mean revert to lower profits in the future due to an increase in competition or a decrease in the barriers to entry. Investing in profitable companies at any cost runs the risk of overpaying for expected future profits. The illiquidity factor earns a premium by providing liquidity, but leaves illiquidity-tilted investors prone to liquidity shocks that could lead to high costs of exiting their positions. The investment factor tilts toward companies with lower asset growth, and thus can risk missing out on potential growth opportunities. Tilting toward the size factor by investing in small-cap stocks can provide diversification away from large caps, but often comes with higher portfolio volatility, potentially lower liquidity, and higher transaction costs.

Figure 3. Risk and Return Characteristics for US Smart Beta Strategies

Panel A. Historical Excess Returns (Gross), Jul 1968–Dec 2016

Panel B. Expected 5-Year Excess Returns (Gross)
Implied by Current Valuations, as of Dec 31, 2016

Source: Research Affiliates, LLC, using CRSP/Compustat and Worldscope/Datastream data.

We also project small-cap and equally weighted strategies to have negative returns over the next five years. After a sharp run-up in small versus large stocks during the second half of 2016, the size factor is now expensive relative to average historical valuations in all regions.

Smart beta strategies with positive forecasted alphas. On the other side of the spectrum, strategies with a value orientation, such as the Fundamental Index™, are projected to have high expected returns in most regions.[II] Unlike low-volatility or small-cap strategies, value strategies produced only mediocre returns over the last decade, scaring many investors away even though the logic should be the opposite: poor past performance implies cheap valuations, positioning these strategies for healthy performance going forward.

Similarly, income-oriented strategies, such as High Dividend and RAFI™ Equity Income, are generally projected to have high expected returns across all regions. Momentum-oriented strategies in all regions—in stark contrast to a year ago—tend to have decent projected returns, gross of trading costs (which we discuss in the next section).

After faltering rather seriously in the second half of 2016, quality has the highest expected return in the US market, attributable in large degree to its being the mirror image of the B/P value factor. Given the current high level of dispersion in profitability across companies, many high-quality companies are trading at reasonably attractive valuations.

Finally, the RAFI Size Factor strategy is projected to have a much higher return in the US and developed markets than other small cap–oriented strategies. It's important to note that "RAFI Size Factor" is not the same as the RAFI 1500 for small companies, but rather is a blend of four factor-tilt strategies, each formed within the universe of small-cap stocks: small value, small momentum, small low volatility, and small quality (a factor

---

[II] One exception is the Gen-1 Value strategy in the US market. The strategy has two Achilles' heels. The first is that because it relies on B/P, its low projected alpha may be associated with low profitability of the companies the strategy favors. The second weakness is that because it is capitalization weighted, it doesn't give correspondingly more weight to the cheapest companies. The Gen-1 Value simulation is based on the Russell 1000 Value Index methodology to select stocks from the parent universe according to a composite value score calculated using B/P, five-year sales per share growth, and two-year earnings per share growth. Stocks are weighted by the product of this score and market capitalization, and rebalanced annually. More information on the Gen-1 Value strategy is available at www.researchaffiliates.com/documents/smart-beta-methodologies.pdf.

that combines profitability and investment metrics). Instead of trying to capture the Fama-French SMB (small minus big) factor, one of the factors with weak long-term empirical support, RAFI Size Factor tries to capture other well-documented factor premia within this segment of small stocks having higher risk and higher potential for mispricing.

Trading Costs Matter!

We quants have the luxury of residing in a world of theory and truly vast data. Investors operate in the real world. As such, no discussion of forecast returns would be complete without addressing the costs associated with implementing an investment strategy. All of our preceding analysis— as well as the backtests and simulated smart beta strategy and factor investing performance touted in the market today—deals with paper portfolios.

No fees or trading costs are considered in these paper portfolios, yet in the real world they are a material drag on investors' performance. Management fees are highly visible and investors are starting to pay a lot more attention to them. We applaud this development. We find it puzzling however that, in order to save a few basis points of visible fees, some investors will eagerly embrace dozens of basis points of trading costs, missed trades, transition costs for changing strategies, and other hidden costs. The impact of these hidden costs is that the investor's performance is often lower than return forecasts had indicated.[12]

Monitoring manager performance relative to an index is insufficient to gauge implementation costs. One of the dirty secrets of the indexing world is that indexers can adjust their portfolios for changes in index composition or weights, and changes in the published index take place

---

[12] The difference between 100 bps and 20 bps is huge, the difference between 20 bps and 4 bps is not. Many strategies incur well over 100 bps in hidden costs, often lumped together in a category called implementation shortfall. We are amused at how many investors will cheerfully pay 2+20 for a hedge fund, with no justification for the fee beyond past returns, but will fight hammer and tongs over 2 bps for a quant product. A cost-minimizing manager can easily charge a few basis points less, and then lose multiples of the difference through careless implementation and sloppy trading.

after these trades have already moved prices. Indexers' costs per trade can be startlingly high; thankfully, their turnover is generally very low.

Another nuance in assessing "hidden" implementation costs is the impact of related strategies. Investors who index to the Russell 1000 and to the S&P 500 Index have 85–90% overlap in holdings, so they impact each other's liquidity and trading costs. Another example is the overlap between minimum variance, low volatility, low beta, and low variance strategies, or to cite our own products, the similarity between FTSE RAFI™ and Russell RAFI™. If significant assets are managed under similar strategies, the *combined* AUM will drive the liquidity and the implementation shortfall of the individual strategies.

To quantify the effect of trading costs on different strategies we use the model developed by our colleagues Aked and Moroz (2015). The price impact defined by their model is linearly proportional to the amount of trading in individual stocks, measured relative to the average daily volume (ADV). They estimate the price impact is about 30 basis points per each 10% of ADV. For our cost estimates we assume $10 billion is invested in each strategy in the US and developed markets, and $1 billion in the emerging markets. A summary of projected alphas, net of trading costs, in the US market is shown in the scatterplot in Figure 4, as of year-end 2016. The same information for the developed and emerging markets is provided in Appendix E.

Many of the strategies still show quite attractive performance. The heaviest toll from trading costs is on the momentum and low-volatility strategies. Momentum strategies, typified by high turnover and by fierce competition to buy the same stocks at the same time on the rebalancing dates, are likely associated with high trading costs. Low-volatility strategies, already operating from a baseline of low projected returns due to their currently rich valuations, are particularly vulnerable to the impact of trading costs. Low-volatility index calculators and managers should pay close attention to ways to reduce turnover. Again, these strategies have merit for risk reduction and diversification, but we would caution against expecting the lofty returns of the past.

Figure 4. Expected 5-Year Excess Returns, Net of Trading Costs, for US Smart Beta Strategies Implied by Current Valuations and Historical Estimated Trading Costs, as of Dec 31, 2016

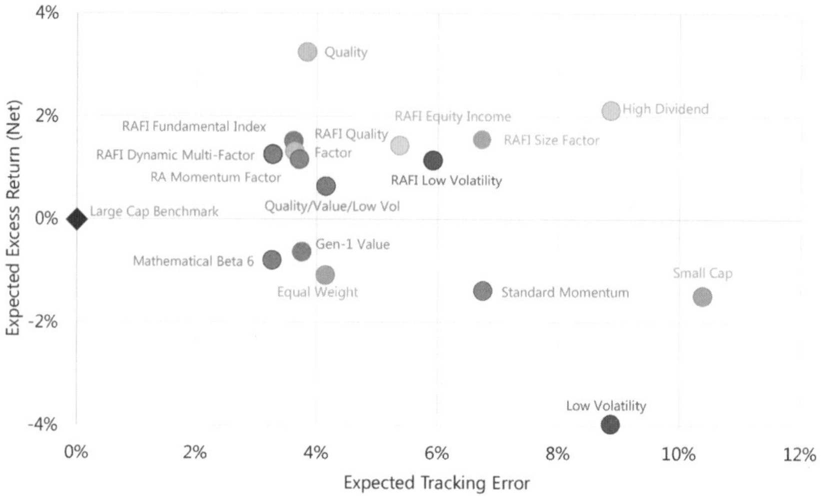

Source: Research Affiliates, LLC, using CRSP/Compustat and Worldscope/Datastream data.

Five-Year Forecasts

We summarize the valuation ratios, historical returns, historical returns net of valuation changes, and expected returns along with estimation errors for the most popular factors and strategies in Table 2. Panel A shows the results for factors, and Panel B shows the results for smart beta strategies. *All of these results reflect our method of calculating relative valuation and relative return forecasts, as described in the published methodology for each of these strategies. We caution against acting on these forecasts without examining the potential considerations that our approach doesn't capture. These forecasts have uncertainty that, in most cases, is larger than the alpha forecast.*

Although large, these tables represent only a portion of the multitude of layers and dimensions that investors should consider when evaluating these strategies. We encourage investors and equity managers to use the tables as a reference point when making factor allocation decisions. As time passes, valuations change, and the expected returns in the table need to be updated to stay relevant. Strategies that seem vulnerable today may be attractively priced tomorrow, and vice versa. The good news is that we will be providing this information, regularly updated, for these and many more strategies and factors on a new interactive section of our website.[13] We encourage readers to visit frequently and to liberally provide feedback.

Table 2. Valuations, Returns, and Expectations of Factors and Smart Beta Strategies, as of Dec 31, 2016

Panel A. Factors

Region	Strategy Name	Current Valuation Ratio	Median Valuation Ratio	Current Valuation Ratio Percentile	Historical Excess Return (ITD)	Historical Alpha Net of Changes in Valuation	Historical Volatility	5-Yr Expected Excess Return (Ann.)	Standard Error of Expected Return	Expected Volatility
United States	Value P/B	0.46	0.37	81%	2.0%	1.1%	11.5%	0.0%	4.0%	11.8%
	Value Composite	0.28	0.27	55%	2.2%	2.5%	12.8%	3.2%	5.3%	11.5%
	Momentum	0.96	1.55	13%	3.0%	2.6%	16.9%	4.9%	5.3%	17.1%
	Illiquidity	1.12	0.99	75%	2.1%	1.6%	8.5%	-0.2%	4.4%	8.0%
	Low Beta	1.13	0.72	89%	1.5%	0.9%	16.8%	-2.0%	7.0%	18.2%
	Gross Profitability	1.63	1.90	27%	0.6%	1.5%	10.1%	3.3%	4.6%	8.3%
	Investment	0.65	0.57	73%	2.5%	1.9%	8.8%	0.3%	3.9%	7.3%
	Size	1.02	0.95	68%	1.7%	1.2%	11.2%	-1.4%	4.9%	9.9%
Developed Market	Value P/B	0.38	0.41	34%	1.9%	1.8%	9.1%	3.1%	4.4%	8.4%
	Value Composite	0.27	0.31	18%	3.6%	3.8%	11.0%	5.2%	4.8%	9.0%
	Momentum	0.93	1.53	4%	3.5%	3.0%	15.6%	5.6%	4.3%	13.9%
	Illiquidity	0.87	0.92	27%	-0.1%	0.0%	6.3%	2.1%	4.1%	5.6%
	Low Beta	1.63	0.93	92%	-0.5%	-3.2%	16.3%	-2.4%	5.2%	16.1%
	Gross Profitability	1.70	1.53	76%	4.2%	3.9%	7.0%	0.6%	4.6%	6.1%
	Investment	0.63	0.69	21%	1.6%	1.5%	7.7%	2.9%	3.0%	6.3%
	Size	0.88	0.85	67%	1.3%	0.6%	7.4%	-1.2%	2.7%	6.1%
Emerging Market	Value P/B	0.29	0.41	13%	5.2%	8.9%	9.6%	6.0%	6.6%	9.5%
	Value Composite	0.24	0.31	15%	8.1%	10.0%	9.3%	6.8%	4.7%	9.6%
	Momentum	0.98	1.54	1%	5.4%	2.2%	14.5%	6.1%	5.8%	13.9%
	Illiquidity	0.94	0.99	37%	3.9%	1.9%	7.0%	2.3%	4.0%	6.5%
	Low Beta	1.43	1.09	86%	-0.1%	-3.9%	15.5%	-1.7%	4.4%	14.9%
	Gross Profitability	1.51	1.35	63%	4.3%	1.6%	9.8%	0.7%	4.5%	9.5%
	Investment	0.52	0.74	14%	0.8%	1.1%	9.4%	4.7%	3.3%	9.2%
	Size	0.89	0.71	87%	-0.9%	-4.2%	8.0%	-3.6%	4.6%	7.5%

Source: Research Affiliates, LLC, using CRSP/Compustat and Worldscope/Datastream data. Note: ITD is inception to date.

[13]   interactive.researchaffiliates.com/smart-beta

Table 2. Valuations, Returns, and Expectations of Factors and Smart Beta Strategies, as of Dec 31, 2016

Panel B. Smart Beta Strategies

Region	Strategy Name	Current Valuation Ratio	Median Valuation Ratio	Current Valuation Ratio Percentile	Historical Excess Return (ITD)	Historical Alpha Net of Changes in Valuation	Historical Tracking Error	5-Yr Expected Excess Return Gross (Ann.)	5-Yr Expected Excess Return Net of Trading Costs (Ann.)	Standard Error of Expected Return	Expected Tracking Error
United States	Gen-1 Value	0.77	0.75	79%	0.9%	0.7%	4.4%	-0.5%	-0.6%	-1.8%	3.8%
	RAFI Fundamental Index	0.71	0.72	47%	1.6%	1.6%	4.1%	1.5%	1.5%	1.7%	3.6%
	High Dividend	0.65	0.67	42%	2.0%	2.9%	8.3%	2.7%	2.1%	3.3%	8.9%
	RAFI Equity Income	0.67	0.68	46%	2.3%	2.1%	6.0%	2.0%	1.4%	2.6%	5.4%
	Low Volatility	1.00	0.81	96%	1.1%	1.0%	9.1%	-2.1%	-4.0%	3.4%	8.9%
	RAFI Low Volatility	0.70	0.67	72%	2.4%	2.5%	6.9%	1.2%	1.2%	3.9%	5.9%
	Quality	1.15	1.46	10%	1.1%	1.8%	5.1%	3.6%	3.2%	2.6%	3.8%
	RAFI Quality Factor	0.96	0.94	63%	1.5%	1.9%	3.9%	1.4%	1.3%	1.7%	3.6%
	Standard Momentum	1.20	1.27	36%	1.8%	1.5%	7.4%	1.3%	-1.4%	2.7%	6.7%
	RA Momentum Factor	0.88	1.02	13%	1.5%	1.4%	4.3%	2.5%	1.2%	1.8%	3.7%
	Quality/Value/Low Vol	1.11	1.11	50%	1.3%	1.3%	3.7%	0.9%	0.6%	1.5%	4.2%
	Mathematical Beta 6	0.96	0.87	83%	1.5%	1.2%	4.0%	-0.7%	-0.8%	1.9%	3.3%
	RAFI Dynamic Multi-Factor	0.82	0.80	66%	2.5%	2.3%	3.7%	1.5%	1.3%	2.0%	3.3%
	Equal Weight	1.00	0.94	77%	0.8%	0.6%	4.6%	-0.9%	-1.1%	2.0%	4.1%
	Small Cap	0.90	0.93	46%	0.4%	-0.1%	13.2%	-0.9%	-1.5%	5.8%	10.4%
	RAFI Size Factor	0.90	0.93	39%	3.2%	2.6%	7.5%	2.4%	1.6%	3.9%	6.7%
Developed Market	Gen-1 Value	0.78	0.78	43%	0.2%	0.2%	3.4%	0.9%	0.8%	1.3%	2.8%
	RAFI Fundamental Index	0.71	0.71	50%	2.3%	2.0%	4.3%	1.7%	1.6%	1.6%	3.1%
	High Dividend	0.66	0.62	63%	2.9%	1.9%	8.6%	1.5%	0.8%	2.6%	6.5%
	RAFI Equity Income	0.66	0.66	49%	3.4%	3.0%	6.3%	2.1%	1.7%	2.5%	4.7%
	Low Volatility	1.11	0.83	92%	2.4%	0.3%	9.9%	-2.0%	-3.9%	3.4%	8.9%
	RAFI Low Volatility	0.76	0.66	77%	3.2%	1.8%	7.0%	0.9%	0.8%	3.1%	6.0%
	Quality	1.42	1.33	66%	3.0%	2.3%	5.5%	0.5%	0.4%	2.3%	3.9%
	RAFI Quality Factor	0.92	0.86	79%	2.7%	2.0%	4.6%	1.1%	1.1%	1.8%	3.4%
	Standard Momentum	1.32	1.19	67%	1.4%	0.9%	6.8%	0.5%	-1.0%	2.8%	5.7%
	RA Momentum Factor	0.88	1.01	7%	2.0%	1.8%	4.0%	3.0%	2.2%	1.6%	3.3%
	Quality/Value/Low Vol	1.29	1.08	92%	1.7%	0.6%	4.6%	-1.0%	-1.1%	1.7%	4.6%
	Mathematical Beta 6	1.01	0.90	93%	1.6%	0.9%	3.0%	-1.0%	-1.1%	1.7%	2.3%
	RAFI Dynamic Multi-Factor	0.85	0.80	73%	2.9%	1.9%	4.1%	1.4%	1.2%	1.9%	3.0%
	Equal Weight	0.87	0.90	32%	0.6%	0.2%	4.0%	0.4%	0.1%	2.4%	3.4%
	Small Cap	1.01	0.90	92%	1.7%	1.0%	6.5%	-3.3%	-3.7%	3.1%	5.8%
	RAFI Size Factor	0.99	0.83	74%	2.9%	1.3%	5.9%	0.3%	-0.6%	4.1%	4.8%
Emerging Market	Gen-1 Value	0.73	0.83	5%	1.7%	2.2%	4.2%	3.7%	3.4%	1.6%	4.1%
	RAFI Fundamental Index	0.62	0.68	25%	2.8%	3.3%	4.6%	2.7%	2.7%	1.9%	5.3%
	High Dividend	0.66	0.69	43%	3.8%	4.0%	6.0%	3.4%	1.7%	2.0%	5.7%
	RAFI Equity Income	0.65	0.65	50%	2.7%	2.4%	5.6%	2.8%	2.3%	1.8%	5.5%
	Low Volatility	1.18	0.93	98%	1.3%	-0.9%	8.3%	-2.6%	-4.7%	2.8%	7.4%
	RAFI Low Volatility	0.75	0.68	77%	4.1%	2.1%	6.8%	0.8%	0.6%	2.3%	6.4%
	Quality	1.39	1.17	87%	0.5%	-1.3%	4.3%	-0.7%	-1.0%	1.6%	4.1%
	RAFI Quality Factor	0.75	0.72	69%	2.2%	1.6%	5.7%	1.3%	1.2%	1.6%	5.5%
	Standard Momentum	1.12	1.30	16%	1.0%	-1.0%	6.5%	2.5%	0.5%	2.6%	6.2%
	RA Momentum Factor	0.91	1.05	6%	1.0%	0.4%	4.8%	3.0%	1.9%	1.5%	4.4%
	Quality/Value/Low Vol	1.28	1.03	85%	1.3%	-1.1%	5.1%	-0.8%	-1.1%	1.8%	4.8%
	Mathematical Beta 6	0.96	0.91	71%	1.6%	0.0%	3.4%	-0.2%	-0.5%	1.2%	3.1%
	RAFI Dynamic Multi-Factor	0.67	0.69	43%	3.1%	2.6%	4.1%	2.6%	2.4%	1.7%	3.9%
	Equal Weight	0.96	0.91	85%	0.9%	-0.2%	4.1%	-1.2%	-1.6%	1.8%	3.6%
	Small Cap	0.87	0.76	79%	-0.3%	-2.9%	8.0%	-3.6%	-4.5%	4.2%	7.3%

Source: Research Affiliates, LLC, using CRSP/Compustat and Worldscope/Datastream data. Note: ITD is inception to date.

Putting It All Together

In the brave new "smart beta" world, with the rapid proliferation of factor tilts and quant strategies, investors should be vigilant to the pitfalls of data mining and performance chasing. Our 2016 three-part series covers the topics we believe investors should consider before allocating to such strategies.

In our earlier research, we explained how smart beta can go horribly wrong if investors anchor performance expectations on recent returns. Expecting the past to be prologue sets up two dangerous traps. First, if past performance was fueled by rising valuations, that component of historical performance—revaluation alpha—is not likely to repeat in the future. Worse, we should expect this revaluation alpha to mean revert because strong recent performance frequently leads to poor subsequent performance, and vice versa.

We discussed that winning with smart beta begins by asking if the price is right. Valuations are as important in the performance of factors and smart beta strategies as they are in the performance of stocks, bonds, sectors, regions, asset classes, or any other investment-related category. Starting valuation ratios matter for factor performance regardless of region, regardless of time horizon, and regardless of the valuation metric being used.

We showed how valuations can be used to time smart beta strategies. We know factors can be a source of excess return for equity investors, but that potential excess return is easily wiped out (or worse!) when investors chase the latest hot factor. Investors fare better if we diversify across factors and strategies, with a preference for those that have recently *underperformed* and are now relatively cheap because of it.

In this article, we offer our estimation of expected returns going forward, based on the logic and the framework we develop in our prior three articles. We hope investors find our five-year forecasts useful in managing expectations about their existing portfolios, and perhaps also in creating winning combinations of strategies, positioned for future—not based on past—success.

Appendix A
Technical description of Model 4.

Model 4 modifies valuation-dependent Model 3, shrinking the parameters to less extreme values,

$$E(r)_{P,R,T} = \alpha_{struct,P} + avg(\beta_P, \beta_{group}) * z\big(\ln\big(val\ ratio_{P,R,T}\big)\big)_P$$

where we:

1. use the independent variable Z-score of log valuation ratio (the modification on its own should be neutral to the model), which provides an intuitive interpretation to valuations and allows for pooling of parameters across different portfolios (P) and regions (R) that may have different levels of average valuation.

2. use as the intercept the structural alpha for the factor or strategy (P); by definition structural alpha is expected return at a neutral valuation. Using structural alpha instead of the in-sample fit intercept should make the model less sensitive to trending valuations in the period of model calibration and to valuation ratio distribution uncertainty.

3. use as the slope the average of P specific slope and the average slope for all factors or all strategies (*group*). In our previous articles, we observe with very high consistency the strong relationship between valuation richness and subsequent performance. We expect that extreme values of slopes estimated for different factors or strategies are statistical outliers. Based on this assumption, we have a prior that individual factor or strategy slopes shrunk half way to the average slope for factors or strategies should provide a better estimate on a forward-looking basis.

4. average both intercepts and slopes across regions (R) proportional to the time period of historical observations for each region.

A more detailed description of the expected returns methodology is available at www.researchaffiliates.com/documents/smart-beta-methodologies.pdf.

Appendix B

Simulation Methodology Used in "Forecasting Factor and Smart Beta Returns"

For Factors

For factor simulations in the United States we use the universe of US stocks from the CRSP/Compustat Merged Database. We define the US large-cap equity universe as stocks whose market capitalizations are greater than the median market cap on the NYSE. For international factors (developed and emerging markets) we use the universe of stocks from the Worldscope/Datastream Merged Database. We define the international large-cap equity universe as stocks whose market caps put them in the top 90% by cumulative market cap within their region, where regions are defined as North America, Japan, Asia Pacific, Europe, and Emerging Markets.

The large-cap universe is then subdivided by various factor signals to construct high-characteristic and low-characteristic portfolios, following Fama and French (1993) for the US, and Fama and French (2012) for international markets. (Note that slight variations in data cleaning and lagging, as well as different investability screens, could lead to slight differences between our factors and those of Fama and French.) As an example, in order to simulate the value factor in the United States, we construct the value stock portfolio from stocks above the 70th percentile on the NYSE by book-to-market ratio, and we construct the growth stock portfolio from stocks below the 30th percentile by the same measure. Internationally, we construct the value stock portfolio from stocks above the 70th percentile in their region (North America, Japan, Asia Pacific, Europe, and Emerging Markets) by book to market, and the growth stock portfolio from stocks below the 30th percentile in their region.

The stocks are then market-cap weighted within each of the two portfolios, which are used to form a long–short factor portfolio. Portfolios are rebalanced annually each July with the exception of momentum, low beta, and illiquidity, which are rebalanced monthly. The US data extend from July 1968 to December 2016, developed data from July 1989 to December 2016, and emerging markets data from July 2002 to December 2016, and has been filtered to exclude ETFs and uninvestable securities such as state-owned enterprises and stocks with little to no liquidity. The signals used to sort the various factor portfolios are:

Factor	Signal	Definition
Value (Blend)	Composite of four value measures	Equally weighted average z-scores (deviation from past norms, divided by standard deviation) for four measures: • Book/Price • Five-Year Average Earnings/Price • Five-Year Average Sales/Price • Five-Year Average Dividends/Price If a company was not paying dividends in the last five years the average of the other three measures is used.
Value (P/B)	Book-to-Price Ratio	Book Value/Market Cap
Momentum	–2 –to –12 Month Return	Prior 12 month returns, skilling most recent month, $$\text{mom}_i = \prod_{t=-12}^{-2}(1+r_{it})$$
Small Cap	Market Cap	Market Cap
Illiquidity	Amihud (2002) Illiquidity	Annual average daily price impact of order flow $$\text{Illiq}_i = \frac{1}{T}\sum_{t=1}^{T}\frac{|r_{it}|}{\text{vol}_{it}}$$
Low Beta	Beta	Frazzini & Pedersen (2014) definition $\beta_i = \rho\frac{\sigma_i}{\sigma_m}$ where ρ is estimated with five years of daily returns and σ with one year of daily returns.
Gross Profitability	Gross Profitability	(Revenue – COGS)/Assets
Investment	Change in Book Value of Assets	Year-over-year percentage change in book value of assets

For Smart Beta Strategies

Gen-1 Value	The Gen-1 Value simulation is based on the Russell 1000 Value Index methodology to select stocks from the top 1,000 by market capitalization according to a composite value score calculated using book to price, five-year sales per share growth, and two-year earnings per share growth. Stocks are weighted by the product of this score and market capitalization, and rebalanced annually.
RAFI Fundamental Index	The RAFI Fundamental Index simulation is based on the RAFI Fundamental Index methodology to select and weight companies according to four fundamental measures of company size: book value, cash flow, dividends + buybacks, and adjusted sales. Four tranches are each rebalanced annually for a quarterly staggered rebalance.
High Dividend	The High Dividend simulation is based on the Dow Jones Select Dividend Index methodology to select 100 stocks by dividend yield from the Large + Mid + Small-Cap universe, after screens for dividend growth and dividend coverage. Stocks are weighted by indicated dividend yield, and rebalanced annually.
RAFI Equity Income	The RAFI Equity Income simulation is based on the FTSE RAFI Equity Income Index methodology to select the top 50% of stocks by dividend yield from the top 98% of stocks by fundamental weight, screening out the bottom quintiles by growth (return on assets), distress (debt coverage ratio), and conservative accounting (net operating assets). Stocks are weighted by the product of fundamental weight and dividend yield, and are rebalanced annually.
Low Volatility	The Low Volatility simulation is based on the S&P Low Volatility Index methodology to select the 100 lowest-volatility stocks from the top 500 by market cap, where volatility is defined as the standard deviation of daily returns over the prior year. Stocks are weighted by 1/volatility, and rebalanced quarterly.
RAFI Low Volatility	The RAFI Low Volatility simulation is based on the FTSE RAFI Low Volatility Index methodology to select companies from the top 1,000 US stocks by fundamental weight with low valuations and low systematic betas (measured relative to global, country, and industry indices). Stocks are weighted by fundamental weights. Four tranches are each rebalanced annually for a quarterly staggered rebalance.
Quality	The Quality simulation is based on the MSCI Quality Index methodology to select companies from the Large + Mid-Cap universe based on a quality score. Quality score combines high return on equity with low debt to equity and low earnings variability. Stocks are weighted by market cap times quality score, and are rebalanced semi-annually.
RAFI Quality Factor	The RAFI Quality Factor simulation is based on the RAFI Quality Factor Index methodology to select the top quarter of large companies with high profitability (operating profitability, ROE, and ROA) and low investment (asset growth and book growth) and weighted by fundamental measures of company size. Four tranches are each rebalanced annually for a quarterly staggered rebalance.
Standard Momentum	The Standard Momentum simulation is based on the AQR Momentum Index methodology to select the top third of companies by momentum from the top 1,000 US stocks by market cap, where momentum is defined as prior-year return, skipping the most recent month. Stocks are weighted by market cap, and are rebalanced quarterly.
RA Momentum Factor	The RA Momentum Factor simulation is based on the RA Momentum Factor Index methodology to select the top half of large companies with a high-momentum score. Momentum score combines standard momentum (prior-year return, skipping the most recent month), beta-adjusted momentum, and fresh momentum that adjusts for the previous-year return. Stocks are weighted by market cap, and rebalanced quarterly.
Quality/Value/Low Vol	The Quality/Value/Low Vol simulation is based on the MSCI Factor Mix A-Series Index methodology to equally weight the Quality Index (high ROE and low debt to equity, weighted by market cap times quality score), Value-Weighted Index (large caps weighted by fundamentals), and Minimum Volatility Index (constrained optimization where constraints include minimum and maximum constituent, country, and sector weights, and turnover).
Mathematical Beta 6	The Mathematical Beta 6 simulation is based on the EDHEC SciBeta Six-Factor methodology to equally weight six factor indices: value (top half by book to price), momentum (top half by prior-year return, skipping most recent month), mid-cap (bottom half by market cap), low volatility (bottom half by prior two-year standard deviation of weekly returns), profitability (top half by gross profits/assets), and investment (bottom half by asset growth). Stocks within each factor are diversified via five diversification methods. The portfolio is rebalanced quarterly.
RAFI Dynamic Multi-Factor	The RAFI Dynamic Multi-Factor simulation is based on the RAFI Dynamic Multi-Factor Index methodology to dynamically weight the RAFI Value Factor, RAFI LV Factor, RAFI Quality Factor, RA Momentum Factor, and RAFI Size Factor indices based on long-term reversal and short-term momentum.
Equal Weight	The Equal Weight simulation is based on the S&P 500 Equal Weight Index (US) and the MSCI Equal Weighted Index (developed and EM) methodologies to equally weight all stocks in the top 500 by market cap (US) or Large + Mid-Cap universe (developed and EM), and rebalanced quarterly (US) or semi-annually (developed and EM).
Small Cap	The Small Cap simulation is based on the Russell 2000 Index (US) and MSCI Small Cap Index (developed and EM) methodologies to select companies 1,001 through 3,000 by market cap (US) or small-cap universe (developed and EM), and weighted by market cap. Stocks are rebalanced annually (US) or semi-annually (developed and EM).
RAFI Size Factor	The RAFI Size Factor simulation is based on the RAFI Size Factor Index methodology to equally weight the RAFI Value Factor, RAFI Low Vol Factor, RAFI Quality Factor and RA Momentum Factor indices within the small-cap universe.

Appendix C

Figure C1. Expected Risk and Return Characteristics for Developed Markets Factors

Panel A. Historical Returns, Jul 1989–Dec 2016

Panel B. Expected 5-Year Returns Implied by Current Valuations, as of Dec 31, 2016

Source: Research Affiliates, LLC, using CRSP/Compustat and Worldscope/Datastream data.

Figure C2. Expected Risk and Return Characteristics for Emerging Markets Factors

Panel A. Historical Returns, July 2002–Dec 2016

Panel B. Expected 5-Year Returns Implied by Current Valuations, as of Dec 31, 2016

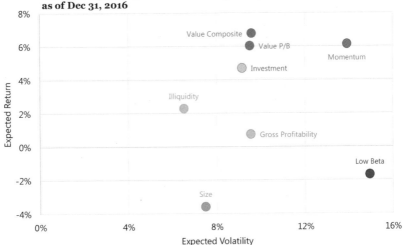

Source: Research Affiliates, LLC, using CRSP/Compustat and Worldscope/Datastream data.

Appendix D

Figure D1. Risk and Return Characteristics for Developed Markets Smart Beta Strategies

Panel A. Historical Excess Returns (Gross), Jul 1989–Dec 2016

Panel B. Expected 5-Year Excess Returns (Gross) Implied by Current Valuations, as of Dec 31, 2016

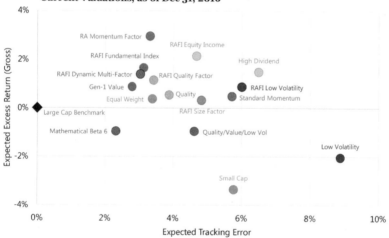

Source: Research Affiliates, LLC, using CRSP/Compustat and Worldscope/Datastream data.

Figure D2. Risk and Return Characteristics for Emerging Markets Smart Beta Strategies

Panel A. Historical Excess Returns (Gross), Jul 2002–Dec 2016

Panel B. Expected 5-Year Excess Returns (Gross) Implied by Current Valuations, as of Dec 31, 2016

Source: Research Affiliates, LLC, using CRSP/Compustat and Worldscope/Datastream data.

Appendix E

Figure E. Expected 5-Year Excess Returns, Net of Trading Costs, for Developed and Emerging Markets Smart Beta Strategies, as of Dec 31, 2016

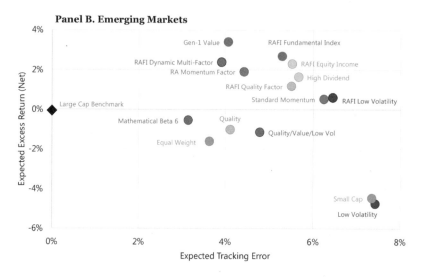

Source: Research Affiliates, LLC, using CRSP/Compustat and Worldscope/Datastream data.

References

Aked, Michael. 2016. "The Dirty Little Secret of Passive Investing." Research Affiliates (January).

Aked, Michael, and Max Moroz. 2015. "The Market Impact of Passive Trading." Research Affiliates (August).

Arnott, Rob, Noah Beck, and Vitali Kalesnik. 2016a. "To Win with 'Smart Beta' Ask If the Price Is Right." Research Affiliates (June).

———. 2016b. "Timing 'Smart Beta' Strategies? Of Course! Buy Low, Sell High!" Research Affiliates (September).

Arnott, Rob, Noah Beck, Vitali Kalesnik, and John West. 2016. "How Can 'Smart Beta' Go Horribly Wrong?" Research Affiliates (February).

Frazzini, Andrea, and Lasse Heje Pedersen. 2014. "Betting against Beta." *Journal of Financial Economics*, vol. 111, no. 1 (January):1–25.

Originally published February 2017; www.researchaffiliates.com/en_us/publications/articles/595-forecasting-factor-and-smart-beta-returns.html.

ABOUT ROB ARNOTT, NOAH BECK AND VITALI KALESNIK

Rob Arnott is the founder and chairman of Research Affiliates. He is also portfolio manager on the PIMCO All Asset and All Asset All Authority family of funds and the PIMCO RAE™ suite of funds.

Rob managed two asset management firms before founding Research Affiliates. As chairman of First Quadrant, LP, he built up the former internal money manager for Crum & Forster into a highly regarded quantitative asset management firm. He also was global equity strategist at Salomon Brothers (now part of Citigroup), the founding president and CEO of TSA Capital Management (now part of Analytic Investors, LLC), and a vice president at The Boston Company.

In 2002, Rob established Research Affiliates as a research-intensive asset management firm that focuses on innovative products. The firm explores novel approaches to active asset allocation, optimal portfolio construction, efficient forms of indexation, and other quantitative strategies. Research Affiliates delivers investment solutions globally in partnership with leading financial institutions.

Rob has published more than 100 articles in such journals as the *Journal of Portfolio Management*, *Harvard Business Review*, and *Financial Analysts Journal*, where he also served as editor in chief from 2002 through 2006. In recognition of his achievements as a financial writer, Rob has received seven Graham and Dodd Scrolls, awarded annually by CFA Institute to the top *Financial Analysts Journal* articles of the year. He also has received four Bernstein Fabozzi/Jacobs Levy awards from the *Journal of Portfolio Management*. He is co-author of *The Fundamental Index: A Better Way to Invest* (Wiley 2008).

Rob Arnott received a BS *summa cum laude* in economics, applied mathematics, and computer science from the University of California, Santa Barbara.

Noah Beck conducts quantitative equity research relating to dynamic factor investing and smart beta strategies for Research Affiliates. He supports existing portfolios and advances research for product development.

Prior to joining Research Affiliates, Noah was a systems engineer at Boeing responsible for the final test and evaluation of ICBM guidance systems.

Noah received a BS in physics from Harvey Mudd College and a Master of Financial Engineering from the Anderson School of Management at UCLA.

Vitali Kalesnik focuses on developing Research Affiliates' research agenda in the European region as well as supporting the firm's business relationships in the region. He leads the Equity Research team located in Newport Beach, CA, and its investigations into equity return predictability, timing of equity factor returns, efficient portfolio construction techniques, smart beta strategy analysis, governance, and other aspects of equity investing.

Articles he has co-authored with others have been recognized with two Graham and Dodd Scroll Awards, a *Financial Analysts Journal* Readers' Choice Award, a William F. Sharpe Indexing Achievement Award, and a Bernstein Fabozzi/Jacobs Levy Award. His research strengthens and expands Research Affiliates' products—in particular, RAFI™ Fundamental Index™ strategies— and supports our global tactical asset allocation products.

Vitali earned his PhD in economics from the University of California, Los Angeles, where he was a winner of the UCLA Graduate Division Fellowship for 2001–2005. He speaks fluent English, Russian, and French.

Catching Up With The Tiger Cubs

STAN ALTSHULLER

How are Julian Robertson's protégés faring today? Market cap, overlap, position sizing, & popular names reveal insight into Cub performance.

Challenging Environment

In February 2017 the *Wall Street Journal* ran "Tiger Hedge Funds Become Wall Street Prey," an article citing the losses of some prominent funds of Tiger lineage.[1] While Tiger Cubs aren't immune to the challenges facing all active managers, it is much too early to call them the "prey" of Wall Street or imply that they've lost their touch. In this article, we'll examine data from the markets and public filings of the Tiger Cubs to unpack what's really going on.

It's no secret that stock pickers, especially those using bottom-up strategies, have struggled in recent years. Many Tiger Cubs follow in Julian Robertson's footsteps by using that very strategy. Most hedge funds that last long enough experience rough periods, so it's natural for a few managers using a strategy that's under pressure to have a tough year. That doesn't, however, mean that something has fundamentally changed.

Why are these strategies struggling? Certain market factors directly influence managers that use a stock-picking approach. One such factor is dispersion (how much the average outperformer gains over the average underperformer), and another is correlation (how much securities move in lockstep).

---

[1] on.wsj.com/2IvMtyA

Last year was notoriously difficult for stock pickers due to low dispersion and high correlation. (The reverse is optimal for generating robust performance.) Other factors including market breadth, interest rates, volatility, risk-free rates, and quantitative easing all aligned in what looked like a perfect storm—the worst possible environment for a long short equity manager picking stocks.

But currently some of these factors are changing. Correlations are crashing, while dispersion is on the rise. Stock pickers—including the Tiger Cubs—will most likely take advantage of these shifting winds.

Overlap in the Tiger Cub Portfolio

To study their portfolios, we aggregated all historical public holdings reports filed by Tiger Cubs (managers that worked with Mr. Robertson), Tiger Seeds (managers seeded by Mr. Robertson), and Grand Cubs (managers that have worked at either a Cub, Seed, or another Grand Cub.) The portfolio's market value is $143B split by pedigree as presented below:

Asset Split and Split Market Value (2017)

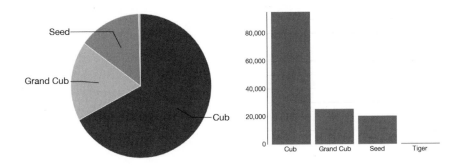

We have been fine-tuning this Tiger Family list for years, weeding out Fund of Funds, non-equity managers, non-U.S. or Global managers, and closures. We were also mindful to include newly launched managers. Today we capture 49 managers including Tiger Management.

The first thing you might notice when comparing portfolio holdings is the high number of shared stocks. Makes sense when you consider they have matured under the same investing legend and have evolved similar processes. Here are the Tiger Cub portfolios with the most overlap:

Tiger Cub Portfolio Overlap (2017)

	Lone Pine	Coatue	Steadfast Financial	Tiger	Foxhaven	Conatus	Valinor	Bloom Tree	Tiger Eye	Tiger Global	Falcon Edge	Miura Global	Blue Ridge	Viking Global	Marble Arch	White Elm	Hoplite
Lone Pine Capital, L.L.C.		30	25	24	20	20	20	19	19	19	18	18	17	17	17	15	15
Coatue Capital, L.L.C.	30		11	23	17	13	21	11	10	16	20	20	17	26	5	9	18
Steadfast Financial, L.L.C.	25	11		12	13	11	8	18	9	13	19	10	15	19	11	22	18
Tiger Management, L.L.C.	24	23	12		14	10	16	22	16	20	12	11	13	19	5	3	22
Foxhaven Asset Management, LP	20	17	13	14		7	10	11	24	17	15	18	16	13	9	28	17
Conatus Capital Management LP	20	13	11	10	7		17	11	20	8	24	16	15	14	15	7	20
Valinor Management, LLC	20	21	8	16	10	17		9	9	10	11	10	15	15	3	15	12
Bloom Tree Partners, LLC	19	11	18	22	11	11	9		12	9	19	3	15	16	11	5	20
Tiger Eye Partners, LP	19	10	9	16	24	20	9	12		7	12	22	13	8	10	15	9
Tiger Global Management, LLC	19	16	13	20	17	8	10	9	7		16	11	20	18	20	21	12
Falcon Edge Capital, LP	18	20	19	12	15	24	11	19	12	16		11	25	21	20	15	23
Miura Global Management, L.L.C.	18	20	10	11	18	16	10	3	22	11	11		15	12	13	12	5
Blue Ridge Capital	17	17	15	13	16	15	15	15	13	20	25	15		21	17	26	22
Viking Global Investors LP	17	26	19	13	14	15	16	8	18	21	12	21	21		17	10	26
Marble Arch Investments, LP	17	5	11	5	9	15	3	11	10	20	20	13	17	17		17	8
White Elm Capital, LLC	15	9	22	3	28	7	15	5	15	21	15	12	26	10	17		9
Hoplite Capital Management, L.L.C.	15	18	18	22	17	20	12	20	9	12	23	5	22	26	8	9	

As an example, the numeral 30 at the intersection of Lone Pine and Coatue means that at least 30% of the value of these portfolios are identical. We can dig deeper to look at the securities in common and sizing:

Position Size % (2017)

	Coatue Capital	Lone Pine Capital	Overlap Calculation
Alibaba Group Holding Ltd	6.65	7.42	6.65
Activision Blizzard Inc	6.18	5.59	5.59
Broadcom Ltd	6.12	5.59	5.59
Facebook Inc	8.99	4.20	4.20
Symantec Corp	4.56	2.69	2.69
Equinix Inc	2.05	2.47	2.05
ServiceNow Inc	1.66	1.54	1.54
salesforce.com Inc	0.85	1.03	0.85
SNAP INC	3.51	0.61	0.61
Liberty Media Corp Media Group	1.98	0.48	0.48
Min Overlap			30.26

The force-field diagram below displays the managers as one would analyze a social network. Instead of media "likes" we use portfolio holdings. The managers in the center (Lone Pine, Viking, Tiger Global, and Blue Ridge) have more positions overlapping with their peers, while those on the periphery (Impala, Deerfield, and Bridger) are more unique. Dot size represents portfolio market value for each manager.

Tiger Cub Network Diagram (2017)

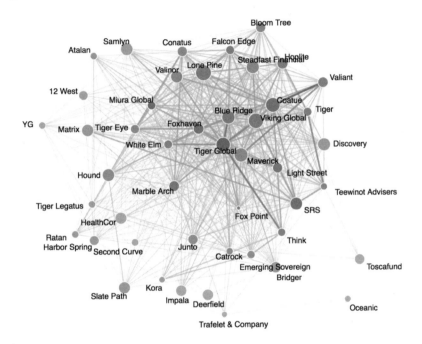

Constructing the Tiger Portfolio

To construct the Tiger portfolio, we merged all holdings together using reported market values. We simulated performance, risk, and other attributes of the Tiger Cubs' portfolio using holdings and market data. Here are the results:

Tiger Cub Returns vs. Market Indices (January 2006–August 2017)

The Tiger Cub portfolio, the top line in the chart, compounds well beyond the S&P 500 total return index and trumps the MSCI World since 2006. While 2016 was a tough year, the YTD 2017 portfolio of Tiger Cub longs has doubled the return of the S&P 500.

Let's study some more data to see how their portfolios are positioned moving forward.

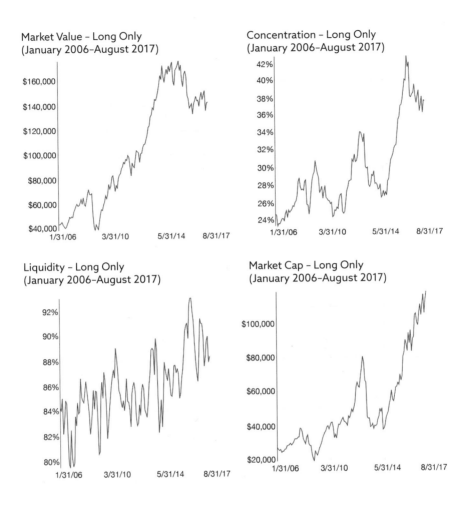

Above we can see four metrics we use when analyzing any portfolio: Assets (market value of longs), concentration, liquidity, and weighted market capitalization. These key metrics are closely linked to a manager's performance.

While the dollars controlled by Tiger Cubs are down from their 2015 peaks, they've stabilized and even grown since early 2016. As we've mentioned, the Cubs control in aggregate $143B in long equity value. The next chart is particularly telling. Concentration of their portfolios has been increasing. This means that the Tiger cubs are expressing a lot of conviction in their top stock picks, putting more of their portfolios to work in top trades. In addition, the average Overlap has increased—they are investing more dollars in the same group of names. Currently 37% of the portfolio is invested in the top 20 stocks. That's down from a peak of 42% in early 2016, but significantly higher than historical average.

Another trend you may notice is that the portfolio is still very liquid; even if all Tiger Cubs sell their longs at once, they can liquidate 88% of their longs in 30 consecutive days. This is because the portfolio is invested in liquid mega cap names—the market capitalization of the portfolio has skyrocketed from $37B in 2014 to $117B today.

So, what does all this mean?

Let's take a closer look at concentration. If Tiger Cubs are getting more concentrated and deploying more capital in their top names, is that a good thing?

Position Sizing

Position sizing is a portfolio management skill closely linked to concentration. We can capture position sizing for the Tiger cub portfolio as follows (with the assumption being that sizing is a conscious decision to add more capital to the top names or let them appreciate from price action):

Monthly Position Sizing (January 2006–August 2017)

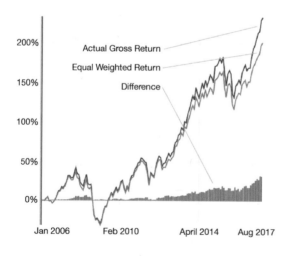

This analysis compares the actual performance of the portfolio to that of an equally weighted portfolio, all else equal. Did the managers benefit from concentration? In aggregate, Tiger Cubs have consistently added value sizing (bars at bottom of chart). In fact, the actual weighted portfolio added almost 32pp over the last decade. This implies there is a relationship between the aggregate position size of Tiger Cubs and the returns of those positions. This can be tested.

Annualized ROIC, by Position Size (January 2006–August 2017)

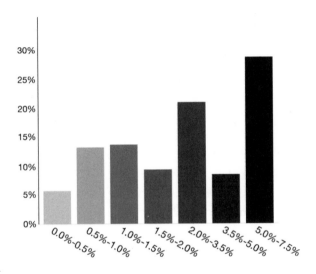

Breaking up the portfolio by position size reveals a clear relationship—the largest positions (>5%) have the highest annualized ROICs (return on invested capital). Increased concentration, where more of the portfolio is invested in the top stocks, is historically a good thing for the Tiger Cubs.

Moving Up Market

Let's consider the increasing market cap trend—is this a problem for the Tiger Cubs? Not according to the empirical evidence. Most of the alpha generated by the portfolio comes from large and mega cap names. Additionally, the names in those buckets have the highest win/loss ratios historically. The following three charts illustrate batting averages (the number of winners per bucket), win/loss ratios (managers earnings vs. manager losses on avg. by bucket), and attribution (how much of the contribution was driven by market and sector volatility vs. security selection in that sector—selection is indicated by the dark shading in the third chart).

Batting Average (January 2006–August 2017)

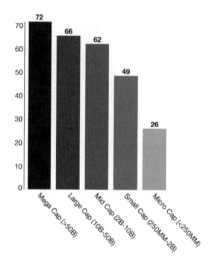

Win/Loss Ratio (January 2006–August 2017)

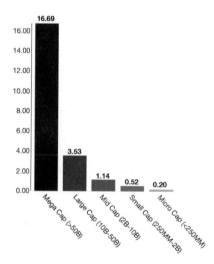

Alpha / Beta Attribution (January 2006–August 2017)

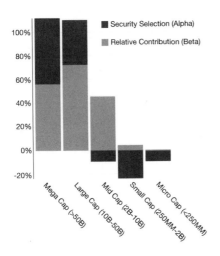

Mega and large caps are winners, while the smaller capitalization names are not so great.

When identifying a trend, we should test its persistence. In the next set of charts, we broke up the attribution analysis into three separate time periods. In all three distinct periods, alpha was generated in mega caps and lost in small and micro:

Alpha / Beta Attribution (2006–2009)

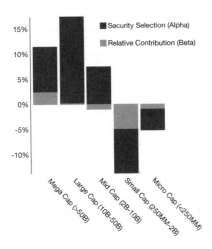

Alpha / Beta Attribution (2010–2013)

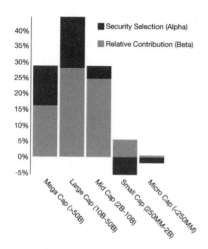

Alpha / Beta Attribution (2014–2017)

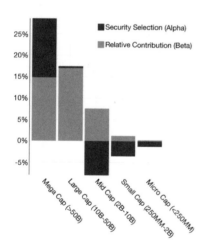

In two of three periods, alpha was generated in large- and mid-cap names (less persistence than mega caps).

Thus, while Tiger Cub portfolios are evolving, most changes have historically positive indications. The increased concentration, increased overlap, and moving up market caps are all changes we expect will help rather than hurt performance.

Most Loved Tiger Cub Stocks

Facebook (FB) is currently the largest bet by dollar value and by number of Tiger Cubs holding it—26 Cub managers hold roughly $6B in the name. In the chart below we observe how the quantity of shares (bars below the price) changed since the IPO in mid-2012.

Facebook Price and Shares Owned by Cubs (June 2012–August 2017)

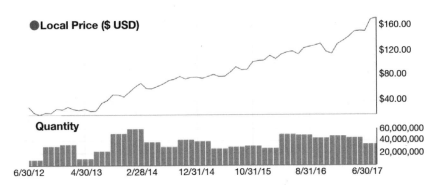

The Cubs held a massive position in early 2014 and then again in 2017, cutting back a bit (likely profit taking) most recently.

We mapped the position size by percent for all managers with a larger than 5% position in FB.

Tiger Cubs March to Facebook (December 2012–August 2017)

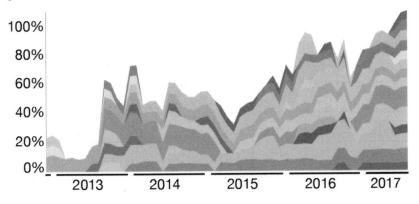

The first managers to invest with conviction (5% or more) were Valiant, Conatus, and Slate Path, all the way back in 2012. We estimate that FB has created $2.36B in profits for the group of Tiger Cubs that held it just this year and $5.36B since the IPO.

Here's a quick rundown of some other Tiger-favored stocks:

Most popular Tiger Cub Stocks

Security Name	# Holders	% of Total Portfolio	% Avg. Manager Size	Max. % Position Belongs To
Facebook Inc	27	4.00	4.88	SRS Investment Management, LLC
Alibaba Group Holding Ltd	16	2.72	5.36	Miura Global Management, LLC
Microsoft Corp	14	2.68	4.72	Viking Global Investors, LP
Amazon.com Inc	18	2.33	4.88	Light Street Capital Management, LLC
Charter Communications Ltd	23	2.31	3.32	Marble Arch Investments, LP
Broadcom Ltd	8	2.28	3.76	Coatue Capital, LLC
JD.com Inc	9	2.22	10.40	Think Investments, LLC
Netflix Inc	11	2.13	6.76	SRS Investment Management, LLC
Alphabet Inc	18	1.90	3.93	Foxhaven Asset Management, LP
Priceline Group Inc (The)	15	1.84	4.35	Tiger Global Management, LLC
Constellation Brands Inc	14	1.76	3.71	Valinor Management, LLC
Activision Blizzard Inc	7	1.67	3.06	Coatue Capital, LLC
TransDigm Group Inc	11	1.54	6.91	Catrock Capital Management, LLC

Security Name	# Holders	% of Total Portfolio	% Avg. Manager Size	Max. % Position Belongs To
FleetCor Technologies Inc	14	1.54	3.25	12 West Capital Management, LP
Comcast Corp	8	1.20	2.87	Marble Arch Investments, LP
Average	14		4.81	

Top winners this year besides FB are Alibaba, JD.com, and Charter Communications.

Originally published October 17, 2017; www.novus.com/blog/catching-up-with-the-tiger-cubs-in-2017.

ABOUT STAN ALTSHULLER

Stan is Co-Founder and Chief Research Officer at Novus. In his current role, he's charged with spearheading research & content initiatives at Novus and frequently contributes to product development. His cutting-edge research is followed by nearly 50,000 investment management professionals, spanning across hedge funds, foundations & endowments, pensions, and other asset owners. To follow his work, visit Novus' research library at www.novus.com/research-library.

Before co-founding Novus in 2007, Stan worked in Ivy Asset Management's Portfolio Management Group as part of a team responsible for constructing, monitoring and managing all of Ivy's portfolios. At Ivy, he designed and implemented a set of tools and processes for analyzing multi-manager portfolios focusing on key drivers and risks across the entire product line. Prior to Ivy, Stan served at Lyster Watson & Co., where he was responsible for quantitative analysis, manager screening and portfolio modeling. Stan holds a B.S. in Mathematics and a B.A. in Economics from Brandeis University.

@saltshuller

INVESTMENT PORTFOLIOS, STRATEGIES

—— & ——

EDGES

You Still Have Made a Choice

────

RUSTY GUINN

Drummers are really nothing more than time-keepers. They're the time of the band. I don't consider I should have as much recognition as say a brilliant guitar player. I think the best thing a drummer can have is restraint when he's playing—and so few have today. They think playing loud is playing best. Of course, I don't think I've reached my best yet. The day I don't move on I stop playing. I don't practice ever. I can only play with other people, I need to feel them around me.

— **Ginger Baker (founder of Cream),
from a 1970 interview with** *Disc Magazine*

La cuisine, c'est quand les choses ont le goût de ce qu'elles sont. (Good cooking is when things taste of what they are.)

— **Maurice Edmond Sailland (Curnonsky)—1872–1956**

There are those who think that life
Has nothing left to chance
A host of holy horrors
To direct our aimless dance

A planet of playthings
We dance on the strings
Of powers we cannot perceive
The stars aren't aligned
Or the gods are malign
Blame is better to give than receive

You can choose a ready guide
In some celestial voice
If you choose not to decide

You still have made a choice

— **Rush,** "Freewill," *Permanent Waves* (1980)

For the kingdom of heaven is like a man traveling to a far country, who called his own servants and delivered his goods to them. And to one he gave five talents, to another two, and to another one, to each according to his own ability; and immediately he went on a journey. Then he who had received the five talents went and traded with them, and made another five talents. And likewise, he who had received two gained two more also. But he who had received one went and dug in the ground, and hid his lord's money. After a long time the lord of those servants came and settled accounts with them.

So he who had received five talents came and brought five other talents, saying, 'Lord, you delivered to me five talents; look, I have gained five more talents besides them.' His lord said to him, 'Well done, good and faithful servant; you were faithful over a few things, I will make you ruler over many things. Enter into the joy of your lord.' He also who had received two talents came and said, 'Lord, you delivered to me two talents; look, I have gained two more talents besides them.' His lord said to him, 'Well done, good and faithful servant; you have been faithful over a few things, I will make you ruler over many things. Enter into the joy of your lord.'

Then he who had received the one talent came and said, 'Lord, I knew you to be a hard man, reaping where you have not sown, and gathering where you have not scattered seed. And I was afraid, and went and hid your talent in the ground. Look, there you have what is yours.'

But his lord answered and said to him, 'You wicked and lazy servant, you knew that I reap where I have not sown, and gather where I have not scattered seed. So you ought to have deposited my money with the bankers, and at my coming I would have received back my own with interest. Therefore, take the talent from him, and give it to him who has ten talents.

For to everyone who has, more will be given, and he will have abundance; but from him who does not have, even what he has will be taken away. And cast the unprofitable servant into the outer darkness. There will be weeping and gnashing of teeth.

— *The Bible*, The Gospel of Matthew 25:14-30

will never understand why more people don't revere Rush.

With the possible exception of Led Zeppelin,[1] I'm not sure there has been another band with such extraordinary instrumentalists across the board, such synergy between those members and their musical style and such a consistent approach to both lyrical and melodic construction. And yet they were only inducted into the Rock & Roll Hall of Fame in 2013. A short list of bands and singers the selection committee thought were more deserving: ABBA, Madonna, Jackson Browne, the Moonglows, Run DMC. At least they got in when Randy Newman did. I remember the first time I heard "YYZ", the Rush tune named after the IATA airport code for Toronto's Pearson International Airport, pronounced "Why Why Zed" in the charming manner of the Commonwealth. It was then that I decided I would be a drummer. I did play for a while, and reached what I would describe as just above a baseline threshold of competence.

That's not a throwaway line.

There's a clear, explicit line that every drummer (hopefully) crosses at one point. A step-change in his understanding of the role of the instrument. The true novice drummer always picks up the sticks and plays the same thing. Common time. Somewhere between 90–100 beats per minute. Eighth note closed hi-hat throughout. Bass drum on the down and upbeat of the first beat. Snare on second down beat. And then it's all jazzy up-beat doodling on the snare for the rest of that bar until the down beat of four. Same thing for three measures, and on the fourth measure it's time for that awesome fill he's been practicing. I don't know how many subscribers are drummers, but I assure you, literally couples of you are nodding your heads.

The fills and off-beat snare hits are all superfluous and not necessary to the principal role of a drummer in rock and roll: to keep the damned beat. But there are a number of reasons why every neophyte does these same things. Mimicry of more advanced players who can do the creative and interesting things without losing the beat, for one. We see Tony Williams, John Bonham, or Bill Bruford and do what it is we *think* they

---

[1] I don't want to hear it from the "but they stole people's music and weren't super nice about it" crowd. Zep played better rock and roll music than anyone before or after, and it's not even close.

are doing to make the music sound good. The amateur often also thinks that these are the necessary things to be perceived as a more advanced player, for another. He doesn't just imagine that his mimicry will make him sound more like the excellent players, but imagines himself *looking like* them to others. More than anything, the amateur does these things because he hasn't quite figured out that keeping a good beat is so much more important than anything else he will do that he's willing to sacrifice it for what he thinks is impressive.

This thought process dominates so many other fields as well. Consider the number of amateur cooks who hit every sauce or piece of meat with a handful of garlic powder, onion powder, oregano, salt, pepper and cayenne, when the simplicity of salt as seasoning dominates most of the world's great cuisine. There is an instinct to think that complexity and depth must come from a huge range of ingredients[2] or from complexity in preparation, but most extraordinary cooking begins from an understanding of a small number of methods for heating, seasoning and establishing bases for sauces. Inventiveness, creativity and passion can take cuisine in millions of directions from there, but many home cooks see the celebrity chef's flamboyant recipe and internalize that the creative flourishes are *what matters* to the dish, and not the fact that he cooked a high-quality piece of meat at the right heat for the right amount of time.

If you're not much of a cook, consider instead the 30-handicap golfer who wouldn't be caught dead without a full complement of four lob wedges in his bag. You know, so that he can address every possible situation on the course. The trilling singer of the national anthem who can't hold a pitch but sees every word of the song as an opportunity to sing an entire scale's worth of notes. The karate novice who addresses his opponent with a convoluted stance. The writer who doesn't know when to stop giving examples to an audience who understood what he was getting at halfway through the one about cooking.

---

[2]   And it can. Pueblan and Oaxacan cuisine feature moles with extraordinary complexity that does come from the melding of a range of seasonings and ingredients. Traditional American chilis, South Asian curries and soups from around the world often do as well. Dishes en croute (e.g. pate en croute, coulibiac, etc.) are notoriously tricky, too.

I'm guessing at least one of these things pisses you off, or at the very least makes you do an internal eye roll. And yet, as investors we are guilty of doing this kind of thing all the time, any time the topic of diversification comes up.

It comes from a good place. We know from what we've been taught (and from watching the experts) that we should diversify, but we don't have a particularly good way of knowing what that means. And so we fill our portfolios with multiple flavors of funds, accounts and individual securities. Three international equity funds with different strategies. Multiple different styles in emerging markets. Some value. Some growth. Some minimum volatility. Some call writing strategies. Some sector funds. Maybe some long/short hedge funds. Some passively managed index funds, some actively managed funds. Definitely some sexy stock picks. And in the end, the portfolio that we end up with looks very much like the global equity market, maybe with a tilt here or there to express uniqueness—that flashy extra little hit on the snare drum to look impressive.

This piece isn't about the time we waste on these things. I already wrote a piece about that: "Chili P is My Signature."[3] This is about the harm we do to our portfolios when we play at diversifying instead of actually doing it.

The Parable of the Two FAs

So what does *actually diversifying* look like?

There are lot of not-very-useful definitions out there. The eggs-in-one-basket definition we're all familiar with benefits from simplicity, which is not nothing. In addition, it *does* work if people have a good concept of what the *basket* is in the analogy. Most people don't. Say you have $100, and you decide that a *basket* is an advisor or a fund. So you split the money between the two, and they invest in the same thing. You have not diversified.[4] The other definitions for diversification tend to be more complicated, more quantitative in nature. That doesn't make them bad, and we'll be leaning on some of them. But we need a rule of thumb, some

[3]   epsilontheory.com/chili-p-signature
[4]   Cue the fund-of-funds due diligence analyst pointing out that we would have, in fact, diversified our fraud risk. Die on that hill if you want to, friend.

heuristic for describing what diversification *ought to look like* so that we know it when we see it. For the overwhelming majority of investors, that rule of thumb should go something like this:

> Diversification is reducing how much you expect to lose when risky assets do poorly or very poorly without necessarily reducing how much total return you expect to generate.

Now, this is not exactly true, and it's very obviously not the *whole* definition. But by and large it is the part of the definition that matters most. The more nuanced way to think about diversification, of course, is to describe it as all the benefits you get from the fact that things in your portfolio don't always move together, even if they're both generally going up in value. But most investors are so concentrated in general exposure to risky assets—securities whose value rises and falls with the fortunes and profitability of companies, and how other investors perceive those fortunes—that this distinction is mostly an academic one. Investors live and die by home country equity risk. Period. Most investors understand this to one degree or another, but the way they respond in their portfolios doesn't reflect it.

I want to describe this to you in a parable.

> There was once a rich lord who held $10 million in a S&P 500 ETF. He knew that he would be occupied with his growing business over the next year. Before he left, he met with his two financial advisors and gave them $1 million of his wealth and told them to "diversify his holdings."

> He returned after a year and came before the first financial advisor. "My lord, I put the $1 million you gave me in a Russell 1000 Value ETF. Here is your $1.1 million." The rich man replied, "Dude, that's almost exactly what my other ETF did over the same period. What if the market had crashed? I wasn't diversified at all!" And the financial advisor was ashamed.

> Furious and frustrated, the rich man then summoned his second financial advisor. "Sir, I put your $1 million in a Short-Duration Fixed Income mutual fund of impeccable reputation. Here's your $1 million back."

> "Oh my God," the lord replied, "Are you being serious right now? If I wanted to reduce my risk by stuffing my money in a mattress

I could have done that without paying you a 65bp wrap fee. How do you sleep at night? I'm going to open a robo-advisor account."

Most of us know we shouldn't just hold a local equity index. We usually buy something else to diversify, because *that's what you do.* But what we usually do falls short either because (1) the thing we buy to diversify isn't actually all that different from what we already owned, or (2) the thing we buy to diversify reduces our risk *and* our return, which defeats the purpose. There's nothing novel in what I'm saying here. Modern portfolio theory's fundamental formula helps us to isolate how much of the variation in our portfolio's returns comes from the riskiness of the stuff we invested in vs. the fact that this stuff doesn't always move together.

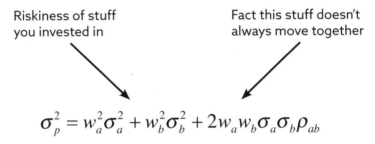

Riskiness of stuff you invested in

Fact this stuff doesn't always move together

$$\sigma_p^2 = w_a^2\sigma_a^2 + w_b^2\sigma_b^2 + 2w_a w_b \sigma_a \sigma_b \rho_{ab}$$

Source: Salient 2017. For illustrative purposes only.

The Free Lunch Effect

So assuming we didn't have any special knowledge about what assets would generate the highest risk-adjusted returns over the year our rich client was away on business, what answer would have made us the good guy in the parable? Maximizing how much benefit we get from that second expression above—*the fact that this stuff doesn't always move together*.

Before we jump into the math on this, it's important to reinforce the caveat above: we're assuming we don't have any knowledge about risk-adjusted returns, which isn't always true. Stay with me, because we will get back to that. For the time being, however, let's take as a given that we don't know what the future holds. Let's also assume that, like the Parable of the Two FAs, our client holds $10 million in S&P 500 ETFs. Also like the parable, we have been asked to reallocate $1 million of those assets to what will be most diversifying. In other words, it's a marginal analysis.

The measure we're looking to maximize is the *Free Lunch Effect*, which we define as the difference between the portfolio's volatility after our change at the margin and the raw weighted average volatility of the underlying components. If the two assets both had volatility of 10%, for example, and the resulting portfolio volatility was 9%, the Free Lunch Effect would be 1%.

If maximizing the Free Lunch Effect is the goal, here's the relative attractiveness of various things the two FAs could have allocated to (based on characteristics of these markets between January 2000 and July 2017).

Volatility Reduction from Diversification—Adding 10% to a Portfolio of S&P 500

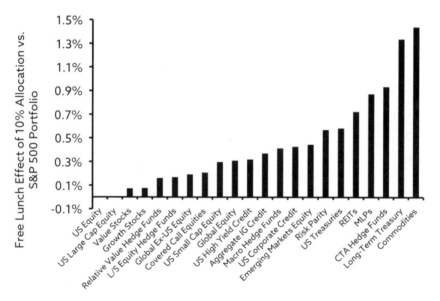

Source: Salient 2017.

The two FAs failed for two different reasons. The first failed because he selected an asset which was too similar. The second failed because he selected an asset which was **not risky enough for its differentness to matter.** The first concept is intuitive to most of us, but the second is a bit more esoteric. I think it's best thought of by considering how much the risk of a portfolio is reduced by adding an asset with varying levels of correlation and volatility. To stop playing at diversification, this is where you start.

Volatility Reduction by Correlation and Volatility of Diversifying Asset

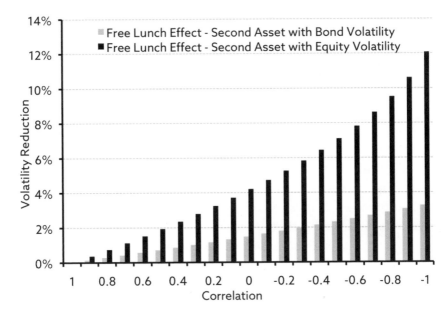

Source: Salient 2017.

If You Choose not to Decide

If there are some complaints that can be leveled against this approach, two of them, I think, are valid and worthy of exploration.

The first is that diversification cannot be fully captured in measures of correlation. If you read "Whom Fortune Favors,"[5] you'll know that our code recognizes that we live in a behaviorally-influenced, non-ergodic world. While I think we'd all recognize that U.S. value stocks are *almost* always going to be a poor diversifier against global equities (and vice versa), clearly there are events outside of the historical record or *what we know today* that could completely change that. And so the proper reading of this should always be in context of an adaptive portfolio management process.

The second complaint, as I alluded to earlier, is the fact that we are not always indifferent in our risk-adjusted return expectations for different

---

[5] epsilontheory.com/whom-fortune-favors-five-things-matter

assets. I'm sure many of you looked at the above chart and said to yourself, "Yeah, I'm not piling into commodities." I don't blame you (I'm still not satisfied with explanations for why I ought to be paid for being long contracts on many commodities), but that is the point. Not owning commodities or MLPs because you don't get them isn't the same as *not* expressing an opinion. If you choose not to decide, you still have made a choice.

When investors choose to forgo diversification, on any basis, they are *implicitly betting that decisions that they make will outperform* what diversification would have yielded them. It may not be optimal to own the most diversified portfolio you can possibly own, because anti-diversifying decisions might, in fact, be worth it. But it is exactly that thought process that must become part of our code as investors. It's OK to turn down a free lunch, but you'd damn well better know that what you're going to spend your money on is better.

So how do you quantify that implicit bet? Again, the Free Lunch Effect gives us our easiest answer. Consider the following case: let's assume we had two investment options, both with similar risk of around 15%. For simplicity's sake we'll start from our naïve assumption that our assets produce, say, 0.5 units of return for every unit of risk we take. If the two assets are perfectly uncorrelated, how much more return would we need to demand from Asset 1 vs. Asset 2 to own more of it than the other? To own 100% Asset 1?

Well, the next chart shows it. In the case above, if you invest 100% of your portfolio in Asset 1, an investor who thinks about his portfolio in risk-adjusted terms is *implicitly betting* that Asset 1 will generate more than 3% more return per year, or an incremental 0.21 in return/risk units. If the assets are less similar, this implicit view grows exponentially.

Implied Incremental Return Expectation from Overweighted Asset

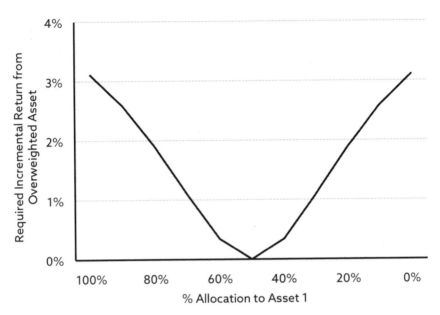

Source: Salient 2017.

A Chain of Linked Engagements

> If we do not learn to regard a war, and the separate campaigns of which it is composed, as a chain of linked engagements each leading to the next, but instead succumb to the idea that the capture of certain geographical points or the seizure of undefended provinces are of value in themselves, we are liable to regard them as windfall profits.
>
> — *On War*, **Carl von Clausewitz**

The point of this note isn't to try to convince you to focus your portfolio construction efforts on higher volatility diversifiers like those highlighted earlier (although many of you should). It's also not to argue that maximizing diversification should be your first objective (although most of us are so far from the optimum that moving in this direction wouldn't hurt). It is to emphasize that portfolio construction and the decisions we make are a chain of linked engagements. It is to give you pause when you or your client asks for a "best new investment idea." If your experiences are like mine, the question is nearly always expressed in isolation—recommend me a stock, a mutual fund, a hedge fund. These questions can never be answered in isolation. If you really must tinker with your allocation, sure, I can give you my view, but only if I know what else you own, and only if I know what you intend to sell in order to buy the thing.

Anyone who will make a recommendation to you without knowing those things is an idiot, a charlatan, or both.

Most of us, whether we are entrenched in financial markets or not, think about our decisions not in a vacuum but in terms of opportunity cost. If we buy A, we're giving up B. If we invest in A, we're giving up on B. If we do A, we won't have time for B. Opportunity cost is fundamental to thinking about nearly every aspect of human endeavor but for some reason is completely absent from the way many investors typically think about building portfolios.

Look, if you didn't completely follow where I was going with "Whom Fortune Favors," I get it.[6] Telling you to think about risk and diversification separately is more than a little bit arcane. But here's where it comes together: an investor can only make wise decisions about asset allocation, about selecting fund managers, about tactical bets and about individual investments when he has an objective opportunity cost to assess those decisions against that allows him to make his portfolio decisions intentionally, not implicitly. That opportunity cost is the free lunch provided by diversification.

If we take this way of thinking to its natural extreme, we must recognize that we can, at any point, identify the portfolio that would have provided the maximum diversification, at least using the tools we've outlined here. For most periods, if you run through that analysis, you are very likely to find that a portfolio of those assets in which every investment contributes a comparable amount of risk to the whole—a risk parity portfolio, in other words—typically provides something near to that maximum level of diversification. I am not suggesting that your portfolio be the maximum diversification portfolio or risk parity. But I am suggesting that

---

[6] epsilontheory.com/whom-fortune-favors-continued-five-things-that-matter

a risk parity portfolio of your investable universe is an excellent place to use as an anchor for this necessary analysis.

If you don't favor it for various reasons (e.g. using volatility as a proxy for risk is the devil, it's just levered bonds, etc.), then find your home portfolio that accomplishes similar goals in a way that is rules-based and sensible. Maybe it's the true market portfolio we highlight in "I am Spartacus."[7] If you're conservative, maybe it's the tangency portfolio from the efficient frontier. And if you're more aggressive, maybe it is something closer to the Kelly Optimal portfolio we discussed in "Whom Fortune Favors." From there, your portfolio construction exercise becomes relatively simple: does the benefit I expect from this action exceed its diversification opportunity cost?

How do you measure it? If you have capital markets assumptions or projections, feel free to use them. Perhaps simpler, assume a particular Sharpe Ratio, say 0.25 or 0.30, and multiply it times the drop in diversification impact from the action you're taking. Are you confident that the change you're making to the portfolio is going to have more of an impact than that? That's ... really it. Now the shrewd among you might be saying, "Rusty, isn't that kind of like what a mean-variance optimization model would do?" It isn't kind of like that, it's literally that. And so what? We're not reinventing portfolio science here, we're trying to unpack it so that we can use it more effectively as investors.

Recognize that this isn't just a relevant approach to scenarios where you're changing things around because you think it will improve returns dramatically. This is also a useful construct for understanding whether all the shenanigans in search of diversification, all that Chili P you're adding, are really worth the headache. Is that fifth emerging markets manager really adding something? Is sub-dividing your regions to add country managers really worth the time?

In the end, it's all about being intentional. With as many decisions as we have to manage, the worst thing we can do is let our portfolios make our decisions for us. Given the benefits of diversification, investors ought to put the burden of proof on anything that makes a portfolio

---

7   epsilontheory.com/spartacus-five-things-dont-matter-part-1

less diversified. In doing so, they will recognize why this code recognizes the intentional pursuit of real diversification as the #2 Thing that Matters.

Originally published August 10, 2017; epsilontheory.com/you-still-have-made-a-choice.

ABOUT RUSTY GUINN

Rusty Guinn is the executive vice president of asset management at Salient. He oversees Salient's retail and institutional asset management business, including investment teams, products, and strategy. Rusty shares his perspective and experience as an investor on the Epsilon Theory website.

Prior to joining Salient in 2013, Rusty was the head of strategic partnerships and opportunistic investments at the Teacher Retirement System of Texas. In this role, he was directly responsible for more than $11 billion of Trust capital and commitments across a multi-asset portfolio consisting of equity, fixed income, credit, private equity, real estate, and commodity investments, and oversight of the plan's Strategic Partnership Program. Rusty started his career in roles with the Asset Management Finance affiliate of Credit Suisse and with De Guardiola Advisors, an investment bank advising the asset management industry.

Rusty earned a Bachelor of Science in economics from the Wharton School of the University of Pennsylvania.

@WRGuinn

The Three-Body Problem

—

BEN HUNT

As much as I dislike the chickens on our farm, I love my bees. Do they sting? Of course they sting. The swarm is a wild animal. But after a few painful years I'm no longer a ham-handed goofball with my hives, and a morning spent in sync with this amazing animal is never a bad morning. Not only are bees low maintenance, not only do they pay a wonderful rent, but they demonstrate a genius and an *optimism*—there's just no other word for it—that makes *me* feel more creative and alive.

The Connecticut winters are tough, though. I do what I can to support the bees, which is mostly just building a wind break with bales of straw, making sure that the hive stays ventilated enough to prevent water vapor condensation, and preventing mice from taking up residence. That and avoiding original sins like poor hive placement or collecting too much rent. But ultimately it's a battle between the animal and Mother Nature. It's up to them to survive. Or not.

Honeybees don't hibernate (bumblebees do, but hive colony bees don't), and they can't fly south for the winter. To survive a Northern winter, bees change the composition of the swarm by shrinking the overall population, caulking the hive, getting rid of the deadweight males (i.e., ALL of the males), and laying just enough eggs to preserve a minimal survivable population through the winter and into spring. They cluster together in the center of the hive, keeping the queen in the center, shivering their wings to create kinetic energy, occasionally sending out suicide squads to retrieve honey stores from the outer combs. They lower their metabolism by creating a cloud of carbon dioxide in the hive. Yes, a carbon dioxide cloud.

All of this preparation takes time. To survive winter, the swarm starts to change its behaviors—from brood patterns to pollen collection to comb creation—not when the weather starts getting cold, but in the middle of summer when the dog days of August are still in front of us. And not just on some random date, but on a completely predictable day.

In 2018 my bees will begin to prepare for winter on Friday, June 22nd.

Why? Because bees can measure the angle of the sun's rays. They can remember this from one day to the next. When today's midday sun is ever so slightly lower in the sky than yesterday's midday sun, a bee will know it. And the entire colony will begin to change.

Bees recognize the freakin' summer solstice with as much accuracy as any human civilization ever did.

See? Genius. But we're just getting started.

When bees act on their awareness of the summer solstice, they are trading a *derivative*. And they expertly manage the *basis risk* of that trade.

Huh? Time out, Ben. What are you talking about?

A *derivative*, in the broadest sense of the word, is something that's related to something else you care about (the "underlying"), but for whatever reason you choose to interact with the derivative-something rather than the underlying-something. For humans, you might care about the stock price of company XYZ, so that's the underlying, but you think something momentous is going to happen to the company three months from now, so you interact with a derivative on the stock, in this case a three-month option contract. For bees, the thing they truly care about is how cold it gets, so from their perspective the temperature is the underlying and the sunlight angles are the derivative thing that they analyze and interact with. In truth, of course, it's the tilt of the Earth's axis and the resultant sunlight angles that cause seasonality and temperature changes, so a curmudgeonly reader might accurately say that actually, it's the temperature that's the derivative here, but I trust we're all open-minded enough to take a bee's eye view of the world for the duration of this note.

Why do bees take their behavioral cues from sunlight angles rather than temperature change directly? Because the algorithm for predicting seasonality—IF (maximum incident angle of sunlight today < maximum incident angle of sunlight yesterday), THEN (prepare for winter)—is enormously simpler, more predictive, more timely, and less volatile than any sort of temperature time-series analysis, or at least any temperature time-series analysis available to bees and pre-weather satellite humans. The genius (and fatal flaw) of bees and humans is their ability to create complex social systems on the basis of simple algorithms like this. Modern computing systems of the Big Data sort have a very different type of genius.

Hold that thought.

But first let's make sure we understand what *basis risk* means, and why it's The Most Important Thing to understand when you're dealing with derivatives. "Basis" is the relationship between the derivative and the underlying, and so basis risk is how bad things could get if the relationship between derivative and underlying isn't as tight as you thought it was. For bees, basis risk takes the form of cold weather coming sooner or later than normal. Shrinking the colony like clockwork based on the summer solstice works great if the first big freeze comes in November, not so well if you get a big snow in mid-October.

The key to managing basis risk is to keep your risk antennae (literally antennae when it comes to bees) focused on how well the derivative thing is tracking with the underlying thing. You need to watch the *correlation*. So to manage their basis risk, bees are also sensitive to temperature (the underlying) and all of the other derivative things related to changing temperature, like flower bloom patterns or prevailing winds. Nothing will totally override the summer solstice trade (even tropical bees make some small colony adjustments based on seasonality), but bees are *adaptive investors*, able to accelerate their winter preparation if cold weather comes early or delay it if cold weather comes late. Efficient management of basis risk is a balancing act between sticking with the original trade and adapting your behavior to changing correlations (you don't want to mistake an Indian Summer for spring!), but that's the beauty of evolution—billions of bee colonies over millions of years have lived and died and reproduced to naturally select the combination of hard-wired nervous system algorithms that allows honeybee species to thrive across a wide range of ecosystems and a wide range of seasonal weather variations.

But it's only a range. Bees can't live in as wide a range of ecosystems and weather variations as, say, ants. I doubt there's a bee colony on Earth that can survive six months straight of sub-50 degree weather. If you're a bee colony and you've moved that far north and that's the magnitude of your downside basis risk, it really doesn't matter how amazing you are in your solar declination calculations … you're not going to make it. Maybe you get lucky for a couple of years, but if it's *possible* that you could have four or five months of harshly cold weather, then sooner or later that severe basis risk catches up with you. This is a basis risk that you can't insure against, that you can't hedge against with extra preparation or precaution. It's an unmanageable basis risk. For most of North America, though, even pretty far up into Canada, cold weather is a manageable basis risk, particularly if you've got a beekeeper able to lend a helping hand. Sometimes the bees will get a bad roll of the weather dice and you'll lose a hive to basis risk, but it doesn't threaten the species.

Species risk comes into play when you get a major climactic event that lasts for a long time in terms of a colony's lifespan but not long at all in terms of evolution, genetic mutation, and natural selection. Like, say, what if spring no longer followed winter? What if it snowed in August and flowers bloomed in January? What if winter disappeared for a decade? What if it lasted that long? What if your weather basis risk was *unknowable*, as in *Game of Thrones*? Even a short Westerosi winter of a couple of years would kill every bee colony on the continent, which is why I don't think I've ever seen a bee hive on *Game of Thrones*. [Hmm … I've just been informed by Grand Master Guinn that "one of the Baratheon vassal houses of the Reach is House Beesbury, with a family seat of Honeyholt and a family motto of *Beware Our Sting*." Sigh. You see what I have to put up with? Okay, we'll stipulate that Dornish latitudes are safe. But The North is no place for bees when winter comes!]

This is *basis uncertainty*, where you're not even sure that any basis *exists at all*, as opposed to mere basis risk. Basis uncertainty is an *unknowable* basis risk, which is much more damaging to species development than the occasional bout of severe basis risk.

[Long parenthetical: understanding the distinction between risk and uncertainty is crucial in every aspect of life. A risky decision is when you have a pretty good sense of the odds and the pay-offs. It lends itself to statistical analysis and econometrics, particularly if it's a decision you will have the opportunity to make multiple times. An uncertain decision is when you don't have a good sense of odds and pay-offs. Here, statistical analysis may very well kill you, particularly if you're not going to get many cracks at the game, or if you don't know how many times you'll get to make a choice. You need game theory to make sense of decisions made under uncertainty.]

Basis uncertainty is the core problem facing every investor today.

It's not just that we endure large basis risks here in the Hollow Market, unmanageable for many. It's not just that all of our old signposts and moorings for navigating markets aren't working very well. It's not just *difficult* to identify predictive/derivative patterns in today's markets. **There is a non-trivial chance that structural changes in our social worlds of politics and markets have made it** *impossible* **to identify predictive/derivative patterns.** THIS is basis uncertainty, and it's as problematic for humans facing markets that don't make sense as it is for bees facing weather patterns that don't make sense.

Well, that's just crazy talk, Ben. What do you mean that it might be *impossible* to identify predictive/derivative patterns? What do you mean that basis might not exist at all? Of course there's a pattern to markets and everything else. Of course spring follows winter.

Nope. This is the Three-Body Problem.

Or rather, the Three-Body Problem is a famous example of a system which has no derivative pattern with any predictive power, no applicable algorithm that a human (or a bee) could discover to adapt successfully and turn basis uncertainty into basis risk. In the lingo, there is no "general closed-form solution" to the Three-Body Problem. (It's also the title of the best science fiction book I've read in the past 20 years, by Cixin Liu. Truly a masterpiece. Life and perspective-changing, in fact, both in its depiction of China and its depiction of the game theory of civilization.)

What is the "problem"? Imagine three massive objects in space ... stars, planets, something like that. They're in the same system, meaning that they can't entirely escape each other's gravitational pull. You know the position, mass, speed, and direction of travel for each of the objects. You know how gravity works, so you know *precisely* how each object is acting on the other two objects. Now predict for me, using a formula, where the objects will be at some point in the future.

Answer: you can't. In 1887, Henri Poincaré proved that the motion of the three objects, with the exception of a few special starting cases, is *non-repeating*. This is a chaotic system, meaning that the historical pattern of object positions has ZERO predictive power in figuring out where these objects will be in the future. There is no algorithm that a human can possibly discover to solve this problem. It does not exist.

To visualize the Three-Body Problem, here's a simulation of the orbits of green, blue, and red objects with random starting conditions, each exerting a gravitational pull on the others. What Poincaré proved is that *there is no formula* where you can plug in the initial information and get the right answer for where any of the objects will be at any future point in time. **No human can predict the future of this system.**

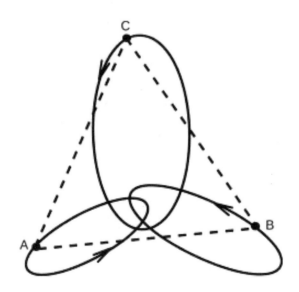

But a computer can. Not by using an algorithm, which is how biological brains—human and bee alike—evolved to make sense of the world, but by brute force calculations. Remember, you know everything about these three objects … none of the physics here is a mystery. If you can do the calculation quickly enough, you can compute where all three objects will be one second from now. And one second from then. And one second from then. And so on and so on. With enough processing power (and this can require a LOT of processing power) you can *calculate* where the three objects will be 100 years from now, even though it is impossible to *solve* for this outcome.

It's a hard concept to wrap your head around, this difference between *calculating the future* **and** *predicting the future*, **but it will change the way you see the world. And your place in it.**

Now here's an observation that I can't emphasize strongly enough, although I'll try:

THIS IS NOT HOW WE USE COMPUTERS IN OUR INVESTING STRATEGIES TODAY.

The way that computers can calculate an answer to the Three-Body Problem is straightforward—they can be programmed with the physics rules for how one object influences another object, so they can simulate where each object will go next. There is ZERO examination of where the objects have been in the past. *This is entirely forward looking.*

The way that computers can NOT calculate an answer to the Three-Body Problem is by examining the historical data of where the objects have been. In a chaotic system, it doesn't matter how hard or how fast or how deeply you look at the historical data. There is NO predictive pattern, NO secret algorithm hiding in the data. And yet this is exactly what we all have our computers doing … examining historical data to look for patterns that will give us the magic algorithm for predicting what's next! The only thing that the past gives you in a chaotic system is inertia, which can look like a pattern or an algorithm for some period of time, depending on how all the objects are aligned. But it's a mirage. It will not last. Examining the past of a chaotic system can give you lots of little answers, like sparks off a bonfire, none lasting more than a few seconds. And certainly if you're efficient with your inertia-identifying spark-capturing effort, you can make some money using computers this way. But this examination of the past through naïve induction will never give you The Answer. Because The Answer does not exist in the past. The Answer—which is another word for algorithm, which is another word for "general closed-end solution"—doesn't exist at all in a chaotic Three-Body System.

But we can approximate The Answer. We can *calculate* the future in small computational chunks even if we can't *predict* the future in one big algorithmic swoop, but only if we can program the computer with the "physics" of how "gravity" works in social systems like markets. **What's our financial world equivalent of a theory of gravity? I think it's a theory of narrative.** This, to me, is a more interesting research program than identifying small inertias or capturing brief sparks. But it's not where our computing resources are being allocated, because there's no money in it. Yet.

Exploring a theory of narrative, what I've called the Narrative Machine,[1] is basic research. Like all basic research, it's not immediately remunerative and thus is difficult to fund. But that's not the biggest obstacle. No, the biggest obstacle to basic research in computational finance is that humans are hard-wired to look for algorithms and have a really hard time imagining that it's even *possible* to pursue a non-anthropomorphic (how about that for a $10 word) research design that doesn't pore through historical data looking for predictive algorithms at every turn. We can't help ourselves!

What if I told you that algorithms and derivatives are as much at the heart of how humans prepare for their financial future as they are for bees preparing for their seasonal future? What if I told you that the dominant strategies for human discretionary investing are, without exception, algorithms and derivatives? And what if I told you that these algorithms and derivatives were perhaps "evolved" under a "benign" configuration of the Three-Body Problem that not only might never repeat, but in fact is *certain* to never repeat because it is a chaotic system?

I'll give you two examples of influential investment algorithms/ derivatives. There are many more.

GOOD COMPANIES => GOOD STOCKS

GOOD COUNTRIES => GOOD GOVERNMENT BONDS

These are the central tenets of stock-picking and sovereign bond-picking, respectively. In both cases, goodness (like beauty) is in the eye of the beholder, so I'm not saying that there is some single standard for what makes a "good" company or what makes a "good" set of macroeconomic policies. What I'm saying is that everyone reading this note (including

---

[1]   See my piece, "The Narrative Machine," epsilontheory.com/the-narrative-machine.

me!) believes that there is a direct relationship between the *quality* of a company or an economy (however you define quality) and the future price of whatever stocks or bonds are connected to that company or economy. What I'm saying is that everyone reading this note believes that tracking the measurable quality of a company or an economy (the derivative) according to some standardized and repeatable process (the algorithm) will, over time, have a predictive correlation with the future price of the related stock and bond securities (the underlying).

What stocks do we want to own? Why, the stocks of high-quality companies, of course … companies with stellar management teams, fortress balance sheets, and wonderful products or services that everyone wants to buy. Ditto for government bonds and currencies and broad market indices and the like. Maybe it will take some time for this faith in Quality to pay off, but we all believe that it WILL pay off. It's only natural, right? As natural as spring following winter. As natural as flowers blooming in May and snow falling in December. Maybe the flowers will bloom a few weeks late and maybe the snows will fall a few weeks early, but that's just basis risk, and we can manage for that.

But what if spring doesn't follow winter anymore?

Look, I'm not asking us to abandon our faith in Quality. One of the key corollaries of the Three-Body Problem is that we don't have to reject our belief that Objects 1 and 2 exist. We don't have to deny our faith that the Quality-of-Companies is an actual thing and that it has a big gravitational pull on the price of stocks. We don't have to deny our faith that the Quality-of-Governments is an actual thing and that it has a big gravitational pull on the price of government bonds.

What we have to accept is that there is an Object 3 that has moved into a position such that its gravity absolutely swamps the impact of Objects 1 and 2. This Object 3, of course, is extraordinary monetary policy, specifically the purchase of $20 TRILLION worth of financial assets by the Big 4 central banks—the Fed, the ECB, the BOJ, and the PBOC.

$20 trillion is a lot of mass. $20 trillion is a lot of gravity.

Here's the impact of all that gravity on the Quality-of-Companies derivative investment strategy.

The chart below shows the S&P 500 index and a Quality Index sponsored by Deutsche Bank. They look at 1,000 global large cap companies and evaluate them for return on equity, return on invested capital, and accounting accruals – quantifiable proxies for the most common ways that investors think about quality. Because the goal is to isolate the Quality factor, the index is long in equal amounts the top 20% of measured companies and short the bottom 20% (so market neutral), and has equal amounts invested long and short in the component sectors of the market (so sector neutral). The chart begins on March 9, 2009, when the Fed launched its first QE program.

S&P 500 vs. Market Neutral Quality Index (% return)

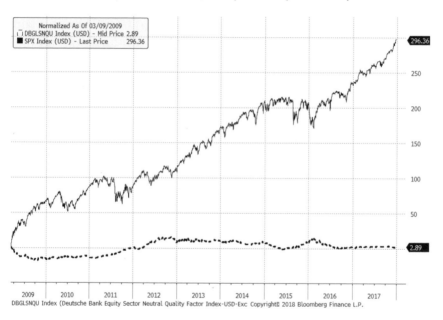

Source: Bloomberg.

Over the past *eight and a half years*, Quality has been absolutely useless as an investment derivative. You've made a grand total of not quite 3% on your investment, while the S&P 500 is up almost 300%.

This is not a typo.

Have the Quality stocks in your portfolio gone up over the past eight and a half years? Sure, but it's not because of the Quality-ness of the companies. It's because ALL stocks have gone up ever since Object 3, the balance sheets of central banks, started exerting its massive gravity on everything BUT Quality. That's not an accident, by the way. Central banks don't care about rewarding "good" companies. In fact, if they care about anything on this dimension, they care about keeping "bad" companies from going under.

This is what it looks like when spring does not follow winter.

And here's the impact of all that gravity on the Quality-of-Countries derivative investment strategy.

The chart below shows the spread (difference) between Portugal's 10-year bond yield and the U.S. 10-year bond yield, and the the spread between Italy's 10-year note yield and the U.S. equivalent. In "normal" times, a country with a weaker set of macroeconomic characteristics (high levels of national debt, say, or maybe low productivity) will have to offer investors a higher rate of interest to borrow their money than a country with a stronger set of macroeconomic characteristics. So in the summer of 2012, when Portugal and Italy were both looking like deadbeat countries, they had to pay investors a much higher rate of interest than the U.S. did to attract the investment – about 9% more (this is per year, mind you) for Portugal and 4% more for Italy. Those are enormous spreads in the world of sovereign debt!

This chart begins in the summer of 2012, when the ECB announced its intentions to prop up the European sovereign debt market directly. Since that announcement—*even though both Portugal and Italy have higher debt-to-GDP ratios today than in 2012*—the spread versus U.S. interest rates has done nothing but decline. Driven by the commitment of the ECB to "do whatever it takes" and to be not only a last-resort buyer but also a first-in-line buyer of Portuguese and Italian debt, it now costs LESS for these countries to borrow money for 10 years than the U.S.

Difference in 10-Yr Yields: Portugal vs. U.S. and Italy vs. U.S.

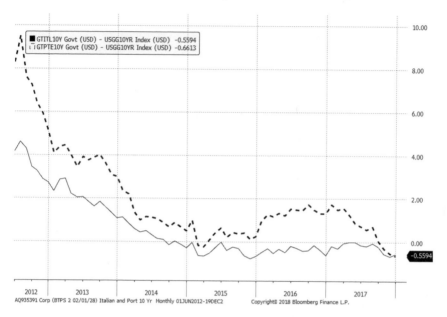

Source: Bloomberg.

This is nuts. It's an understandable nuts when you consider that the German 10-year bond yield is currently about 30 basis points, and was actually negative (meaning that you had to pay the German government for the privilege of lending them money for the next ten years) for about six months in 2016. Meaning that at least with Italian and Portuguese debt you're being paid something (a little less than 2% per year). It's an understandable nuts when you consider that the Swiss 10-year bond still sports a negative interest rate and has been negative for the past two and a half years. **There's about $10 trillion worth of negative yielding sovereign bonds out there today, something that is IMPOSSIBLE under a [good country => good bond] derivative algorithm. No country is that good!** But it's entirely possible under the immense gravitational force of massive central bank asset purchases.

Here's the kicker. Below is the spread between Greek 10-year sovereign bonds and U.S. 10-year notes. In 2012 you were paid 24% more to lend money to Greece. Per year! Today you are paid less than 2% more to lend money to Greece rather than the United States. For ten years. To Greece.

Difference in 10-Yr Yields: Greece vs. U.S.

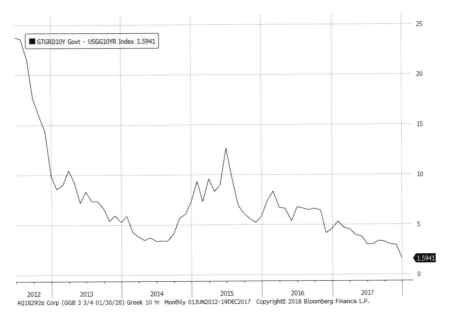

Source: Bloomberg.

Again, I'm not saying that the Quality derivative doesn't exist as a real thing or that it isn't an important factor in the *history* of successful stock-picking or bond-picking. **What I'm saying is that the Quality derivative hasn't mattered for eight and a half years with stocks and five years with sovereign debt.** What I'm saying is that it might not matter for another eighty years. Or it might matter again in eight months. A Three-Body System is a chaotic system. As the boilerplate says, past performance is not a guarantee of future results. In fact, the only thing I can promise you is that past performance will NEVER give you a predictive algorithm for future results in a chaotic system.

This is basis uncertainty. This is the biggest concern that every investor should have, that the signals (derivatives) and processes (algorithms) that we ALL use to make sense of the investing world are no longer connected to security prices.

… Okay, Ben, you've exhausted me. It's a weird and strange way of looking at the world, but let's go with it for a minute. What's the pay-off here? What

do we DO in a chaotic system? What does that even mean, to say that we are investors in a chaotic system?

Four suggestions.

First, I think we should adopt a philosophy of what I've called *profound agnosticism*[2] when it comes to investing, where we don't just embrace the notion that no one has a crystal ball in this system, but we actually get kinda annoyed with those who insist they do. **I think that risk balancing strategies make a ton of sense in a chaotic system,** so that we think first about budgeting our risk agnostically across geographies and asset classes and sectors, and secondarily think about budgeting our dollars.

Second, and relatedly, I think we should adopt a classic game theory strategy for dealing with uncertain systems—*minimax regret*. The idea is simple, but the implications profound: **instead of seeking to maximize returns, we seek to minimize our maximum regret.** Keep in mind that our maximum regret may not be ruinous loss! I know plenty of people whose maximum regret is not keeping up with the Joneses. In fact, from a business model perspective, that's more common than not. Or if you've bought into Bitcoin north of $15,000 per coin, I think you know what I'm talking about, too. The point being that we need to be painfully honest with ourselves about our sources of regret and target our investments accordingly. If we can be this honest with ourselves, it's a VERY powerful strategy.

Third, I think we should reconsider our approach to computer-directed investment strategies. **Using computers in an anthropomorphic way, where we treat them like a smarter, faster human, set loose in a vast field of historical data to search for patterns and algorithms … it's a snipe hunt.** Or at least I think we've squeezed just about all the juice out of this inductive orange that we're likely to get. With the massive processing power at our fingertips today, not to mention the orders-of-magnitude-greater processing power that quantum computing will bring to bear in the future, there's much bigger game afoot with computational approaches that take a more deductive, forward-looking strategy.

---

[2] See my piece, "Don't Fear the Reaper," epsilontheory.com/dont-fear-the-reaper.

Fourth, and perhaps most importantly, I think we need to accept that we're never going to fully understand the reality of a chaotic system, but that it's never been more important to try. The brains of both bees and humans are hard-wired for algorithms. Both species see patterns even when patterns don't exist, and both species tend to do poorly in environments where derivative signals are plagued by basis uncertainty rather than mere basis risk. **Every bee in the world will follow its hard-wired algorithms even unto death.** *And most humans will, too.* **But humans have the capacity to think** *beyond* **their biological and cultural programming … if they work at it.**

Where do we lose good people? When they convince themselves that they've found The Answer—either in the form of a charismatic person or, more dangerously still, a charismatic idea—in a chaotic system where no Answer exists. A chaotic system like markets, yes, but also a chaotic system like politics.

The Answer is, by nature, totalitarian. Why? Because it's a general closed-form solution. That's the technical definition of The Answer, and that's the practical definition of totalitarian thought. We're hard-wired to want the all-encompassing algorithm, which is why it's so difficult to resist. But if we care about liberty. If we care about justice. If we care about liberty and justice *for all* … we have to resist The Answer.

Because we've lost enough good people.

Originally published December 21, 2017; epsilontheory.com/three-body-problem.

ABOUT BEN HUNT

Ben Hunt is the chief investment strategist at Salient and the author of Epsilon Theory, a newsletter and website that examines markets through the lenses of game theory and history. Over 100,000 professional investors and allocators across 180 countries read Epsilon Theory for its fresh perspective and novel insights into market dynamics. As chief investment strategist, Dr. Hunt helps develop investment strategy for the firm, works with portfolio managers and key clients to incorporate his investment views into their decision-making process, and manages certain portfolios directly. Dr. Hunt is a featured contributor to a wide range of investment publications and media programming.

Dr. Hunt received his Ph.D. in Government from Harvard University in 1991. He taught political science for ten years: at New York University from 1991 until 1997 and (with tenure) at Southern Methodist University from 1997 until 2000. Dr. Hunt wrote two academic books: *Getting to War* (University of Michigan Press, 1997) and *Policy and Party Competition* (Routledge, 1992), which he co-authored with Michael Laver. Dr. Hunt is the founder of two technology companies and the co-founder of SmartEquip, Inc., a software company for the construction equipment industry that provides intelligent schematics and parts diagrams to facilitate e-commerce in spare parts.

Dr. Hunt began his investment career in 2003, first in venture capital and subsequently on two long/short equity hedge funds. He worked at Iridian Asset Management from 2006 until 2011 and TIG Advisors from 2012 until 2013. Dr. Hunt joined Salient in 2013, where he combines his background as a portfolio manager, risk manager, and entrepreneur with academic experience in game theory and econometrics to provide a unique perspective on investment risk and reward on behalf of Salient and its clients.

@EpsilonTheory

Passive Investing Misconceptions

_____

LARRY SWEDROE

Howard Marks is one of the financial industry's most respected investment managers—for good reason. In 1995, he co-founded Oaktree Capital Management and built an enviable track record, with an emphasis on high-yield bonds, distressed debt, private equity and other nontraditional strategies.

His "memos" to Oaktree clients are the only ones of their kind I read (other than market analyses on which I'm asked to comment by our clients). I make it a point to read them because they are almost always filled with investment wisdom that every investor, whether active or passive, can put to work.

Key Insights

Marks's latest, "There They Go Again ... Again," is no exception. Like many of his memos, this one contains cautionary tales, advising investors to not get caught up in fads. He warns investors:

- "The uncertainties are unusual in terms of number, scale and insolubility in areas including secular economic growth; the impact of central banks; interest rates and inflation; political dysfunction; geopolitical trouble spots; and the long-term impact of technology.

- In the vast majority of asset classes, prospective returns are just about the lowest they've ever been.

- Asset prices are high across the board. Almost nothing can be bought below its intrinsic value, and there are few bargains. In general, the best we can do is look for things that are less overpriced than others.

- Pro-risk behavior is commonplace, as the majority of investors embrace increased risk as the route to the returns they want or need."

He then added the following points about U.S. equities:

- "The S&P 500 is selling at 25 times trailing-12-month earnings, compared to a long-term median of 15.

- The Shiller Cyclically Adjusted PE Ratio stands at almost 30 versus a historic median of 16. This multiple was exceeded only in 1929 and 2000—both clearly bubbles.

- While the 'p' in p/e ratios is high today, the 'e' has probably been inflated by cost cutting, stock buybacks, and merger and acquisition activity. Thus today's reported valuations, while high, may actually be understated relative to underlying profits.

- The 'Buffett Yardstick'—total U.S. stock market capitalization as a percentage of GDP—is immune to company-level accounting issues (although it isn't perfect either). It hit a new all-time high last month of around 145, as opposed to a 1970–95 norm of about 60 and a 1995–2017 median of about 100.

- Finally, it can be argued that even the normal historic valuations aren't merited, since economic growth may be slower in the coming years than it was in the post-World War II period when those norms were established."

He also added a warning about "super-stocks" (FAANG: Facebook, Amazon, Apple, Netflix, Google) and warned that, while these are great companies, they are selling at historically high multiples and aren't invulnerable to competition and change.

So far, so good. Investors should be aware that valuations are high. That means forward-looking return expectations are now much lower than historical returns. And just as once nifty-fifty, "sure-thing" stocks such as Polaroid, Eastman Kodak, Digital Equipment, Burroughs and Xerox have "gone with the wind," the FAANGs could suffer similar fates. In other words, valuations matter, and investors should not be caught up in fads, or chase recent great returns.

Perspective on Passive

Marks then turned his thoughts to the trend toward passive investing. He writes: "Like all investment fashions, passive investing is being warmly embraced for its positives:

- Passive portfolios have outperformed active investing over the last decade or so.

- With passive investing you're guaranteed not to underperform the index.

- Finally, the much lower fees and expenses on passive vehicles are certain to constitute a permanent advantage relative to active management."

He then added: "Does that mean passive investing, index funds and ETFs are a no-lose proposition? Certainly not:

- While passive investors protect against the risk of underperforming, they also surrender the possibility of outperforming.

- The recent underperformance on the part of active investors may well prove to be cyclical rather than permanent."

He continued with what he called "a few more things worth thinking about."

Marks writes: "Remember, the wisdom of passive investing stems from the belief that the efforts of active investors cause assets to be fairly priced—that's why there are no bargains to find. But what happens when the majority of equity investment comes to be managed passively? Then prices will be freer to diverge from 'fair,' and bargains (and over-pricings) should become more commonplace. This won't assure success for active managers, but certainly it will satisfy a necessary condition for their efforts to be effective."

He added this: "One of my clients, the chief investment officer of a pension fund, told me the treasurer had proposed dumping all active managers and putting the whole fund into index funds and ETFs. My response was simple: ask him how much of the fund he's comfortable having in assets no one is analyzing."

Then Mark noted: "Passive funds that emphasize stocks reflecting specific factors are called 'smart-beta funds,' but who can say the people setting their selection rules are any smarter than the active managers who are so disrespected these days? [Horizon Kinetics' Steven] Bregman calls this 'semantic investing,' meaning stocks are chosen on the basis of labels, not quantitative analysis. There are no absolute standards for which stocks represent many of the characteristics listed above."

A Rebuttal

Let me suggest another perspective on passive investing. I'll begin by addressing Marks' statement on passive investing not being a no-lose proposition and his supporting points.

First, as Marks correctly noted, passive investing certainly isn't a no-lose proposition. But what passive investing does do is provide the opportunity to earn the return of the markets, asset classes or factors in which you are investing, less low costs.

While that means you give up the possibility of outperforming your benchmark, you're also virtually certain to outperform the vast majority of active investors trying to beat the market. The only reason it's not completely certain is that you would have to maintain the same type of discipline Warren Buffett has exhibited over the years—intelligence is the necessary condition for successful investing, but discipline is the sufficient condition.

The bottom line is this: You put the odds of meeting your financial goals greatly in your favor by accepting the returns the markets offer and giving up the hope of outperforming benchmarks.

Second, there is nothing cyclical about the underperformance of active managers. That's a permanent condition, and has been so for a long time.

In his brilliant, and short, 1991 paper, "The Arithmetic of Active Management," Nobel Prize-winner William Sharpe showed why this must be the case. And each and every year, the S&P Dow Jones Indices Versus Active (SPIVA) scorecards demonstrate that the majority—in most cases a very large majority—of active managers underperform their appropriate risk-adjusted benchmarks in every asset class.

For example, the 2016 SPIVA Institutional Scorecard, which covered the ten-year period ending in 2016, found that while active institutional funds produced better results than active mutual funds, across all asset classes within the domestic equity space, the overwhelming majority of active managers lagged their respective benchmarks. For example, the percentage of institutional funds underperforming their benchmark ranged from 63% (large value) to 96% (small growth).

The results in international markets were no better, with 81% of international institutional funds failing to provide value and 84% of mutual funds failing to do so. The performance was somewhat better in international small stocks, where "only" about two-thirds of active institutional and active mutual fund managers underperformed.

In the supposedly inefficient asset class of emerging markets, which has traditionally been thought to be one area where active management can add value, 79% of institutional managers fell short of the benchmark. Mutual funds performed even worse, with 86% of them underperforming.

And the results in bond markets were not encouraging either. In the 13 bond categories examined, mutual fund underperformance ranged from 59% (investment-grade bonds) to as high as 97% (high-yield bonds). For institutional managers, the results were similar.

Looking at Factors

I'll now address Marks's comments on investment factors, smart beta and the fund construction rules of passive vehicles.

First, I agree with Marks that a fund's construction rules matter—a great deal. Furthermore, not all passively managed funds are created equal. Some have superior fund construction strategies.

That said, fund families such as DFA, AQR Capital Management and Bridgeway Capital Management, the three fund families my firm, Buckingham Strategic Wealth, uses to implement equity strategies, all base their fund construction rules on decades of academic, peer-reviewed research.

This research shows which factors (traits or characteristics of stocks) demonstrate: persistence of a premium over long periods of time and across economic regimes; pervasiveness across the globe; robustness to various definitions; implementability (meaning they survive transactions costs); and have intuitive risk- or behavioral-based explanations giving us confidence that the premiums are likely to persist.

Once identified, specific portfolio construction rules are created and followed. And they also use patient-trading strategies to avoid some of the negatives of pure indexing.

Second, much of the academic research that has uncovered these factors (or what is often referred to as "smart beta") can be viewed as reverse engineering. It identified the characteristics (such as low price-to-cash flow ratio, earnings, EBITDA or book value) that the most successful active managers have exploited. Once identified, other investors can access the same factors, though in a more highly diversified way.

This process effectively converts what was once alpha (a scarce resource) into beta (a common factor). And because beta is cheap to access, investors no longer need to pay the high fees of active management to benefit from exposure to stocks with these traits.

A good example of this process of converting alpha into beta is the 2012 study "Buffett's Alpha," authored by AQR researchers Andrea Frazzini, David Kabiller and Lasse Pedersen.

They found that, in addition to benefiting from the use of cheap leverage provided by Berkshire Hathaway's insurance operations, Warren Buffett bought stocks that are safe, cheap, high-quality and large.

The most interesting finding in the study was that stocks with these characteristics tend to perform well in general, not just the stocks with these characteristics that Buffett buys. Thus, the quality factor was "born." And now many passive funds incorporate it into their fund construction rules.

When Analysis Doesn't Help Performance

Let's turn now to Marks' query about investing in a fund in which no one is analyzing anything. Let me offer a very different perspective on the question. Today we have more actively managed mutual funds, and more hedge funds, than we have individual stocks. Active funds still control perhaps two-thirds of investment dollars. These active managers analyze the valuations of stocks. It's their actions that are setting prices. If they think a stock is overvalued, they will either avoid it or sell the stock short.

In other words, passive investors aren't investing in something no one is analyzing. Instead, they are investing in assets on which tens of thousands of active managers have offered their opinions through their actions. That's the wisdom of crowds at work.

The evidence shows that such wisdom—the wisdom of the market's collective opinion—is very hard to beat.

As my co-author Andrew Berkin and I showed in our book, *The Incredible Shrinking Alpha*, today only about 2% of active managers are generating statistically significant alpha. I would add that active managers have performed just as poorly in bear markets as they have in bull markets. In other words, while passive funds go down in bear markets, the average active fund goes down even more.

Given the trend toward passive management, one might ask: At what point will there not be sufficient managers analyzing stocks to ensure that prices are the best estimate of the right price?

While I don't think anyone knows that answer, surely it's far less than the tens of thousands we have today. Perhaps even a few hundred would be enough. In fact, it wasn't until 1950 when the number of mutual funds topped 100. That number was still only at about 150 in 1960. And we didn't seem to have any problems allocating capital and setting prices efficiently then.

Today we have more than 9,000 mutual funds and probably more than 10,000 hedge funds. Do investors really need all those active managers to ensure capital is allocated efficiently? It doesn't seem likely.

Markets Are Pretty Efficient

There is one other point to make. At least as of today, the fact that companies that report better- or worse-than-expected results still see higher volumes and larger same-day price moves implies there are still plenty of investors making the markets highly efficient.

As I noted, 50 years ago, there was a small fraction of the number of mutual funds we have today, and the hedge fund industry was in its infancy. On top of that, individuals dominated the market, because the majority of stocks were held directly by investors in brokerage accounts.

The research shows that retail money is "dumb"—active managers exploit its pricing errors. But even back then, the evidence was that on a risk-adjusted basis, in aggregate, mutual funds underperformed—though not anywhere close to as poorly as they are doing today.

For example, about 20 years ago, roughly 20% of active managers were generating statistically significant alpha. As noted above, the figure today is just 2%, with no evidence the trend is reversing. In fact, as Andrew Berkin and I explain in our book, the evidence suggests that, because the competition is getting ever tougher (more skilled), fewer and fewer active managers are able to outperform.

In summary, passive investing has been the winning strategy for decades, and it will continue to be the winning strategy. As William Sharpe showed, that's simple math.

That said, investors should be aware of the concerns Marks has raised and ensure that their portfolio is highly diversified across many different unique sources of risk and return. Investors should avoid concentrating all of their risk in U.S. equities (due to a home-country bias), and also make sure all of their eggs aren't in the single basket of market beta.

Diversifying across other unique factors and investments (such as reinsurance) that also meet all the criteria I listed (persistent, pervasive, robust, implementable and intuitive) creates a more efficient portfolio, and one with less volatility. You can see the benefits of doing so in my books, *Your Complete Guide to Factor-Based Investing* (co-authored with Andrew Berkin) and *Reducing the Risk of Black Swans* (co-authored with Kevin Grogan).

Originally published September 5, 2017; etf.com/sections/index-investor-corner/swedroe-passive-investing-misconceptions.

ABOUT LARRY SWEDROE

Larry Swedroe is the director of research for Buckingham Strategic Wealth and The BAM Alliance, a community of more than 140 independent registered investment advisors throughout the country.

@larryswedroe

How to Become a Professional Trader

ANDREAS F. CLENOW

Would you like to trade for a living? Of course you do. That's why you are here, reading this article. Professional trading is the subject of much lore and myths, and it can be difficult sometimes to tell reality from fiction. Before you read this article, you need to make a decision. Do you want to become a professional trader? Or do you want to fantasize about becoming one?

The common fantasy of what professional traders do is very appealing. But it is also far from reality. If you would like to maintain the illusion and stay with the fantasy, this article is not for you. This article is for those who want the real thing.

Still with me?

How Much does a Good Trader Make?

I want you to think of a number. What do you think a good trader should make per year? Not in terms of salary or bonus or something like that. No, rather how many percent per year on average a solid trader should produce.

When speaking at conferences, I often ask the audience this question. It's very interesting that I will get very different answers depending on if the audience are primarily industry professionals or hobby traders. The latter group tends to suggest five to ten times higher return numbers.

Here's the most important sentence in this article: The very best traders in the world have achieved annualized return numbers of about 20% p.a.

That doesn't mean that every year hits such a number of course. Some years could be more, some years less. Some years negative. In any given year, returns of much higher is possible. Those hitting yearly return numbers of 18–23% kind of range over a few decades are the very best in the world. This is what we have come to expect from the likes of Buffett, Soros, Lynch, Einhorn, Jones, Koulajian, Harding, etc.

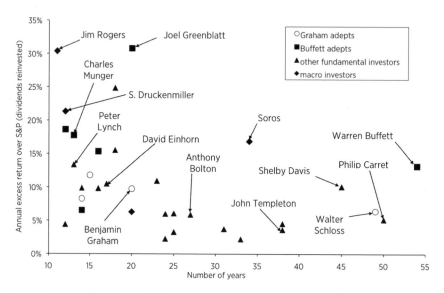

Source: Frederik Vanhaverbeke, *Excess Returns* (Harriman House).

So if the number you thought was 40, 50, 60 or even 100%, you should now start worrying. What you need to ask yourself is this. Do you have a real world, rational reason, for assuming that you can do more than double of what the very best in the world can do?

The Math of Impossibility

Imagine for a moment that we live in a fantasy world where it is possible to compound at 100% p.a. After all, there is no shortage of bloggers out there who make such claims. Let's assume that this is actually true, as insane as that might sound.

So we'll put a small amount of cash into this insane sounding money making machine that some self proclaimed market wizard sells, and start trading. Let's put up 10k.

In a year, our account is at 20,000 and after two years the account stands at 40,000. Great! Let's keep the ball rolling. In seven years, we've got a million bucks. But why stop there?

From our first million, there's only a couple of years to eight digits. By year 10, we have over 10 million cold ones, and of course by year 11 we've got 20 million smackaroos.

It's a little disappointing that we have to wait all the way to year 17 before we see a billion. But clocking the first ten billion in year 20 should call for some champagne.

$10,000 at 100% Annual Compounding

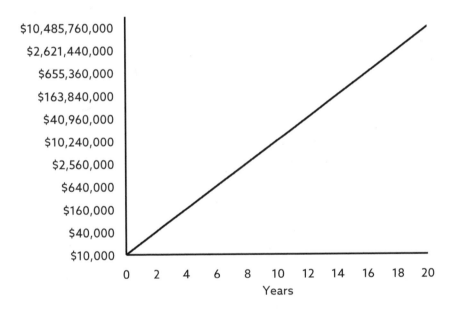

This makes for a very attractive daydream. Of course, no one has ever done this in history.

Hitting 100% in a single year is possible, through skill, hard work, dumb luck or a combination. But it's an outlier. No one averages at such numbers.

But what about Mr. XYZ who claims to have turned a tiny amount into a massive amount in no time at all, and is now offering to teach me how to achieve hundreds of percent a year if I pay him?

Well, good luck with that.

Back to Reality

Let's go back to the real world again. For the sake of this article, I'm going to assume that you have a trading methodology that you're happy with, and that you are looking at ways to turn this into a living.

You probably spent quite a bit of time already learning trading. You've read the books, you did your research, you ran your simulations. Perhaps you even traded for some time, and have strong results to show for it. Great! Now let's see what options this leaves you.

The way I see it, you have three main routes to consider.

1. Get a job in the financial industry.
2. Trade your own money, aka day trading.
3. Start a business.

Getting a Job

There's much to be said for getting a good job in the business. There are very few professions where the earning potential is as high as in the financial industry. How many other sectors let 20-something punks pull seven digit bonuses?

It's not easy getting the kind of job roles that can net you seven figures. Then again, most rational people are happy with mid-six digits, and that's a whole lot easier.

Don't underestimate the value of a salary. If you work in the financial industry, you will likely earn a decent six figure amount even for a fairly junior position. The safety and stability of a paycheck shouldn't be underestimated. You will also learn from being inside the business. Even if you eventually want to go out on your own, the insights that be only be gained from working in the business can be of very high value.

The jobs in the financial industry may not be exactly what people outside it think though. Most people with the word trader in their job title do nothing even remotely similar to pop culture perception. Most are execution traders, handling the execution of other people's orders, and similar.

There are very few people in the business who are simply given a pile of money to trade any way they like. Extremely few. Working in the financial industry can be very rewarding, but for the vast majority it's just a job like any other.

Will They Steal Your Strategies?

Perhaps you have built some solid trading code, and you're considering using it to land a high paying job with a financial institution. But you're worried that they might simply steal your code. How secretive should you be?

This is largely a misconception. They will not be interested in stealing your code. And if they are, they are amateurs you don't want to deal with anyhow. It's not even a matter of ethics. It's completely irrational.

Even if you have built something really great, it's likely not completely revolutionary. A rational manager would be very impressed if you build something similar to what they're using, even if it's less good. Being outside the business, you wouldn't be expected to have something actually better than whatever they're already using.

Even if it is better, and even if it is really revolutionary, stealing it makes no sense. If you did something really unique, it makes sense to hire you. Taking your code would mean that they would need to spend time and money reverse engineering and understanding it, adapting it to their needs, instead of simply hiring the guy who built it.

And besides, if you built something great once, chances are you'll do it again. Of course they'll want to hire you, and not steal the code.

The concept of super secret code worth massive amounts of money is largely a myth. It doesn't work like that.

So how do you get a job in the business?

Same way you get to Carnegie Hall, I suppose.

The competition is tough. If you didn't attend top schools, have top grades and have a solid contact grid in the market, you'll need to compensate with very hard work. Make yourself visible. Stand out. Get the right people to notice you.

There are no easy answers. It is very tough to get a good job in the business, and you are likely to be rejected many times. Don't let that stop you.

What about Trading for Myself?

I have written before about my view on how trading your own money is a bad trade.[1] If you make a living off trading your own money, you will be forced to take too high risk, to get enough money out to live on. That in turn will lead to economic downfall.

Almost all day traders end up losing most or all of their money.

If you go this route, the odds are strongly against you. When you hear stories of extremely successful day traders, people trading their own money, making very high returns and building wealth, you can be sure that you're dealing with one of two scenarios. Either they are extreme statistical outliers or the stories are *beaucoup de merde*, if you pardon my French.

Daytraders tend to advertise their success, while being very quiet about losses. The article about the trader who made 500% in a year isn't likely to be updated when he lost everything the following year.

The problem with daytrading comes down to risk.

Assume for a moment that you are all set to start your path as a daytrader. You've got your trading strategy, and you've done your research well. You have been working hard and saved up 100,000 bucks to start off trading with.

So what kind of returns will you be aiming for? How much money do you need to live on?

I suppose that very much depends on where in the world you live. An entry level finance job here in Zurich would pay you in the low six

---

[1] "Why managing your own money is a bad trade," followingthetrend. com/2014/10/why-managing-your-own-money-is-a-bad-trade

figures, and that's probably the case in Manhattan as well. But if you're happy living somewhere cheaper, you could probably get by with 50k.

With that target, you would need to achieve a 50% return on your 100k. More than double of what Buffett has achieved.

In order to be able to reach such returns, you need to take on a high degree of risk. Return isn't free. Never was, never will be. Unless your dad is the union representative at Bluestar Airlines. Risk is the currency we all use to buy performance.

Skill and hard work will let you buy a little more performance for a little less risk, but to be able to hit 50% trading returns you will need to take on a very high amount of risk.

It is a very reasonable assumption that your worst drawdown will be somewhere between two to three times your long-term annual return. That is what most experience at some point. Remember that the only people who never have losses are the liars.

Aiming for a 50% average yearly return will end up in wiping out your entire account, sooner or later. It is the equivalent of betting all your money on red on the roulette table. You might get lucky a couple of times, but if you stay at the table you will lose everything sooner or later.

Trading for a living means living off your returns. That implies taking out the gains to pay for basic needs, such as rent, food, alimony and cocaine, depending on your personal situation. There are two main implications of this.

First, withdrawing gains for living expenses means that you will not be compounding the returns. This will make a substantial difference in the long run.

Second, reliance on gains to cover living expenses will absolutely push you to take on too high risk, aiming for too high returns. Daytraders rarely have realistic aims, but are rather aiming for 50–100% p.a. This is sure to lead to disaster in the long run.

To be clear, the main reason why daytraders fail is not a lack of trading skill. The issue is that they take on such high risk, that trading skill becomes irrelevant.

The Good News

The bad news is that realistic long-term results are in the 10–15% range. But the good news is that returns in this range can make you quite wealthy.

The money in this business is not in high return numbers. Never was. That's an illusion, marketed to hobby traders. The best in the business have become billionaires by achieving around 20% p.a. *You can become a millionaire in this field by achieving 10–15%.*

Trading Other People's Money

The truth is that the interesting money in this business is in managing other people's money. There is a great demand for such services and it can be a very rewarding field to be in.

When you manage other people's money, you naturally get paid for this. The base fee you get, usually referred to as a management fee, provides a steady income. Do not underestimate the value that this provides.

Having a base income will allow you to make rational decisions, and not chase unrealistic results. It will allow you to aim for realistic returns, without risking disaster.

Now you can trade your own money, along with clients', and make money for everyone.

A common misunderstanding is that clients, or potential clients, will invest with managers who have the highest return. Too high return targets are a major warning sign for sophisticated investors.

If someone claims to achieve 50% yearly return with Sharpe ratio of 10, nobody will take them seriously. That's like some guy claiming to run 100 meter dash on two seconds. Extraordinary claims require extraordinary proof. And no one has ever managed that so far.

No, what you will find is that informed investors will pay more attention if you target 15% p.a. with a Sharpe of 0.8, for example. Responsible, long-term, realistic asset management.

You can still trade your own money of course. But by managing other people's assets as well, you have stability and can make a good living off trading without the irrational risks of daytrading.

Comparing the Approaches

So let's assume you've got 100k to trade, and a solid trading strategy. Now you want to go and be a daytrader.

Since you plan on living off the returns, you would need to aim for very high returns. Here's a very likely scenario for what may follow.

Year 1, you start off really well. In this example, shown in the image below, you get a 40% realized return the first year. That's an amazing return. Far above reasonable, long-term average. Good job, buddy!

Now you take out the return, 40k, and pay off your bookie and get the repo man off your back.

Next year, we start again with 100k, and make a 20% net return. Still a very good year. But is 20k enough to live on? Well, at least we made a gain.

Daytrading at High Risk

Year 1 ➡️ **Year 2** ➡️ **Year 3**

Year 1	Year 2	Year 3
• 100k start	• 100k start	• 100k start
• 40% profit	• 20% profit	• 30% loss
• Take out 40k living exp.	• Take out 20k living exp.	• Now what?

Then comes the inevitable. Sooner or later, there will be a losing year. Year 3, we start off with the 100k again, and make a 30% loss. That's not even a big loss in the context of the previous gains. This doesn't mean that there is anything wrong with your trading strategy.

But, now your initial 100k is down to 70. You have less money than when you started three years ago, and you didn't get a cent for yourself this year. You can't pay your rent, your five hungry kids are screaming for food and a career in telemarketing looks better and better.

This is a career killing year. It might happen year 3, or year 1 or year 7. But it will happen.

Now look at the alternative.

Start over on these three years. This time around, we raise some external assets, and manage other people's money along with our own. Let's go out there and find 10 million. How do we raise ten mil? Given the current word count on this article, that might become a subject of the next article…

For managing the external assets, we're going to charge a fairly reasonable 1+10. That is, 1% management fee and 10% performance fee. And since we now have a base income, we can afford to trade a little more responsibly. Let's cut the volatility in half. We're going to take on half the risk, for half the return.

In year 1, we start off with 10.1 million. The external 10, plus our own 100k. With half the risk, we'll end up with a return of 20%. You think a 20% is ridiculously low? Think again. It's much higher than industry average, and any rational client will be very happy.

Instead of making a mere 40k, as we did daytrading this year on high risk, we now make a lot more. We're clocking 100k management fee, 200k performance fee and 20k personal gain. That should cover your bad habits.

In the second year, we start off with 11.8 million, since there was no need to withdraw money. Your client is likely very happy and staying with you, and you got paid without having to take out your own money. At half risk, we're making 10% this year. Still a good result, and both you and your client are making good money.

With External Assets

Year 1 ➡ **Year 2** ➡ **Year 3**

Year 1	Year 2	Year 3
• 10.1m start	• 11.8m start	• 12.6m start
• 20% profit	• 10% profit	• 15% loss
• 100k management fee	• 117k management fee	• 125k management fee
• 200k performance fee	• 117k performance fee	• 0 performance fee
• 20k personal gain	• 12k personal gain	• 20k personal gain

But what about the career killing year 3?

Now you start off year 3 with 12.6 million, having compounded the returns. By the same logic, you're now seeing a 15% loss. That's not a fun year, but certainly not a career killer. After +20 and +10, a -15 year is very much in proportion and reasonable. If you have properly explained your strategy and potential gains and losses to your client, he'll stay with you. And you still made 125k management fee, minus the 20k personal loss.

You can now live to fight another day. Perhaps year 4 will be another +20% year. You and your client still made money over time, and there's no need to polish up your CV.

Step by Step

The first step towards becoming a professional trader is to understand how the business works. Learn to see past the usual platitudes of hobby trading lore and understand where the real money is made, and lost.

There are more steps to be overcome of course. Another extremely important point, which deserves an article by itself, is to understand risk. What the word means in a financial context, and how it is misunderstood by practically all trading books.

Then there is the point on how to approach methodology and model origination. And once all of this is done, you need to learn about how to approach asset raising, how to present yourself and your strategy, and how to market your investment services. More articles will come on these topics.

Make no mistake, this is a business like any other. A very interesting and highly rewarding one, but it is still a business and that is the way it should be approached.

Lower returns and responsible asset management may not sound as sexy as extreme leverage forex daytrading and similar get-rich-quick schemes. But one is real and the other is not.

So the question is if you want to be a trader, or daydream about becoming one. Your call.

Originally published January 4, 2018; followingthetrend.com/2018/01/how-to-become-a-professional-trader.

ABOUT ANDREAS F. CLENOW

Andreas F. Clenow is a Swiss financier and the CIO of Acies Asset Management, a Zurich based investment group with a nine figure asset base.

Starting out as an IT entrepreneur in the 90s, he had a management career as the global head of commodity and equity quant modeling for Reuters before leaving for the hedge fund world.

Having founded, managed and seeded multiple hedge funds, Mr. Clenow is now overseeing investment management across all asset classes, covering quant trading, private equity and venture capital.

He is the author of the critically acclaimed book *Following the Trend* and can be reached through his website www.FollowingTheTrend.com.

@clenow

The One Business I'll Teach My Children

PORTER STANSBERRY

If you were going to limit all of your investments to only one sector of the economy – only one type of business or one kind of stock – what would you buy?

We've come to believe that, for outside and passive investors (common shareholders), only three sectors offer truly extraordinary rates of return and don't require taking *any* material risk.

Let me be clear about what I mean...

There are three sectors of the economy where companies can establish and maintain a truly *lasting* competitive advantage and where outside investors can identify attractive values.

As I teach my children about investing, I focus almost entirely on examples from these three sectors. And truly... *I spend most of my time explaining only one business to my children.*

If they come to understand this business thoroughly, I know that with a reasonable amount of saving discipline, they will be financially secure by the time they are 30 years old... and wealthy long before they reach 50.

I want to show you *why* the investment returns in these businesses are so incredibly good over the long term. I want you to know how to think about these businesses... how they work... and a few simple keys to making great investments in these sectors.

I promise... this is all far easier than you're imagining right now. Let's start with this chart...

What Kind of Business Always Beats the Market?

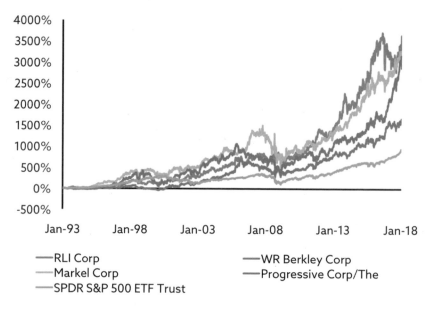

Legend:
- RLI Corp
- Markel Corp
- SPDR S&P 500 ETF Trust
- WR Berkley Corp
- Progressive Corp/The

Source: Bloomberg.

This chart shows four of the best-managed property and casualty (P&C) insurance companies in the United States.

RLI Corp started in the 1930s insuring jitney buses and, later, long-haul truckers. In 2017, it serves niche markets and underwrites specialty insurance products. The company is worth $12 billion.

Markel Corp got its start insuring contact lenses. In 2017, it focuses on things that other companies won't touch, like oil rigs and summer camps. It's a small public company worth $2.7 billion.

The Progressive Corp was founded by a Harvard Business School graduate 50 years ago. It's still mostly a family business (even though it has public shareholders and is worth $7.3 billion). It insures almost anything commercial, from yachts to elevators.

WR Berkeley Corp is a major global company that insures virtually anything and is worth $31 billion.

You might think that outside of being in the insurance industry, these companies have almost nothing in common. Some are small and insure essentially niche items. Others are huge, operate globally, and insure virtually anything. Yet to us, these companies look nearly the same: *They are among the best underwriters in the world.*

That means these insurance companies almost always demand more in insurance premiums than they will end up spending on insurance claims. As you will soon learn, nothing is more valuable in the financial world than having the skill and the discipline to underwrite insurance profitably.

Over the long term, all these companies have generated returns that are *more than double the S&P 500.* They did so without taking any risk. And here's the best part... their success was both *inevitable and repeatable.* These are not "lucky guesses" or fad-driven product sales.

Knowing what I know now about finance, I wouldn't have gotten into the investment newsletter business. I would have gotten into insurance.

Let me say it one more time... I believe if individuals limit themselves to only investing in P&C insurance companies, they would greatly increase their average annual returns. We don't believe that's true of any other sector of the market.

There's a simple reason for this. If you think about it for a minute, it should become intuitive... Here's why insurance is the world's best business: *Insurance is the only business in the world that enjoys a positive cost of capital.*

In every other business, companies must pay for capital. They borrow through loans. They raise equity (and pay dividends). They pay depositors. Everywhere else you look, in every other sector, in every other type of business, the cost of capital is one of the primary business considerations. Often, it's the dominant consideration.

But a well-run insurance company will routinely not only get all the capital it needs for free, *it will actually get paid to accept it.*

I want to make sure you understand this point. All the people who make their living providing financial services – banks, brokers, hedge-fund managers – pay for the capital they use to earn a living.

Banks borrow from depositors, investors who buy CDs, and other banks. They have to pay interest for that capital. Likewise, virtually every actor in the financial-services food chain must pay for the right to use capital. Everyone, that is, except insurance companies.

Now just follow me here for a second... Insurance companies take the premiums they've collected and invest that capital in a range of financial assets.

Assume, just for the sake of argument, that they earn 10% each year on their premiums. (That is, they make 10% on their underwriting.) And assume they invest only in the S&P 500... What do you think the average return on their assets will be each year? In this hypothetical example, their return would be 10% plus whatever the S&P 500 returned.

In reality, of course, few insurance companies can make such a large underwriting return. And few insurance companies invest a large percentage of their portfolio in stocks. Most stick to fixed income to make sure they can always pay claims. But the point remains valid. By compounding underwriting profits over time, year after year, into the financial markets, insurance companies can produce very high returns.

Here's the best part: Insurance companies don't really own most of the money they're investing. They invest the "float" they hold on behalf of their policyholders.

Float is the money they've received in premiums, but haven't paid out yet. Underwritten appropriately, this is a risk-free way to leverage their investments and can result in astronomical returns on equity over time.

Just look at RLI Corp in the earlier chart.

It has produced five times the S&P 500's long-term return. Can you think of any investor, anywhere, who has done anything like that? There isn't one. *That kind of performance was only possible because, using a small equity base, the firm has profitably invested underwritten float into solid investments, year after year.*

Do you like paying taxes? If you do... well, you won't like insurance stocks. They have *huge* tax advantages. Insurance is, far and away, the most tax-privileged industry in the world. *Many of their investment products are totally protected from taxes.*

And their earnings are sheltered, too. *Insurance companies don't have to pay taxes on the cash flow they receive through premiums because, on paper, they haven't technically earned any of that money*. It's not until all the possible claims on the capital have expired that the money is "earned."

So unlike most companies that have to pay taxes on revenue and profits before investing capital, insurance companies get to invest all the money first. *This is a stupendous advantage*. It's like being able to invest all the money in your paycheck – without any taxes coming out – and then paying your tax bill ten years from now.

I realize that I can't make you (or anyone else) actually invest in insurance stocks. And I know that no matter what I say, you probably never will. It's a tough industry to understand, filled with financial concepts and tons of jargon. But there are two reasons the smartest guys in finance wind up in insurance, one way or another...

1. It pays the best.

2. It takes real genius to understand.

But my goal is to make it so easy to understand and follow that any reasonably diligent person can do so. I want to simply show you the one number you've got to know to invest safely and successfully.

The One Number You Need to Know to Invest Safely and Successfully

Normal measures of valuation don't apply to insurance companies. Why not? Because regular accounting considers the "float" an insurance company holds as a liability. And technically, of course, it is. Sooner or later, most (but not all) of that float will go out the door to cover claims.

But because more premiums are always coming in the door, float tends to grow over time, not shrink. So in this way, in real life, float can be an important asset – by far the most valuable thing an insurance company owns. But there's one important catch...

Float is only valuable if the company can produce an underwriting profit. If it can't, float can turn into an expensive liability.

That's why the ability to consistently underwrite at a profit is the key – the whole key – to understanding what insurance stocks to own. Outside of underwriting discipline, almost nothing differentiates insurance companies. And they have no other way to gain a competitive advantage.

Warren Buffett – who built his fortune at Berkshire Hathaway largely on the back of profitable insurance companies – explained this in his 1977 shareholder letter:

> Insurance companies offer standardized policies, which can be copied by anyone. Their only products are promises. It is not difficult to be licensed, and rates are an open book. There are no important advantages from trademarks, patents, location, corporate longevity, raw material sources, etc., and very little consumer differentiation to produce insulation from competition.

Thus, the basis of competition between insurance companies is *underwriting*. That is… to be successful, insurance companies must develop the ability to accurately forecast and price risk. And they must maintain their underwriting discipline even during "soft" periods in the insurance market when premiums fall.

Our team tracks nearly every major P&C insurance company in the U.S. and in Bermuda (where many operate to avoid U.S. corporate taxes completely). We rank every firm by long-term underwriting discipline. We've done the legwork for you. All you have to do is know what price to pay.

So if normal accounting doesn't apply for insurance stocks, how do you value them? Again, we went to the master, Warren Buffett, to see what he was willing to pay for well-run insurance companies.

Back in 2012, we found data on three of Buffett's biggest insurance purchases. In 1998, he bought General Re for $21 billion, which added $15.2 billion to Berkshire's float and $8 billion in additional book value. So Buffett paid $0.94 for every $1 of float and book value.

Before that, in 1995, Buffett bought 49% of GEICO for $2.3 billion, which added $3 billion to Berkshire's float and $750 million in additional book value. So Buffett paid $0.61 for every dollar of float and book value.

And way back in 1967, Buffett paid $9 million for $17 million worth of National Indemnity float. That's $0.51 for every $1 of float.

Looking at these numbers, we expect to pay something between $0.75 and $1 for every dollar of float and book value.

In short, there are two fundamental rules to investing in insurance stocks:

Rule No. 1: Make sure the company earns an underwriting profit almost every year, no exceptions.

Rule No. 2: Never pay more than 75% of book value plus float.

Originally published in *The American Jubilee, A National Nightmare is Closer Thank You Think* (Stansberry Research, 2017).

ABOUT PORTER STANSBERRY

Porter Stansberry founded Stansberry Research in 1999 with the firm's flagship newsletter, *Stansberry's Investment Advisory*. He is also the co-host of Stansberry Investor Hour, a broadcast that has quickly become one of the most popular online financial radio shows.

Prior to launching Stansberry Research, Porter was the first American editor of the *Fleet Street Letter*, the world's oldest English-language financial newsletter.

At Stansberry Research, Porter oversees more than a dozen of the best editors and analysts in the business, who do an exhaustive amount of real-world, independent research. Together, his group has visited hundreds of publicly traded companies to bring Stansberry Research subscribers the safest, most profitable investment ideas in the world, no matter what's happening in the markets.

@PorterStansber

Factor Investing is More Art, and Less Science

WESLEY R. GRAY

Albert Einstein is reported to have said the following:
"The more I learn, the more I realize how much I don't know."

I can relate.

Having studied finance for a long time (PhD, professor, books, articles, etc.), I think I now know *less* about how the stock market works.

In fact, I probably should have stopped studying finance after I read Ben Graham's *Intelligent Investor*, over 20 years ago. Life would be a lot easier, or at least less complicated. Adhering to Graham's straightforward value investing ethos certainly worked out for Warren Buffett:

> What I'm doing today, at age 76, is running things through the same thought process I learned from the book [*The Intelligent Investor*] I read at 19.

And why should investing be complex, anyway? Asset pricing, or figuring out what something should be worth, seems easy in theory. And yet, when you review the vast swath of research dedicated to this question, there doesn't seem to be any clear silver bullet answer.

Some might retort, "Valuation is easy," figure out the expected cash flows and discount back to the present with an appropriate cost of capital, or "discount rate."

Well, what's the discount rate?

The discount rate is supposed to account for the risk of the expected cash flows, but what is risk? How do we measure it?

Warren Buffett had this to say about the issue:

> Charlie and I don't know our cost of capital. It's taught at business schools, but we're sceptical … I've never seen a cost of capital calculation that made sense to me.

While cost of capital is a notoriously imprecise valuation tool, there is still hope. Of the many ideas on the playing field, factor-based risk models seem to have captured the imagination of most empirical asset pricing researchers.[1]

But what is a factor-based model approach?

We answer this question – and many related questions – throughout this article.[2]

Jim Cramer Factor Investing: An Illustration

The factor approach has roots in what is deemed the arbitrage pricing theory, or APT. Researchers seek to identify a set of factors (e.g., value, momentum, size, market, quality, low-vol, and so forth) that explain the so-called "cross-section" of returns, or the distribution of returns at a given point in time.

A simple example can clarify the concept. Let's assume that the decibel level of Jim Cramer's voice on CNBC is a proxy for systematic risk in the economy. So a stock that moves stronger when Jim Cramer is louder corresponds to more systematic risk, and should therefore require higher expected returns (i.e., more risk should equal more reward). The simple relationship is outlined below.

expected_Stock_return = risk_free_rate + B × Jim_Cramer_decible + randomness

Besides randomness and the baseline risk-free rate, the only thing that should drive expected performance is the exposure to the Jim_Cramer_decible factor. If a stock has a strong "beta" with respect to the Jim_

---

[1]   See our discussion of Berkin/Swedroe's new book – *Your Complete Guide to Factor-Based Investing*: alphaarchitect.com/2017/02/01/berkin-and-swedroes-factor-based-investing-book.

[2]   David Foulke helped out a lot in drafting this article.

Cramer_decible factor, then the expected stock return should be higher in the future, all else equal.

With this factor investing model in hand we can now assess the risk and return associated with a stock by simply looking at the Jim_Cramer_Decibel risk factor exposure. If a stock earns high expected returns and has high Jim Cramer exposure – great – the model seems to work because it explains what happens in the real world. And if a stock earns low expected returns, and has low Jim Cramer exposure – great– again, the model seems to work. If a researcher conducts this analysis across a large sample of stocks, across a long sample period, and confirms the result through lots of robustness analysis, the model would be deemed the new Fama and French 1-Factor Cramer model in an academic paper.

Consultants would use it. Investors would use it. And the market efficiency world would be complete.

However, *what if the Jim Cramer asset pricing model broke down?*

Let's say the model doesn't always predict what happens in asset pricing markets. Perhaps we start seeing situations where the expected returns don't match the risk profile; in other words, we see situations where stocks earn high expected returns but *don't have any measurable exposure* to the Jim_Cramer_Decibel factor. The model no longer fits our observations. Oh no – Looks like we need a better model. Researchers will now scramble to identify a better model that explains why stocks act like they act. Maybe they'll add new factors, delete old factors, and grind on regressions until the numbers sing.

Mission complete. Or is it?

The Jim_Cramer_Decibel risk factor identified above is obviously an attempt at finance humor (I know, pretty terrible. I get it). Nonetheless, the description of the process mirrors the basic approach serious academic researchers have used to identify factors that theoretically and empirically determine why stocks move, in expectation. And while the Jim Cramer decibel factor is tongue-in-cheek, some of the wilder explanatory "factors" that have been earnestly explored by reputable academics are not that far from it conceptually. In short, not all factors are created equal. Some factors are more reasonable than others.

The Original Factor Gangsta: The Capital Asset Pricing Model (CAPM)

One of the earliest attempts to explain how stocks move was posited in 1964, when Sharpe, Lintner and Black (SLB) developed their Capital Asset Pricing Model. The CAPM proposed something remarkable: all expected stock returns could be described via beta, which quantified the extent to which a stock return moved with the so-called market portfolio's return (often approximated by a broad passive index, such as the S&P 500).[3]

Think about that – the CAPM suggests that ALL expected stock price movements revolve around a single, relatively simple, statistical metric. The elegance of the concept is arguably on par with $E = mc 2$ and the 1990 Nobel prize awarded to Markowitz and Sharpe[4] was probably well deserved.[5]

Unfortunately, while the CAPM theory was beautiful, the evidence in support of the theory was flawed.[6] Academic research demonstrated that the relationship between beta and expected stock returns was too "flat": Low-beta assets' returns were higher than the risk-free rate, while high-beta assets showed returns that were lower than those suggested by the model. (Fama and French provide a good overview of the research.)[7]

The Figure below highlights the problem with the CAPM's predictions versus reality:

---

[3]   Technically, beta is calculated with respect to the excess market portfolio return (i.e., MKT – RF).

[4]   Merton Miller was in the mix as well.

[5]   Here is a crash course on the concept, if you'd like to refresh: alphaarchitect. com/2014/08/16/introduction-to-finance-class-8.

[6]   Richard Roll (en.wikipedia.org/wiki/Roll's_critique) argued that the theory is untestable, but that doesn't really help us learn anything.

[7]   faculty.chicagobooth.edu/finance/papers/capm2004a.pdf

Average Annualized Monthly Return vs Beta for Value Weighted Portfolios Formed on Prior Beta (1928–2003)

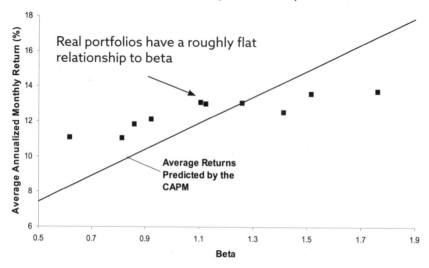

Source: faculty.chicagobooth.edu/finance/papers/capm2004a.pdf The results are hypothetical results and are NOT an indicator of future results and do NOT represent returns that any investor actually attained. Indexes are unmanaged, do not reflect management or trading fees, and one cannot invest directly in an index.

Note that real portfolios had a flat relationship with beta. In other words, knowing your beta didn't tell you anything about expected returns. D'oh!

The CAPM was quickly dumped in the graveyard of great theories that don't work in practice. Along came the CAPM apologists and new models with more factors that could help explain how and why stocks move. The primary puzzle to solve was why small-cap stocks and cheap "value" stocks were doing so much better than the CAPM predicted. On one hand, small-caps and value-stocks might reflect systematic mispricing (anti-efficient market hypothesis), but on the other hand, these styles of stocks may simply be more risky (pro-efficient market hypothesis). Fama and French came to the rescue…

Fama and French Lay the Foundation for Factor Investing

In response to the failure of the CAPM to explain the world, in 1992 Eugene Fama and Ken French, arguably the two greatest empirical financial economists of our time, established the empirical foundations for the Fama and French three-factor model, which did a much better job explaining anomalies, such as size and value.

The three-factor model included the original market factor from the CAPM, but added two new factors:

- A long/short size factor portfolio (small-minus-big, or SMB).

- A long/short value factor porfolio (high-minus-low, or HML).

The following table is Table III from the original paper, covering the 1963–1990 period, highlighting the relationship between stock returns and beta (i.e., β), size (i.e., ln(ME)), and value (i.e., ln(BE/ME)) for NYSE, AMEX and NASDAQ stocks:

β	ln(ME)	ln(BE/ME)
0.15		
−0.46		
	−0.15	
	(−2.58)	
−0.37	−0.17	
(−1.21)	(−3.41)	
		0.5
		−5.71

The results are hypothetical results and are NOT an indicator of future results and do NOT represent returns that any investor actually attained. Indexes are unmanaged, do not reflect management or trading fees, and one cannot invest directly in an index.

There are a few things to note.

1. The slope of beta alone is 0.15% per month, with a t-statistic of 0.46. From this, Fama and French conclude that beta does not help explain

average stock returns over the period. Fama and French described this as "a shot straight at the heart of the SLB model" (or CAPM).

2. The slope for size (ln(ME)) is -0.15%, with a t-statistic of -2.58. Thus, Fama and French conclude that size has statistically significant explanatory power.

3. The slope for value (ln(BE/ME)) is 0.50, with a t-statistic of 5.71. This suggests a very statistically strong relationship between returns and book-to-market equity.

Here is a visualization that highlights how poorly the CAPM predicted returns when portfolios are sorted on size and value. The chart plots excess returns against beta. The blue dots reflect realized returns associated with the so-called "Fama and French 25 portfolios," which sort stocks into portfolios based on value and size. The red dots plot the CAPM predicted portfolio returns, had these portfolios earned their theoretically predicted premiums.

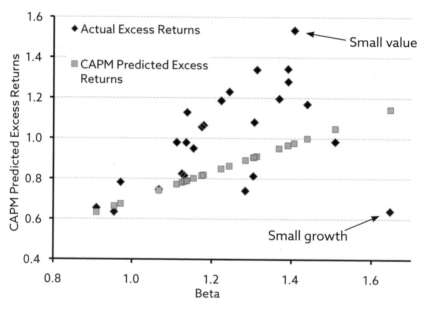

The results are hypothetical results and are NOT an indicator of future results and do NOT represent returns that any investor actually attained. Indexes are unmanaged, do not reflect management or trading fees, and one cannot invest directly in an index.

Note that the portfolios don't line up very nicely along the CAPM predicted red-dots. The relationship is really screwed up for small-cap value (earn way too much) and small-cap growth stocks (earn way too little).[8] The Fama and French three-factor model rescued factor investing from the graveyard and helped researchers understand what characteristics drove stock returns.

Wait a minute: Active managers have alpha when we use the FF three-factor model!

As factor analysis became more commonplace, thanks to the illuminating analysis from Fama and French 1992 and 1993, academics now had a tool to explain stock return movements. Researchers decided to apply these enhanced tools to explain mutual fund manager performance. Unfortunately, the early results concluded that mutual funds had persistent performance – winners kept winning and losers kept losing. These results also suggest that active managers may exhibit some level of skill.

But if active managers exhibit skill, this might imply markets aren't efficiently pricing risk, which means markets aren't efficient. Uh-oh!

In order to fix this problem, the research literature came up with a solution: when a factor investing model doesn't work, simply add more factors.

In 1997, Mark Carhart followed the academic factor research modus operandi and created a new "four-factor model." Carhart added a momentum factor (2-12 momentum, or "PR1YR," also referred to as "UMD" or "MOM" depending on the researcher) to the Fama and French three-factor model, which significantly enhanced the explanatory power of the original model. The following table is Table II from the original paper, which sets forth performance statistics from 1963 to 1993:

---

[8]   For those curious, we posted "How to use the Fama French Model" about how to use the Fama and French model in practice (alphaarchitect. com/2011/08/01/how-to-use-the-fama-french-model). An in-depth discussion is available at home.uchicago.edu/~taelee/fama_french.pdf. Finally, to examine some of these ideas in practice, we recommend Portfolio Visualizer (portfoliovisualizer.com).

Factor Portfolio	Monthly Excess Return	Std Dev	t-stat for Mean= 0	Cross-Correlations				
				VWRF	RMRF	SMB	HML	PRIYR
VWRF	0.44	4.39	1.93	1				
RMRF	0.47	4.43	2.01	1	1			
SMB	0.29	2.89	1.89	0.35	0.32	1		
HML	0.46	2.59	3.42	−0.36	−0.37	0.1	1	
PRIYR	0.82	3.49	4.46	0.01	0.01	−0.29	−0.16	1

The results are hypothetical results and are NOT an indicator of future results and do NOT represent returns that any investor actually attained. Indexes are unmanaged, do not reflect management or trading fees, and one cannot invest directly in an index.

In Carhart's new four-factor model, SMB, HML, and PRıYR (momentum) had high mean average excess returns. Also, the factors have high variance and low correlation, which suggests they might do a good job in jointly explaining variation in stock returns and mutual fund manager performance.

Carhart applies his new factor model in the context of understanding mutual fund manager performance persistence. The key results from Carhart's paper are highlighted in the graphic below (Figure 2 from the original paper). The past mutual fund winners (decile 1) seem to win in the future, but the reversion to the mean is strong and hard to distinguish from the other groups. However, if you are a past loser (decile 10), you tend to be a loser in the future.

Carhart identifies some fascinating insights. Carhart highlights that winning active managers don't win because they are skilled at identifying stocks that outperform, but rather, "Some mutual funds just happen by chance to hold relatively larger positions in last year's winning stocks." In short, winning mutual fund managers were momentum investors and didn't even know it. And because the winning managers didn't really know they won because of momentum exposure, we can't attribute their performance to their skill (convoluted argument, I know!).

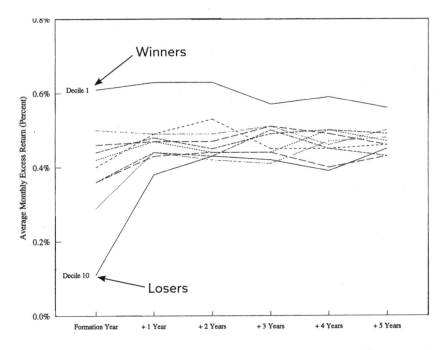

The results are hypothetical results and are NOT an indicator of future results and do NOT represent returns that any investor actually attained. Indexes are unmanaged, do not reflect management or trading fees, and one cannot invest directly in an index.

The takeaway from Carhart's "momentum" factor is clear with respect to understanding mutual fund manager performance, but muddied with respect to how we can think about his four-factor model in the context of using it to understand stock returns. In fact, Carhart highlights in his paper that the inclusion of momentum in his four-factor model is confusing. On the one hand, his model could be interpreted as a "risk" attribution model that suggests high performance is due to exposure to higher risk, which is proxied by exposures to beta, size, value, and momentum. However, on the other hand, his four-factor model could also be viewed as a performance attribution model, which doesn't make the claim that size, value, and momentum reflect risk factors (i.e., maybe they are "mispricing" factors), but rather, these factors simply do a good job of explaining performance.

Carhart's paper leaves readers with a nagging question: *Are factor models capturing risk exposures or mispricing effects?*

Carhart's momentum factor really opened up the discussion on the so-called "factor wars." Momentum, or investing based on past prices, went directly to the heart of the weakest form of the efficient market hypothesis. Clearly, researchers needed to head back to the drawing board. One could not simply add more factors and claim victory that the market was efficient, without identifying why the factors explaining the performance reflected a genuine risk premium. In other words, factor models can't reflect a game of throwing spaghetti against the wall and seeing what sticks. Economists needed to better understand *why* factors matter.

Less Data-Mining and More Economic Theory

The three- and four-factor models ran the show for over a decade following their respective publications. Within academia, Fama and French and Carhart's factor models were generally considered to be part of the *empirical* asset pricing discipline. However, critics were concerned that data-dredging drove the discipline and whatever results that had the highest t-stats won the day. At some level, there was nothing wrong with this approach – understanding the historical facts can be an important baseline for our understanding of how the world works (the core innovation from Fama and French 1992).

But correlation doesn't help us fully understand causation.

The three-factor model was a perfect example of the problem. Sure, the model was great at explaining stock market movements, but what were the theoretical underpinnings as to why size and value characteristics determined expected returns? Size might be understandable – smaller stocks are less liquid, potentially have more business risk, etc. But value was more controversial – were these stocks actually riskier? Or were they simply suffering from mispricing as described by Ben Graham?

The financial economics profession was suffering and needed answers. First, their cherished CAPM model, which was elegant and grounded in rational economic theory, was no longer believable on empirical grounds. And now there were the three- and four-factor models highlighting that the stock market is more confusing than originally thought. Asset pricing theorists needed to take on the challenge of putting more rigor around factor models to try understand why, for example, size and value, were able to describe stock market movements.

The natural itch to have a sound theory behind multi-factor models needed to be scratched. Luckily, neoclassical economic theories, in particular the "q-theory of investment," as advanced by James Tobin in the 1960s, explored a fundamentals-based approach to reconciling market prices with investment in corporate assets. In 2007, a paper by Lu Zhang and Long Chen, entitled "Neoclassical factors," offered hints that a new combination of factors, based on "investment" and "profitability," might explain returns better than the early ad-hoc factor models and, importantly, its theoretical basis drew from a different branch of financial economics–corporate finance, not asset pricing. Lu Zhang and colleagues continued their research trying to build a unified asset pricing theory that established economic logic behind a factor model. He set out on a stream of articles that hit on the same theme, but changed titles over time:[9]

- Neoclassical factors (July 2007)

- An Equilibrium three-factor model (January 2009)

- Production-based factors (April 2009)

- A better three-factor model that explains more anomalies (June 2009)

- An alternative three-factor model (April 2010, April 2011)

- Digesting anomalies: An investment approach (October 2012, August 2014)

As these new neoclassical "q factors" were further refined, it became clear that they offered a powerful alternative explanation for the cross section of returns. Unfortunately, the powers that ran the top-tier academic journals were not interested in rocking the Fama and French three-factor boat and Prof. Zhang and his colleagues had a challenging time getting their ideas published. But this situation would change when Fama and French decided to embrace the idea of creating an enhanced factor model with ties to economic theory.

[9] Source: Lu Zhang.

Fama and French Adapt to New Research Findings

Perhaps seeing the handwriting on the wall that the three-factor model rested on a shaky theoretical foundation, Fama and French offered an enhancement to their three-factor model, in hopes of heading off competition from the q-factor concept developed by Zhang and others. By 2014, the dynamic Fama and French duo extended their model to include five factors, by adding two additional factors:

1. Operating profitability (robust-minus-weak, or RMW), which is measured as revenues – COGS – SGA – interest expense, scaled by book value (t-1).

2. Investment (conservative-minus-aggressive, or CMA), which is measured as YoY asset growth, scaled by total assets (t-1).

For those paying attention, these appeared to be thematically similar to the new q-factors proposed by Zhang et al.:

• Operating profitability ~ "ROE," which is net income divided by lagged book value (very similar to Fama and French).

• Investment ~ "real investment factor," which is the same YoY asset growth scaled by lagged total assets (the same as Fama and French).

Had Zhang & Co. been cut off at the academic pass by Fama and French? We will never know. Nonetheless, Hou, Xue, and Zhang ran a horse race on the competing factor models with a keen eye on the performance between their Q-factor model and the new Fama and French five-factor model.[10]

The abstract from the Hou, Xue, and Zhang paper says it all:

This paper conducts a gigantic replication study of asset pricing anomalies by compiling an extensive data library with 437 variables… the *q-factor model* and a closely related *five-factor model* are the two best performing models among a long list of models. Investment and profitability are the dominating driving forces in the broad cross section of average stock returns.[11]

---

[10] Covered briefly in our article, "Using Profitability as a Factor? Perhaps You Should Think Twice…", alphaarchitect.com/2015/06/10/using-profitability-factor-perhaps-think-twice.

[11] papers.ssrn.com/sol3/papers.cfm?abstract_id=2520929

Here is the key table from the paper:

	m	α	β_{MKT}	β_{SMB}	β_{HML}	β_{UMD}	R^2
			Panel B: The FF five factors				
SMB	0.28	−0.02	0.01	1.00	0.13	0.00	0.99
	(2.02)	(−1.26)	(0.99)	(88.07)	(8.12)	(0.11)	
HML	0.37	0.00	−0.00	0.00	1.00	0.00	1.00
	(2.63)	(1.49)	(−0.68)	(0.37)	(1752.68)	(0.97)	
RMW	0.27	0.34	−0.04	−0.27	−0.00	0.04	0.19
	(2.58)	(3.36)	(−1.38)	(−3.08)	(−0.07)	(0.83)	
CMA	0.36	0.19	−0.09	0.04	0.46	0.04	0.55
	(3.68)	(2.82)	(−4.42)	(0.90)	(13.43)	(1.52)	
		α_q	β_{MKT}	β_{ME}	$\beta_{I/A}$	β_{ROE}	R^2
SMB		0.05	−0.00	0.94	−0.09	−0.10	0.96
		(1.58)	(−0.48)	(58.83)	(−4.72)	(−5.61)	
HML		0.04	−0.05	0.00	1.03	−0.17	0.50
		(0.36)	(−1.37)	(0.01)	(11.67)	(−2.19)	
RMW		0.04	−0.03	−0.12	−0.03	0.52	0.49
		(0.49)	(−1.07)	(−1.70)	(−0.37)	(8.54)	
CMA		0.02	−0.05	0.04	0.93	−0.11	0.85
		(0.45)	(−3.65)	(1.58)	(33.68)	(−3.90)	

The results are hypothetical results and are NOT an indicator of future results and do NOT represent returns that any investor actually attained. Indexes are unmanaged, do not reflect management or trading fees, and one cannot invest directly in an index. Additional information regarding the construction of these results is available upon request.

The Hou, Xue, and Zhang four-factor model captures all the returns associated with the new five-factor model outlined by Fama and French. Note the alpha estimates above. The yellow box highlights the alphas associated with the Fama and French factors, controlling for the Hou, Xue, and Zhang four factors and the blue blox highlights the alphas associated with the Hou, Xue, and Zhang factors, controlling for the FF five factors. The Hou, Xue, and Zhang factors do a good job explaining the Fama and French factors (there are no statistically significant intercepts), but *the Fama and French factors cannot explain the Hou, Xue, and Zhang factors*. This suggests that Fama and French's "new" profitability factor may not be a new dimension at all, since it can be explained quite well via exposures to the market, size, and Hou, Xue, and Zhang's investment and ROE factors.

Interestingly enough, while the two research teams debated the merits of their respective models, one fact stood out: both researchers found that *the value effect may not be real!*

How can this be? Value had always been part of the factor literature! The new factor research suggested that value was simply a proxy for risk exposures to profitability and investment factors. And once you control for the new profitability and investment exposures, value ceased to have explanatory power. In short, value was dead.

The comments below, taken directly from source papers, describe their findings:

First, Fama and French highlight that value is dead:

> With the addition of profitability and investment factors, the *value factor* of the Fama and French three-factor model *becomes redundant* for describing average returns in the sample we examine.

Hou, Xue, and Zhang take things a step further and suggest that *both* value and momentum are dead:

> The alphas of HML and UMD [momentum] in the q-factor model are small and insignificant, but the alphas of the investment and ROE factors in the Carhart model (that augments the Fama and French model with UMD) are large and significant. As such, *HML and UMD* might be *noisy versions of the q-factors*.

Step Aside Ivory Tower: Practitioners Offer Their Opinion

At this point the argument over the king of factor investing models was limited to the domain of uber-geeks like Fama and French, and the Hou, Xue, and Zhang team. The Hou, Xue, and Zhang model is arguably better on both empirical and theoretical grounds. Of course, outside of academic researcher circles, practitioners started to add their 2 cents. For example, a newer paper from a joint team of academics and researchers at Robeco Asset Management, aptly named, "Five Concerns with the Five-Factor Model," goes straight to the heart of these models.

Here is the abridged abstract:

> ... Although the *5-factor* model exhibits significantly improved explanatory power, we identify five concerns with regard to the new model. First, it maintains the CAPM relation between market beta and return ... Second, it continues to ignore the ... momentum effect. Third, there are a number of robustness concerns ... Fourth

… the economic rationale for the two new factors is much less clear … Fifth … it does not seem likely that the *5-factor* model is going to settle the main asset pricing debates…

And of course, there isn't a real factor debate unless Cliff Asness and his team at AQR weigh in. Asness was struck by the reported redundancy of the so-called "value" factor, or "HML" factor, described in Fama and French and Hou, Xue, and Zhang. He decided to investigate the issue on his own in his article, "Our Model Goes to Six and Saves Value from Redundancy Along the Way."

First, Cliff replicated Fama-French's findings. Sure enough, they checked out. The evidence also highlighted that HML doesn't matter once RMW (profitability factor) and CMA (investment factor) are included.

	Intercept	RM-RF	SMB	HML	RMW	CMA	R²
RM-RF	9.8% (4.94)		0.25 (4.45)	0.03 (0.37)	−0.40 (−4.84)	−0.91 (−7.82)	24%
SMB	4.6% (3.22)	0.13 (4.45)		0.05 (0.81)	−0.48 (−8.42)	−0.17 (−1.92)	18%
HML	−0.5% (−0.46)	0.01 (0.37)	0.02 (0.81)		0.23 (5.39)	1.04 (23.04)	52%
RMW	5.2% (5.44)	−0.09 (−4.84)	−0.22 (−8.42)	0.20 (5.39)		−0.44 (−7.85)	22%
CMA	3.3% (5.03)	−0.10 (−7.82)	−0.04 (−1.92)	0.45 (23.04)	−0.21 (−7.85)		57%

The results are hypothetical results and are NOT an indicator of future results and do NOT represent returns that any investor actually attained. Indexes are unmanaged, do not reflect management or trading fees, and one cannot invest directly in an index. Additional information regarding the construction of these results is available upon request.

Next, he considered the elephant in the room that all factor models need to address, but rarely do: *Momentum* (described early in the Carhart discussion). In other words, Asness decided to see what would happen if he added momentum to the Fama and French five-factor model, and created a six-factor model.[12]

Perhaps not surprisingly, Asness found that adding momentum enhanced the explanatory power of the model (strong t-stat of 4.11), however, value still seemed to be redundant (i.e., low t-stat of 0.51!).

	Intercept	RM-RF	SMB	HML	RMW	CMA	UMD	R^2
RM-RF	10.7% (5.36)		0.25 (4.55)	−0.03 (−0.35)	−0.36 (−4.36)	−0.85 (−7.24)	−0.12 (−3.03)	25%
SMB	4.3% (2.98)	0.13 (4.55)		0.06 (1.05)	−0.49 (−8.49)	−0.18 (−2.05)	0.03 (1.10)	18%
HML	0.5% (0.51)	−0.01 (−0.35)	0.03 (1.05)		0.24 (5.97)	1.03 (23.38)	−0.11 (−5.92)	54%
RMW	4.6% (4.76)	−0.08 (−4.36)	−0.22 (−8.49)	0.23 (5.97)		−0.46 (−8.17)	0.06 (3.12)	23%
CMA	2.9% (4.36)	−0.09 (−7.24)	−0.04 (−2.05)	0.46 (23.38)	−0.22 (−8.17)		0.04 (3.20)	58%
UMD	8.7% (4.11)	−0.13 (−3.03)	0.07 (1.10)	−0.50 (−5.92)	0.28 (3.12)	0.41 (3.20)		8%

The results are hypothetical results and are NOT an indicator of future results and do NOT represent returns that any investor actually attained. Indexes are unmanaged, do not reflect management or trading fees, and one cannot invest directly in an index. Additional information regarding the construction of these results is available upon request.

Was value simply a proxy for exposure to profitability and investment risk factors? That is what the evidence suggested, but Asness wasn't done with his investigation.

---

[12] Asness does not investigate the Hou, Xue, and Zhang model directly.

Questioning the Value Factor's ("HML") Construction

Asness had some fundamental questions about what constituted "value". He pointed out in a 2013 paper, "The Devil in HML's Details," that when Fama-French construct HML, they need two pieces of information:

1. Book value of equity.

2. Price.

How do Fama and French calculate these?

1. **Book Value**. Fama and French portfolios assume a *six-month lag* on **book equity** data, since sometimes it takes time for this accounting information to be disseminated into the market. The idea here is that this reduces the risk of "look-ahead" bias.

2. **Price**. Fama and French portfolios *also assume a six-month lag* on **price**. The idea here is that the price matches the book value, so you are working with the actual book-to-price at a given date.

Why Fama and French went with this original construction is a bit odd: Why input a six-month lag on price, when price would be readily known when the B/M portfolios are formed?

Sidestepping the reasons why Fama and French rationalized the use of lagged prices for sorting value portfolios – which seem to make no sense – Asness and Frazzini found that using a more realistic value sorting technique – with updated prices – created a more effective value premium.

The Devil in HML's Details Actually Matter

Asness re-ran his six-factor model (Fama and French five-factor + momentum), and made two changes to HML:

1. He used up-to-date price information.

2. He used a monthly rebalance.

The "new" HML factor is referred to as "HML-Devil." The output from the regressions are below, covering 1963-2013:

	Intercept	RM-RF	SMB	HML-DEV	RMW	CMA	R²
RM-RF	9.7% (4.91)		0.25 (4.44)	0.11 (2.05)	−0.39 (−4.83)	−0.97 (−10.35)	25%
SMB	4.6% (3.21)	0.13 (4.44)		0.00 (0.12)	−0.47 (−8.43)	−0.12 (−1.68)	18%
HML-DEV	0.2% (0.15)	0.06 (2.05)	0.00 (0.12)		−0.02 (−0.29)	0.95 (14.24)	28%
RMW	5.4% (5.47)	−0.10 (−4.83)	−0.23 (−8.43)	−0.01 (−0.29)		−0.23 (−4.64)	18%
CMA	4.3% (5.53)	−0.16 (−10.35)	−0.04 (−1.68)	0.27 (14.24)	−0.15 (−4.64)		40%

The results are hypothetical results and are NOT an indicator of future results and do NOT represent returns that any investor actually attained. Indexes are unmanaged, do not reflect management or trading fees, and one cannot invest directly in an index. Additional information regarding the construction of these results is available upon request.

As Asness put it, "Shazam, shazam, shazam!" The HML factor was back and UMD (momentum) was even more powerful.[13]

Asness argues that the way Fama and French construct their HML factor diminishes the true relationship between value and momentum. After including a more pragmatic value factor, it is the investment factor (i.e., CMA) that becomes redundant – not the value factor – and now we have come full circle and are back to where we started – value and momentum are back as factor kings. But now we are faced with the original critique of the three-factor model: the empirical evidence is clear that value and momentum matter, but there are no rational economic theories that explain why! The q-theory approach was a commendable effort, but has holes and this raises questions about both the empirical design and theoretical foundations for the five-factor model. D'oh![14]

[13]   This research doesn't consider that HML, constructed using book-to-market, isn't even the king of value factors. See our paper on the enterprise multiple factor, papers.ssrn.com/sol3/papers.cfm?abstract_id=2847874.
[14]   The new paper, "The Profitability and Investment Premium: Pre-1963 Evidence" looks at the out of sample of the investment and profitability factors

What Next? Factor Investing Wars Will Probably Last Forever

Hou, Xue, and Zhang moved the factor investing discussion to a higher level and took on the challenge of trying to tie factor models to rational economic theory. Their approach outlines the q-factor model, which uses two simple accounting variables, representing "investment" and "quality," or ROE. The goal of their research was bold: Create a theoretically sound factor model that was empirically superior to ad-hoc factor models studied in the past. Their efforts are commendable and arguably influenced Fama and French to develop their new five-factor.

But then evidence happened. And behavioral-based explanations were never really ever considered.

Small changes on model design (e.g., HML_Devil versus HML, or the enterprise multiple factor, which we didn't even cover!) allowed value and momentum anomalies to rear their ugly heads into the picture again. These tweaks also made the q-factor concepts (profitability and investment) less impressive and/or redundant. Other research on the subject also shows that profitability, for example, is not very robust.[15] On the investment side, authors question the empirical validity of the finding. For example, Fangjian Fu finds that how one controls for delisting data can dramatically alter the empirical results associated with the "investment factor." Also, Fama and French, who include investment as a factor in their five-factor model, published a paper in 2008 that questions the robustness of the investment factor, suggesting that it is entirely driven by micro-cap stocks.[16]

---

finds that profitability is robust, investment is not robust, and value still matters, papers.ssrn.com/sol3/papers.cfm?abstract_id=2891491.

[15] See our previous articles, "Value Investing: Accruals, Cash Flows, and Operating Profitability," alphaarchitect.com/2016/01/14/value-investing-accruals-cash-flows-and-operating-profitability; "Using Profitability as a Factor? Perhaps You Should Think Twice…", alphaarchitect.com/2015/06/10/using-profitability-factor-perhaps-think-twice; and "Daily Academic Alpha: International 5-Factor Evidence from Fama and French," alphaarchitect.com/2015/07/13/daily-academic-alpha-international-5-factor-evidence-from-fama-and-french.

[16] schwert.ssb.rochester.edu/f532/ff_JF08.pdf

So despite the herculean mental efforts on behalf of academic researchers to better understand how stocks move, it seems that value and momentum still matter (as does size, beta, and profitability). But this truth doesn't sit well with the mental models of many who study financial markets (i.e., the market efficiency crew).

Will we ever understand why factors exist? I think there is hope.

An alternative approach is to change the mental model for understanding the theoretical underpinnings for factor models. For example, in order to explain the value and momentum factors, one must wander beyond the realm of traditional rational economic theories. To understand these anomalies one must loosen theoretical constraints to encompass the view that 1) investors are irrational (behavior can be wack) and 2) frictional costs matter (limits of arbitrage). This train of thought is often referred to as behavioral finance. But relaxing the assumption that investors can be irrational, does not imply there is easy money lying around, which we explain in our article, "The Sustainable Active Investing Framework: Simple, But Not Easy."[17] However, relaxing these assumptions may help us better understand why risk/mispricing factors like value and momentum continue to "stick" in factor models.

Of course, relaxing rational constraints adds degrees of freedom for modelers and makes the challenge of understanding reality more difficult. Perhaps this trade-off is best outlined by Eugene Fama in his incredibly insightful piece, "Market Efficiency, Long-Term Returns, and Behavioral Finance."

Here is the abstract from the paper:

> Market efficiency survives the challenge from the literature on long-term return anomalies. Consistent with the market efficiency hypothesis that the anomalies are chance results, apparent over-reaction to information is about as common as under-reaction. And post-event continuation of pre-event abnormal returns is about as frequent as post-event reversal. Consistent with the market efficiency prediction that apparent anomalies can also be due to

---

[17] alphaarchitect.com/2015/08/17/the-sustainable-active-investing-framework-simple-but-not-easy

methodology, the anomalies are sensitive to the techniques used to measure them, and many disappear with reasonable changes in technique.

For fun, I did a thought experiment. What would happen if someone simply reversed the wording from Fama's abstract and communicated the behavioral message:

> *Long-term return anomalies* survive the challenge from the literature on market efficiency. Consistent with the market *inefficiency* hypothesis that *instances of market efficiency* are chance results, *evidence that prices react appropriately to information are sparse.* And *evidence that* post-event *prices are efficient following pre-event information are few and far between.* Consistent with the market *inefficiency* prediction that *instances of market efficiency* can also be due to methodology, *evidence for market efficiency* is sensitive to the techniques used to measure them, and *much of this evidence* disappears with reasonable changes in technique.

The "behavioral" version of Fama's abstract could arguably stand as strong based on the collective evidence – if not stronger – than the statement put forth by Fama.[18]

My conclusion is that we are still a long way away from understanding the so-called "science" of investing. We're probably better off understanding the insanity of investors and the incentives of delegated asset managers if we want to understand the science of investing, but this is controversial among many financial economists.

I think Fama says it best in a recent 2016 interview with Joel Stern.[19]

A few highlights from their conversation:

- After a half-century of research and refinements, *most asset-pricing models have failed empirically.*

---

[18]   For example, Prof. Stambaugh, a stalwart of the efficient market hypothesis and thought leader in the space for decades, has even loosened his stance on the "old way" of viewing the world. See the paper "Mispricing Factors" as an example, papers.ssrn.com/sol3/papers.cfm?abstract_id=2626701.

[19]   papers.ssrn.com/sol3/papers.cfm?abstract_id=2902370

- Estimating something as apparently simple as the cost of capital *remains fraught with difficulty.*

- The wide range of estimates for the market risk premium – anywhere from 2% to 10% – *casts doubt on their reliability and practical usefulness.*

Sure sounds to me like we are about as close to understanding the science of finance as we are to understanding the science of astrology.

The painful reality is that factor investing is mostly art, and maybe a little bit of science…

Originally published February 3, 2017; alphaarchitect.com/2017/02/03/factor-models-are-more-art-and-less-science.

ABOUT WESLEY R. GRAY

After serving as a Captain in the United States Marine Corps, Dr. Gray earned a PhD, and worked as a finance professor at Drexel University. Dr. Gray's interest in bridging the research gap between academia and industry led him to found Alpha Architect, an asset management that delivers affordable active exposures for tax-sensitive investors. Dr. Gray has published four books and a number of academic articles. Wes is a regular contributor to multiple industry outlets, to include the following: *Wall Street Journal, Forbes,* ETF.com, and the CFA Institute. Dr. Gray earned an MBA and a PhD in finance from the University of Chicago and graduated magna cum laude with a BS from The Wharton School of the University of Pennsylvania.

@alphaarchitect

Waiting for the Market to Crash
is a Terrible Strategy

SAMUEL LEE

In my experience, investors sitting on a lot of cash are usually worried about equity valuations or the economy, and tell themselves and others that they're going to buy gobs of stock *after* a crash. The strategy sounds prudent and has commonsense appeal—everyone knows that one should be fearful when others are greedy, greedy when others are fearful. But historically waiting for the market to fall has been an abysmal strategy, far worse than buying and holding in both absolute and risk-adjusted terms.

Using monthly U.S. stock market total returns from mid-1926 to 2016-end (from the ever-useful French Data Library), I simulated variations of the strategy, changing both the drawdown thresholds before buying and the holding periods after a buy. For example, a simple version of the strategy is to wait for a 10% peak-to-trough loss before buying, then holding for at least 12 months or until the drawdown threshold is exceeded before returning to cash. This strategy would have put you in cash about 47% of the time, so if our switches were random, we'd expect to earn about half the market return with half the volatility.

The chart below shows the cumulative excess return (that is, return above cash) of this variation of the strategy versus the market. Buy-the-dip returned 2.2% annualized with a 15.7% annualized standard deviation, while buy-and-hold returned 6.3% with an 18.6% standard deviation. Their respective Sharpe ratios, a measure of risk-adjusted return, are 0.14 and 0.34, meaning for each percentage point of volatility buy-the-dip yielded 0.14% in additional annualized return and buy-and-hold yielded 0.34%.

Cumulative Excess Return (Log Scale)

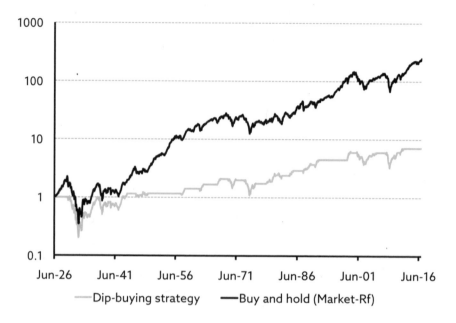

The above chart understates the terribleness of the strategy. In the next chart I plot the cumulative wealth ratio of the strategy over the market to show their relative performances. When the line is sloping down, dip-buying is underperforming; when it's sloping up, it's overperforming. As you can see, the line shows small jags of outperformance, expansive plateaus of neutral performance, and long rolling slopes of underperformance.

Buy-the-dip/buy-and-hold Relative Wealth (Log Scale)

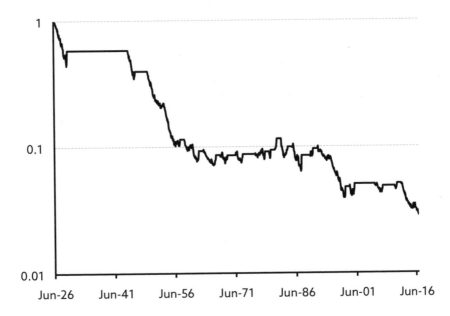

What about waiting for a deeper crash? For every drawdown level from –10% to –50% (in increments of 5%), waiting for a crash before buying results in lower absolute and risk-adjusted returns.

12-Month Holding Period

Drawdown Threshold	-10%	-15%	-20%	-25%	-35%	-40%	-45%	-50%
Excess Return	2.19%	2.41%	0.73%	1.22%	0.78%	1.79%	1.97%	1.54%
Standard Dev.	15.74%	15.29%	14.45%	13.80%	12.95%	12.31%	11.86%	11.00%
Sharpe Ratio	0.14	0.16	0.05	0.09	0.06	0.15	0.17	0.14

What about holding on longer? This helps, but not enough to make it a winning strategy. Here's what holding for three years after a crash produces:

36-Month Holding Period

Drawdown Threshold	-10%	-15%	-20%	-25%	-35%	-40%	-45%	-50%
Excess Return	3.24%	3.43%	1.36%	1.24%	1.74%	2.11%	3.06%	2.61%
Standard Dev.	16.62%	16.11%	15.00%	14.40%	13.66%	13.14%	13.01%	12.13%
Sharpe Ratio	0.19	0.21	0.09	0.09	0.13	0.16	0.24	0.22

Holding for five years helps, too, but now we're getting closer to buy and hold:

60-Month Holding Period

Drawdown Threshold	-10%	-15%	-20%	-25%	-35%	-40%	-45%	-50%
Excess Return	3.08%	3.50%	2.69%	2.25%	2.47%	3.31%	3.64%	2.09%
Standard Dev.	16.88%	16.60%	15.79%	15.06%	13.97%	13.82%	13.79%	12.08%
Sharpe Ratio	0.18	0.21	0.17	0.15	0.18	0.24	0.26	0.17

None of the variations tested produces higher absolute or risk-adjusted returns than buy and hold.

The strategy fails for two reasons. First, the historical equity risk premium was high and decades could pass before a big-enough crash, making it very costly to sit in cash. Second, the market tended to exhibit momentum more than mean reversion over years-long horizons. As strange as it sounds, you would have been better off buying when the market was going up and selling when it was going down, using a trend-following rule.

The closest thing to a success is waiting for a 40% or 45% crash before buying, and then holding on for at least five years. That strategy would have captured more than half the market's return while being exposed to the market only a third of the time. However, 40%+ crashes are rare, occurring only five times in our sample, or about once every 18 years. The best that can be said for our strategy is that medium-term returns after a big crash tended to be above average, so it's probably a good time to buy equities if you have cash sitting around and a multi-year horizon.

This data does not say you should always buy and hold, no matter what. It simply says that a mechanical strategy of waiting for a crash *on average* resulted in much worse absolute and risk-adjusted returns than buying and holding. It is conceivable that you could have some piece of information—say, market valuations or economic conditions or technicals—that indicates a big crash is more likely to occur. In fact, a drawdown from a prior peak is itself just such a piece of information, because bad returns tend to clump together.

Originally published May 19, 2017; svrn.co/blog/2017/5/14/waiting-for-the-market-to-crash-is-a-terrible-strategy.

ABOUT SAMUEL LEE

Before striking out on his own, Sam was a strategist at Morningstar, where he wrote about funds, asset class valuations, and the application of the scientific method to investing. He has been quoted by the *Wall Street Journal*, *Financial Times*, *Barron's*, and other financial publications.

He graduated from Grinnell College with a bachelor's degree in economics. He is a recovering efficient-market purist.

@svrnco

The Best Way to Add Yield to Your Portfolio

—

MEB FABER

Many investors dream of passive income. They picture themselves on the beach sipping a pina colada, and enjoying the income of their portfolio rolling in. (But let's be honest, the Hans Gruber yield days are long gone…)[1] What would you do to achieve an extra 1% or 2% a year, and consequently, an extra $10,000 or $20,000 on your portfolio?

I know what the investment management industry would spend. Billions of dollars and a gazillion man hours of time trying to add just a smidgen of yield. David Swensen's old book *Pioneering Portfolio Management* depicts the spread of top quartile vs. median returns for active managers across a handful of asset classes and strategies. If you're a stock manager you are top quartile if you just add 0.9% percentage points. In bonds it's 0.3 percentage points. (Granted this argument also applies to the reality that it makes more sense to be active where active helps, i.e. private equity, small/foreign, absolute return, and real estate.)

So, if I could tell you there is a way to add a little yield, but five or even ten percentage points to your annual returns? You'd be interested right?

Well, here's my advice.

Do nothing. Actually, don't just do nothing, stop doing what you were doing before. Let me explain.

I think it is a great endeavor for investors to spend time learning about investing, and the history of markets. Bill Bernstein and I talked about

---

[1] See my piece, "Earning 20% From The Beach," bit.ly/2wpjE1N.

this at length on my podcast.[2] Having realistic expectations, and knowing how markets have performed in the past, will keep you from doing really stupid things in the future. Well, hopefully at least.

Lots of people study markets in the hopes of *beating the market*. What a lot of people don't factor into their equation is the *time spent* to achieve that goal.

So, instead of figuring out how much extra juice we can squeeze out of that portfolio, let's flip the equation around.

How much alpha do you HAVE to generate to break even on the time spent to achieve it?

Below, we take a look at a handful of scenarios for investors making between $50,000 to $500,000 per year, with portfolios ranging from $100k, to $10,000,000. We examine an investor who spends eight hours a week studying markets in hopes of beating a basic portfolio allocation. We chose eight hours based on responses to a poll of mine with over 500 votes on Twitter.[3]

In nearly every case, it is a more realistic scenario to spend zero hours on investing, and simply work a few more hours and achieve a much higher yield on your entire portfolio.

Only once you achieve family office levels of wealth does it make sense to be spending ANY time on your portfolio. The best way to add yield to a portfolio is to ignore it!

This is one reason we are such strong advocates of the new digital advisors … not only do they automate the entire process, but they are low-cost, tax-efficient, and in many cases, commission free. And from someone who has automated his own process, as well as running it for over 400 clients, I cannot fathom ever going back.

So, the simple advice is this: Implement a low-cost, tax-efficient, rules-based portfolio. Pay low or no commissions. Automate it if you can. Invest in yourself. And then move on and order up that pina colada…

---

2   bit.ly/2rupU3q
3   twitter.com/MebFaber/status/882981016431808514

BTW, the final column is extra returns in PERCENTAGE POINTS needed to break even...

Salary	Portfolio	Time Value/ Hour	Portfolio Return	Portfolio Return $	8 Hours of Research Per Week Cost	Total Return to Break Even	Extra Returns Needed To Break Even
$50,000	$100,000	$25	6%	$6,000	$10,000	16.00%	10.00%
$100,000	$100,000	$50	6%	$6,000	$20,000	26.00%	20.00%
$200,000	$100,000	$100	6%	$6,000	$40,000	46.00%	40.00%
$500,000	$100,000	$250	6%	$6,000	$100,000	106.00%	100.00%

Salary	Portfolio	Time Value/ Hour	Portfolio Return	Portfolio Return $	8 Hours of Research Per Week Cost	Total Return to Break Even	Extra Returns Needed To Break Even
$50,000	$500,000	$25	6%	$30,000	$10,000	8.00%	2.00%
$100,000	$500,000	$50	6%	$30,000	$20,000	10.00%	4.00%
$200,000	$500,000	$100	6%	$30,000	$40,000	14.00%	8.00%
$500,000	$500,000	$250	6%	$30,000	$100,000	26.00%	20.00%

Salary	Portfolio	Time Value/ Hour	Portfolio Return	Portfolio Return $	8 Hours of Research Per Week Cost	Total Return to Break Even	Extra Returns Needed To Break Even
$50,000	$1m	$25	6%	$60,000	$10,000	7.00%	1.00%
$100,000	$1m	$50	6%	$60,000	$20,000	8.00%	2.00%
$200,000	$1m	$100	6%	$60,000	$40,000	10.00%	4.00%
$500,000	$1m	$250	6%	$60,000	$100,000	16.00%	10.00%

Salary	Portfolio	Time Value/ Hour	Portfolio Return	Portfolio Return $	8 Hours of Research Per Week Cost	Total Return to Break Even	Extra Returns Needed To Break Even
$50,000	$10m	$25	6%	$600,000	$10,000	6.10%	0.10%
$100,000	$10m	$50	6%	$600,000	$20,000	6.20%	0.20%
$200,000	$10m	$100	6%	$600,000	$40,000	6.40%	0.40%
$500,000	$10m	$250	6%	$600,000	$100,000	7.00%	1.00%

Originally published July 6, 2017; mebfaber.com/2017/07/06/best-way-add-yield-portfolio

ABOUT MEB FABER

Meb Faber is a co-founder and the Chief Investment Officer of Cambria Investment Management. Faber is the manager of Cambria's ETFs, separate accounts and private investment funds. Mr. Faber has authored numerous white papers and five books. He is a frequent speaker and writer on investment strategies and has been featured in *Barron's*, *The New York Times*, and *The New Yorker*. Mr. Faber graduated from the University of Virginia with a double major in Engineering Science and Biology.

@MebFaber

Skis and Bikes: The Untold Story
of Diversification

ADAM BUTLER, MICHAEL PHILBRICK AND
RODRIGO GORDILLO

The most fundamental principle of investing is diversification. But in our experience, few investors understand what diversification means. Sure, investors typically understand that diversification means "don't put all your eggs in one basket." Some also understand that diversification is about owning a combination of investments that zig and zag at different times. But when we probe a little deeper, it seems many investors are still confused about how diversification works in practice. They wonder, "If I'm buying something that makes money when the other is losing money, doesn't that just give me a zero return?"

In this report we hope to clear up some of the more nuanced complexities of diversification with a few simple examples.

Section 1: Skis and bikes

In most parts of Canada we have very distinct seasons. Some months of the year are temperate and relatively dry, while other months are cold and snowy. As a result, most Canadian towns of any size have stores that sell skis and bikes.

Of course, they don't inventory both skis and bikes at the same time. Rather, in the spring they sell off all their ski related inventory and set out their bike gear, and in the fall they clear out the bike gear to make room for skis. Pretty creative, right? Let's observe a simplified example of bike sales and ski sales over several years.

Figure 1. Sales of skis and bikes

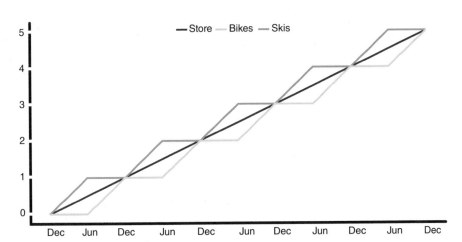

Source: ReSolve Asset Management. For illustrative purposes only.

As winter approaches, ski sales accelerate while bike sales drop off. As summer approaches people stop buying skis, but ramp up their purchases of bikes. One line of business is thriving while the other is flat. In some years, winter might come late and produce very little snow, stifling ski sales.

But the subsequent spring might be warm and dry, and encourage bumper bike sales. This is the nature of diversification.

This same effect plays out in markets. Economic news that is good for one type of investment is often bad news for another. In fact, the hallmark of a diversified portfolio is the observation that one or more investments is disappointing you most of the time. A portfolio that consists of assets that all produce gains at similar times for similar reasons will probably produce their worst losses at the same time too.

Section 2: Well-executed diversification is indistinguishable from magic

The skis and bikes example above shows how deriving cash-flows from two *independently profitable businesses*, which produce returns at different times, reduces the variability of cash-flows throughout the year. This is helpful because it makes it easier for the business owner to manage investments in the business, and stabilizes the owner's income. In other words, diversifying across two return sources—skis and bikes—lowers the overall risk of the business. Let's examine why this is so important.

If the business owner simply wanted to reduce his risk, he could have abandoned the business altogether, and kept his savings in safe bonds or cash. But the business owner needs to take some risks to earn a higher income. Both the ski business and the bike business are risky enterprises on their own, with highly fickle cash-flows. Either one might have been too risky for the shop owner to earn a stable income. But when the businesses are combined, the resulting "portfolio" of businesses is much more stable.

The skis and bikes example extends quite intuitively to the domain of investment portfolios. In investing, it is a simple thing to build a low-risk portfolio by holding lower risk assets, like short- term government bonds. Unfortunately, this portfolio would not be expected to generate much in the way of returns. Remember, the reason investors own higher risk assets like stocks instead of clinging to the safety of short-term bonds or cash is that higher risk assets are expected to produce higher returns. Figure 2 illustrates this relationship for a broad universe of global asset classes.

Figure 2. Return vs. risk for global asset classes

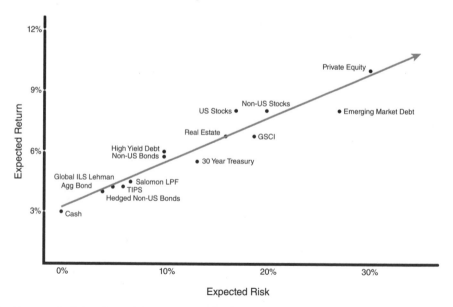

Source: ReSolve Asset Management, Bridgewater Associates.

The long-term return we can expect to earn from any one investment is proportional to that investment's risk. If we seek to lower portfolio risk by investing a large portion of capital in lower risk assets, this will necessarily lower the expected return on the portfolio.

In order to generate returns above cash, investors need to take on risk.

The magic of diversification is that it allows investors to keep more of their money invested in higher risk assets, with commensurately higher expected returns, while lowering the overall risk of the portfolio.

Section 3 below illustrates this concept with a theoretical example, while Section 4 provides evidence with real asset classes. Section 5 illustrates the power of diversification to produce stable returns across most investment environments.

Section 3: Diversification in theory

The central advantage of diversification is that it allows investors to hold many risky assets, while maintaining a tolerable level of portfolio risk. But many investors express confusion about how two investments can both be expected to rise in value, even while they are uncorrelated. After all, if they are uncorrelated, shouldn't we expect them to move in different directions? The skis and bikes example offers some perspective on this apparent contradiction. The revenues accumulated from both skis and bikes are rising over time. But they are rising at precisely opposite times. As a result, the shop owner can even out his revenue streams across the different seasons of the year.

Now let's apply this same phenomenon to two investments. In Figure 3 both Market 1 and Market 2 grow at the same rate of 10% per year for three years. We know this is true because the assets' prices begin and end in the same place. In addition, the assets fluctuate the exact same average amount from day to day—that is, they have the same "volatility". However, Market 1 and Market 2 take a very different path to the same final destination. Market 1 shoots up early on but then returns flatten out and become choppy. Market 2 endures a steady decline over the first half of the period, but then shoots higher. Market 1 inflicts a 26% maximum peak-to-trough loss while Market 2 forces investors to endure an even steeper decline of 34% before recovering.

Figure 3. Two uncorrelated markets

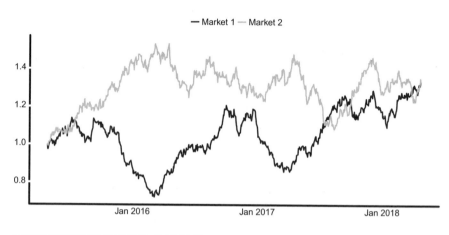

	Market 1	Market 2
Compound Return	10.00%	10.00%
Volatility	20.00%	20.00%
Return Risk Ratio	0.5	0.5
Maximum Peak Trough Loss	−26%	−34%

Source: ReSolve Asset Management. For illustrative purposes only. Simulated results.

To make this example more real, assume that the markets in Figure 3 represent the returns to a long-duration bond index (Market 1) and a diversified stock index (Market 2) over the three-year period from April 2013 through March 2016. By the middle of the period, investors in the stock index are extremely anxious, as their wealth has declined by 25%. They are also envious of investors in bonds, who have outperformed them by over 50%. Meanwhile investors in bonds are convinced that their outperformance was inevitable in retrospect, given their superior talent and good sense. Of course, by the end of the period those investors in stocks who kept faith with their investment ended with exactly the same wealth as investors in bonds.

Remember that both Market 1 and Market 2 have the same expected average returns over the long term. However, they move in different directions at different times for different reasons. In other words, they are uncorrelated. If we expect the same average outcome from both markets, and they are different, then we should take advantage of the opportunity for diversification. Consider the experience of an investor that places half of her capital in Market 1 and half in Market 2 over the same period.

Figure 4. Combining two uncorrelated markets

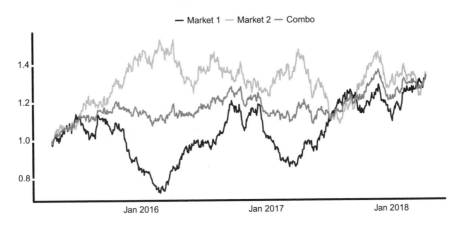

	Market 1	Market 2	Combo
Compound Return	10.00%	10.00%	10.00%
Volatility	20.00%	20.00%	13.70%
Return Risk Ratio	0.5	0.5	0.73
Maximum Peak Trough Loss	−26%	−34%	−18%

Source: ReSolve Asset Management. For illustrative purposes only. Simulated results.

When we examine the full three-year experience of a diversified investor relative to investors with concentrated investments in just one market, it's clear that diversification produces a gentler ride. While the diversified portfolio produced the same return, it did so with about one-third less volatility. Even better, because the declines in the two markets occurred at different times, the diversified portfolio achieved its returns with a 40% smaller peak-to-trough loss than that endured by investors in either of the individual markets.

However, while it's clear with the benefit of perfect hindsight that diversified investors were better off over the entire period, it's illustrative to revisit how each investor might have felt halfway through. At that time, investors who chose to diversify were probably regretting their decision, as Market 1 had produced about 25% in extra returns. They were wishing that they had never even heard of Market 2! Only after the completion of the period, once Market 1 experienced its own 26% decline, would diversified investors finally have felt vindicated.

What makes investing so incredibly challenging is that we can't know for sure in advance whether two investments will produce the same returns, or whether one investment will produce higher returns than another. And even if there is a high degree of confidence that one investment will beat another in the long term, there is no guarantee that returns will converge over a time horizon that investors can live with. For example, over the two decades from 1981 through 2001, safe U.S. government Treasury bonds produced higher returns than stocks, without inflicting the pain and anxiety of two major bear markets.[1]

Ironically, this uncertainty about the true average return is actually a good thing. If investors knew the true average return of their investments in advance, it's likely that these investments would attract a lot more capital. This would drive the price of the investments so high that future investors would necessarily earn a much lower return.

As a thought experiment, it's interesting to see how introducing more uncorrelated investments can make the experience even smoother. For example, in the event an investor could construct five uncorrelated investments with the same 10% expected compound return and 20% volatility, an equally weighted portfolio would have the same return, but less than half the volatility, of any of the individual investments. Even better, while the average peak-to-trough loss of each individual investment is close to 30%, the peak-to-trough loss of the portfolio is well under 10%.

[1]   Source: Global Financial Data.

Figure 5. Combining five uncorrelated sources of return

	Investment 1	Investment 2	Investment 3	Investment 4	Investment 5	Combo
Compound Return	10.00%	10.00%	10.00%	10.00%	10.00%	10.00%
Volatility	20.00%	20.00%	20.00%	20.00%	20.00%	8.70%
Return Risk Ratio	0.5	0.5	0.5	0.5	0.5	1.14
Maximum Peak Trough Loss	−26%	−34%	−30%	−27%	−25%	−7.20%

Source: ReSolve Asset Management. For illustrative purposes only. Simulated results.

As you can see, the "Holy Grail" of diversification is the ability to introduce streams of investment returns from many diverse sources. The emphasis here is on the word "diverse", as it is unhelpful, from a diversification standpoint, to add many investments that are highly correlated. However, the diversification advantage from adding many uncorrelated investments to a portfolio is indistinguishable from magic.

Section 4: Diversification in practice

We've seen that by combining investments with uncorrelated return streams, we can create a portfolio that preserves returns while dramatically reducing risk. This is interesting in theory, but it prompts the question: how can we make diversification work for us in practice?

There are two parts to this answer. The first part addresses how to fit together assets with different risk profiles. The second part deals with finding truly uncorrelated investments. It turns out this is harder than people think, and most investors get it wrong.

Step one: Balance

Diversification is about balance. Unfortunately, while many investors own products that are labeled "balanced", the portfolios underlying those products are anything but. The imbalance occurs because the assets in the portfolio have wildly different risk profiles. As Figure 6 shows, when you hold an equal portion of stocks and bonds in a portfolio, the portfolio is completely dominated by stock risk, because stocks are so much more volatile than bonds.

This large imbalance is not just a theoretical curiosity. It has a very real economic impact on portfolios. Remember, portfolios should be engineered to be resilient to all major economic environments. But stocks are designed to produce positive returns only during periods of sustained positive growth shocks, with benign inflation and abundant liquidity conditions.

When these conditions are present, the portfolio does well. However, when growth plummets unexpectedly, or inflation spirals out of control, the true personality of this portfolio reveals itself. Consider the performance of this 50/50 portfolio of U.S. stocks and high-grade bonds during the global growth shock in 2008–09 (Figure 7.).

Figure 6. A portfolio equally divided between U.S. stocks and Treasuries is dominated by stock risk

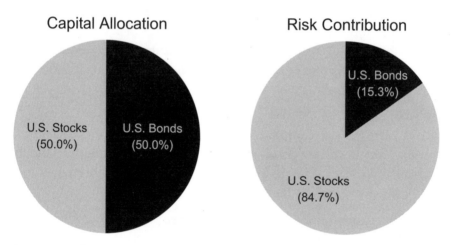

Source: ReSolve Asset Management. Data from CSI.

Figure 7. Equal weight U.S. stocks and high grade corporate bonds: Daily inflation adjusted total returns, Oct 2007–Mar 2009, log-scale

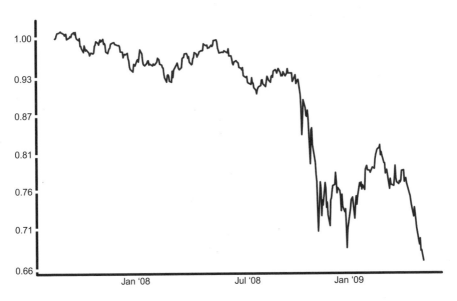

Source: ReSolve Asset Management. Data from CSI.

The Global Financial Crisis of 2008 inflicted a 33% peak-to-trough loss on U.S. investors holding equal weight portfolios of high grade bonds and stocks. Investors outside the U.S. fared approximately the same with a similar portfolio configuration. This despite the fact that the bond portion of the portfolio held its value throughout.

Another way to observe the fact that an equally weighted portfolio of stocks and bonds is just a diluted stock portfolio is to examine the correlation between this portfolio and stocks over time. From Figure 7 it's obvious that despite having 50% in bonds, the portfolio is almost perfectly correlated with stocks most of the time. The average correlation is 0.9, and the portfolio's correlation with stocks has never dropped below 0.8 since 1993.

Figure 8. Rolling three-year correlation between U.S. stocks and equally weighted portfolio of stocks and bonds, 1993–2017

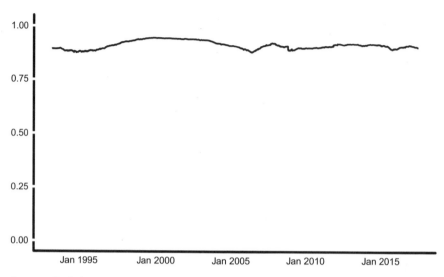

Source: ReSolve Asset Management. Data from CSI.

It's clear that traditional "balanced" portfolios are not balanced at all. The much higher volatility of stocks relative to bonds means that bonds have no opportunity to express their diversification benefits. This is no trivial matter because, as we'll see in the next section, bonds can provide substantial diversification with the right amount of balance.

Step two: Diversity

Unfortunately, most investors seek diversification in the wrong places. For example, many investors perceive that holding many different stocks or stock mutual funds in a portfolio will produce strong diversification benefits. This is like seeking greater diversification and lower risk from buying several ski stores across Canada. Sure, different parts of Canada may have better or worse ski seasons in different years, but summer months are still going to be tough.

It works the same way for stocks and stock mutual funds, because all of the stocks in a market are influenced by the same force: economic growth expectations. Stocks will all fall together if economic growth is weaker than expected, and vice versa. This is even true for stocks in different countries, because economic growth for individual countries is often tied to general global economic trends.

To illustrate this point, let's examine whether we can achieve meaningful diversification by combining the 14 largest global stock markets in the MSCI All-Cap World Index (ACWI). The ACWI is constructed to represent over 99% of total global equity market capitalization, and the 14 markets that we've chosen represent over 75%. (Note: we excluded China due to lack of long-term index data.) Figure 6 shows the annualized volatility over the 26-year period ending October 31, 2016 for each index (in USD).[2]

How can we measure the available diversification opportunity? A simple method would be to observe the ratio between the average of the volatilities across each individual market, and the volatility of the equally weighted portfolio of the same constituents. We'll call this the "diversification ratio". The average of the individual volatilities does not account for the diversification benefit, while the volatility of the equally weighted portfolio does, so the ratio measures the risk reduction advantage of diversification.

From Figure 9, we see that the average of individual market volatilities is 26.4%, while the volatility of the equally weighted portfolio is 19.8%. Thus, the diversification ratio is 26.4%/19.8% = 1.33. In other words, we achieve a 33% diversification advantage from dividing capital equally among 15 of the largest global equity market indexes.

[2]   Where daily index histories did not extend to 1991 we calculated from inception. Portfolio volatility was calculated from pairwise complete covariances.

Figure 9. Annualized volatility of ACWI constituents, 1991–2017

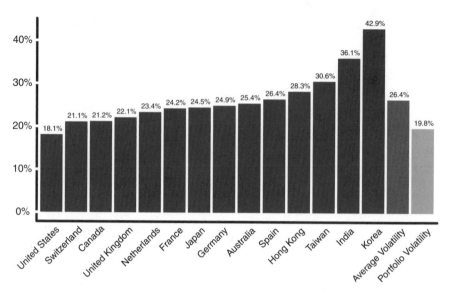

Source: ReSolve Asset Management. Data from CSI and MSCI.

You may be surprised to learn that earning a 33% risk-adjusted performance advantage from diversification is relatively thin gruel. Remember that diversification benefits are a function of low correlation between the assets in the portfolio. However, over the past 26 years the average correlation between these global equity markets is about 0.6. Worse, since the proliferation of index products has made it easy to invest in international markets, correlations have steadily increased. Figure 10 shows the rolling average annual pairwise correlations between these markets from 1999 through 2016, and the trend of these correlations. High correlations between global equity markets might be here to stay, which further dilutes the diversification opportunities within the global equity asset class.

Figure 10. Rolling average annual pairwise correlations of ACWI constituent indexes

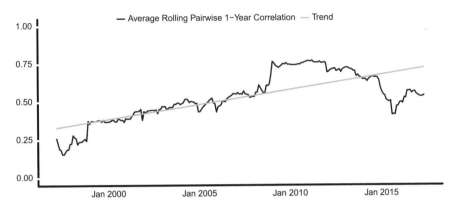

Source: ReSolve Asset Management. Data from CSI and MSCI.

While investors focused on global stock markets are likely to experience diminishing returns on diversification, other opportunities for diversification abound. However, investors seeking diversification must be willing to look further afield.

Remember, investment environments are generally defined by unexpected changes to inflation and growth expectations. Figure 10 divides economic environments along these two dimensions to create four distinct economic states of the world. Diverse global asset classes are embedded in the quadrants in which they would be fundamentally expected to perform well. Assets near the middle have low sensitivity to the corresponding economic dynamics, while those near the edge are highly sensitive and volatile. You can see that stocks would be expected to flourish during periods of unexpectedly strong growth, while other assets like government bonds, TIPs, commodities, REITs and gold are designed to produce their best returns in very different economic periods.

Figure 11. Global asset class sensitivities to growth and inflation

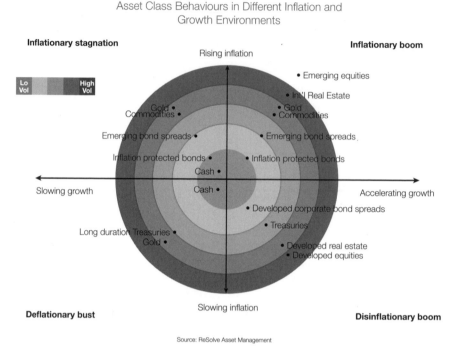

Source: ReSolve Asset Management.

Since there are assets available to investors that can be expected to produce positive returns in any environment, the investment universe in Figure 10 is truly diversified. Let's extend our analysis of diversification benefits using this more diverse group of assets. Specifically, consider a universe of global assets consisting of U.S., European, Asian and emerging market stock indexes; U.S. and international real estate securities (REITs); gold; commodities; Treasury Inflation Protected Securities (TIPs); U.S. government bonds (Treasuries), foreign bonds, and; USD denominated emerging market bonds. Figure 12 quantifies the annualized volatility of each of these asset class indexes over the period 1991 through 2016.[3]

---

[3] Where daily index histories did not extend to 1991 we calculated from inception. Portfolio volatility was calculated from pairwise complete covariances.

Figure 12. Annualized volatility of global asset classes

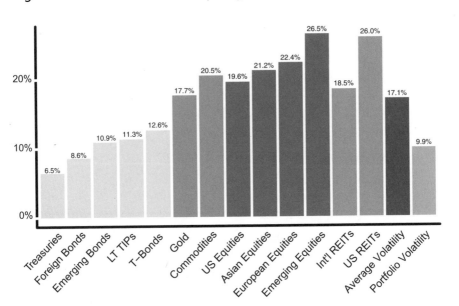

Source: ReSolve Asset Management. Data from CSI and Bloomberg.

Recall from Figure 9 that, because global equity markets are highly correlated with one another, investors accrue a rather small (33%) advantage from holding them all together in a portfolio. In contrast, it's clear from Figure 10 that our diversified universe provides much larger benefits. The average of individual asset class volatilities is 17.1% (red bar), while the volatility of the equally weighted portfolio is 9.9% (green bar). Thus, the diversification ratio is 19.8%/12% = 1.73. In other words, we achieve a 73% diversification advantage from dividing capital equally among 13 major global asset classes.

Even better, there is no reason to believe that this diversification benefit from investing in diverse global asset classes will go away anytime soon. Figure 13 clearly shows that the average annual pairwise correlations between these diverse asset classes have been persistently low, averaging 0.25 compared to the average 0.6 correlations across global equity markets. And, in contrast to what we observe across global equity markets, the trend does not appear to be increasing materially over time.

Figure 13. Rolling average annual pairwise correlations of global asset classes

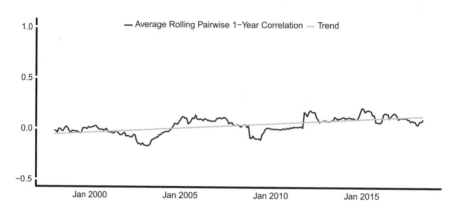

Source: ReSolve Asset Management. Data from CSI and Bloomberg.

The lesson from this section is that diversification has very practical benefits, but only for investors who can think more broadly about the world's many sources of returns. Investors who are uncomfortable investing outside their borders, or in unfamiliar asset classes, will incur large opportunity costs. Either they will own a portfolio that is much more vulnerable to risk in order to earn the returns they need, or they will own a portfolio that earns a lower return at the level of risk they can tolerate.

Section 5: Diversification for stable returns in all environments

This paper has made the case that the primary advantage of diversification is that it allows an investor to hold many risky assets in a portfolio—with commensurately high expected returns—but with much less risk than would be experienced by holding any single asset on its own. We laid the foundation for this concept using theoretical uncorrelated return streams, and discovered that it is possible to combine many risky, but sufficiently uncorrelated assets in a portfolio to dramatically lower portfolio risk. Finally, we observed the practical benefits of diversification by combining two different universes of asset classes. We saw that it is challenging to achieve meaningful diversification from investments across global equity markets, but that there are significant diversification opportunities from investing in a broader universe of global asset classes.

In this final section, we will explore how to combine all of the concepts discussed so far to create robust portfolios that are designed to thrive in most economic environments. Specifically, we will analyse how to use the diverse universe of asset classes described in Figures 11 and 12 to create maximum balance in a portfolio.

First, let's revisit the historical personalities of our assets by reflecting on their long-term volatilities, and their average correlations with all of the other assets. Figure 12 summarized the long-term average volatilities of major markets. Recall that that Treasury bonds produced just one quarter the volatility of most risky assets like stocks and commodities over the past 25 years. On the correlation front, Figure 14 shows that U.S. Treasuries in general have exhibited the lowest correlation with other assets, followed by gold and commodities. Mostly as a function of currency effects (we use unhedged bond indexes), foreign bonds are grouped between equities and commodities in terms of average correlations.

Figure 14. Average pairwise correlations with other assets, 1991–2017

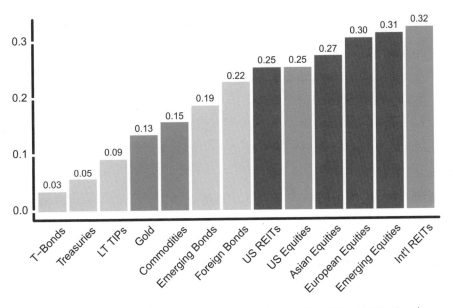

Source: ReSolve Asset Management. Data from CSI, S&P, MSCI, Barclays, Deutsche Bank.

It's clear that asset classes have varied risk profiles, and diverse relationships with other assets. The question is, how can we maximize these diversification opportunities in a portfolio, to achieve steady returns in all economic environments?

Let's start with perhaps the most common interpretation of a "balanced" portfolio—the 60/40 stock/bond portfolio. We can use the 13 assets in our asset universe to create a very close approximation of a global "balanced" portfolio by holding all the assets in equal weight. There are eight risky assets and five fixed income assets, so the mix is very close to 60/40, with all assets having a 7.7% weight in the portfolio per Figure 15.

Figure 15. Equal weight portfolio is a global "balanced" portfolio

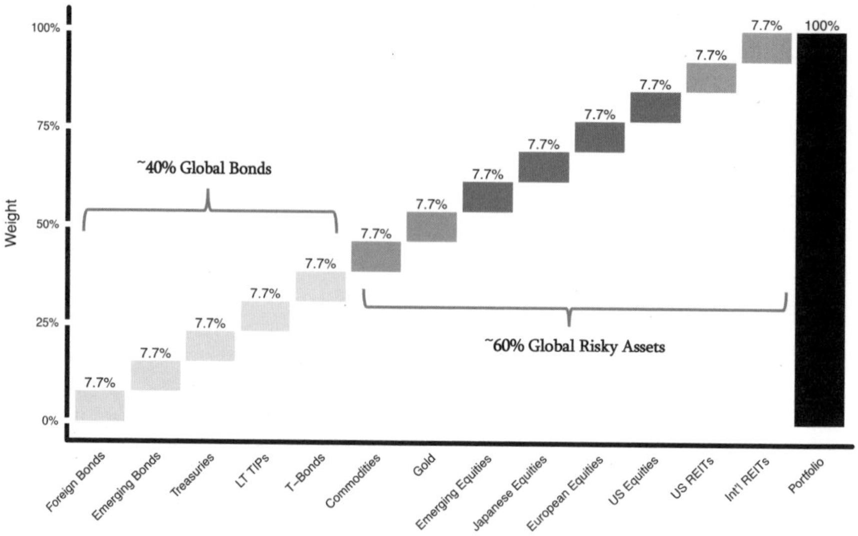

Source: ReSolve Asset Management.

Is this so-called "balanced" portfolio truly balanced? Rather than stopping at a surface level view of asset weights, let's examine the portfolio through the lens of the assets' risk contributions. Remember, asset classes in this diverse universe have different risk properties.

Some assets are much more volatile and/or highly correlated than others. If we mix volatile assets with high correlations to other assets alongside stable assets with low correlations, how can we expect each asset to contribute the same amount of diversification benefits? Per Figure 16, it turns out that this portfolio is not very balanced at all.

Let's take a moment to interpret this waterfall chart in Figure 16. Each bar shows the total risk contribution, in units of volatility, for that asset as a constituent of the portfolio. The portfolio volatility above the black bar on the right-hand side is the sum of all of the constituent asset volatilities. As a quick sanity check, you'll note that the total portfolio volatility of the equalweight multi-asset portfolio in Figure 16 below is exactly the same as the portfolio volatility in Figure 12 (quick—go confirm this—it will help to cement the concept).

It's clear that the risk contributions from fixed income assets in light blue are completely dominated by the risk contributions from the other risky assets. In fact, the sum of risk contributions from bonds is just 0.6%, which means the other assets cumulatively contribute 9.3% of the 9.9% in total portfolio volatility. While it might seem strange that an asset can contribute negative risk to the portfolio (see T-Bonds in Figure 16), this is a simple consequence of the fact that the asset is negatively correlated with the portfolio itself. The direction of risk from this asset marginally offsets volatility contributions from the other assets in the portfolio.

Figure 16. Risk contributions of the global "balanced" portfolio, based on average volatility and correlations from 1991–2017

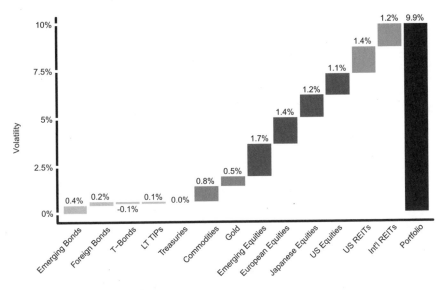

Source: ReSolve Asset Management.

If a traditional "balanced" portfolio isn't actually balanced, what method can we use to create a truly balanced portfolio from these diverse assets? Risk Parity is the concept of constructing a portfolio so that each asset has an equal opportunity to express its diverse character. Quantitatively, this occurs when each asset contributes the same amount of risk to the portfolio. Intuitively, for assets with different risk profiles to contribute the same amount of risk, a portfolio must hold a larger weighting in low risk assets, and a smaller weighting in higher risk assets. To maximize diversity, assets with low correlation to other assets would also receive a higher weighting.

Based on this logic, and with a quick glance at Figures 12 and 14 above, one might expect a Risk Parity portfolio to have its largest weights in U.S. Treasuries and T-Bonds, since they exhibit the lowest combination of volatility and correlation relative to the other assets. On the other end of the spectrum, we might expect emerging market stocks and REITs to have the smallest weights in the portfolio.

Figure 17. Risk contributions of the global "balanced" portfolio, based on average volatility and correlations from 1991–2017

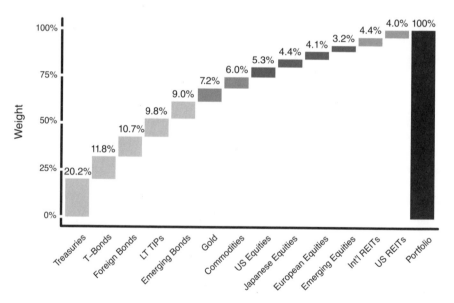

Source: ReSolve Asset Management. Data from CSI, S&P, MSCI, Barclays, Deutsche Bank.

Figure 17 shows the true optimal Risk Parity portfolio weights using average volatilities and correlations from 1991–2017. Conveniently, asset weights in the portfolio are broadly aligned with what we would expect, given their volatility and correlation profiles. Bond type assets are on the left with the most weight, while risky assets are on the right with less weight. When we view this portfolio through the lens of risk contributions in Figure 18, we see that all of the assets are now contributing the same amount of risk to the portfolio. The portfolio is in perfect balance.

Figure 18. Risk contributions for the Global Risk Parity portfolio, based on average volatility and correlations from 1991–2017

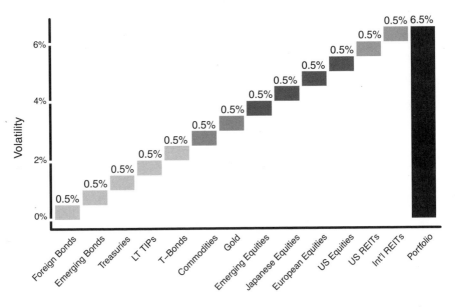

Source: ReSolve Asset Management. Data from CSI, S&P, MSCI, Barclays, Deutsche Bank.

The truly balanced Global Risk Parity portfolio has significantly less volatility than the global 60/40 portfolio. In fact, the Global Risk Parity portfolio has the same volatility as 10-year Treasury bonds over the period studied, despite the fact that 80% of the portfolio is comprised of assets with much higher volatility. Even so, astute readers might wonder what proportion of the reduction in volatility is simply due to the larger weight in bonds.

We can invoke the "diversification ratio" concept discussed above to disentangle how much of the reduction in volatility is due to better diversification rather than a higher weighting in bonds. Recall that the diversification ratio is the ratio of the weighted average volatility of the constituent assets divided by portfolio volatility. The weighted average volatility of the equally weighted asset classes was 17.1% (see Figure 10), while the volatility of the equally weighted portfolio was 9.9%, reflecting a diversification ratio of 1.73. The weighted average volatility of the assets in the Global Risk Parity portfolio is 13.65%, reflecting a higher weighting in bonds. However, the portfolio volatility is just 6.5%, so the diversification ratio is 13.65%/6.5% = 2.1.

But so far this is just theory. Let's face it, few investors care about esoteric objectives like maximizing the diversification opportunity in a portfolio. Investors care about results.

Specifically, they want to maximize their returns with minimal risk.[4] In Figure 19, we examine the historical character of the global 60/40 portfolio and the Global Risk Parity portfolio over the past quarter century to see what diversification means in terms of real dollars and cents. Specifically, let's use a prudent amount of leverage to scale both strategies to target 10% portfolio volatility. For simplicity, we assumed investors can borrow (with margin) at the T-bill rate.

This is where theory meets economic reality. The enhanced diversification properties of the Global Risk Parity portfolio produce higher returns when scaled to the same level of risk as the Global 60/40 portfolio. In fact, over a quarter century the Global Risk Parity portfolio produces almost twice as much wealth at the same level of volatility, and with a smaller peak-to-trough loss (Max Drawdown) along the way.

---

[4]   More accurately, investors want to maximize the probability that they will achieve their financial objectives. However, expected risk-adjusted performance is a good proxy for this probability for investors with reasonable goals.

Figure 19. Global Risk Parity vs. Global 60/40 portfolio, scaled to 10% volatility, 1991–2017

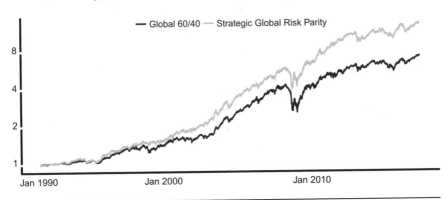

Statistics	Global 60 / 40	Strategic Global Risk Parity
Compound Return	8.32%	10.97%
Volatility	10.00%	10.00%
Sharpe Ratio	0.62	0.86
Maximum Drawdown	−40.95%	−34.40%
Positive Rolling Yrs	82.00%	82.00%
Growth of $1	$8.14	$15.39

Source: ReSolve Asset Management. For illustrative purposes only. Simulated results.

Summary

This paper set out to correct a variety of misconceptions about diversification. Many investors are fundamentally confused about how two assets can move in different directions without canceling each other out. In the first section, we described a simple business that sold skis in the winter and bikes in the summer. The revenues from these two sales channels arrive at different times of the year, but they both contribute to the bottom line. When combined, the business is able to earn much more stable cash-flows, perhaps allowing the owner to scale the business more aggressively for growth.

Diversified investments work the same way in portfolios. As more uncorrelated sources of return are introduced, portfolios experience lower volatility and smaller peak-to-trough losses. This is important because investors seek returns by investing in risky assets. Diversification provides the opportunity to invest in a variety of risky assets—with commensurately high expected returns—but at a fraction of the total risk that an investor would endure from an investment in any single asset on its own.

Unfortunately, traditional portfolios get diversification wrong, for two reasons. First, they fail to account for the fact that asset classes have very different risk profiles. As a result, popular products like "balanced" funds are completely dominated by the riskier assets in the portfolio, like stocks. Bonds have no opportunity to provide their diversification "ballast". That's why typical "balanced" portfolios lost between 35%–40% of their value during the Global Financial Crisis in 2008–09.

Second, most portfolios fail to invest in diverse assets that thrive in different economic states. Portfolios that are heavily concentrated in equity risk will only do well during periods of sustained global growth, benign inflation, and abundant liquidity. Thankfully, with some notable exceptions, these conditions largely characterize investors' experience over the past three decades. But such a long period of conditions favourable to stocks is the exception, not the rule. There have been three periods over the past century or so, each lasting between 14 and 21 years, where "balanced" portfolios have produced flat or negative real growth. These periods are real, and they lie somewhere ahead of us.

ABOUT ADAM BUTLER, MICHAEL PHILBRICK AND RODRIGO GORDILLO

Adam Butler, CFA, CAIA, is Co-Founder and Chief Investment Officer of ReSolve Asset Management. ReSolve manages funds and accounts in Canada, the United States, and internationally. The firm employs quantitative methods in the management of three multi-asset factor strategies in including Systematic Global Macro and Global Risk Parity strategies. Adam has 14 years of experience in investment management including 11 years as a Portfolio Manager, and is a sub-advisor for the ReSolve Adaptive Asset Allocation Fund (Canada), the Horizons Global Risk Parity ETF, and the ReSolve Online Advisor. Adam is lead author of the book *Adaptive Asset Allocation: Dynamic Global Portfolios to Profit in Good Times – And Bad* (Wiley, 2016), and many investment related articles and whitepapers.

@GestaltU

Michael Philbrick has over 25 years of experience in investment management, including nine years as a Portfolio Manager, and is a Chartered Investment Manager and Accredited Investment Fiduciary.

He is currently one of the Portfolio Managers for the ReSolve Adaptive Asset Allocation Fund, the Horizons Global Risk Parity ETF, and ReSolve's managed accounts. Prior to co-founding the ReSolve in 2015, Mike was a Portfolio Manager at Dundee Private Wealth, Richardson GMP and Macquarie Private Wealth. Mike also served as Branch Manager at Scotia McLeod, Richardson GMP and Macquarie Private Wealth. Mike is co-author of the book *Adaptive Asset Allocation: Dynamic Global Portfolios to Profit in Good Times – And Bad* (Wiley, 2016), and many investment related articles and whitepapers. Mr. Philbrick graduated from Carlton University with a degree in Economics, and has earned both Chartered Investment Manager® and Accredited Investment Fiduciary® credentials.

@MikePhilbrick99

Rodrigo Gordillo is a Co-Founder, Managing Partner and Portfolio Manager of ReSolve Asset Management and has over 13 years of experience in investment management.

He has co-authored the book *Adaptive Asset Allocation: Dynamic Global Portfolios to Profit in Good Times – and Bad* (Wiley) as well several whitepapers and research focused on adding new insights to the quantitative global asset allocation space. Rodrigo began his career on the institutional side with John Hancock before transitioning to the ultra-high net worth space at a boutique wealth management firm. Subsequently, Rodrigo, along with his partners, Mike and Adam, continued to evolve their quantitatively focused investment methodology as Portfolio Managers at Macquarie Private Wealth and Dundee Goodman Private wealth before launching ReSolve Asset Management in 2015.

@RodGordilloP

A Benchmark for Efficient Asset Allocation

PETER MLADINA, CHARLES GRANT AND
STEVEN GERMANI

Asset allocation is the most important decision in portfolio construction. It aligns investment assets with investment objectives. More than 60 years ago, Harry Markowitz developed modern portfolio theory (MPT) and demonstrated the diversification benefit of combining different assets. For each level of possible return, there is an optimal mix of assets – a portfolio – that offers the lowest risk. Together, these portfolios comprise an efficient frontier. Optimizing investors select a portfolio from the efficient frontier.

Around the same time, other researchers were developing the efficient market theory, which holds that market prices fully reflect all available information. This basic notion has profound implications, including that the market value of a security is the best estimate of its fair value and there is no opportunity for a skilled investor to earn a risk-adjusted excess return.

In the 1960s, William Sharpe extended efficient market theory to MPT with the capital asset pricing model (CAPM). If investors optimize their portfolios per MPT and markets are efficient, an efficient equilibrium of asset values is reached. This equilibrium is represented by the market portfolio of all capital assets—the average asset allocation of all investors.[1] It would be the optimal portfolio under CAPM theory, offering the

---

[1]   A capital asset has a positive market value and a cost of capital (and thus a positive expected return). Capital assets finance the economy. In contrast, derivatives are not capital assets. Their market values sum to zero.

highest expected return per unit of risk. This return-to-risk efficiency ratio is known as the Sharpe ratio, where return and risk (standard deviation) are defined in excess of the risk-free cash return. Investors who want more return would leverage the market portfolio. Investors who want less risk would combine it with cash.

If markets are competitive, the equilibrium global market portfolio of capital assets provides a *theoretically* sound benchmark for asset allocation. The global market portfolio results from an ongoing optimization process, incorporating the forward-looking return and risk expectations of all investors. Therefore, the global market weights of asset classes contain information investors can use when setting their own asset allocation policy. From this perspective, the global market portfolio can serve as a benchmark for strategic asset allocation just as strategic asset allocation serves as a benchmark for tactical asset allocation. But how efficient has the asset allocation of the global market portfolio been, and is it an *empirically* sound benchmark for asset allocation?

We test the efficiency of the global market portfolio by constructing a proxy that serves as a benchmark to evaluate asset allocation mutual funds. Our proxy for global market equity is the MSCI All Country World Investable Market Index (ACWI IMI).[2] The index represents approximately 99% of the market value of all publicly traded equities, including developed and emerging market stocks, large and small stocks, and growth and value stocks. It also includes sectors commonly considered distinct asset classes, such as listed real estate, infrastructure and natural resources. Our proxy for global market bonds is the Bloomberg Barclays Multiverse Bond Index (Multiverse), a global fixed income index that includes the market values of a broad base of investment-grade and high-yield bonds across maturities from government, corporate and other issuers in both developed and emerging markets.[3]

[2] ACWI IMI market values are backfilled to 1997 by grossing up ACWI market values, which represent approximately 85% of capitalization-weighted market value.

[3] Multiverse market values and returns are backfilled to 1997 using the Bloomberg Barclays Global Aggregate and Global High Yield indices.

Hedge funds are not included in the global market portfolio because they own capital assets, and we do not want to double count. Our proxy is missing the market values of investable private equity (and debt) and commercial private real estate. Based on data from Preqin, we estimate that about 3% of the global market portfolio is investable private equity (and debt).[4] And based on Doeswijk *et al* (2014), we estimate that about 4% of the global market portfolio is investable commercial private real estate.[5] These omissions do not affect the results of our efficiency tests of asset allocation mutual funds because the funds do not hold private assets. The global market portfolio of capital assets is largely composed of the combined market values of ACWI IMI and Multiverse, enabling us to reconstruct its monthly returns going back 20 years to 1997.

Exhibit 1 displays the equilibrium mix of global stocks versus global bonds since 1997. As of May 2017, the equilibrium-weighted global market portfolio was 48% global equities and 52% global bonds. The 48% in global equities was approximately 52% U.S. equity, 37% developed ex-U.S. equity and 11% emerging markets equity. Of the 52% in global bonds, approximately 94% was investment-grade and 6% was high-yield. U.S. fixed income comprised about 39% of global bonds. Over the 20-year period, the allocation to global equities ranged between 67% and 38%. The allocation changes through time as return and risk expectations evolve and securities are issued and redeemed.

The returns of the global market portfolio represent a global market benchmark. Our efficiency tests compare the Sharpe ratio of the global market benchmark with the Sharpe ratio of each asset allocation fund in Morningstar's World Allocation category, comparing both over each fund's unique history. The World Allocation category includes asset allocation funds that can explore the world to allocate across asset classes with broad discretion. We add expense ratios back to the net returns of each fund to better isolate a fund's asset allocation efficiency. The final sample includes 151 live and dead funds (to reduce survivorship bias) with at least 24 months of gross returns.

---

[4] *2017 Preqin Global Private Equity and Venture Capital Report* and *2017 Preqin Global Private Debt Report.*
[5] Ronald Doeswijk, Trevin Lam, and Laurens Swinkels; "The Global Multi-Asset Portfolio," *Financial Analysts Journal,* 2014.

Exhibit 1: Stocks vs. bonds in the global market portfolio

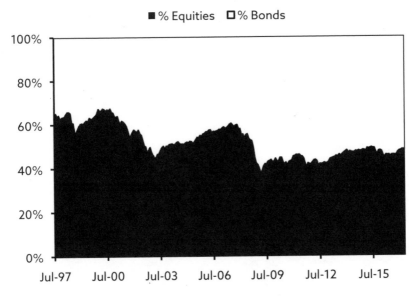

Source: Northern Trust Research, Morningstar, Barclays.

Since it is common to hedge the currency risk of foreign bonds (see our research article "Go Global and Diversify"), we created a second version of the global market benchmark using U.S. dollar-hedged returns for foreign bonds.

Of the funds in our sample, 65% had a higher correlation to this version of the benchmark. This result is consistent with an intertemporal version of the CAPM, where investors align part of an implicit or explicit multi-period liability with safe fixed income assets denominated in the same currency. We chose the version of the benchmark with the higher correlation to a fund as that fund's benchmark.

The histogram in Exhibit 2 shows the difference in Sharpe ratios between the global market portfolio and each fund. The difference is negative for 68% of funds, indicating that their asset allocation was less efficient than that of the global market portfolio.

Exhibit 2: Efficiency of the global market portfolio

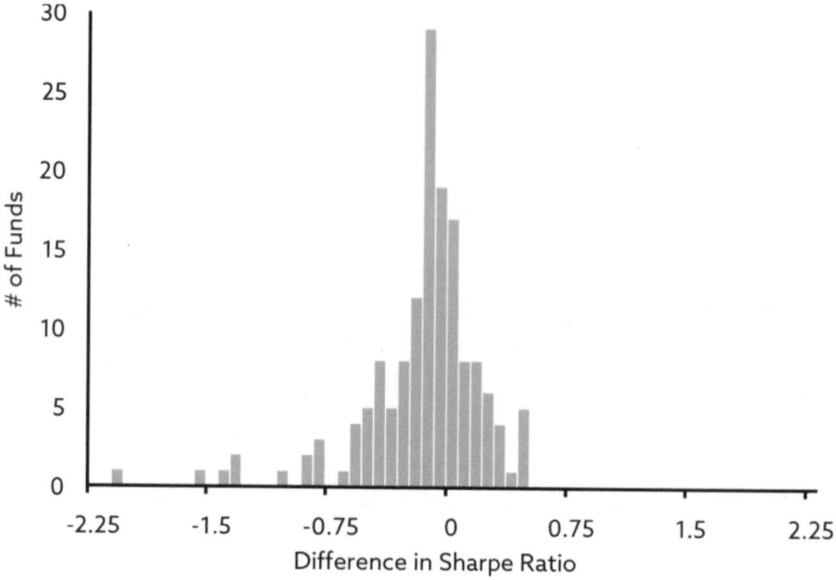

Source: Northern Trust Research, Morningstar, Barclays.

The average expense ratio of the funds in our sample is 1.34%, representing the cost of seeking alpha from active asset allocation and security selection decisions. If we repeat the efficiency test using net fund returns, we find that 83% of funds are less efficient than the global market portfolio. This result is notable because the information contained in the global market portfolio is readily available at low cost.

The overall results suggest that the global market portfolio is indeed a sound theoretical and empirical benchmark for asset allocation. The relative weights of asset classes within the global market portfolio can serve as a good starting point to develop a customized asset allocation based on an investor's unique goals (liabilities) and risk preferences. Consistent with an intertemporal version of the CAPM, the main element of customization should be the alignment of safe fixed income assets with an investor's unique set of lifetime goals.

Originally published July 2017; northerntrust.com/insights-research/detail?c=90b266c5081dbfcbcdf32abcf98b808d.

ABOUT PETER MLADINA, CHARLES GRANT AND STEVEN GERMANI

Peter Mladina is the Director of Portfolio Research for Northern Trust Wealth Management. He is responsible for the application of leading research to the wealth management investment process. This includes research, tools and methods that support asset allocation, portfolio construction, investment selection and best practices in portfolio management.

Previously, Mr. Mladina was the Director of Research at Waterline, a boutique wealth manager acquired by Northern Trust in 2010. In addition to advising high-net-worth clients, Mr. Mladina helped Waterline develop an innovative goals-based asset allocation solution and an empirical investment approach rooted in academic research.

Mr. Mladina is an Adjunct Professor of Economics at UCLA, where he teaches applied finance for the Master of Applied Economics program. His research on asset allocation and portfolio construction has been awarded publication in peer-reviewed journals, and he is a co-author of the CFA Institute's revised Level III asset allocation curriculum. He received a BA in Economics from UCLA and an MBA from Edinburgh Business School (UK).

Charles Grant is Senior Vice President at Northern Trust. He is responsible for the research, analytical tools, software development and education that support the Wealth Management investments practice. This includes research, tools and software that inform goals-based and strategic asset allocation, portfolio construction, manager selection and monitoring, and the development of investment capabilities and products.

Mr. Grant is a CFA Charterholder and received a BA in Economics from the University of Dayton and an MBA from Northwestern University's Kellogg School of Management.

Steven Germani is a Senior Investment Research Analyst in the Wealth Management Portfolio Research group at Northern Trust. He is responsible for quantitative research, data analysis and education to support the Wealth Management investment practice. This includes asset allocation, portfolio construction, manager selection and monitoring, and authoring research articles.

Mr. Germani received a MS in Computational Finance and Risk Management from the University of Washington and a BS in Finance from Indiana University. He is a CFA charterholder and holds the CFP® certification.

Revenge of the Humans

How Discretionary Managers
Can Crush Systematics

LEIGH DROGEN

One day, I found myself in the Estimize office sitting across the table from a hedge fund portfolio manager (PM) who said something I honestly couldn't believe. According to this PM who runs a $500M long/short book at a large multi-manager fund, he was taking a data science course at night, after work. He told me, "If I don't learn how to do quantitative analysis I'm not going to have a job in two years."

A second said the same thing to me a week later.

Two weeks after that I received an email from the "school" providing that very course, inquiring if I could teach a data science class, specifically for finance, to 25 members of a hedge fund who had contracted them.

These are just a few anecdotes among many in the absolutely massive transformation taking place right now within the discretionary institutional management industry. Discretionary managers have woken up, and are now scrambling to understand what's taking place and how they must change in relation to it. Many will not survive the shift. Others will take advantage and be better off for it.

This piece takes a deep dive into the following themes and how institutional managers can begin to effectively redirect themselves:

1. Investors have woken up to the asymmetric risk they were taking on with active discretionary mutual funds, hedge funds and registered

investment advisers (RIAs) who were basically playing with beta instead of generating alpha. Now they are pulling their money.

2. Asset flows are moving into "passive" ETF strategies and will continue to move further into smart beta ETF strategies, long only active management is headed to the grave.

3. Hedge fund assets are flowing out of discretionary and into quantitative systematic strategies which have produced far more consistent alpha. They also blow-up less often.

4. Most classic systematic alpha strategies are based on price; volume and fundamentals have been arbitraged out and are now betas. This has precipitated a race to build new alphas with new data sets.

5. Discretionary managers are scurrying to incorporate new data sets, but lack the understanding of how to analyze their efficacy and more importantly, how to incorporate them into their discretionary trading processes.

6. If discretionary managers remain disciplined and execute their rubric faithfully, they can crush systematic quants, but they must solve the religion vs. science question first.

7. The organizational structure of discretionary management teams along with the type of people they hire is broken and outdated for today's challenges. Changes are starting to take place, but all too slowly for many players to survive.

8. Building the right infrastructure will remain pertinent to surviving this shift. Both quant and discretionary firms must hire teams that include engineers, product managers and quants to suss out new data sets.

Let's take a deeper dive into these topics.

1. Getting Paid For Playing With Beta Is Over

Looking back, it's hard to understand why anyone was willing to give most discretionary fund managers money in the first place. The truth is, most PMs were simply playing with beta, whether it be momentum, mean reversion, value, growth, sector or market cap. Managers were leveraging these far more often than they were actually generating alpha. Now we can all argue over whether correctly timing the use of betas is in itself alpha, but that argument is made moot by the fact that the vast majority of PMs were unsuccessful at this in the long run and eventually blew up.

The greatest trick the industry ever pulled was making limited partners (LPs) believe that they could consistently leverage beta and not get caught with their hand in the cookie jar, giving up years of returns in a matter of months. Over and over, fund managers took their "two and twenty" to the bank in the years they happened to be on the right side of that equation. Then they blew up. Instead of fighting back to their hurdle, they just closed shop and opened up a new one, somehow convincing investors to play the same asymmetric game of risk once again. Heads I win, tails I take a vacation for a year and someone gives me another coin to flip later.

Don't get me wrong, there are managers who have proven track records of not blowing up while playing with beta, and some even generate true alpha, but they are few and far between. Good luck picking the correct fund manager.

Why did it take the market so long to wake up? We can start with the great answers you'll hear from friends of mine like wealth manager, Josh Brown. He fully understands the social and egotistical aspect of being invested in these funds, not because it's the rational thing to do, but because of the accompanying prestige. The same can be said for managing your own personal portfolio; it's something to talk about at a cocktail party. And while it seems our current political climate echoes the movie *Idiocracy*, financial market education and investor behavior have actually taken a huge leap forward since the '08 crash. I find it interesting that retail investors actually got smart before pension funds, pulling money from active managers, closing their brokerage accounts, and investing in passive low cost ETF strategies.

As for the tens of thousands of small RIAs, why would I give them my money either if I can buy a smart beta ETF for 20bps that does basically the same thing they were for 100bps? You're gonna tell me that all those mom and pop RIAs managing $40M are executing those smart beta strategies as efficiently and accurately as iShares? Please. It's only a matter of time before Betterment or some other robo-advisor allows its clients to algorithmically allocate a portion of their portfolio to these strategies.

Heck, I wouldn't be surprised if one of them also provided the ability to use simple, proven, market timing overlays in order to rotate in and out or long and short certain smart beta strategies.

Hedge fund PMs have to realize that even though they are in last car on this disruption train, the conductor is coming to clip their ticket as well. They will either evolve or die, like any other industry disrupted by better efficiency. I think it's obvious that there will be far fewer of them as most will not successfully shift to generating alpha.

2. All Investing Is Active, Even The Passive Kind

Let's clear something up, there's no such thing as "passive investing." The words we use matter because they form the basis for how we think about things and the actions we take. The developed western world is ripping itself apart over an inability to win a "war on terrorism" because, for propaganda purposes, we decided to say we were fighting a war on a military tactic (you didn't have to study war theory in school like me to know you can't win a war against a tactic).

All investing is active, even the decision of how to weight an index, what goes into that index, and how to allocate your capital amongst different asset classes. Just because the computer keeps your allocation levels static does not mean you've abdicated responsibility for investment decisions. This is why I'm such a big fan of smart beta, because it does away with the ignorant notion that you can avoid making a decision on beta to begin with. We all have to, so we might as well make that decision in an informed and active way.

In any event, we're going to continue to see massive flows of capital out of "active" long only mutual fund and long/short hedge fund strategies and into these. The question on everyone's mind is, how will this affect the market? My best guess is that we're not going to see the downside of massive systemic risks some are warning about when everyone is indexing. The latter part of 2016 and beginning of 2017 prove that even with all the indexed money, correlations can still drop quickly when macro factors evolve. After the 2016 US Presidential election, cross-asset correlations that had existed for the past decade began to break down.

3. Assets Are Flowing From Discretionary to Systematic

You don't have to look too deeply to see this massive trend in strategy allocations playing out. WorldQuant LLC, with its growing team of over 600 employees, including more than 120 PhDs and 275 researchers, has been managing systematic investment strategies for Millennium Management since 2007. At Point72 (SAC) we've seen Cubist outpace the discretionary side of the firm by a wide margin with now over 40 systematic PMs. Balyasny has quickly shifted focus and is building a stable of systematic managers to effectively do something with their huge assets under management (AUM) growth. Other multi-manager platforms like Schonfeld, Paloma, AHL, Engineer's Gate and GSA have added significant assets. Paul Tudor Jones is attempting to remake his firm by hiring a bunch of systematic managers, and others are following suit. And let's not even get started with the continued dominance of firms like Renaissance, AQR and Two Sigma, where you probably can't even give them your money if you tried.

I would say that the nerds are the new kings of Wall Street (Midtown), but frankly they (myself included) would cringe at that statement given their propensity to run in very different circles than the rest of the money manager crowd. This group is mostly made up of unassuming nerdy PhD types that you would probably take for accountants on the subway. They have serious mathematical and scientific training and have usually honed their craft on other data sets before coming to the financial world.

The fact of the matter is that there's simply more efficacy to what these managers are doing than the vast majority of the discretionary trading world, and they've (mostly) put up the numbers to prove it. And I'm not just talking about returns, these groups are producing real alpha. Their strategies are meticulously backtested in and out of sample before going live, and are scaled up over time. Many discretionary managers launch a book with $500m in play from day one, I can count on one hand the number of systematic funds that have done that in the past five years.

And while some systematic funds don't perform well, you'll be hard pressed to find any massive blow-ups akin to what's regularly seen on the discretionary side. Pension funds can certainly deal with paying 2 and 20 if they have more confidence that their returns from year 1 through 3 aren't going to all disappear in year 4.

The flow of capital from discretionary to systematic strategies is going to continue, as it should. That will have its own repercussions, which we're already starting to see.

4. Quants Dig For New Alpha

A 2012 tell-all book from a former Goldman Sachs trader revealed how the Great Vampire Squid often endearingly referred to their unsophisticated clients as "muppets." While they rightfully got skewered for that comparison, they were certainly onto something when their trading desks would remark internally that they were basically taking candy from babies.

However, many of the muppets are gone now and that's left far less alpha in the market to capture. Relative value and statistical arbitrage strategies are about capturing asset mispricings associated with the irrational behavioral aspects of fear and greed. This isn't going to change any time soon, the muppets aren't coming back, they've wised up. Less alpha overall will lead to a drop in the number of hedge funds and the amount of hedge fund assets that can generate enough alpha to command high fees.

It truly is amazing to watch a data set go from being an alpha to a beta over time. I've seen the sell-side analyst estimates data set owned by Thomson Reuters IBES travel this path over the past 15 years. Yes, there will always be alpha available to be arbitraged which is associated with the irrational behavior of humans in markets, but most alpha generated by systematic traders is associated with an informational advantage.

About five years ago many of the classic stat-arb strategies stopped working due to an influx of competitors. There simply wasn't enough alpha to go around. This precipitated the smartest firms to search for new data sets with predictive power, or reflexivity. Fast-forward a few years and an all out arms race is now under way.

I love to use the example of the company that is selling data captured from new car insurance registrations. They get this data daily, and it's incredibly accurate at calling new car sales. So instead of waiting until the end of the quarter to find out how many vehicles GM sold, you can basically get a running count of growth on a daily basis. Obviously that's going to give you an advantage in trading those auto names, that is until everyone else is using that data. At that point, the data set goes from providing alpha you can capture, to a data set that you must be looking at in order to avoid an informational disadvantage. In a sense, it becomes beta.

So the arms race is in full swing, and there is now a serious lack of qualified talent to analyze all of these different data sets and incorporate them into the existing multi-factor models. While the quantitative research process into the efficacy of a data set hasn't changed much, firms are struggling to build a process around the testing pipeline. The most efficient firms like WorldQuant have been able to take advantage of that competency to move quickly and decisively to incorporate new alphas.

This brings me to my last point about the systematic testing process. In the next section of this article, I'm going to heavily malign the discretionary buy-side for being fairly clueless about how to undertake this entire process. The truth is, even most (but not all) systematic quants suffer from a severe lack of creativity and original thought when it comes to generating hypotheses around how to take advantage of a given data set. From our experience working with discretionary firms at Estimize, they are two steps even further behind the quants as it relates to incorporating new data sets.

Let's just go back to the car sales example for a second. Would you know exactly how to take advantage of that data to run an event study and generate alpha? Probably not. You'd likely want to talk with someone who's been trading autos for ten plus years to get their take on what they think moves auto stocks and how having a good projection of sales would impact those names. A good quantitative research process requires an ex-ante hypothesis for some level of causation and not just correlation. We need to know roughly why something works, not just that it works, or else we won't know why it stops working, and as history has proven, everything stops working at some point.

Being able to hand over an easily testable clean data set, and a bunch of original thoughts about how to generate alpha, is imperative for data firms to succeed at this process.

5. Quantamental, Systamental, Factor Aware... Call It What You Want

The rise of the systematic quants and their use of these new data sets also had an impact on the poor returns of the discretionary world over recent years. First, the HFT guys killed the day traders making it impossible to pick up pennies. Next, the stat-arb guys crushed the swing traders playing in the couple of hours to one week timeframe. Were they the primary factor of poor discretionary returns? Probably not, but significant none of the less.

A few years ago the first big discretionary firms started making attempts to hire data scientists and acquire new data sources. They've mostly failed to integrate any of this into an actual investment process. Then in the second half of 2016 another chunk of the more forward thinking discretionary firms gave in to the realization that they needed to make big changes. It's not as if discretionary PMs weren't using data driven statistical approaches to gain an edge, or that none of them had quants on the desk to help, they were just very few and far between.

You may have seen Paul Tudor Jones almost publicly berating his organization in a strange showing of frustration from such a legendary investor. Steve Cohen has been very public about his attempt to shift Point72 in the data driven direction, even commenting that it's incredibly hard to find good talent these days (we'll get to this in a minute). The guys who have been successful in this game historically see the writing on the wall. Hell, even the first episode of season two for the show *Billions* features main character Bobby "Axe" Axelrod giving his team the condensed three-minute version of this piece, albeit in a much louder tone. So whomever the producers of that show are talking to, this whole thing has seeped into the mainstream buy-side consciousness now.

The shift that needs to happen is similar to the way players were drafted in Michael Lewis' book, *Moneyball*. Consider how hard the scouts fought against being replaced by algorithms that were far more accurate than they were, and even in the face of all this evidence, refusing to change. Then consider how much money was on the line in baseball, and the astronomically larger amount on the line in our world. You would think that would precipitate a much quicker shift, but in fact, it will only mean a slower one due to the fear of change when dealing with so much money.

As quants, we are taught how to go through the research process to validate the efficacy of a data set or tool. Everything is derived from this process, and there isn't too much leeway, it is designed as good science. Yes, as mentioned above, you still need a level of creativity in order to do good research. However, discretionary managers don't even have the framework for understanding how to do that research, or incorporate new things into their decision making process. This is the largest hurdle to making the shift, and I believe less than 20% of managers will clear it.

This shift isn't just about using new data sets, like Estimize, or the car sales example, it's about fundamentally buying into the notion that PMs need to be making investment decisions based on putting the odds in their favor by looking at statistics, and not just being gunslingers or bottoms up value guys. That's an affront to their entire way of doing things, just as it was for the baseball scouts.

6. Algorithms + Human Experience = Optimal Trading

A passage from Michael Lewis' latest book, *The Undoing Project*, speaks so directly to the issue discretionary firms face today. Lewis writes about a specific behavioral experiment performed on a set of first year residents and accomplished oncologists. In the experiment, the scientists asked the accomplished doctors to tell them how they make a decision regarding whether a patient has cancer from looking at an X-ray. The doctors all tended to give the scientists a ten-point checklist with a 1–10 rating for each of the ten points, add up the points and you can accurately determine whether it's cancer or benign. The scientists proceed to give a set of X-rays (the outcomes of which are known only to them) to the doctors and the residents, asking them to determine whether each is cancer or not. They also give the doctor's checklist to the residents to use.

I think you can guess what happens next. The oncologists who supplied the rubric in the first place show almost zero ability above random to accurately determine whether the X-ray was cancer or not. They didn't follow their own rubric, suffered from an astounding amount of representative heuristic, and failed to do their job well. Meanwhile, the first year residents were able to score far higher accuracy rates on average and therefore would have been able to help their patients. They were simply acting as the human measurement component of an algorithm.

Similarly, most discretionary PMs would likely supply a rubric for how they make decisions, but when it comes down to it, they don't actually adhere to it. No set of new data or analytical tools thrown into the "mosaic of information" that the PM is supposed to be paying attention to will matter unless they are disciplined enough to remove their ego from the equation and reduce themselves to being a human algorithm.

There's an inevitable question that arises from the above, what's the point of the human PM if we're going to ask humans to basically be algorithms? Why not just run a fully systematic strategy and remove the human all together after the quantitative research process is complete? Could a first year analyst and some good portfolio construction software more faithfully execute the signals than a PM with 20 years of experience? Science would seem to say yes. That said, there's obviously a more optimal scenario where that 20 years of experience alongside the discipline to execute the rubric faithfully results in better outcomes due to the ability to see regime changes in the market, something quantitative strategies built on linear analysis have a hard time doing.

It's my belief that good quantamental/systamental/factor-aware PMs can crush the systematic quants if they are disciplined. Systematic strategies are designed to make small bets across a lot of names using half a dozen or more different signals that each have a weighting in the stock selection and exposure model. A lot of them hit for singles, consistently. But that also means that when a really fat pitch comes down the plate based on all the data, they can't swing for the fences. This is the advantage of discretionary managers. With the right discipline, they can take a big cut with a 7% position in their book when all the data lines up, and reap the rewards of the hard work.

While it's been a tough run of it recently, there are reasons to believe this is a great time to enter the market with a solid quantitative approach to discretionary trading. While there may be many secular headwinds for the discretionary investing world at the time of writing, the cyclical nature of this industry is extremely strong, and we're certainly at the deepest part of the trough regarding performance, with only one direction to go.

7. There's Plenty of Talent, You're Just Hiring the Wrong People

The last part of this puzzle is obviously the people. And here's the sad truth: the way that discretionary hedge funds have staffed themselves historically is almost criminal (there were actually some real criminals in there too!).

Picture the normal funnel to becoming a PM running a $500m long/short equity book. You grew up in a wealthy family in a wealthy town, usually in the New York metropolitan area, parts of Silicon Valley, Chicago or Michigan. You went to Harvard, Yale or Princeton. You took an IB analyst position at Goldman or another bulge bracket. You spent a few years there learning how to build a financial model before a hedge fund picked you up for an analyst spot. You made friends with your PM, who if you were lucky did well, and five years later when the firm had more capital than it knew what to do with, your PM told the firm to give you $200m to play with.

At no point in this process did you ever have to exhibit a lick of skill for the job that you've just been given. Yes, you are probably a very smart individual, and you worked hard, but we all know that smart does not equal good in the investment world. Every step along the way you were selected not for the trait which would make you the best qualified to do that job, you were selected because you jumped through the hoops which lead to the correct selection bias. The sad truth is that hedge funds are run by white dudes who grew up in Greenwich, and they like (and trust) working with white dudes who grew up in Greenwich and look like them.

And look, this isn't some idealistic push for equality bullshit comment, it's about results. If you are hiring these people exclusively, you are not selecting for skill and you will not be able to make the shift to a more data driven quantitative approach, I guarantee it. If I were starting a fund from scratch, I'd rather have a more racially, socioeconomically diverse group of kids from schools other than the Ivy's than those from Yale who studied political science.

And don't get me started on the lack of women running money. Every single study ever done says that they are more successful than men due to a range of behavioral and psychological factors. Yet firms tend to overlook women for PM positions due to their inability to play the game that gets them the capital allocation. And of course, we come back to the fact that the entire industry is designed to hire for people that look like the people who are currently in charge.

Firms need to start incorporating measurement of variables pre-hiring that actually correlate to success as a PM. They need to start selecting for skill, not just smarts. Our Forcerank platform is beginning to be used for this purpose, and I expect others will pop up over time. I also expect some kind of psychometric testing firm to be created soon which has done the research to identify certain skills and traits that correspond to success in different strategies. You don't want the same kind of people running momentum models as the ones running deep value.

There isn't a lack of talent, you just need to look in the right places and be willing to elevate people who might not look, talk, or act like you.

8. Building the Right Team

The other major personnel issue we're seeing firms grapple with is the question of how to structure their teams to incorporate the quantitative research and data science capability. Some approaches have been successful, and others have failed.

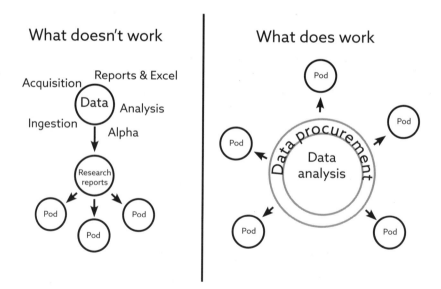

Each firm, whether quant or discretionary, is going to need a centralized infrastructure that is capable of imbibing a new data set and making it available across the firm. Many systematic multi-manager funds, and large centralized managers are already setting up data teams to search for, ingest, clean, and quickly analyze new data sets to test for alpha in their multi-factor models. The heads of these teams are getting paid big dollars, upwards of $2m a year to run this process that feeds the heart of the machine—and there aren't many good ones out there. The imbalance of supply and demand for this position is causing some funds to make poor hiring decisions in order to simply get someone in the door. The role itself is incredibly multidisciplinary in nature and requires a strong understanding of the quantitative research process, a decent technical background, the ability to travel across the globe to conferences meeting with hundreds of potential vendors, sniffing out what's real from what's bullshit, determining what start-ups will be around tomorrow and which won't, and then haggling over price. Please tell me which previous role prepares you for all of that?

The firms that don't hire well here are going to fall behind and see their returns suffer as data sets more quickly than ever move from being alphas to betas as they get arbed. This doesn't happen overnight, it takes years for alpha to get arbitraged from a data set, but many won't have as much capacity as those previously, along with a larger stable of systematic managers, things will speed up.

The centralized infrastructure and data acquisition team is going to also house engineers, a product manager, and optimally a quant who can do basic descriptive work on a data set to determine whether it's clean and reliable enough to have PMs use.

And that's where the centralized team should end.

Each PM or "pod" should then have a quant, an engineer or two, and a data analyst placed on their desk directly. Here's why. Each PM is going to be trading different names, and have a need to access different sets of information. Fighting over centralized quantitative research capacity with other pods is a disaster. And then receiving some kind of report that doesn't fit into your actual process is useless. Each PM is going to have a different checklist or rubric with different signals. And the key is the data analyst, they need to have a deep understanding of the industries the PM is trading so that they can work in coordination with the PM and the quant to build a process that can be effectively utilized. I've seen people in this role who also have some coding experience so that they can rapidly prototype stuff for the quant before the centralized team goes out and does the job in a production-ready way. The quant, of course, will be testing different data sets for efficacy, and handing them over to the engineers to build factor models.

A quantitative approach and a commitment to data science by firms is not a thing you do in some other room. The only way this is going to work is if you build cross functional teams on the PM's desk and support them with a data and infrastructure team at the top.

How Far Down the Rabbit Hole?

So if you're a PM, do you need to take that data science class at night? Yes, but not for the reason you think. PMs aren't going to be writing python code and working in R to do quantitative research, that's not their job. But in order to effectively communicate and run their teams they are going to have to understand all the pieces to the process. And most of all, if they aren't educated as to how all of this works, how are they ever going to trust the data and signals coming out of the process when the time comes to make buy and sell decisions?

This is the entirety of a three part series that was originally published by Integrity Research and titled "The Great Quant Makeover - Part 1: How Discretionary Managers Can Cope with the New Systematic Realities," "Part 2: The Rise of the Quants and How Some Successful Discretionary Managers are Responding," "Part 3: Revenge of the Humans or How Discretionary Managers Can Crush Systematics."

Part 2 of this article, "Revenge of the Humans Part II: A New Blueprint For Discretionary Management," can be found on LinkedIn: linkedin.com/pulse/revenge-humans-part-ii-new-blueprint-discretionary-leigh-drogen.

Originally published May 11, 2017; blog.estimize.com/post/160556636987/revenge-of-the-humans-how-discretionary-managers.

ABOUT LEIGH DROGEN

Leigh Drogen is the Founder and CEO at Estimize.

@LDrogen

"Passive" Investing: Theory and Practice in a Global Market

JONATHAN SEED

Purely passive investing is theoretically plausible, but practically impossible. That said, the practical implementations can often be "good enough."

As a theoretical index investor, you deploy capital passively, take a long snooze, and wake up some day to consume your portfolio.

Unfortunately, the world doesn't work like. Allocations change because life happens, and as we cover in this blog post, there are really no indexes that are truly passive.

For example, recently the index giant FTSE Russell proposed to exclude the popular social media app, Snapchat, from its index. In fact, in their memo any company with no voting rights (like Snap) could be excluded from their indexes.[1] This is something that other large index providers have also discussed. The knee-jerk reaction might be, "Who cares about Snapchat?" Well, there is a "small" firm called Alphabet (e.g. "Google" as most know it), a stock representing over 1% of the S&P 500, and their shareholders have effectively no voting rights.[2] So perhaps this is a big deal?

This recent example is a good anecdote, but there are arguably even bigger issues. Consider index investors invested in many Emerging Market ETFs, like Vanguard's VWO. These investors may notice that

---

[1]   www.ftse.com/products/index-notices/home/getmethodology/?id=2122858
[2]   bit.ly/2KMUCgn

they don't own Chinese internet juggernauts Alibaba and Baidu, either.[3] But if index investors think they can go back to sleep after finding a fund like the MSCI Emerging Market ETF (ticker: EEM), that *does* include Chinese overseas listings like Alibaba, perhaps they should be made aware of MSCI's most recent proposal.[4] MSCI will likely continue to largely ignore the $7 trillion dollar China A-shares market comprising most Chinese domestic companies. Instead of the near 40%[5] of their emerging markets index holding A-shares, China could maintain its more modest 28–29% weighting in the MSCI Emerging Markets Index.

The below pie charts are where we now are likely to stand with MSCI:

Pro-Forma Weight of A-Shares Based on New Connect Based Proposal

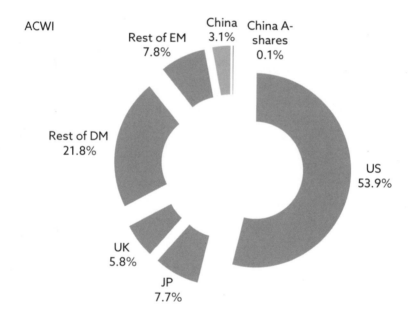

ACWI

Rest of EM 7.8% · China 3.1% · China A-shares 0.1% · US 53.9% · JP 7.7% · UK 5.8% · Rest of DM 21.8%

---

[3] Alibaba, at $350bn, is China's second largest company by market cap and 10% of its investable market. FTSE and by extension the Vanguard Emerging Market ETF VWO started to include Alibaba in October 2017, after the initial publication of this article.

[4] bit.ly/2KLzdUA

[5] bit.ly/2Io9ES1

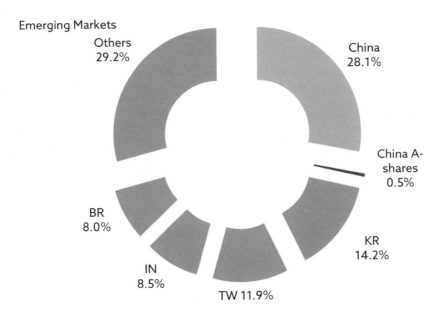

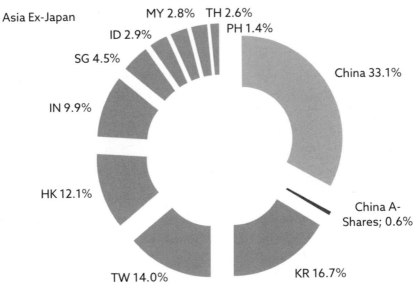

If this all seems pretty arbitrary, well, that's because the process is fairly arbitrary. But a natural question is whether or not these details matter for the passive investor? Are these passive approximations good enough?

Let's take a step back with a little theory before we address this question.

The Theoretical Global Market Portfolio

Modern Portfolio Theory (MPT) argues that a rational investor who cared about minimizing volatility while maximizing returns should own the so-called "global market portfolio." Of course, a major assumption (of many) underlying all of this is that markets are efficient—a highly contentious assumption.[6]

The challenge is that the global market portfolio theoretically includes every risk asset, including everything from your human capital to Afghanistan Light-Rail Bonds.[7] These probably don't exist, but you get the point. Setting aside incredibly esoteric assets that probably don't have much weight in the theoretical global market portfolio, we will own the investable universe. The research suggests there is a 91 trillion dollar investable universe (as calculated by Doeswijk, et al 2014[8]) and the portfolio looks something like the following.

Perhaps surprisingly, only 40% is tied up in public/private equity and roughly 29% is in government bonds. To simplify the chart even further, you have ~40% equity, ~30% government bonds, and ~30% "other." Dumping 30% into government bonds is not exactly appealing given the historically current low and often negative yields on government bonds. Only a 40% allocation to equities, in contrast, seems light given their historical high risk adjusted returns. So in theory this allocation makes sense, but in practice this might be questionable. Luckily, theory and practice don't need to clash.

---

[6] See bit.ly/2KKaYWS.

[7] Eugene F. Fama, and Merton H. Miller, *The Theory of Finance* (Holt, Rinehart & Winston, 1972), pp. 20–1.

[8] www.cfapubs.org/doi/abs/10.2469/faj.v70.n2.1

Estimated Market Values (US$ trillions) and Weights in the Global Market Portfolio at the End of 2012

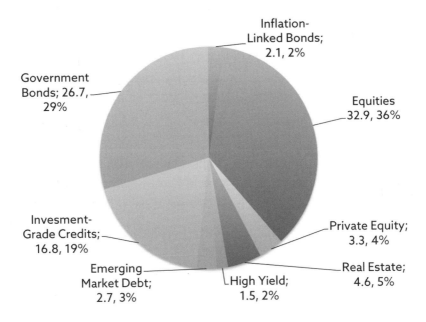

Nobel Laurette Gene Fama told the Chicago Booth Magazine on his 50th anniversary at Booth[9] that the best advice he ever got, from Harry Roberts, was that:

> You do empirical work to learn from the data…but no hypothesis that you ever test is strictly true…

Likewise, although we need perfect capital markets to truly test the hypotheses stemming from Modern Portfolio Theory (MPT), the proxies for the global market portfolio—often constructed by CRSP, S&P, MSCI or FTSE—can be considered "close enough."[10] Consider by analogy (used by Fama) that true predictions coming from the laws of motion require a perfect vacuum: Does an anvil falling from the Earth's sky, instead of an anvil falling through a vacuum to replicate the theoretically correct environment to measure gravity, change your reaction to step aside?

---

9   "Father of Modern Finance," *Chicago Booth Magazine*, Fall 2013, www. chicagobooth.edu/magazine/35/3/feature4.aspx
10   Fama, and Miller, *Theory of Finance*, p. 22.

Likewise, an inability to replicate the perfect global market portfolio doesn't mean we shouldn't attempt to achieve this goal of maximizing diversification via indexing.

The Global Market Portfolio in Practice

Let's start with the equity vs fixed income mix. The standard 60/40 split between equities and fixed income for a moderately risk adverse investor still seems an "adequate" start. An investor can adjust from there according to his/her risk tolerance and cash flow needs.

But peeling back the onion a bit further, what should allocations look like within the equity bucket? In other words, what does the global market portfolio theory say about our international stock exposure?

Composition of the Global Stock Market: More International than U.S.

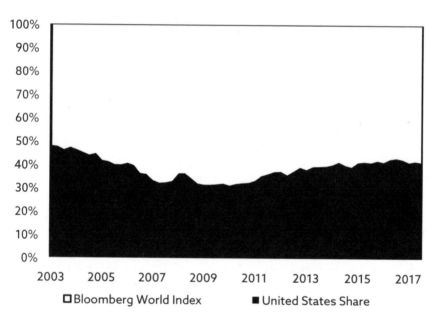

International equity as measured by Bloomberg now represents well over half of the global equity portfolio (~59% as of March 2018) so should theoretically represent the majority of an investor's equity exposure if they are trying to allocate to the global market portfolio (largely because of its lower weight in China and adjustments for free float, MSCI measures the US weight as 52%).[11] A 59% international equities as measured by Bloomberg feels high and judging from other investors who have only 21% invested internationally, I'm not the only one with a home bias.[12] So many of us aren't following the theoretical advice presented by the academia. Of course, if we blindly followed the advice of the global market portfolio allocations, then back in 1989 more of your holdings would have been held in Japan than in the US.[13] Any investor with equity allocations based on global market weights would have been shot following the epic Japanese equity market fallout in the ensuing three years (they've probably been beat up the past few years as well, as US equity has dominated while international returns have been lacklustre).

Allocate 59% to International Equities? Or is there Wiggle Room?

In theory, we should have our equity book roughly 59% allocated to international markets. But is that an iron-clad rule? Perhaps not. Adding to the argument against a full theoretical allocation to international equities, a team from AQR shows that the volatility of currencies can swamp the diversification benefits in AQR's "Risk Without Reward" white paper.[14] Correlations between currencies and US equities are found to be just too unstable, and often positive.

Vanguard also takes look at the question of optimal international diversification. While Vanguard recognizes that the diversification benefits of international equities are real, they suggest that anywhere between 20–40% is "adequate." Vanguard buttresses this conclusion by showing that most of the benefits of international equity diversification dissipates quickly.[15] So perhaps the "theoretical" allocation isn't a hard and fast rule?

11 bit.ly/2rx5d6l
12 vgi.vg/2IrIzGR
13 The scale to which depends on your source, bit.ly/2KLzWoM.
14 bit.ly/2KO6xuk
15 advisors.vanguard.com/iwe/pdf/ISGGAA.pdf

Concluding Thoughts

There are theories and then there are practical realities. Theoretically I should have 1 basis point allocated to Afghani Light-Rail-Bonds, but practically accessing that paper probably isn't worth it for my portfolio. (Or my life expectancy!)

In this short piece, I highlight the concept of the global market portfolio, identify some of the recommendations stemming from this theoretical construct, and discuss some arguments for why we may not need to consider this theory the gospel. The general takeaway is that we often invest in markets in a theoretically suboptimal way, but in a way that is adequate from a practical standpoint. We also focused on equity allocations. Fixed income can get trickier. The 17.4 trillion dollars of bonds represented by the Bloomberg Barclays Aggregate Index is less than half of the investable $39.1 trillion universe of US domestic bonds (as reported by Guggenheim).[16] Is the AGG index good enough? Or do we need to dig deep into the 39.1 trillion dollars to maintain our tie with the global market portfolio's theory? Possibly, but perhaps not. We can punt that discussion to another article.

In the end, investors should focus on what they can measure and control with more certainty, namely fees and taxes. Luckily, that task doesn't take a PhD (or a high priced investment advisor). Most ETFs are already structured to minimize capital gains and have relatively low fees. Tax loss harvesting strategies[17] and maximizing the tax deferral nature of 401Ks and IRAs are also straightforward.[18] So forget about optimizing your portfolio to match a global market portfolio construct and go back to sleep. You probably won't miss much during your slumber.

Originally published June 14, 2017; alphaarchitect.com/2017/06/14/passive-investing-theory-practice-global-market.

---

[16]   bit.ly/2rvwG9g
[17]   bit.ly/2I1XWGK
[18]   bit.ly/2K4uw7d

ABOUT JONATHAN SEED

Jonathan Seed began his career at Franklin Resources where he was an Assistant Portfolio Manager for their then quantitative asset arm, Franklin Asset Management Systems. There, he helped build value biased equity portfolios. After graduating with honors from the University of Chicago Booth School of Business, he began a 20 year career on Wall Street focused on fixed income, with an emphasis on structured products. He started in fixed income research before switching to institutional sales, leaving Credit Suisse as Managing Director in 2009 for RBS Securities and leaving the industry altogether in 2014, after which he started Seed Wealth Management, Inc., a Registered Investment Advisor incorporated in the state of Illinois.

A Smoother Path to Outperformance with Multi-Factor Smart Beta Investing

CHRIS BRIGHTMAN, VITALI KALESNIK, FEIFEI LI AND JOSEPH SHIM

Key Points

- Researchers have identified hundreds of factors that purport to predict equity returns; we find a half dozen that provide an opportunity to outperform the market.

- To maximize risk-adjusted returns, diversify across smart beta strategies that access the value, low beta, profitability, investment, momentum, and size factors.

- Systematic rebalancing to fixed weights—reducing exposure to popular factors that have outperformed over recent years, while increasing exposure to the out-of-favor factors that have underperformed—in a portfolio of smart betas will likely improve performance relative to a buy-and-hold weighting.

- Dynamically rebalancing factor exposures using short-term momentum and long-term reversal signals further improves the return.

Factor investing, also called smart beta, is rapidly displacing traditional stock picking—and for good reason. Traditional active management of equity mutual funds has delivered returns persistently below passive benchmarks. In contrast, many factor-based smart beta strategies have persistently outperformed the same capitalization-weighted benchmarks. As you consider migrating your public equity holdings away from traditional active management to smart beta, two portfolio construction questions come to the fore: which smart beta strategies should you include, and how should you manage those strategy allocations through time? We find that a smart beta strategy diversified across factors substantially reduces tracking error relative to the average of the single-factor strategies, and dynamic rebalancing materially increases expected return relative to rebalancing to equal weights.

US Multi-Factor Smart Beta Strategies Value-Add and Tracking Error, Jul 1973–Sep 2016

Source: Research Affiliates, LLC, using data from CRSP and Compustat.

Look Before You Leap

The advantages associated with systematic factor investing, such as low costs and transparency, have driven rapid growth in the number of smart beta funds. At the end of 2015 we counted more than 800 smart beta ETFs, not including mutual funds, separately managed accounts, and other investment vehicles. This nascent smart beta category does not come without its challenges, however.

Many factors are mirages that result from datamining. According to Harvey, Liu, and Zhu's (2015) survey of the literature, top-tier academic journals document over 300 distinct factors and the number grows every year. We are not surprised. Professional success of an army of professors, assistant professors, and graduate students depends on publishing articles that "discover" new factors. Because the number of potential factors is practically unlimited, and stock price changes are largely random, hundreds of false positives are inevitable. To combat these datamining outcomes, academia is increasing the pressure on publications to institute stricter criteria in evaluating research that purports to identify new factors.

Many seemingly robust factors are simply exhausted past opportunities. Active quantitative investors are constantly searching for investment opportunities, and by the time academic researchers document a factor, investors have often already recognized it and deployed sufficient capital to eliminate its future profitability. No surprise that MacLean and Pontiff (2015) document significant reduction of factor efficacy after publication.

Some otherwise robust factors may even be dangerous. After a factor strategy has proved sufficiently profitable, investment flows attracted by its popularity can drive up the prices of stocks with that factor characteristic. Factors thereby become overvalued. Arnott, Beck, and Kalesnik (2016a,b) and Arnott et al. (2016) empirically demonstrate that strategies with rich valuations tend to provide poor subsequent performance. To avoid such underperformance, we suggest you look before you leap.

The Distinction between Factors and Smart Betas

Before we continue, let's clarify how we define the following terms: factor, factor portfolio, smart beta, and smart beta strategy. *Factor* is a generic label for company and stock price characteristics that provide the common sources of return across the broad universe of equity securities.

We construct *factor portfolios* to measure and study factor returns. Factor portfolios are long stocks with the desired characteristic and short stocks with the undesired characteristic. For example, the value factor portfolio is long cheap stocks and short expensive stocks, and the size factor portfolio is long small stocks and short large stocks. An investor cannot practically invest in factor portfolios because of restrictions on shorting and leverage.

Smart beta is a label for simple, transparent, low-cost, systematic investment strategies, often designed to exploit factor research. *Smart beta strategies* are long-only portfolios that can be carefully engineered to avoid excessive implementation costs. Smart beta strategies are easy and inexpensive to invest in.

The Six Factors with the Most Robust Returns

Our research leads us to conclude that only a handful of factors represent genuine future return opportunities—strategies with the potential to outperform in the decades ahead. Following the findings of Fama and French (1993, 2012, 2015), we include in this group of six the four factors in their current model (looking beyond the market factor)—value, profitability, investment, and size—as well as low beta and momentum, two factors widely deemed robust in academic publications (Frazzini and Pedersen, 2014, and Carhart, 1997).

We construct these six factor portfolios in accordance with widely accepted academic practice. We summarize our factor portfolio construction method in Appendix A. All six factors demonstrate both statistically and practically significant returns. The average annualized factor return in the United States over our study period July 1973–September 2016 is 4.86%. The correlations across these factor returns are predominantly low or negative, with an average cross-correlation of 0.08, suggesting they are independent and thus able to provide strong diversification benefits.

In Appendix B we replicate the same six factor portfolios in three international markets—Japan, the United Kingdom, and Europe ex UK—over the period July 1993–September 2016. We choose these markets for their lengthy history and homogeneity of corporate domicile. Whereas not all factors display positive returns in all geographies, taken as a group the factors do show consistently strong out-of-sample returns. We intend to elaborate on our research validating these six factors in future publications; many of our detailed research findings on these equity factors are beyond the scope of this article.

Performance Characteristics of US Long–Short Portfolios for the Most Accepted Factors in Academic Literature, Jul 1973–Sep 2016

Strategy	Annualized Return	Annualized Volatility	Sharpe Ratio	t-stat (Return)
Value	3.70%	10.0%	0.37	2.69
Low Beta	10.13	11.7	0.86	5.81
Profitability	2.63	8.0	0.33	2.38
Investment	3.74	6.6	0.56	3.87
Momentum	6.18	15.5	0.40	3.08
Size	2.80	10.4	0.27	2.11
Average	4.86	10.4	0.47	3.32

Cross-Correlation between Factor Returns, United States, Jul 1973–Sep 2016

	Value	Low Beta	Profitability	Investment	Momentum	Size
Value	1.00	0.32	0.09	0.54	-0.20	0.01
Low Beta	0.32	1.00	0.31	0.19	0.23	0.01
Profitability	0.09	0.31	1.00	-0.13	0.13	-0.43
Investment	0.54	0.19	-0.13	1.00	0.06	0.08
Momentum	-0.20	0.23	0.13	0.06	1.00	-0.02
Size	0.01	0.01	-0.43	0.08	-0.02	1.00

Source: Research Affiliates, LLC, using data from CRSP and Compustat.

A Few Observations about Factors

Drawing on the abundant literature dealing with factors, as well as our own research, we can make several observations relevant to factor portfolio construction; we refer primarily here to the US market. First, the low beta factor's exceptionally strong return can be explained in part by its rising valuations. From today's baseline of elevated prices in low-volatility stocks, the low beta factor may well provide disappointing returns over the next decade.

A second observation is that, on its own, profitability generates a low return. Despite its low return, however, profitability's low and negative correlation with the other factors makes it a helpful addition to a diversified portfolio of factor strategies. Perhaps for this reason many smart beta providers combine profitability with other characteristics to create a composite quality factor.[1]

We also observe the relatively strong correlation between value and investment factor returns, which suggests that in combination the two factors may be redundant. This higher correlation is primarily the result of similar sector exposures. But, controlling for sector composition, we find that value and investment are robust independent factors.

We find that smaller stocks do not necessarily provide higher returns than larger stocks, consistent with Shumway and Warther (1999). We find that small size does provide such excess returns, however, when combined with other factors. Beck and Kalesnik (2014) argue that other factors provide stronger returns when applied to small companies because of the higher volatility and less-efficient pricing of small stocks. Similarly, Asness et al. (2015) find a strong factor return from a small-size factor after controlling for the quality characteristics of the issuing companies.

Finally, the factor returns demonstrated by academics using long–short portfolios offer an unrealistic assessment of the returns an investor is likely to earn in practice. The returns are before trading costs such as price impact, the cost of shorting stocks, and management fees. These real-world costs are not identical across all factors; Novy–Marx and Velikov (2015) and Beck et al. (2016) find that for some factors the trading costs are high enough to wipe out all the benefits, even if the strategy does not attract a large following.

Factor-Based Smart Betas

The prospect of an average annualized excess return of nearly 5% across six robust and largely independent factors helps explain the strong investor demand for factor investing. Alas, as we explained in the introduction, factor portfolios are impractical real-world investment strategies due to

---

[1]   Beck et al. (2016) find various specifications of a quality factor are not robust to variations in factor definition and market geography. In a follow-up article to Beck et al., Hsu, Kalesnik, and Kose (2017) examine subgroups within the broad "quality" umbrella, finding that among the many characteristics used to define quality, only profitability and investment are robust to variations in factor definition and market geography.

constraints on shorting and leverage. We can, however, apply our factor research to create simple, transparent, low-cost smart beta strategies that you can easily and inexpensively invest in.

We illustrate the opportunities for investing in real-world factor-based strategies by constructing six very simple long-only investable portfolios: value, low beta, profitability, investment, momentum, and size. Our factor-based smart beta portfolio construction methodology is explained in Appendix C.

As expected, real-world constraints dramatically reduce the simulated outperformance of our factor-based smart beta strategies relative to long–short factor portfolios. Yet the evidence of robustness remains impressive. The historical results for the US market suggest investors can earn an average value-add of 2.19% a year across these six smart beta strategies. The average tracking error is 7.10% and the average information ratio is 0.30. Most strategies produce results which pass tests of statistical significance at 95% confidence. A couple do not.

Out-of-sample robustness tests in Japan, United Kingdom, and Europe ex UK provide confirming, if somewhat weaker, evidence. Most strategies earn an excess return over the market benchmark, but in each of the international markets we study, a couple of the factor-based smart beta strategies generate mildly negative value-add. The average value-add of the six strategies remains well above 1.00% a year in all three out-of-sample geographies.

Correlations across our six smart betas are generally low and sometimes negative. Nine of the 15 strategy correlations of our six smart betas in the United States are near zero or negative, with an average excess return cross-correlation of 0.02. As with the six factors, these factor-based strategies capture independent sources of return and should provide strong benefits from diversification.

We confidently conclude from our study of factors that such smart beta strategies offer a significant opportunity for future value-add relative to the capitalization-weighted equity market. The magnitude of opportunity is in line with the historical simulation results we present here. Our decade of success in producing strong value-add, after fees and expenses, in live smart beta portfolios for many billions of dollars invested by real investors adds to our conviction.

Performance Characteristics of US Long-Only Factor-Based Smart Betas, Jul 1973–Sep 2016

Strategy	Annualized Return	Annualized Volatility	Sharpe Ratio	Value-Add	Tracking Error	IR	t-stat (VA)
Market	11.05%	15.60%	0.40				
Value	13.37	18.50	0.46	2.32%	9.35%	0.25	1.83
Low Beta	13.43	12.60	0.68	2.39	8.03	0.30	1.41
Profitability	11.26	15.00	0.43	0.21	3.25	0.07	0.20
Investment	13.70	15.40	0.58	2.65	5.10	0.52	3.01
Momentum	13.41	17.10	0.50	2.36	6.82	0.35	2.29
Size	14.23	19.90	0.47	3.19	10.03	0.32	2.39
Average of Six Factors	13.23%	16.40%	0.52	2.19%	7.10%	0.30	1.85

Cross-Correlation between Factor Excess Returns, United States, Jul 1973–Sep 2016

	Value	Low Beta	Profitability	Investment	Momentum	Size
Value	1.00	0.23	-0.33	0.42	-0.18	0.23
Low Beta	0.23	1.00	0.07	0.42	-0.06	0.06
Profitability	-0.33	0.07	1.00	0.01	0.13	-0.59
Investment	0.42	0.42	0.01	1.00	-0.09	-0.05
Momentum	-0.18	-0.06	0.13	-0.09	1.00	0.05
Size	0.23	0.06	-0.59	-0.05	0.05	1.00

Note: VA is value-add.

Source: Research Affiliates, LLC, using data from CRSP and Compustat.

Additional Risk Measures for US Long-Only Factor-Based Smart Betas, Jul 1973–Sep 2016

Strategy	Absolute Risk			Relative Risk		
	Skewness	Maximum Drawdown	Longest Drawdown (Years)	Skewness	Maximum Drawdown	Longest Drawdown (Years)
Market	-0.52	-50%	5.3			
Value	-0.58	-63	6.3	-0.05	-37%	15.0+
Low Beta	-0.51	-37	3.3	0.10	-57	22.2
Profitability	-0.38	-43	5.3	0.17	-24	25.2
Investment	-0.34	-49	3.4	0.27	-21	12.7+
Momentum	-0.43	-48	5.3	-0.31	-21	11.0
Size	-0.50	-54	3.5	0.52	-52	20.0
Average of Six Factors	-0.46	-49%	4.5	0.12	-35%	17.7+

Source: Research Affiliates, LLC, using data from CRSP and Compustat.

Multi-Factor Smart Beta Strategies

The low and negative correlations across the excess returns of the six factor-based smart betas indicates strong diversification benefits by combining the strategies into a multi-factor portfolio. Theory suggests that the returns and value-add of a multi-factor smart beta portfolio should be similar to the average values of the factor strategies, but achieved at significantly lower risk levels. Lower relative risk would also be a reasonable expectation, experienced by lower tracking error and shorter periods of underperformance relative to the market.

We consider three different methods of combining smart beta strategies:

1. **Buy and Hold**: Allocate one-sixth of a portfolio to each of the six factor-based smart beta strategies and do not subsequently rebalance this mix.

2. **Systematic Rebalancing**: Allocate one-sixth of a portfolio to each of the six strategies and then rebalance back to a one-sixth allocation every quarter.

3. **Dynamic Rebalancing**: Set a default weight of one-sixth to each strategy and then modestly tilt allocations based on short-term price momentum and long-term price mean-reversion signals at each quarterly rebalance.

We provide more information about our factor timing methodology in Appendix D.

Performance Characteristics of US Multi-Factor Smart Beta Strategies, Jul 1973–Sep 2016

Strategy	Annualized Return	Annualized Volatility	Sharpe Ratio	Value-Add	Tracking Error	IR	t-stat (VA)
Market	11.05%	15.6%	0.40				
Average of Six Factors	13.23	16.4	0.52	2.19%	7.10%	0.30	1.85
Buy and Hold	13.35	15.6	0.55	2.31	3.82	0.60	3.58
Systematic Rebalancing	13.49	15.2	0.57	2.45	3.41	0.72	4.13
Dynamic Rebalancing	14.21	15.3	0.61	3.16	4.00	0.79	4.58

Additional Risk Measures for US Multi-Factor Smart Beta Strategies, Jul 1973–Sep 2016

Strategy	Absolute Risk			Relative Risk		
	Skewness	Maximum Drawdown	Longest Drawdown (Years)	Skewness	Maximum Drawdown	Longest Drawdown (Years)
Market	-0.52	-50%	5.3			
Average of Six Factors	-0.46	-49	4.5	0.12	-35%	17.7+
Buy and Hold	-0.69	-50	3.8	0.56	-15	8.0+
Systematic Rebalancing	-0.64	-48	3.3	0.84	-15	7.9+
Dynamic Rebalancing	-0.60	-47	3.3	1.00	-13	6.8

Note: VA is value-add.
Source: Research Affiliates, LLC, using data from CRSP and Compustat.

As expected, our diversified multi-factor smart beta strategies provide large and meaningful risk reduction. For the US portfolios, volatility is reduced by a full percentage point, from 16.4% for the average smart beta to between 15.2% and 15.6% for the multi-factor strategies. We cut tracking error in half, from an average of 7.10% to between 3.41%

and 4.00% for the multi-factor portfolios. We double or better our information ratios from 0.30 to between 0.60 and 0.79.

Also, as we expect, buy-and-hold weighting produces value-add relatively close to the average individual factor strategy, 2.31% compared to 2.19%. The advantage of drifting into the highest performing strategy over the sample period is offset by the disadvantage of failing to profit from rebalancing. A move to simple systematic rebalancing to fixed weights increases the value add by 0.14% and 0.26% relative to the buy-and-hold and average factor strategies, respectively. Systematic rebalancing also provides the lowest risk and tracking error by ensuring the most consistent diversification.

Nearly a full percentage point in return, however, is produced by dynamic rebalancing relative to the average individual factor strategy, with value-add rising from 2.19% to 3.16%. The extra value added from dynamic rebalancing relative to systematic rebalancing is also substantial, rising from 2.45% to 3.16%. If we consider trading costs, however, the improvement in value-add erodes slightly. Appendix E provides our method for estimating trading costs when applying the three weighting methods used in creating the diversified multi-factor smart beta strategies in the United States, Japan, United Kingdom, and Europe ex UK.

Importantly, the additional return captured by more strategic rebalancing changes the risk experience. For our US smart beta portfolios, we find that relative to systematic rebalancing, dynamic rebalancing slightly increases volatility and tracking error, but lowers drawdowns and the duration of periods of underperformance. Simply put, higher returns lower relative drawdowns.

As reported in Appendix F, the evidence of risk reduction is similarly strong across geographies, approximately halving tracking error from the range of 8–9% to 3–5%. The value added from both systematic and dynamic rebalancing is also significant relative to the average individual smart beta strategy, adding from about 0.3% to 1.2% of excess return.

Our international evidence does not confirm higher returns from rebalancing relative to a buy-and-hold weighting. In these markets with shorter histories, the benefit of sticking with the strategy with the best in-sample performance (i.e., low beta) offsets the return advantage of systematic rebalancing. We remain convinced that mean reversion will prevail over a long time horizon and that rebalancing will generate higher future returns.

A Smoother Path

You *can* outperform the market by investing in factor-based smart beta strategies, and you can obtain this outperformance with a smoother ride—that is, with substantially lower tracking error and shorter periods of underperformance—when you invest in a diversified portfolio of smart betas. In addition, our findings indicate you should benefit from the highest return and value-add, highest Sharpe and information ratio, and lowest drawdown and shortest period of underperformance if you dynamically rebalance your diversified portfolio of smart betas.[2] Multi-factor equity investing combined with either dynamic or systematic rebalancing is a reliable strategy for outperforming the market without the burden of excessive volatility. We believe the evidence shows a smoother path to outperformance is paved through multi-factor smart beta investing.

Appendix A: Factor Portfolio Construction Methodology

To construct our portfolios in the United States we use the universe of US stocks from the CRSP/Compustat database. We define the US large-cap equity universe as stocks whose market capitalizations are greater than the median market capitalization on the NYSE, and the small-cap universe as stocks whose market capitalizations are smaller than the NYSE median. The US data extend from July 1973 to September 2016.

For international factor portfolios, we use the universe of stocks from the Worldscope/Datastream database. We define the international large-cap equity universe as stocks with market capitalization in the top 90% by cumulative market-cap within their region, where regions are defined as Japan, United Kingdom, and Europe ex UK. The small-cap universe is defined as the bottom 10% by cumulative market-cap. The international data extend from July 1993 to September 2016.

---

[2] We point to further evidence of the benefits of timing smart betas described in the series of articles published by Arnott, Beck, and Kalesnik in 2016.

We divide each universe by the various factor signals to construct desired-characteristic (the long side) and undesired-characteristic (the short side) portfolios. We follow Fama and French (1993, 2012, 2015) in constructing value, size, profitability, investment, and momentum factor portfolios in both large- and small-cap universes. For example, to simulate the large-cap value factor in the United States, we construct the value portfolio from large-cap stocks above the 70th NYSE percentile by book-to-market ratio (desired characteristic), and we construct the growth portfolio from large-cap stocks below the 30th NYSE percentile (undesired characteristic). To simulate the small-value factor in the international markets, we construct the value portfolio from small-cap stocks above the 70th percentile in their respective region (Japan, United Kingdom, and Europe ex UK) by book-to-market ratio, and the growth portfolio from small-cap stocks below the 30thpercentile in their respective region.

Each long-side or short-side portfolio is defined as the equal-weighted average of large- and small-cap portfolios. These portfolios are weighted by market capitalization and rebalanced annually each July, with the exception of momentum, which is rebalanced monthly. The long- and short-side portfolios are then used to form a long–short factor portfolio without leverage. For example, the value factor is the average return on small-value and large-value portfolios minus the average return on small-growth and large-growth portfolios:

$$Value\ Factor = \frac{(Small\ Value + Large\ Value)}{2} - \frac{(Small\ Growth + Large\ Growth)}{2}$$

We follow Frazzini and Pedersen (2014) in constructing the low beta factor. We use the median value as the breakpoint instead of the 70th and 30th percentiles. The high beta and low beta portfolios are weighted by the difference between beta ranks and average rank, and rebalanced monthly. The long–short portfolio is a self-financing zero-beta portfolio with leverage:

$$Low\ Beta\ Factor$$

$$= \frac{1}{Beta\ of\ Low\ Beta\ Portfolio}(Low\ Beta - Risk\ Free)$$

$$- \frac{1}{Beta\ of\ High\ Beta\ Portfolio}(High\ Beta - Risk\ Free)$$

The signals used to sort the various factor portfolios are:

Factor	Signal	Definition
Value	Book-to-Price Ratio	Book Value/Market Cap
Low Beta	Market Beta	Frazzini and Pederson (2014) definition, in which correlation is estimated with five years of daily returns and volatility with one year of daily returns
Profitability	Operating Profitability	Annual revenues minus cost of goods sold, interest expense, and selling, general, and administrative expenses divided by book equity for the last fiscal year
Investment	Change in Assets	Year-over-year percentage change in total assets
Momentum	-12 to -2 Month Return	Prior 12 month returns, skipping most recent month
Size	Market Cap	Market Cap

Source: Research Affiliates, LLC.

Note that slight variations in data cleaning and lagging could lead to slight differences between our factors and those of Fama and French and of Frazzini and Pedersen.

Appendix B: International Markets Factor Portfolios and Smart Beta Strategies

Performance Characteristics of Long–Short Factor Portfolios, International Markets, Jul 1993–Sep 2016

Strategy	Annualized Excess Return	Annualized Volatility	Sharpe Ratio	t-stat (Return)
Japan				
Value	5.66%	10.5%	0.54	2.78
Low Beta	4.64	14.9	0.31	1.83
Profitability	-1.79	9.4	-0.19	-0.70
Investment	-0.24	8.7	-0.03	0.08
Momentum	1.45	17.1	0.09	0.84
Size	-0.11	10.8	-0.01	0.21
United Kingdom				
Value	1.74%	13.3%	0.13	0.94
Low Beta	8.96	18.2	0.49	2.73
Profitability	8.40	12.8	0.66	3.36
Investment	2.87	9.0	0.32	1.73
Momentum	14.62	23.6	0.62	3.40
Size	1.79	10.8	0.17	1.05
Europe ex UK				
Value	3.68%	10.3%	0.36	1.94
Low Beta	15.94	13.2	1.21	5.77
Profitability	2.40	6.2	0.39	1.99
Investment	3.01	8.1	0.37	1.96
Momentum	13.79	17.8	0.78	3.96
Size	0.72	7.7	0.09	0.63

Source: Research Affiliates, LLC, using data from Worldscope and Datastream.

Performance Characteristics of Long-Only Factor-Based Smart Beta Strategies, International Markets, Jul 1993–Sep 2016

Strategy	Annualized Return	Annualized Volatility	Sharpe Ratio	Value-Add	Tracking Error	IR	t-stat (VA)
Japan							
Market	1.49%	18.0%	-0.06				
Value	6.25	22.6	0.17	4.76%	12.65%	0.38	2.09
Low Beta	3.61	15.0	0.07	2.12	10.37	0.20	0.74
Profitability	0.00	19.0	-0.13	-1.49	4.23	-0.35	-1.47
Investment	0.26	19.7	-0.11	-1.23	7.15	-0.17	-0.60
Momentum	3.22	20.0	0.04	1.73	8.36	0.21	1.18
Size	2.25	21.0	-0.01	0.75	10.82	0.07	0.59
Average of Six Factors	2.60	19.6	0.01	1.11	8.93	0.06	0.42
United Kingdom							
Market	7.50%	16.0%	0.31				
Value	6.48	24.9	0.16	-1.03%	15.59%	-0.07	0.33
Low Beta	10.66	13.4	0.61	3.16	8.08	0.39	1.51
Profitability	7.33	16.9	0.28	-0.17	3.94	-0.04	0.00
Investment	8.86	17.7	0.36	1.36	8.46	0.16	0.89
Momentum	11.07	17.9	0.48	3.57	9.46	0.38	1.84
Size	8.48	19.1	0.31	0.97	10.01	0.10	0.71
Average of Six Factors	8.81	18.3	0.37	1.31	9.26	0.15	0.88
Europe ex UK							
Market	8.86%	18.4%	0.34				
Value	7.91	25.7	0.21	-0.94%	11.99%	-0.08	0.32
Low Beta	11.93	13.6	0.69	3.07	8.13	0.38	1.20
Profitability	7.94	20.7	0.26	-0.92	5.19	-0.18	-0.35
Investment	11.26	19.8	0.44	2.40	7.73	0.31	1.52
Momentum	12.30	17.9	0.55	3.44	7.40	0.46	1.97
Size	10.17	17.7	0.43	1.31	7.18	0.18	0.73
Average of Six Factors	10.25	19.2	0.43	1.39	7.94	0.18	0.90

Note: VA is value-add.

Source: Research Affiliates, LLC, using data from Worldscope and Datastream.

Additional Risk Measures for Long-Only Factor-Based Smart Beta Strategies, International Markets, Jul 1993–Sep 2016

Strategy		Absolute Risk			Relative Risk	
	Skewness	Maximum Drawdown	Longest Drawdown (Years)	Skewness	Maximum Drawdown	Longest Drawdown (Years)
Japan						
Market	0.09	-57%	8.1			
Value	0.50	-61	9.5	-0.27	-40%	6.7
Low Beta	0.10	-51	11.2	-0.10	-42	9.0
Profitability	0.15	-62	16.5	0.62	-31	15.9
Investment	0.07	-70	20.4	-0.17	-41	20.4
Momentum	0.34	-61	15.3	0.47	-26	7.8
Size	0.34	-71	11.4	-0.18	-54	10.4
Average of Six Factors	0.25	-63	14.0	0.06	-39	11.7
United Kingdom						
Market	-0.50	-59%	5.9			
Value	-0.84	-84	8.9	-0.38	-63%	9.3
Low Beta	-0.48	-49	4.8	0.07	-40	6.2
Profitability	-0.41	-58	6.3	-0.51	-25	17.6
Investment	-0.58	-55	8.9	0.19	-33	6.7
Momentum	-0.35	-52	4.7	-0.41	-33	7.5
Size	-0.64	-67	6.3	0.16	-39	9.6
Average of Six Factors	-0.55	-61	6.6	-0.15	-39	9.5
Europe ex UK						
Market	-0.60	-58%	6.3			
Value	-0.42	-70	8.9	-0.15	-45%	7.0
Low Beta	-0.78	-45	3.4	-0.12	-37	7.9
Profitability	-0.57	-62	8.9	-0.13	-25	18.2
Investment	0.01	-52	5.8	1.85	-12	4.5
Momentum	-0.31	-53	5.8	-0.48	-24	7.6
Size	-0.82	-59	6.3	-0.17	-36	11.6
Average of Six Factors	-0.48	-57	6.5	0.13	-30	9.5

Source: Research Affiliates, LLC, using data from Worldscope and Datastream.

Appendix C: Smart Beta Strategy Construction Methodology

The factor-based smart beta portfolios, except the size strategy, are constructed from the large-cap universes only. We define the US large-cap equity universe as stocks whose market capitalizations are greater than the median market capitalization on the NYSE. We define the international large-cap equity universe as stocks with market capitalization in the top 90% by cumulative market-cap within their region, where regions are defined as Japan, United Kingdom, and Europe ex UK.

For the long-only investable portfolios, we select the top 30% of the large-cap universe for each of the factor characteristics, except for the low beta strategies for which we select the top 50%. For example, to simulate the value smart-beta strategy in the United States, we construct the portfolio from large-cap stocks above the 70th NYSE percentile by book-to-market ratio. To simulate the value smart-beta strategy in the international markets, we construct the portfolio from large-cap stocks above the 70th percentile in their respective region (Japan, United Kingdom, and Europe ex UK) by book-to-market ratio.

We then capitalization weight the selected stocks, except for low beta, which we weight by the difference between beta rank and average rank. The portfolios are rebalanced annually, except for momentum and low beta, which are rebalanced monthly.

Appendix D: Factor Timing Methodology

The following timing methods are employed across factors:

Timing Method	Signal	Description
Systematic	Equal-Weight	Equal-weight of six factors
Dynamic	Momentum	Prior 12-month returns, skipping most recent month
	Reversal	Prior five-year returns, skipping most recent year

Source: Research Affiliates, LLC.

In the systematic timing method, we rebalance factor allocations to equal weights every quarter. In the dynamic timing method, we compute the cross-factor Z-score of the two timing signals every quarter, and take the average of the two. The Z-scores are capped at -3 and $+3$, and then used to adjust the systematic allocations as follows:

$$Dynamic\ Weight = \begin{cases} Systematic\ Weight \times (1 + Z\_score), & Z\_score \geq 0 \\ Systematic\ Weight \div (1 - Z\_score), & Z\_score, < 0 \end{cases}$$

The factor allocations are renormalized after these adjustments.

Appendix E: Trading Cost Estimation

Trading cost, measured as a percentage reduction in portfolio return, is defined as

$$Cost = \sum_i 0.03 \times \Delta w_i^2 \times \frac{AUM}{ADV_i}$$

The number 0.03 derives from the empirical observation that trading 10% of average daily volume has 30 basis points of market impact. We assume \$1B AUM for the current portfolios and retrospectively adjust the historical AUM in accordance with past market returns.

Estimated Trading Costs for US Long-Only Factor-Based Smart Betas, Jul 1973–Sep 2016

Strategy	Current N	WAMC ($Bil)	Turnover One-Way	Average T-Cost (at $1Bil)
Market	3,447	120.6	4.2%	0.01%
Value	156	117.1	45.2	0.30
Low Beta	457	29.8	87.1	0.33
Profitability	344	140.8	16.3	0.04
Investment	212	84.6	67.3	0.37
Momentum	368	158.8	298.9	1.18
Size	2,477	1.4	21.4	0.11

Estimated Trading Costs for US Multi-Factor Smart Beta Strategies, Jul 1973–Sep 2016

Strategy	Current N	WAMC ($Bil)	Turnover One-Way	Average T-Cost (at $1Bil)
Market	3,447	120.6	4.2%	0.01%
Buy and Hold	3,310	78.4	82.7	0.17
Systematic Rebalancing	3,310	88.6	85.5	0.16
Dynamic Rebalancing	3,310	89.6	103.5	0.20

Note: WAMC is weighted-average market capitalization. T-Cost is trading cost.
Source: Research Affiliates, LLC, using data from CRSP and Compustat.

Estimated Trading Costs for Long-Only Factor-Based Smart Betas, International Markets, Jul 1993–Sep 2016

Strategy	Current N	WAMC ($Bil)	Turnover One-Way	Average T-Cost (at $1Bil)
Japan				
Market	3,437	29.4	2.9%	0.01%
Value	73	36.3	64.1	0.51
Low Beta	334	4.7	97.8	0.60
Profitability	286	45.8	23.4	0.15
Investment	141	31.7	71.6	0.56
Momentum	262	27.6	308.0	2.07
Size	2,739	0.4	18.7	0.14
United Kingdom				
Market	1,188	58.6	8.9%	0.03%
Value	29	101.4	44.1	0.35
Low Beta	77	26.3	111.6	0.63
Profitability	88	58.9	19.2	0.10
Investment	31	43.8	80.0	0.63
Momentum	72	78.9	378.6	2.61
Size	1,038	1.2	22.5	0.17
Europe ex UK				
Market	3,435	50.4	5.6%	0.02%
Value	67	31.8	47.8	0.36
Low Beta	266	14.4	118.8	0.68
Profitability	234	50.7	16.1	0.07
Investment	110	25.3	77.9	0.55
Momentum	188	48.5	287.3	1.36
Size	2,880	1.2	20.8	0.16

Note: WAMC is weighted-average market capitalization. T-Cost is trading cost.
Source: Research Affiliates, LLC, using data from Worldscope and Datastream.

Appendix F: International Markets Multi-Factor Strategies

Performance Characteristics of Multi-Factor Strategies, International Markets, Jul 1993–Sep 2016

Strategy	Annualized Return	Annualized Volatility	Sharpe Ratio	Value Add	Tracking Error	IR	t-Stat (VA)
Japan							
Market	1.49%	18.0%	-0.06				
Average of Six Factors	2.60	19.6	0.01	1.11%	8.93%	0.06	0.42
Buy and Hold	3.10	18.2	0.03	1.61	4.95	0.32	1.56
Systematic Rebalancing	2.98	18.0	0.03	1.49	4.73	0.31	1.47
Dynamic Rebalancing	2.98	17.8	0.03	1.49	5.19	0.29	1.32
United Kingdom							
Market	7.50%	16.0%	0.31				
Average of Six Factors	8.81	18.3	0.37	1.31%	9.26%	0.15	0.88
Buy and Hold	9.10	16.3	0.40	1.59	4.07	0.39	1.84
Systematic Rebalancing	9.35	16.3	0.42	1.84	3.94	0.47	2.17
Dynamic Rebalancing	10.02	16.3	0.46	2.51	4.48	0.56	2.56
Europe ex UK							
Market	8.86%	18.4%	0.34				
Average of Six Factors	10.25	19.2	0.43	1.39%	7.94%	0.18	0.90
Buy and Hold	10.53	17.9	0.45	1.68	3.24	0.52	2.15
Systematic Rebalancing	10.56	18.1	0.44	1.70	3.28	0.52	2.22
Dynamic Rebalancing	10.72	18.0	0.45	1.86	4.05	0.46	1.95

Note: VA is value-add.

Source: Research Affiliates, LLC, using data from Worldscope and Datastream.

Additional Risk Measures for Multi-Factor Strategies, International Markets, Jul 1993–Sep 2016

Strategy	Absolute Risk			Relative Risk		
	Skewness	Maximum Drawdown	Longest Drawdown (Years)	Skewness	Maximum Drawdown	Longest Drawdown (Years)
Japan						
Market	0.09	-57%	8.1			
Average of Six Factors	0.25	-63	14.0	0.06	-39%	11.7
Buy and Hold	0.29	-57	11.2	0.25	-16	7.1
Systematic Rebalancing	0.27	-57	11.2	-0.16	-21	7.1
Dynamic Rebalancing	0.23	-55	11.2	-0.69	-24	8.8
United Kingdom						
Market	-0.50	-59%	5.9			
Average of Six Factors	-0.55	-61	6.6	-0.15	-39%	9.5
Buy and Hold	-0.90	-64	6.3	0.61	-17	8.8
Systematic Rebalancing	-0.73	-62	5.9	-0.04	-13	4.9
Dynamic Rebalancing	-0.61	-60	5.8	0.44	-12	2.8
Europe ex UK						
Market	-0.60	-58%	6.3			
Average of Six Factors	-0.48	-57	6.5	0.13	-30%	9.5
Buy and Hold	-0.65	-57	6.1	0.39	-10	4.9
Systematic Rebalancing	-0.64	-57	6.1	0.47	-11	3.8
Dynamic Rebalancing	-0.60	-55	6.1	0.10	-13	7.6

Source: Research Affiliates, LLC, using data from Worldscope and Datastream.

References

Arnott, Rob, Noah Beck, and Vitali Kalesnik. 2016a. "To Win with 'Smart Beta' Ask If the Price Is Right." Research Affiliates (June).

————. 2016b. "Timing 'Smart Beta' Strategies? Of Course! Buy Low, Sell High!" Research Affiliates (September).

Arnott, Rob, Noah Beck, Vitali Kalesnik, and John West. 2016. "How Can 'Smart Beta' Go Horribly Wrong?" Research Affiliates (February).

Asness, Cliff, Andrea Frazzini, Ronen Israel, Tobias Moskowitz, and Lasse H. Pedersen. 2015. "Size Matters, If You Control Your Junk." AQR Working paper (January 22).

Beck, Noah, Jason Hsu, Vitali Kalesnik, and Helge Kostka. 2016. "Will Your Factor Deliver? An Examination of Factor Robustness and Implementation Costs." *Financial Analysts Journal*, vol. 72, no. 5 (September/October):32–56.

Beck, Noah, and Vitali Kalesnik. 2014. "Busting the Myth about Size." Research Affiliates (December).

Carhart, Mark M. 1997. "On Persistence in Mutual Fund Performance." *Journal of Finance*, vol. 52, no. 1 (March):57–82.

Fama, Eugene, and Kenneth R. French. 1993. "Common Risk Factors in the Returns on Stocks and Bonds." *Journal of Financial Economics*, vol. 33:3–56.

————. 2012. "Size, Value, and Momentum in International Stock Returns." *Journal of Financial Economics*, vol. 105, no. 3 (September):457–472.

————. 2015. "Dissecting Anomalies with a Five-Factor Model." Fama–Miller Working Paper (June). Available at SSRN.

Frazzini, Andrea, and Lasse Heje Pedersen (2014). "Betting Against Beta." *Journal of Financial Economics*, vol. 111, no. 1 (January):1–25.

Harvey, Campbell R., Yan Liu, and Heqing Zhu. 2015. "…and the Cross-Section of Expected Returns." *Review of Financial Studies*, vol. 29, no. 1 (October):5–68.

Hsu, Jason, Vitali Kalesnik, and Engin Kose. 2017. "A Survey of Quality Investing." White paper (May 19).

MacLean, R. David, and Jeffrey Pontiff. 2015. "Does Academic Research Destroy Stock Return Predictability?" *Journal of Finance*, Forthcoming. Available at SSRN.

Novy–Marx, Robert, and Mihail Velikov. 2015. "A Taxonomy of Anomalies and Their Trading Costs." *Review of Financial Studies*, vol. 29, no. 1:104–147.

Shumway, Tyler, and Vincent A. Warther. 1999. "The Delisting Bias in CRSP's Nasdaq Data and Its Implications for the Size Effect." *Journal of Finance*, vol. 54, no. 6 (December):2361–2379.

Originally published January 2017; www.researchaffiliates.com/en_us/publications/articles/594-a-smoother-path-to-outperformance-with-multifactor-smart-beta-investing.html.

ABOUT CHRIS BRIGHTMAN, VITALI KALESNIK, FEIFEI LI AND JOSEPH SHIM

Chris Brightman leads the Research and Investment Management team. In this role, he supervises Research Affiliates' research and development activities, provision of index strategies, and management of client portfolios.

Chris has three decades of investment management experience in equities, fixed income, currency, and asset allocation. He has traded securities and derivatives, managed portfolios, supervised quantitative product development, and allocated assets to alternative investment strategies. He also has extensive organizational and people management expertise.

Prior to joining Research Affiliates, Chris served as board chair of The Investment Fund for Foundations (TIFF), vice chair of the Investment Advisory Committee for the Virginia Retirement System, chief executive officer of the University of Virginia Investment Management Company, chief investment officer of Strategic Investment Group, director of global equity strategy at UBS Asset Management, senior portfolio manager at Brinson Partners, vice president and head of asset/liability management at Maryland National Bank, and associate national bank examiner at the Comptroller of the Currency.

Chris holds the Chartered Financial Analyst® designation and is a member of CFA Institute and CFA Society Orange County. He serves on the Board and the Investment Committee of the Virginia Tech Foundation.

Chris received a BS in finance from Virginia Tech and an MBA from Loyola University, Maryland.

Vitali Kalesnik focuses on developing the firm's research agenda in the European region as well as supporting the firm's business relationships in the region. He leads the Equity Research team located in Newport Beach, CA, and its investigations into equity return predictability, timing of equity factor returns, efficient portfolio construction techniques, smart beta strategy analysis, governance, and other aspects of equity investing.

Articles he has co-authored with others have been recognized with two Graham and Dodd Scroll Awards, a *Financial Analysts Journal* Readers' Choice Award, a William F. Sharpe Indexing Achievement Award, and a Bernstein Fabozzi/Jacobs Levy Award. His research strengthens and expands Research Affiliates' products – in particular, RAFI™ Fundamental Index™ strategies – and supports our global tactical asset allocation products.

Vitali earned his PhD in economics from the University of California, Los Angeles, where he was a winner of the UCLA Graduate Division Fellowship for 2001–2005. He speaks fluent English, Russian, and French.

Feifei Li leads the Investment Management group, comprising three teams: Product Research, Portfolio Construction, and Investment Systems. She works closely with researchers in designing all the investment strategies offered by Research Affiliates. She supervises the execution of the approved methodology for our strategies, construction and delivery of model portfolios, as well as risk attributions and analytic support.

Feifei has taught undergraduate and MBA finance classes at the California Institute of Technology and University of California, Irvine. She conducts investment-related research and has published numerous articles in both academic and practitioner journals, as well as chapters in investment-related books. In 2015, Feifei and her co-authors won a Bernstein Fabozzi/Jacobs Levy Outstanding Article award for "A Study of Low-Volatility Portfolio Construction Methods" published in the *Journal of Portfolio Management*. She holds the Financial Risk Manager designation.

Feifei earned a BA from Tsinghua University's School of Management and Economics in Beijing, and a PhD in finance from the University of California, Los Angeles, where she has conducted empirical research on corporate finance and event-driven investment strategies.

Joseph Shim conducts quantitative research to enhance the RAFI™ Fundamental Index™ portfolio and active equity strategies.

Prior to coming to Research Affiliates, Joseph was a consultant at Moody's Analytics and, earlier, at Accenture. In his consulting role, he helped major commercial banks implement Basel II credit risk management and asset-liability management systems.

Joseph has a Master of Financial Engineering degree from the UCLA Anderson School of Management, and a BS in computer science and industrial engineering from Yonsei University.

Microcaps' Factor Spreads, Structural Biases, and the Institutional Imperative

EHREN STANHOPE

The ironic twist to the proliferation of "factor"-based strategies in recent years is that the overwhelming majority of these strategies are[1] launching in U.S. Large Cap Equity – *the most competitive arena for any financial market in the world*. Sure, factors can be effective in large cap but, lately, discerning investors are discovering that the factor research in eclectic corners of the market is much more compelling. This article presents our findings in perhaps the most capacity-constrained of those eclectic corners: microcap. Despite some unique considerations as it relates to liquidity and tradability (see Part 2 of this article: bit. ly/2q4ir9O), the opportunity in Micro is hard to ignore.[2]

Microcap stocks represent only a fraction of the total U.S. market's capitalization (about 1.2%). These stocks are under-covered, un-loved, under-owned, and they offer dedicated investors a unique opportunity. Though it was small to begin with, the microcap portion of the total U.S. equity market has been cut in half in the past two decades. A key culprit, the proliferation of passive and "smart beta" investment products has resulted in disproportionate flows into the large cap space and, therefore, away from small and microcap stocks.

This article's intent is to reveal microcap's inefficiency in some other areas beyond just the low institutional ownership and sell-side analyst

---

[1]   … boldly, or blindly …

[2]   As factor investors continually seeking alpha, we find that "true microcap" can tilt the probabilities of investment success in the investors' favor.

coverage. We start out by reviewing Russell's definition of microcap, then refining that definition to hone in on pure microcap stocks. We explore the composition of the microcap universe to shed light on why it is a less competitive space, and then provide a framework for quality assessment and alpha generation. We close with an argument for the persistence of alpha in the space, based on structural barriers to scale.

What is Microcap?

Russell defines the microcap space using an ordinal ranking methodology. Whereas the Russell 1000® (R1000) consists of the 1,000 largest stocks in the U.S., the Russell 2000®(R2000) contains those ranking from 1,001 to 3,000. The Russell Microcap® Index overlaps with the R2000 since it includes the 2,001st to 4,000th ranked stocks. Russell has conveniently created some overlap to prevent index churn—buying and selling constituents frequently crossing over between index thresholds—because there tends to be a lot of movement in the ranking of stocks at the lower end of the market cap spectrum.

Since these indexes are market cap-weighted, owning the Russell Microcap index is much the same as owning a small tail of the R2000 plus a minor allocation to even smaller names. There is an 88% overlap between the Russell Microcap Index with the R2000. Based on monthly observations from 1982–2016, the correlation of return between the two indexes is 0.96.[3]

A similar picture emerges when reviewing the share of dollar volume in each index. These tables summarize the allocation of the total U.S. market, based on capitalization and dollar volume across the indexes:

[3]   Despite the highly-correlated returns of Russell's 2000 and Microcap indexes, the relevant iShares Russell ETF [IWC] carries a 0.60% expense ratio—three times higher than the fee of its Russell 2000 counterpart [IWD], which costs just 0.20%.

Percentages:[4]

by Market Cap

Stock Rank	Avg. Market Cap ($mil)	Total Market	Russell indexes:		
			1000®	2000®	Microcap®
1–1,000	22,014	93.4%	100.0%	—	—
1,001–2,000	1,269	5.4%	—	83.1%	—
2,001–3,000	258	1.1%	—	16.9%	88.2%
3,001–4,000	35	0.1%	—	—	11.8%

by Dollar Volume

Stock Rank	Average Volume	Total Market	Russell indexes:		
			1000®	2000®	Microcap®
1–1,000	127,803,000	88.8%	100.0%	—	—
1,001–2,000	13,497,000	9.4%	—	84.9%	—
2,001–3,000	2,400,000	1.7%	—	15.1%	94.1%
3,001–4,000	342,000	0.1%	—	—	5.9%

Notice how average dollar volume declines exponentially as you move away from large cap. Also, the small, unique portion of the Russell Microcap index (stocks ranked 3,001st through 4,000th) represents half the dollar volume weight as it does the market cap weight. Low volumes in this corner of the market can lead to significant transaction costs if not managed appropriately. This suggests that the cost of exposure to that small tail is very expensive, and likely a drag on performance of

---

4   1982–2016 (Compustat).

the index. In our own analysis over the period from 1982 through 2016, we found that applying a liquidity floor of $100K average daily volume (inflation-adjusted) improved the index return by 0.8%.

In current form, the performance statistics for microcap certainly do not drive a compelling narrative for adding an allocation to portfolios. The risk-return trade-off is poor enough that commonly used covariance optimization techniques in an institutional asset allocation study would suggest a zero-percent weighing to microcap. In fact, most would suggest little or no weight to the small cap R2000 as well. Given these results, it's little wonder large cap stocks are all the rage.

Risk-Return Trade-Off (1982–2016, Compustat)

	Russell 1000®	Russell 2000®	Russell Microcap®
Return	11.7%	10.8%	10.1%
Volatility	15.1%	19.1%	20.5%
Sharpe Ratio	0.58	0.41	0.35

For the rest of this article, we diverge from the Russell index definitions to get a better sense of the composition of microcap and the alpha opportunity available. We define microcap stocks as those trading on U.S. exchanges with an inflation-adjusted market capitalization between $50 million and $200 million.[5] Also, because our microcap universe is *equal*-weighted, not cap-weighted, we believe investors get a more "pure" view of the microcap market—that is, minimal overlap with small cap stocks. This group of about 1,300 stocks represents a disproportionately small 0.4% of total U.S. market capitalization. With average daily volume of just $700K per stock and a cumulative market cap of about $100 billion, the group is a mixture of exciting growth opportunities on the one hand, and the Land of Misfit Toys on the other. Once we screen out

[5]   The OSAM Microcap Universe would be analogous to the approximately 2,600th to 4,000th stocks using Russell's ordinal market cap ranking methodology.

companies with unreasonable liquidity and non-U.S. domiciled firms (ADRs), the list dwindles to about 500 investable stocks.

For comparative purposes, we periodically refer to a Large Stocks universe comprising U.S. firms with a market capitalization greater than the average for the total market.[6] Large stocks are instructive as they represent the bulk of investor's U.S. equity allocation. It is analogous to the S&P 500 Index on an equal-weighted basis.

Microcaps' Uniqueness

It's hard for investors to fully appreciate the microcap space without understanding how stocks have come to fall on the microcap spectrum. Whereas most **large** stocks have succeeded in attempts to grow their businesses, as recognized by their multi-billion-dollar valuations, microcap stocks are on a completely different playing field. These businesses range from biotech start-ups to failing businesses that have depreciated to their current middling market cap. From an empirical perspective, the result is a lot of noise in the data.

To demonstrate, let's look at one of a firm's most fundamental metrics: sales growth. Though its efficacy as an investment factor is marginal, sales are the lifeblood of any firm and have a cascading effect on all other elements of their financial statements. This chart compares the distribution of three-year sales growth across large and microcap stocks:

---

[6] At present, this includes stocks above an inflation-adjusted $7 billion market cap.

Range of Positive 3-Year Sales Growth (CAGR)

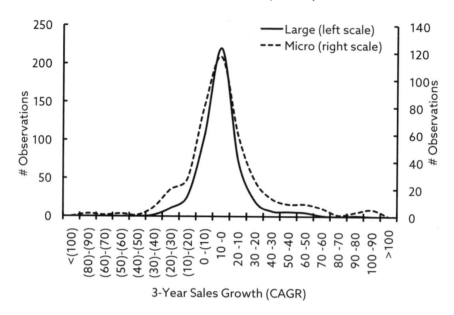

Notice the significantly fatter tails for microcap relative to large stocks. If growth in sales is the most basic way to assess the status of a firm, then this suggests much greater dispersion in the underlying microcap metrics. Popular rhetoric decries small and microcap stocks as being junkier than their large cap counterparts. While this is true on average, a wide dispersion in fundamental metrics means that many phenomenal businesses get hidden behind a wall of meaningless averages.

A deeper dive reveals a disparate group of continually evolving —and devolving—businesses

Investors have widely accepted that there exist many different types of private equity: Angel Investing, Venture, Early Stage, Late Stage, Mezzanine, LBOs, and Distressed. Interestingly, in the private space, these labels represent the need of the firm receiving the investment. Just as there are many sub-classes of venture capital and private equity, such is the case with microcap stocks, but for whatever reason, we do not view these businesses with the same categorical lens as we do private investments.

The microcap universe can be divided into three broad categories: (1) *New Ventures* that have become revenue-generating within the past three years, (2) distressed *Fallen Angels* that have descended into the microcap universe from small cap—and sometimes large cap—and (3) those in a *Steady State* (microcaps for at least three years).

To contextualize microcap, think of a revolving door where firms are constantly entering and leaving for different reasons, as diagrammed here:[7]

The Transitory Microcap Universe

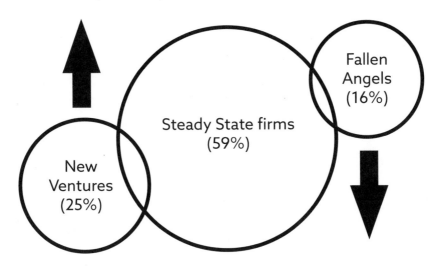

This simplistic perspective on the universe is relevant because it sheds light on the strong inherent biases that skew the underlying fundamental characteristics. Below is the same distribution of Sales Growth for microcap, broken down into those three categories.[8] These disparate groups possess fundamentally different metrics that obscure a lot of noise in microcap stocks when averaged together.

---

7   From 1982 through 2016, New Ventures represented 25% of the microcap universe, while 16% were Fallen Angels, and 59% were Steady State. Effectively, 41% of the universe is in some sort of transition—ranging from start-up to established firm, or from established firm to potential liquidation.

8   An analysis on three-year earnings growth reveals similar patterns, though with greater noise.

Range of Positive 3-Year Sales Growth (CAGR)—Microcap

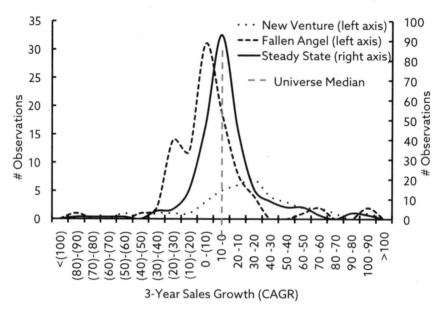

New Ventures, with their small sales bases, are highly skewed towards positive sales growth. Unsurprisingly, New Ventures tend to be comprised of Information Technology and Health Care stocks—most notably biotech, software, and pharmaceuticals. Currently, those industries represent a rather large 20% of the microcap universe. The average annualized return of this group from 1982–2016 is 4.7%, woefully short of the microcap universe average of 8.9%. Adding insult to injury, annualized volatility for this group is 27.8% (likely a result of the nature of outcomes in the space). Biotech firms generally succeed or fail—binary outcomes—giving investors strong gains or staggering losses.

Steady State firms are more centered in the distribution, but still positively skewed. At 60% of the overall universe, a good proportion of Steady State firms are Commercial Banks and Thrifts. These two industries represent 20% of the universe currently. Banks are the *least* volatile microcap industry and one of the top performers. The remainder of firms in this category tend to be widely dispersed across industries. Steady State firms are the highest performing of the three categories with an annualized return of 10.1% and volatility of 22.8%.

Fallen Angels skew significantly in the negative growth direction. This is a group of firms ranging across industries. Currently, the oil & gas industry has the highest representation in this category. It tends to offer representative groups of stocks that suffered in the previous cyclical business downturn. Fallen Angels gave investors an annualized return of 8.0% from 1982–2016, with volatility of 27.4%.

Our task as factor investors is to develop empirical criteria that enable us to cut through the noise to separate the good from the bad. Given the perspective above, we know there are reasonable fundamental explanations for the "junk-*ish*" nature of microcap stocks. Quite simply, a lot of microcap stocks possess poor business characteristics, whether weak cash flow generation, too much leverage, or dwindling and unprofitable revenues. By codifying firms and removing those with poor characteristics, we can improve investors' base rates[9] for success.

Leveling the playing field

We've established that the fundamental drivers of microcap businesses are widely varied, at least in part, due to their state of being—New Venture, Steady State, and Fallen Angel. Let's take a step back to build intuition for stock selection regardless of category. In our research, we have found several quality metrics to be indicative of good businesses. Generally, businesses should be profitable, growing at a reasonable pace, and appropriately capitalized. Individually, these metrics are effective, but when used together thematically, they provide a powerful framework for eliminating poor-quality stocks. The following table compares several characteristics for Large and Microcap stocks.

In each case, a simple average of characteristics for microcap stocks betrays the universe's lower-quality nature relative to Large Stocks. One would assume from looking at the microcap column that these businesses are rapidly growing their asset base, not particularly profitable, taking on tremendous debt, and generating negative free cash flow. Each one of these signals seem to indicate a hunger for cash.

---

[9] Base Rates are batting averages for how often factors outperform the market in rolling periods.

Measures of Quality (1982–2016, Compustat)

	Large Stocks	Microcap Stocks	
		(all)	Quality-Adjusted
Change in Net Operating Assets (%)	25.0	44.3	13.7
One-Year Debt Change (%)	17.7	32.6	12.1
Debt-to-Equity	1.1	1.0	0.8
ROIC (%)	30.7	13.2	23.7
Free Cash Flow-to-Enterprise Value (%)	2.1	−4.5	0.7

Change in Net Operating Assets (NOA) measures the growth in assets required to run the business. If a small consumer products company, for example, hit the jackpot with a new contract at a huge retailer and then had to ramp up production to fulfill the order, this metric would increase. Sales growth requires large investment for raw materials, inventory, delivery of finished goods, and equipment for ongoing production. The challenge with growth is that it requires huge cash outlays. This cash is all outlaid *before* revenue occurs. Dramatic growth in operating assets can be indicative of stress, as it leaves the business in a tenuous cash position. This state of affairs seems to be the norm for microcap stocks with an average change in NOA of 44.3%—almost double the rate for large stocks.

Few small firms have enough internal capital to fund such large investments. They then turn to capital providers to fund growth—issuing equity offerings, or taking on debt. Keep in mind that many microcap stocks have no analyst coverage, so the ability to tap equity capital markets is limited and expensive.[10] Debt becomes the default source of capital. The average one-year change in debt for the universe is 32.6%, and debt-to-equity is on par with Large Stocks. The ROIC of just 13.2% indicates that capital, of which debt is a part, is not being as

---

[10]   See "Microcap as an Alternative to Private Equity" (osamlibrary.com).

efficiently invested as with Large Stocks. A free cash flow yield of -4.5% suggests economic value is being destroyed, rather than created.

Each of these characteristics are components of multi-factor themes that we use to assess the quality of a firm: Earnings Quality (NOA), Financial Strength (D/E, Change in Debt), and Earnings Growth (ROIC).[11] To level the playing field for comparing Micro to Large Stocks, we can rank stocks in the microcap universe based on these multi-factor themes and eliminate the lowest ranking decile. Firms falling into these groups tend to be poorly capitalized and have low profitability and weak earnings quality.

By adjusting the microcap universe, the overall metrics dramatically improve and, in some cases, are actually better than Large Stocks. Quality-adjusted microcap stocks reveal much more moderate growth rates in NOA. An average 13.7% is indicative of businesses that are more likely to handle organic business growth without needing to seek substantial funding from debt or equity issuance. The improvement in the One-Year Debt Change metric after adjusting for quality supports this logic. A large 32.6% increase in debt decreases to just 12.1%—lower than the average for Large Stocks.

Clearly, the universe quality metrics have improved, but how does this translate into investor returns? It turns out that ***eliminating*** *poor quality boosts the return of our universe by 5.3% annualized with a 0.7% reduction in annual volatility,* as shown in this table:

Quality Matters (1982–2016, Compustat)

		Microcap Stocks	
	Large Stocks	(all)	Quality-Adjusted
Return	12.0%	8.9%	14.2%
Volatility	17.0%	24.5%	23.8%
Sharpe Ratio	0.41	0.16	0.39

[11]   For a full description of our multi-factor Quality themes, please request a copy of our "OSAM Guide to Factor Alpha" c/o info@osam.com.

Incorporating quality criteria to eliminate stocks from consideration has a dramatic impact on microcap stocks. Performing a quality assessment highlights the importance of a less appreciated aspect of factor investing. While many researchers focus on the outperformance associated with factors, using factors to avoid groups of stocks can be just as positive a contributor to investor returns. After controlling for quality, the risk-adjusted returns available are in-line with large stocks. Earlier we mentioned that the historical return and risk of the Russell Microcap® Index did not merit an allocation according to mean-variance optimization. This simple quality screen alters the space's characteristics to such an extent that it becomes a viable source of differentiated return for investors.

Originally published August 18, 2017; osam.com/Commentary/microcaps-factor-spreads-structural-biases-and-the-institutional-imperative.

ABOUT EHREN STANHOPE

Ehren Stanhope is a Principal and Client Portfolio Manager at O'Shaughnessy Asset Management (OSAM). Ehren has deep expertise in OSAM's investment philosophy, portfolio construction, and implementation, which enables him to represent the investment process to key clients throughout the United States. He is responsible for positioning the firm's investment capabilities within the context of client needs and the current market environment. Ehren is an equity owner in OSAM and a member of the firm's Operating Committee. He is also the author of the "Factor Investor" blog and is a Yahoo! Finance Contributor.

Prior to joining OSAM, Ehren worked at Western Asset Management Co (WAMCO), where he was a member of the Analytics team in the Client Service/Marketing group. In that role, he specialized in relationships with insurance clients handling inquiries related to portfolio performance, structure, and strategy. Prior to his role at WAMCO, Ehren served as an Account Executive at Indymac Bank in the Mortgage Banking Division and a Regional Director for Sigma Phi Epsilon Fraternity. Ehren holds a B.S. in Management from Tulane University with concentrations in Finance and Legal Studies, and an M.B.A. from the Yale School of

Management with a focus in Asset Management. He is a Chartered Financial Analyst and member of the CFA Society New York.

@FactorInvestor

PRICING

— & —

VALUATION

The Bitcoin Boom:
Asset, Currency, Commodity or Collectible?

ASWATH DAMODARAN

As I have noted with my earlier articles on crypto currencies,[1] in general, and bitcoin, in particular, I find myself disagreeing with both its most virulent critics and its strongest proponents. Unlike Jamie Dimon, I don't believe that bitcoin is a fraud and that people who are "stupid enough to buy it" will pay a price for that stupidity.[2] Unlike its biggest cheerleaders, I don't believe that crypto currencies are now or ever will be an asset class or that these currencies can change fundamental truths about risk, investing and management.[3] The reason for the divide, though, is that the two sides seem to disagree fundamentally on what bitcoin is, and at the risk of raising hackles all the way around, I will argue that bitcoin is not an asset, but a currency, and as such, you cannot value it or invest in it. You can only price it and trade it.

Assets, Commodities, Currencies and Collectibles

Not everything can be valued, but almost everything can be priced. To understand the distinction between value and price, let me start by positing that every investment that I will look at has to fall into one of the following four groupings:

---

[1] aswathdamodaran.blogspot.co.uk/2017/08/the-crypto-currency-debate-future-of.html

[2] cnb.cx/2jXmT7Q

[3] bit.ly/2jXnpTk

1. **Cash Generating Asset**: An asset generates or is expected to generate cash flows in the future. A business that you own is definitely an asset, as is a claim on the cash flows on that business. Those claims can be either contractually set (bonds or debt), residual (equity or stock) or even contingent (options). What assets share in common is that these cash flows can be valued, and assets with high cash flows and less risk should be valued more than assets with lower cash flows and more risk. At the same time, assets can also be priced, relative to each other, by scaling the price that you pay to a common metric. With stocks, this takes the form of comparing pricing multiples (PE ratio, EV/EBITDA, Price to Book or Value/Sales) across similar companies to form pricing judgments of which stocks are cheap and which ones are expensive.

2. **Commodity**: A commodity derives its value from its use as raw material to meet a fundamental need, whether it be energy, food or shelter. While that value can be estimated by looking at the demand for and supply of the commodity, there are long lag and lead times in both that make that valuation process much more difficult than for an asset. Consequently, commodities tend to be priced, often relative to their own history, with normalized oil, coal, wheat or iron ore prices being computed by averaging prices across long cycles.

3. **Currency**: A currency is a medium of exchange that you use to denominate cash flows and is a store of purchasing power, if you choose to not invest. Standing alone, currencies have no cash flows and cannot be valued, but they can be priced against other currencies. In the long term, currencies that are accepted more widely as a medium of exchange and that hold their purchasing power better over time should see their prices rise, relative to currencies that don't have those characteristics. In the short term, though, other forces including governments trying to manipulate exchange rates can dominate. Using a more conventional currency example, you can see this in a graph of the US dollar against other fiat currencies, where over the long term (1995–2017), you can see the Swiss franc and the Chinese yuan increasing in price, relative to the $, and the Japanese yen, Brazilian real, Indian rupee and British pound, dropping in price, again relative to the $.

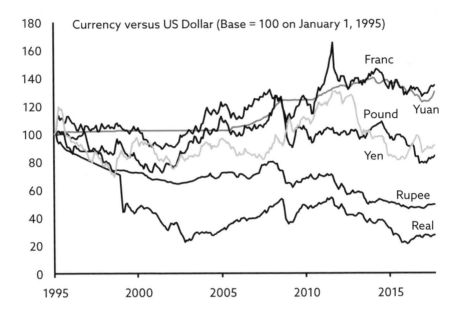

4. **Collectible**: A collectible has no cash flows and is not a medium of exchange but it can sometimes have aesthetic value (as is the case with a master painting or a sculpture) or an emotional attachment (a baseball card or team jersey). A collectible cannot be valued since it too generates no cash flows but it can be priced, based upon *how other people perceive its desirability* and the *scarcity of the collectible*.

Viewed through this prism, Gold is clearly not a cash flow generating asset, but is it a commodity? Since gold's value has little to do with its utilitarian functions and more to do with its longstanding function as a store of value, especially during crises or when you lose faith in paper currencies, it is more currency than commodity. Real estate is an asset, even if it takes the form of a personal home, because you would have had to pay rental expenses (a cash flow), in its absence. Private equity and hedge funds are forms of investing in assets, currencies, commodities or collectibles, and are not separate asset classes.

Investing versus Trading

The key is that cash generating assets can be both valued and priced, commodities can be priced much more easily than valued, and currencies and collectibles can only be priced. So what? I have written before about the divide between investing and trading and it is worth revisiting that contrast. To invest in something, you need to assess its value, compare to the price, and then act on that comparison, buying if the price is less than value and selling if it is greater. Trading is a much simpler exercise, where you price something, make a judgment on whether that price will go up or down in the next time period and then make a pricing bet. While you can be successful at either, the skill sets and tool kits that you use are different for investing and trading, and what makes for a good investor is different from the ingredients needed for good trading. The table below captures the difference between trading (the pricing game) and investing (the value game).

	The Pricing Game	The Value Game
Underlying philosophy	The price is the only real number that you can act on. No one knows what the value of an asset is and estimating it is of little use.	Every asset has a fair or true value. You can estimate that value, albeit with error, and price has to converge on value (eventually).
To play the game	You try to guess which direction the price will move in the next period(s) and trade ahead of the movement. To win the game, you have to be right more often than wrong about direction and to exit before the winds shift.	You try to estimate the value of an asset, and if it is under (over) value, you buy (sell) the asset. To win the game, you have to be right about value (for the most part) and the market price has to move to that value.
Key drivers	Price is determined by demand and supply, which in turn are affected by mood and momentum.	Value is determined by cash flows, growth and risk.
Information effect	Incremental information (news, stories, rumors) that shifts the mood will move the price, even if it has no real consequences for long-term value.	Only information that alter cash flows, growth and risk in a material way can affect value.

	The Pricing Game	The Value Game
Tools of the game	(1) Technical indicators, (2) Price Charts, (3) Investor Psychology.	(1) Ratio analysis, (2) DCF Valuation, (3) Accounting Research.
Time horizon	Can be very short term (minutes) to mildly short term (weeks, months).	Long term
Key skill	Be able to gauge market mood/momentum shifts earlier than the rest of the market.	Be able to "value" assets, given uncertainty.
Key personality traits	(1) Market amnesia, (2) Quick Acting, (3) Gambling Instincts.	(1) Faith in "value," (2) Faith in markets, (3) Patience, (4) Immunity from peer pressure.
Biggest Danger(s)	Momentum shifts can occur quickly, wiping out months of profits in a few hours.	The price may not converge on value, even if your value is "right."
Added bonus	Capacity to move prices (with lots of money and lots of followers).	Can provide the catalyst that can move price to value.
Most Delusional Player	A trader who thinks he is trading based on value.	A value investor who thinks he can reason with markets.

As I see it, you can play either the value or pricing game well, but being delusional about the game you are playing, and using the wrong tools or bringing the wrong skill set to that game, is a recipe for disaster.

What is Bitcoin?

The first step towards a serious debate on Bitcoin then has to be deciding whether it is an asset, a currency, a commodity or collectible. Bitcoin is *not an asset*, since it does not generate cash flows standing alone for those who hold it (until you sell it). It is *not a commodity*, because it is not raw material that can be used in the production of something useful. The only exception that I can think of is that if it becomes a necessary component of smart contracts, it could take on the role of a commodity;

that may be ethereum's saving grace, since it has been marketed less as a currency and more as a smart contracting lubricant. The choice then becomes *whether it is a currency or a collectible,* with its supporters tilting towards the former and its detractors the latter. I argued in my article "The Crypto Currency Debate: Future of Money or Speculative Hype?" that Bitcoin is a currency,[4] but it is not a good one yet, insofar as it has only limited acceptance as a medium of exchange and it is too volatile to be a store of value. Looking forward, there are three possible paths that I see for Bitcoin as a currency, from best case to worst case.

1. **The Global Digital Currency**: In the best case scenario, Bitcoin gains wide acceptance in transactions across the world, becoming a widely used global digital currency. For this to happen, it has to become more stable (relative to other currencies), central banks and governments around the world have to accept its use (or at least not actively try to impede it) and the aura of mystery around it has to fade. If that happens, it could compete with fiat currencies and given the algorithm set limits on its creation, its high price could be justified.

2. **Gold for Millennials**: In this scenario, Bitcoin becomes a haven for those who do not trust central banks, governments and fiat currencies. In short, it takes on the role that gold has, historically, for those who have lost trust in or fear centralized authority. It is interesting that the language of Bitcoin is filled with mining terminology, since it suggests that intentionally or otherwise, the creators of Bitcoin shared this vision. In fact, the hard cap on Bitcoin of 21 million is more compatible with this scenario than the first one. If this scenario unfolds, and Bitcoin shows the same staying power as gold, it will behave like gold does, rising during crises and dropping in more sanguine time periods.

3. **The 21st Century Tulip Bulb**: In this, the worst case scenario, Bitcoin is like a shooting star, attracting more money as it soars, from those who see it as a source of easy profits, but just as quickly flares out as these traders move on to something new and different

---

[4] aswathdamodaran.blogspot.co.uk/2017/08/the-crypto-currency-debate-future-of.html

(which could be a different and better designed digital currency), leaving Bitcoin holders with memories of what might have been. If this happens, Bitcoin could very well become the equivalent of tulip bulbs, a speculative asset that saw its prices soar in the 1600s in Holland, before collapsing in the aftermath.

I would be lying if I said that I knew which of these scenarios will unfold, but they are all still plausible scenarios. If you are trading in Bitcoin, you may very well not care, since your time horizon may be in minutes and hours, not weeks, months or years. If you have a longer-term interest in Bitcoin, though, your focus should be less on the noise of day-to-day price movements and more on advancements on its use as a currency. Note also that you could be a pessimist on Bitcoin and other crypto currencies but be an optimist about the underlying technology, especially block chain, and its potential for disruption.

Reality Checks

Combining the section where I classified investments into assets, commodities, currencies and collectibles with the one where I argued that Bitcoin is a "young" currency allows me to draw the following conclusions:

1. **Bitcoin is not an asset class**: To those who are carving out a portion of their portfolios for Bitcoin, be clear about why you are doing it. It is not because you want to a diversified portfolio and hold all asset classes, it is because you want to use your trading skills on Bitcoin to supercharge your portfolio returns. Lest you view this as a swipe at cryptocurrencies, I would hasten to add that fiat currencies (like the US dollar, euro or yen) are not asset classes either.

2. **You cannot value Bitcoin, you can only price it**: This follows from the acceptance that Bitcoin is a currency, not an asset or a commodity. Anyone who claims to value Bitcoin either has a very different definition of value than I do or is just making up stuff as he or she goes along.

3. **It will be judged as a currency**: In the long term, the price that you attach to Bitcoin will depend on how well it will performs as a currency. If it is accepted widely as a medium of exchange and is stable enough to be a store of value, it should command a high price.

If it becomes gold-like, a fringe currency that investors flee to during crises, its price will be lower. Worse, if it is a transient currency that loses all purchasing power, as it is replaced by something new and different, it will crash and burn.

4. **You don't invest in Bitcoin, you trade it**: Since you cannot value Bitcoin, you don't have a critical ingredient that you need to be an investor. You can trade Bitcoin and become wealthy doing so, but it is because you are a good trader.

5. **Good trader ingredients**: To be a successful trader in Bitcoin, you need to recognize that moves in its price will have little do with fundamentals, everything to do with mood and momentum and big price shifts can happen on incremental information.

Would I buy Bitcoin at $6,100? No, but not for the reasons that you think. It is not because I believe that it is overvalued, since I cannot make that judgment without valuing it and as I noted before, it cannot be valued. It is because I am not and never have been a good trader and, as a consequence, my pricing judgments are suspect. If you have good trading instincts, you should play the pricing game, as long as you recognize that it is a game, where you can win millions or lose millions, based upon your calls on momentum. If you win millions, I wish you the best! If you lose millions, please don't let paranoia lead you to blame the establishment, banks and governments for why you lost. Come easy, go easy!

Originally published October 24, 2017; aswathdamodaran.blogspot.co.uk/2017/10/the-bitcoin-boom-asset-currency.html.

ABOUT ASWATH DAMODARAN

Aswath Damodaran is a Professor of Finance at the Stern School of Business at New York University. He teaches the corporate finance and valuation courses in the MBA program as well as occasional short-term classes around the world on both topics. He received his MBA and Ph.D degrees from the University of California at Los Angeles. His research interests lie in valuation, portfolio management and applied corporate finance. His papers have been published in the *Journal of Financial and*

Quantitative Analysis, the *Journal of Finance,* the *Journal of Financial Economics* and the *Review of Financial Studies.*

Professor Damodaran has written four books on equity valuation (*Damodaran on Valuation, Investment Valuation, The Dark Side of Valuation, The Little Book of Valuation*) and two on corporate finance (*Corporate Finance: Theory and Practice, Applied Corporate Finance: A User's Manual*). He also co-edited a book on investment management with Peter Bernstein (*Investment Management*) and he has two books on portfolio management – one on investment philosophies (*Investment Philosophies*) and one titled *Investment Fables.* His newest book, *Narrative and Numbers,*was published in January 2017.

@AswathDamodaran

Portfolios in Wonderland & The Weird Portfolio

COREY HOFFSTEIN

Summary

- The current outlook for stocks, bonds, and traditionally allocated portfolios is near all-time historical low levels.

- Even though short-term performance may vary, investors looking for long-term success may have to expand their investment palette to earn returns anywhere close to those realized in the past.

- A mean-variance optimal portfolio using the current market forecasts relies heavily on more unique asset classes such as U.S. Small Caps, Emerging Market Debt (Local Currency), and Levered Loans.

- While investors may not be willing to hold such a weird looking "60/40" portfolio, thinking outside the box may be necessary going forward.

Portfolios in Wonderland

"Begin at the beginning," the King said, very gravely, "and go on till you come to the end: then stop."

At the beginning of each year, many institutions publish their capital market assumptions, providing an outlook for expected returns, volatilities, and correlations. These glossy brochures go well beyond data, however, and often veer wildly into what we like to call *macro tourism*: data-based market prognostications about macro-economic conditions and their implications for markets.

Unfortunately, for most investors, while macro tourism makes for an entertaining read, the track record of most predictors is quite poor. Simply put, markets do not behave in the linear, domino-like fashion that most predictions are laid out as. There are simply too many non-linear relationships to make accurate predictions; it is like trying to predict the exact weather in Boston a year out.

That said, if we are willing to restrain ourselves, meaningful forecasts *can* be made. We may not be able to predict the exact weather, but there is a good chance the temperature will be between 65 Fahrenheit and 80 Fahrenheit.

While exact predictions may be futile, evidence suggests that by taking a long-term view (seven to ten years) and focusing on stable variables, we can make similar long-term forecasts for most major asset classes. For U.S. investors, simply getting an understanding of what will likely happen with U.S. stocks and bonds can provide a tremendous amount of insight for the rest of our financial plan.

So, let's begin with U.S. equities. Here, we turn to the Shiller CAPE. For those not familiar yet with this metric, it is a ten-year smoothed price-to-earnings measure for the U.S. equity market. The aim of smoothing over ten-year periods is to get a measure that is less sensitive to market cycles, creating a "cyclically-adjusted" P/E ("CAPE").

We can see that today's CAPE is highly elevated compared to past measures.

The implication of a high CAPE reading is that stocks are expensive: you are paying more per unit of fundamental value.

In our piece "Anatomy of a Bull Market,"[1] and the subsequent follow-up,[2] we demonstrated that over the long-run, valuation changes have contributed little to U.S. equity performance. While they can vary wildly in the short-run, they have historically exhibited *mean-reverting* behavior: cheap tends to get more expensive, and expensive tends to get cheaper.

---

[1] blog.thinknewfound.com/2017/02/anatomy-bull-market
[2] blog.thinknewfound.com/2017/02/anatomy-bull-market-follow

Shiller CAPE

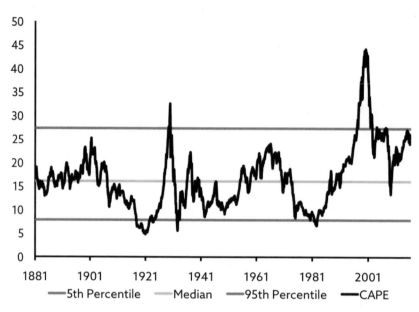

Source: Shiller Data Library. Calculations by Newfound Research. Shiller CAPE is the Shiller cyclically-adjusted price-to-earnings ratio, which uses smoothed earnings over the last ten years.

In the short-run (periods of seven to ten years), however, valuation changes can have a very meaningful impact on returns. Where the Shiller CAPE sits today, if real earnings grew at 2% a year, the market would have to return 0% for the next 13 years for the Shiller CAPE to revert back to its long-term average. Even if earnings accelerate and grow at 4% a year, it would still take nearly a decade of 0% returns.[3]

The other option, of course, is that we experience a bear market and price falls fast enough to cause the Shiller CAPE to revert. A 30% decline in prices would just about do it.

Now, we're not here to forecast gloom and doom. Rather, we believe there are a few simple, potential answers. One is that Shiller CAPE is simply the wrong measurement of valuation. Another is that this time really is different: valuations, for a variety of reasons, are simply structurally

---

[3]   theirrelevantinvestor.com/2017/08/10/stock-bubble

higher and will remain that way. Or, we could simply argue that we expect market returns to be *lower than average* going forward, allowing earnings to catch up.

If we "hope for the best and prepare for the worst," assuming the latter case is prudent. Using earnings growth, dividend yield, and valuation figures, we can forecast expected equity returns over the next seven to ten years. The current estimate—around 3.5% after inflation—is incredibly low by historical standards.

Expected Equity Return

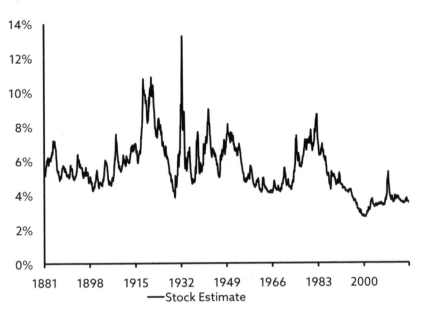

— Stock Estimate

Source: Shiller Data Library. Calculations by Newfound Research. Expected equity return is a 50/50 blend of adjusted earnings yield (inverse of Shiller's CAPE times 1.075) divided by 2 plus 1.5% earnings growth and dividend yield plus 1.5% earnings growth.

Estimating the expected future return for bonds is much easier. Buying a bond today and holding it to maturity ensures that you lock in the yield-to-worst, regardless of what happens with interest rates.

What about bond funds? For most funds—which are near constant maturity/duration in nature—changing rates have not made as large an impact as most people might assume. This was the topic of our prior commentary "Did Declining Rates Actually Matter?",[4] whose results are depicted below.

Return Sources for Constant Maturity Bond Indices

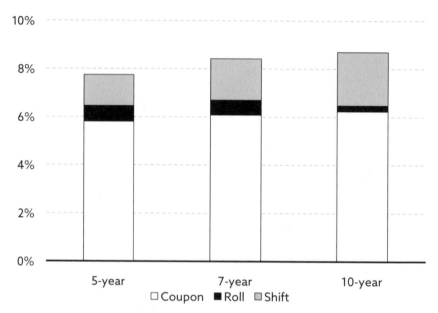

Source: Federal Reserve of St Louis. Calculations by Newfound Research. Indices are hypothetical and are gross of all fees and expenses.

What we find is that while declining rates *did* have an impact on bond index returns, the vast majority of the return was due to the actual coupon level itself. In other words, what we should focus on, in the current environment, is not trying to accurately predict whether rates will go up or down, but rather the coupon yield we will be receiving.

Which is, today, incredibly low.

"Why, sometimes I've believed as many as six impossible things before breakfast."

Believing that traditional core U.S. fixed income will deliver a return profile anything close to what they have historically delivered is misguided at best. We can actually use a very simple rule—the "2x duration minus

---

4   blog.thinknewfound.com/2017/04/declining-rates-actually-matter

1" rule—to forecast bond fund returns. This rule is highly useful because it is derived to provide guidance *regardless* of what interest rates do.[5]

Simply, we take the current year and add to it 2x the duration of the bond fund and subtract one. This provides us the forecast year. The current yield-to-maturity—or, yield-to-worst—is then our estimate through that year.

Asset	Yield to Maturity	Duration	Through	Predicted Nominal Return	Predicted Real Return
U.S. Aggregate Bonds	2.59%	5.7	2028	2.59%	0.29%
1-3 Yr. Treasuries	1.37%	1.9	2020	1.37%	−0.93%
3-7 Yr. Treasuries	1.91%	4.5	2025	1.91%	−0.39%
7-10 Yr. Treasuries	2.34%	7.5	2031	2.34%	0.04%
10-20 Yr. Treasuries	2.55%	10.0	2036	2.55%	0.25%
20+ Yr. Treasuries	3.00%	17.3	2050	3.00%	0.70%
IG Corporates	3.53%	8.2	2032	3.53%	1.23%

Source: iShares. Calculations by Newfound Research. Figures as of June 2017.

It should be no surprise, then, that forecasted U.S. aggregate real returns are near all-time lows.

5   See "For Constant-Duration or Constant-Maturity Bond Portfolios, Initial Yield Forecasts Return Best near Twice Duration," by Gabriel Lozada for technical details.

Bond Expected Real Returns

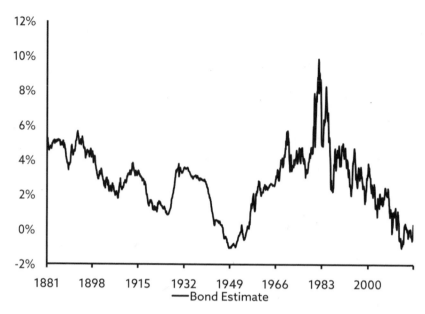

Source: Federal Reserve of St Louis. Calculations by Newfound Research.

What makes the current market environment so strange is that while stock and bond valuations have historically been negatively correlated, they became simultaneously cheap in the 1980s and are now simultaneously expensive.

While the negative correlation allowed a traditionally constructed 60/40 stock/bond mix to provide a semi-constant expected return profile (or, at least, a reasonably floored one) from 1880–1970, the post-1970 period has seen the portfolio shift from very cheap to very expensive.

This means that the outlook for a 60/40 portfolio today is near the lowest it has ever been: our rough math puts the real-return near 2.2%.

60/40 Portfolio Expected Real Returns

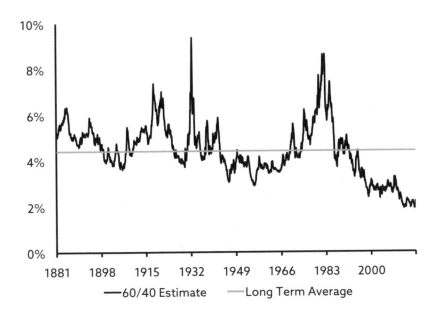

"My dear, here we must run as fast as we can, just to stay in place.
And if you wish to go anywhere you must run twice as fast as that."

There is a significant danger of low expected returns for financial planning. Old rules—using a 60/40 portfolio with a 4% or 5% withdrawal rate—may no longer be safe. We highlighted this risk in our commentary "Impact of High Equity Valuations on Safe Withdrawal Rates."[6] Below are two graphs from that commentary. In the first, the historical results of applying a 4% withdrawal rate to a 60/40 stock/bond allocation. In the second, the same rules applied, but historical results are adjusted downward such that the long-term average return matches the future long-term expected returns.

6   blog.thinknewfound.com/2017/08/impact-high-equity-valuations-safe-retirement-withdrawal-rates

Historical Wealth Paths for a 4% Withdrawal Rate and 60/40 Stock/Bond Allocation with Historical Returns

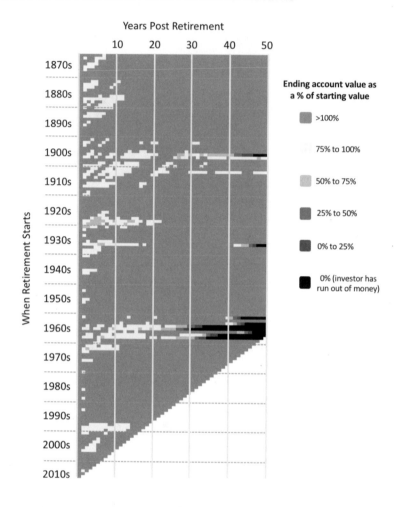

Source: Shiller Data Library. Calculations by Newfound Research. Data from 1870 to 2016. Analysis uses real returns and assumes the reinvestment of dividends. Returns are hypothetical index returns and are gross of all fees and expenses. Results may differ slightly from similar studies due to the data sources and calculation methodologies used for stock and bond returns. Current return expectations are calculated by adjusting the historical returns so that they align with the "Yield and Growth" capital market assumptions from Research Affiliates. These assumptions assume that there is no change in valuations. As of July 2017, these forecasted nominal returns were 5.3% for equities and 3.1% for bonds, compared to the historical averages of 9.0% and 5.3%, respectively.

Historical Wealth Paths for a 4% Withdrawal Rate and 60/40 Stock/Bond Allocation with Current Return Expectations

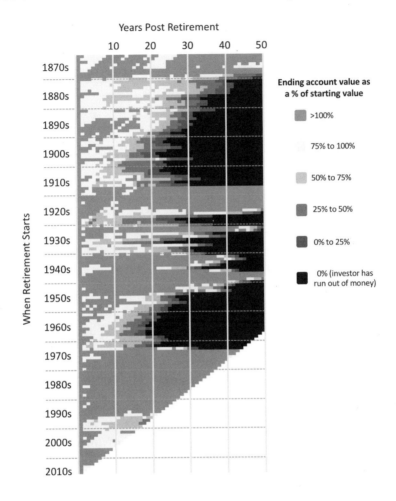

Source: Shiller Data Library. Calculations by Newfound Research. Data from 1870 to 2016. Analysis uses real returns and assumes the reinvestment of dividends. Returns are hypothetical index returns and are gross of all fees and expenses. Results may differ slightly from similar studies due to the data sources and calculation methodologies used for stock and bond returns. Current return expectations are calculated by adjusting the historical returns so that they align with the "Yield and Growth" capital market assumptions from Research Affiliates. These assumptions assume that there is no change in valuations. As of July 2017, these forecasted nominal returns were 5.3% for equities and 3.1% for bonds, compared to the historical averages of 9.0% and 5.3%, respectively.

We see that what was once safe may no-longer be. There is no silver bullet to this problem. Rather, a number of solutions will likely be necessary. Some immediate ideas for dealing with this problem are:

- Increased savings rates during accumulation.

- Significantly reducing fees during retirement.

- Dynamic withdrawal plans.

- Active risk-management plans to address sequence risk.

- Looking outside traditional stocks and bonds for other return generators.

The Weird Portfolio

Fortunately, one of the many positive trends of the last two decades has been the down-stream movement of many asset classes and investment styles once relegated to the world of accredited investors, into low-cost, liquid fund packaging. Exposures like levered loans and emerging market debt, and strategies like equity long/short and global macro, are now available for investor use to complement a traditionally allocated stock/bond portfolio.

If J.P. Morgan's outlook is right, these types of positions may be more important today than ever before.

Plotting expected return versus risk allows us to see that positions like U.S. Large Cap equities and U.S. Aggregate Bonds may no longer be attractive. Rather, positions like U.S. Small Caps, Emerging Market Debt (Local Currency), and Levered Loans may provide much more bang for the investment buck.

J.P. Morgan's 2017 Capital Market Assumptions

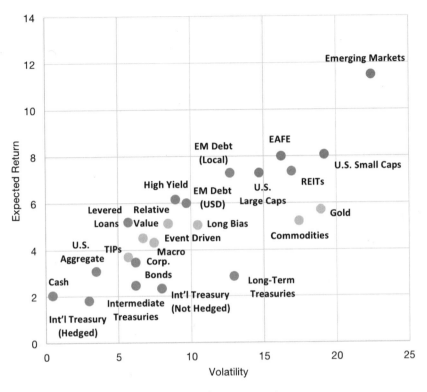

Source: J.P. Morgan's 2017 Capital Market Assumptions

One of our favorite exercises is to take capital market assumptions like these and run them through a traditional mean-variance optimization, targeting the same risk profile of a standard 60/40 stock/bond mix.[7] Unlike us, the optimizer has no attachment to a particular asset class: it simply looks to maximize return for our stated risk target.

The result, today, is a pretty weird looking portfolio.

[7]   Technically, we run a simulation-based mean-variance optimization in effort to account for estimation risk and come up with a more stable allocation profile.

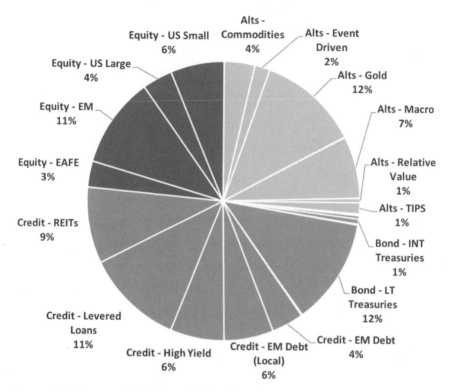

Source: J.P. Morgan. Calculations by Newfound Research. Portfolio constructed using a simulation-based mean-variance optimization and J.P. Morgan's 2017 Capital Market Assumptions.

(We should note that if we perform the same exercise using capital market assumptions from BNY Mellon, BlackRock, or Research Affiliates, the results are very similar).

We see:

- Despite targeting the same risk profile of a 60/40 portfolio, traditional equities and bonds only make up about one-third.

- U.S. large-caps and U.S. aggregate bonds are almost nowhere to be found.

- Equity exposure is dominated by emerging market and U.S. small-cap exposure.

- Bond exposure is almost entirely long-dated U.S. Treasuries. This may seem odd, given that long-term Treasuries offer one of the worst risk-reward trade-offs according to J.P. Morgan's outlook. However, J.P. Morgan's correlation assumptions make them an incredible diversifier to increased volatility of the equity sleeve.

- Traditional "return generators" are largely replaced by credit-like exposures (e.g. high yield bonds, levered loans, emerging market debt, and REITs).

- Traditional "risk mitigators" are largely replaced by diversifying alternative exposures.

We'll be the first to admit that almost *no* investor would be willing to actually hold this portfolio. With nearly 25% of the portfolio in gold and long-term U.S. Treasuries, the tracking error alone would drive most investors mad.

And all just for what amounts to a 1% bump in expected return. While 1% may not seem like much, in a low-return world it is nearly a 25% increase from a traditional stock/bond mix.

While few would feel comfortable implementing this weird portfolio outright, we believe that this exercise provides at least a hint of guidance for investors today: thinking outside the box may be necessary going forward.

Conclusion

"But I don't want to go among mad people," Alice remarked.

"Oh, you can't help that," said the Cat: "we're all mad here. I'm mad. You're mad."

"How do you know I'm mad?" said Alice.

"You must be," said the Cat, "or you wouldn't have come here."

Originally published August 30, 2017;
blog.thinknewfound.com/2017/08/portfolios-wonderland-weird-portfolio.

ABOUT COREY HOFFSTEIN

Corey Hoffstein is co-founder and Chief Investment Officer of Newfound Research, a quantitative asset manager offering a suite of separately managed accounts and mutual funds. At Newfound, Corey is responsible for portfolio management, investment research, strategy development, and communication of the firm's views to clients.

Prior to offering asset management services, Newfound licensed research from the quantitative investment models developed by Corey. At peak, this research helped steer the tactical allocation decisions for upwards of $10bn.

Corey is a frequent speaker on industry panels and contributes to ETF. com, ETF Trends, and Forbes.com's Great Speculations blog. He was named a 2014 ETF All Star by ETF.com.

Corey holds a Master of Science in Computational Finance from Carnegie Mellon University and a Bachelor of Science in Computer Science, cum laude, from Cornell University.

@choffstein

Net Buybacks Supplement Dividend Yields and Support Future Per Share Growth

JEREMY SCHWARTZ

I started working with Wharton finance professor Jeremy Siegel in 2001—right after he started cautioning investors about the very extended valuations in big cap tech stocks when he called them a suckers bet in a Wall Street Journal editorial on March 14, 2000.

Many are worried that the market environment we have currently rhymes with those late 1999 and early 2000 days, with big cap tech stocks again dominating market indexes and pushing up overall market valuation levels.

The most bearish market prognosticators tend to focus on extended market valuations using the cyclically adjusted price-to-earnings (CAPE) ratio.

Robert Shiller and Jack Bogle provide two examples of these forecasters who tend to be more subdued in their outlook for U.S. equities.

I saw Jack Bogle present his outlook for ten-year returns at the 2017 annual Chartered Financial Analyst conference in Philadelphia and Bogle suggested we've seen strong gains in the markets over the last 35 years that resulted from valuation expansion, so he had a subdued outlook. Bogle's model was fairly simple: take the 2% dividend yield on the market today, add in his personal estimates of 4% earnings growth and subtract 2% from speculative market activity or his anticipation of a decline in valuation ratios over the coming decade, and you come up with an outlook for 4% returns over the coming decade. If we assume there is 2% inflation, this would lead to just a 2% real return after inflation. Note that this is largely similar to Shiller's outlook for returns from high CAPE ratios.

One chart that I think is not talked about enough in the context of valuation changes on the market is the dividend payout ratio of the market. I show a smoothed ten-year average dividend payout ratio in the spirit of Shiller's ten-year smoothed earnings for the CAPE ratio. Prior to 2000, the dividend payout ratio averaged 60%. Since 2000, the dividend payout ratio has averaged 40%. This change in the nature of how firms reinvest their earnings, conduct stock buybacks and pay dividends is absolutely critical to the future earnings growth we are likely to get.

Ten-Year Average Smoothed Dividend Payout Ratio

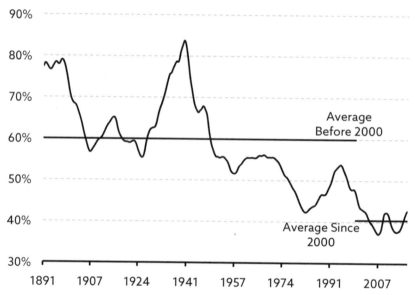

Source: Robert Shiller online data library. Data for the period 2/28/1881–12/31/2017.

Those who assume that earnings growth rates will revert to some historical average growth rate when firms paid out 60% of their earnings as dividends are assuming that all this money not being paid out—used for either buybacks or other reinvestment in business—is being completely wasted. That is an incorrect assumption, in my view.

This chart looks at the rolling ten-year and 20-year earnings growth rates of the CAPE earnings per share (EPS) that Shiller uses to make his dour forecasts on the market. If these numbers were to mean revert, that would be a cautionary tale for the markets. But in my view, the earlier declining dividend payout ratio means we are likely to see upside changes to these earnings figures. What is possible?

Growth Rates in 10- and 20-Year CAPE EPS

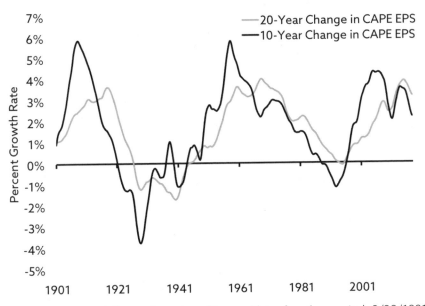

Source: Robert Shiller online data library. Data for the period 2/28/1881–12/31/2017.

Changing dividend payout ratios have already translated to better earnings growth. Prior to 1982, the average dividend yield on the U.S. equity market was approximately 5% per Shiller's data, and we had an average dividend payout rate of nearly two-thirds of earnings paid out as dividends. With only a third of earnings reinvested, firms were still able to achieve earnings growth of 3.3% per year.

	EPS Growth	Avg Div Yield	Avg Payout
1871–1982	3.3%	5.0%	64.7%
1982–2017	5.6%	2.5%	50.9%
Latest Year	16.2%	1.9%	45.6%

Source: Robert Shiller online data library. Data for period 2/1/1871–12/31/2017

Since 1982, payout ratios declined to an average of 51%, while at the same time firms started conducting stock buybacks. The average EPS growth during this period of reducing dividend payout ratios was an increase of 230 basis points (bps) per year, from the previous long-term average of 3.3% per year to 5.6% per year. In just the latest year, there has been a large increase in earnings, with a 16% year-over-year earnings growth in 2017, with an average dividend yield of 2% and average dividend payout ratio of 45.6%.

When we look at the last 20 years, and particularly the last seven, we see consistent signs of 2% dividend yields with 2% net buyback ratios. The latest trailing 12-month net buyback for the S&P 500 was 1.84%. These net buybacks are going to continue to support earnings growth for the ten-year look-ahead period. These firms have locked in future EPS growth because they reduced their shares outstanding.

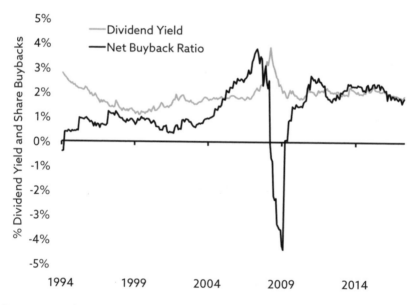

Sources: WisdomTree, Factset. Data for the period 12/30/1994 –12/31/2017. Past performance is not indicative of future results. You cannot invest directly in an index.

Returning to the table above, where I showed the earnings growth since 1982 as being higher than the previous 110 years, the current dividend payout ratios are consistent with an even further drop in the payout ratios from their average since 1982. I can see a case that earnings growth picks up even from that 5.6%-per-year mark that we had for the period 1982–2017. It would not surprise me to see earnings growth of 6% to 7% per year over the next decade.

The standard pushback is that firms are just leveraging up to conduct buybacks—that interest rates are at historical lows, leading to higher margins than are sustainable. The reverse case is that the changing composition of companies—into higher-margin businesses that have more revenue abroad with lower tax rates than in the U.S.—also means margins may not be mean reverting anytime soon either. Of course, no one knows how the future will unfold, including me.

The charts above caution anyone relying on historical patterns of earnings growth trends from over-extrapolating them into the future. Professor Siegel looks at the current earnings yield of the market associated with a 20 price-to-earnings ratio and thinks 5% is a pretty good indicator of long-term, after-inflation real returns. Add in inflation of 2% and you get 7% nominal returns. This is a touch below their historical 6.5% to 7% that he showed in Stocks for the Long Run as being the historical return to U.S. equities, but it is not dramatically different. I think his model for looking at the markets makes more sense than some of these more dour predictions—for what that's worth.

Originally published December 4, 2017; www.wisdomtree.com/blog/2017-12-04/latest-thoughts-on-us-market-valuations.

ABOUT JEREMY SCHWARTZ

Jeremy Schwartz is responsible for the WisdomTree equity index construction process and oversees research across the WisdomTree family. Prior to joining WisdomTree, Jeremy was Professor Jeremy Siegel's head research assistant and helped with the research and writing of *Stocks for the Long Run* and *The Future for Investors*. He is also co-author of the *Financial Analysts Journal* paper "What Happened to the Original Stocks in the S&P 500?" Jeremy is a graduate of The Wharton School of the University of Pennsylvania and currently stays involved with Wharton by hosting the Wharton Business Radio program "Behind the

Markets" on SiriusXM III. Jeremy is also a member of the CFA Society of Philadelphia.

@JeremyDSchwartz

Is Market Valuation Determined By Sectors?

NORBERT KEIMLING

The old business adage "the profit lies in the purchase" also applies to financial markets. Numerous studies show that undervalued equity markets appreciate significantly more than highly valued ones over the long term. For investors, it is therefore an obvious step to compare the valuation levels of different countries and invest primarily in countries with attractive valuations while avoiding expensive markets. For example, if one compares all established equity markets based on the price-to-book ratio (PB), Asian markets such as Singapore and South Korea currently stand out due to their particularly attractive valuations, while Denmark and the US seem expensive. But is it really the case that all countries are comparable with each other in equal measure?

Special case Denmark

In particular, the case of Denmark raises doubts since the healthcare sector dominates the country's equity market in an exceptionally strong way. While this sector accounts for just 9% of the global equity market, it represents almost half of the Danish market (see Chart 1).

Chart 1: Denmark is dominated by the healthcare sector

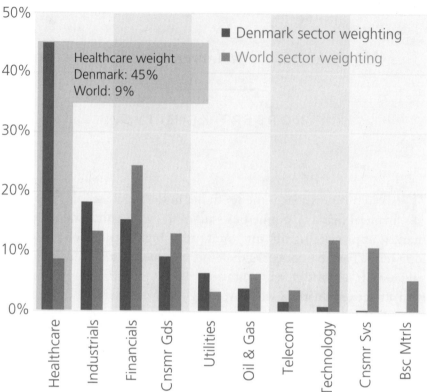

The chart represents the sectoral weighting of the Datastream Denmark Index compared with the Datastream World Index. Source: Thomson Reuters Datastream and StarCapital as of 28/02/2018.

Healthcare raises market valuation

The fact that the global healthcare sector has consistently traded at a significant premium—85% on average—to the global equity market in the past few decades raises the question of whether the Danish equity market with such a high weighting in a traditionally expensive sector will ever be able to return to an average valuation level (see Chart 2).

Assuming that different sectors—e.g. due to industry-specific balance sheet structures—will also have different valuation levels in the future and that the sector structure of a market won't change dramatically in the medium term, it appears worthwhile to analyse the extent to which

Denmark's overvaluation is simply the result of a higher healthcare weighting.

Chart 2: Healthcare sector valuations have been steadily higher

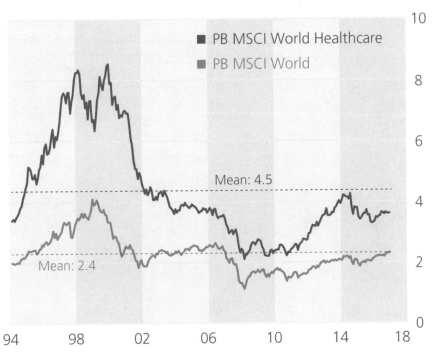

Source: Thomson Reuters Datastream as of 28/02/2018.

This effect can be quantified by comparing Denmark's valuation level with that of a sector-adjusted benchmark. For example, if the global equity market had the same sector composition as Denmark—including the high healthcare weighting—its price-to-book ratio would rise from 2.1 to 2.5. The Danish equity market would no longer be valued 50% higher than the global equity market, but only 28% (see Chart 3). As a result, about half of Denmark's overvaluation is attributable to a divergent sector composition.

Chart 3: Valuation comparison – classical vs. sector adjusted

Country	PB	PB World	PB World sect.-adj.	Discount World	Discount sect.-adj.
Australia	2.0	2.1	1.7	-3%	19%
Austria	1.4	2.1	1.5	-35%	-6%
Belgium	2.0	2.1	2.5	-5%	-20%
Brazil	2.1	2.1	1.6	-1%	27%
Canada	1.8	2.1	1.6	-14%	12%
China	1.1	2.1	1.3	-47%	-14%
Czech	1.5	2.1	1.4	-27%	9%
Denmark	3.2	2.1	2.5	50%	28%
Finland	2.2	2.1	2.0	6%	12%
France	1.8	2.1	2.3	-16%	-23%
Germany	1.8	2.1	2.0	-13%	-10%
Hong Kong	1.7	2.1	1.8	-18%	-6%
Hungary	1.5	2.1	1.5	-27%	5%
India	3.1	2.1	1.9	46%	61%
Ireland	1.9	2.1	1.9	-11%	0%
Israel	1.5	2.1	1.7	-26%	-9%
Italy	1.3	2.1	1.6	-38%	-20%
Japan	1.4	2.1	2.1	-35%	-35%
South Korea	1.1	2.1	2.1	-47%	-48%
Malaysia	1.7	2.1	1.8	-17%	-3%
Mexico	2.3	2.1	2.2	7%	4%
Netherlands	2.0	2.1	2.3	-5%	-12%
New Zealand	1.9	2.1	2.1	-8%	-10%
Norway	1.7	2.1	1.6	-18%	11%
Poland	1.3	2.1	1.5	-36%	-8%
Portugal	1.6	2.1	1.6	-26%	-3%
Russia	0.9	2.1	1.4	-57%	-35%
Singapore	1.2	2.1	1.6	-43%	-25%
South Africa	2.0	2.1	1.7	-4%	19%
Spain	1.6	2.1	1.7	-26%	-8%
Sweden	2.0	2.1	2.0	-4%	1%
Switzerland	2.5	2.1	2.3	20%	9%
Taiwan	2.0	2.1	2.2	-7%	-13%
Thailand	2.3	2.1	1.7	12%	39%
Turkey	1.5	2.1	1.6	-30%	-8%
UK	1.8	2.1	2.0	-15%	-9%
US	3.2	2.1	2.5	53%	30%

"PB World sect.-adj." refers to the sector-adjusted world valuation, i.e. the PB ratio of a notional global equity index that has the identical sector composition to that of the relevant country. Source: StarCapital as of 28/02/2018.

Worldwide sector adjusted valuation

For all other established equity markets, it can be concluded that undervalued markets generally show undervaluations even after a sector adjustment, and vice versa. However, some undervaluations must be put in perspective, for example in Singapore, whose low PB ratio is largely due to a high weighting of (historically attractive) financial stocks (see Chart 4).

Chart 4: Systematically lower PB ratio in the financial sector

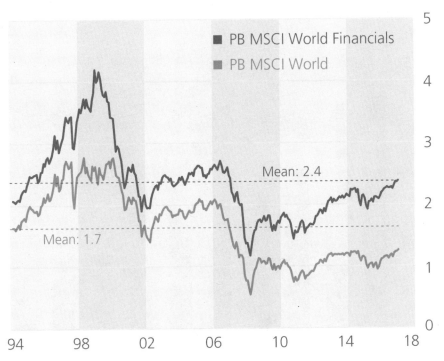

The chart represents the sector weighting of the Datastream US Index compared with the Datastream World Index. Source: Thomson Reuters Datastream as of 28/02/2018.

In the seemingly attractive markets of Norway, Canada and Australia, the undervaluation actually turns into an overvaluation after a sector adjustment due to their high weightings of basic materials stocks and financial stocks. This means that equities in these countries are even valued higher on average compared to their competitors from other countries. However, this remains concealed in a classical PB country comparison.

US overvaluation partially explainable by sectors

The sector structure also has an effect on the high US valuation. Lower exposure to attractively valued financial stocks and an overweighting of comparatively expensive technology stocks inevitably cause the valuation of the US market to rise (see Chart 5).

Chart 5: Sector structure of the US market

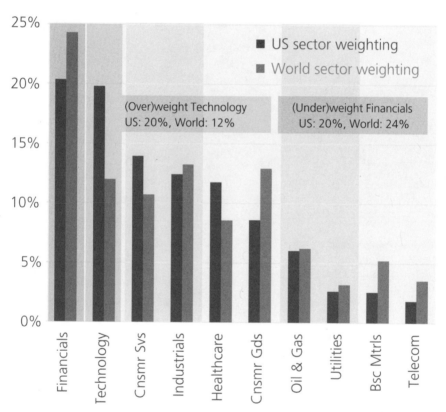

The chart represents the sector weighting of the Datastream US Index compared with the Datastream World Index. Source: Thomson Reuters Datastream and StarCapital as of 28/02/2018.

If the global equity market had the same sector structure as the US market, its PB valuation would rise from 2.1 to 2.5. As a result, about half of the overvaluation is attributable to a divergent sector composition. This effect is similar for other valuation indicators (see Chart 6).

Chart 6: Sector-adjusted valuation of the US market

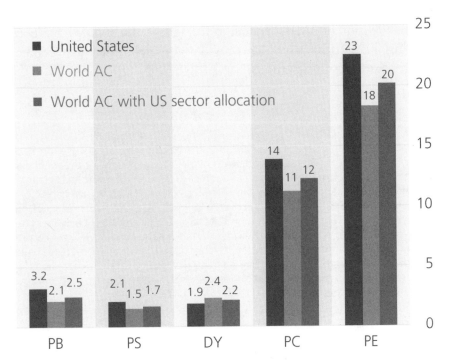

To determine to what extent valuation discounts and premiums of the US market can be explained by its sector weights, we adjust the world's sector weights to match those of the US for five frequently used valuation ratios. United States refers to all US stocks whereas World AC includes all stocks in the Datastream universe. Source: StarCapital as of 28/02/2018.

Conclusion

Investors should therefore scrutinise undervaluations, particularly in smaller countries or in countries with a very divergent sector structure. An equity market with a comparatively attractive valuation does not always include attractive equities.

Originally published April 2018.

ABOUT NORBERT KEIMLING

Norbert Keimling leads the capital markets research section of StarCapital AG. After studying business informatics, he worked for the quantitative research division of AMB Generali in Cologne. Since 2004, he has been working for StarCapital which provides complete asset management services based on mutual funds.

@CAPE_invest

FAANG SCHMAANG

Don't Blame the Overvaluation of the S&P Solely on Information Technology

ANNA CHETOUKHINA AND RICK FRIEDMAN

Introduction

Asmall group of technology stocks have recently delivered stellar returns. Facebook, Apple, Amazon, Netflix, and Alphabet (Google), the so-called "FAANG" stocks, are up 36% on average from January to September 2017. This superlative performance, in such a narrow group of large cap names, has led many to raise questions about the current valuation of the S&P 500, its sector composition, and comparisons to other markets. These questions have included:

- Do the old rules apply? The Information Technology (IT) sector, which has and deserves to trade at a higher multiple, is a larger part of the market today, so comparing today's price multiples to history doesn't make sense, right?

- How can the market be expensive if no sector is trading at extreme valuations relative to its own history as measured by P/E 10 multiples?[1]

---

[1] The P/E 10 ratio, or cyclically adjusted price-to-earnings ratio (also known as the Shiller P/E), is a commonly used valuation measure. It is defined as the current price divided by the average of 10 years of earnings (moving average), adjusted for inflation. The P/E 10 ratio uses smoothed real earnings to eliminate the fluctuations in net income caused by variations in profit margins over a typical business cycle.

373

- Isn't the valuation gap of the US vs. non-US markets justified by the higher weight in IT in the US?

We know that the higher weight in the relatively expensive IT sector is driving some of the expensiveness of the S&P 500, but this does not fully explain the bulk of its high absolute and relative valuation level. In this short note, we'll try to address some of the questions asked above.

Do the old rules apply to a "new" S&P 500?

The sector composition of the S&P 500 has changed meaningfully over the last four decades (see Exhibit 1). As we entered the roaring 1980s, the S&P 500 was dominated by lower-price-multiple, cyclical companies. The Energy, Materials, and Industrials sectors accounted for 45% of the S&P 500 while IT and Health Care made up 15% of the index. IT and Health Care's weight has expanded to 38% today, while the lower-multiple cohort has declined to under 20%.

But that shift to higher-multiple sectors explains only a portion of today's overvaluation as Exhibit 2 suggests. The chart plots the P/E 10 of the S&P 500 based on GMO's bottom-up calculations.[2] The chart also shows the long-term median P/E 10 of the market, essentially the "fair value anchor" for the S&P 500. Today, at 27.3x, the P/E 10 of the S&P 500 is quite elevated, trading 46% above its long-term median dating back to 1970. The static fair value measure, however, doesn't account for the concern we've been hearing so much about recently—the changing sector composition of the market. Comparing today's P/E 10 of the market to its long-term median valuation level makes the assumption that the level the S&P 500 traded at on average in the past is "fair" today. If index composition along some risk dimension one cares about, such as country or sector weights, changed over time, history might not be a very relevant anchor. Or so the argument goes. For any investor, such as GMO, who has considered the fair value of emerging markets, these issues are familiar and part of the assessment process given the dramatic changes the MSCI Emerging Markets index has seen in its country and sector membership over the last few decades.

---

[2] GMO P/E 10 differs from Robert Shiller's data due to a number of implementation choices made in aggregating bottom-up data.

Exhibit 1: S&P 500 Sector Composition Has Evolved Over the Last Four Decades

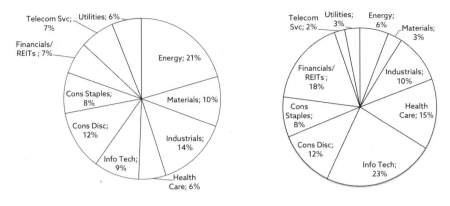

	Median P/E 10 Since 1980
Energy	16.2x
Materials	22.0x
Industrials	20.8x
Financials/REITs	14.3x
Info Tech	28.1x
Health Care	29.4x

Source: GMO. Sector weights rebased to exclude "Other" sectors.

We asked ourselves what the long-term fair value multiple of the S&P 500 would look like if we accounted for the shift in sector weights. This is also captured in the chart by applying long-term, median sector valuations to the shifting weights in the index. As the S&P 500 has rotated in and out of lower- and higher-multiple sectors (based on long-term sector median multiples), the fair value line has shifted between 17.6x and 20.6x P/E 10. The September 30, 2017 "dynamic fair value" multiple of 19.6x, for instance, accounts for the S&P 500's higher concentration in IT and lower weights in Financials and Energy relative to a decade earlier. Incorporating dynamic sector weights acknowledges that some of today's higher valuation is due to a shift in market structure, but it is hardly enough to call the S&P 500 fairly valued. On a dynamic sector basis, the S&P 500 is still a lofty 39% overvalued. While the sector composition of the S&P 500 has migrated to higher-multiple sectors like IT (and Health Care as well), that shift does not render historical multiples useless or relative valuations justified.

Exhibit 2: Current, Long-term Median, and Dynamic Sector-based Median P/E 10 Multiples

As of 9/30/17. Source: GMO. Median P/E 10 line represents median P/E 10 of the S&P 500 from 1970 through September 2017. Dynamic sector-based median P/E 10 tracks the weighted average of the S&P sector weights times the long-term median sector P/E 10 multiples.

If the sector shift to IT accounts for only some of today's expensiveness, what gives? Quite simply, pretty much every other sector, save Energy, is trading expensively relative to its median valuation since 1970 (see Exhibit 3). Yes, more of the S&P 500 is in the IT sector, which is relatively expensive versus other sectors historically and to itself today. But, with every other sector trading at P/E 10 levels far above long-term sector medians, it is easy to see why the overall market is overheated. The Financials, Utilities, and Consumer Discretionary sectors are particularly expensive relative to their own history, trading at premiums of 95%, 80%, and 58%, respectively. We ought to be careful, however, reading too much into valuations of Financials as the sector's ten-year trailing earnings are still materially affected by post-GFC write-offs. Interestingly, the three sectors that don't look particularly expensive, Consumer Staples, Health

Care, and Information Technology, have historically been Growth sectors. Growth prospects for Consumer Staples and Health Care today are far from obvious to us and might not justify valuations normal by historical standards.

Exhibit 3: Long-term Medians vs. Current Valuations

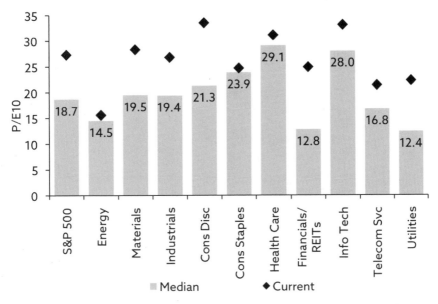

As of 9/30/17. Source: GMO. Medians based on data back to January 1970.

P/E 10 multiples tell only part of the story

While Exhibit 3 makes it clear that S&P sectors are trading expensively relative to the long-term medians, it is true that on a Z-score[3] (or standard deviation) basis current levels are not too extreme. Few sectors, as the display on the left of Exhibit 4 indicates, are trading above 1

[3] A Z-score measures distance from the mean in terms of standard deviations. Z-scores in this exercise are calculated on the natural logarithm of multiples. A log transformation helps map Z-scores to well-defined probabilities given multiples are log-normally distributed. Moreover, log transformation makes Z-scores indifferent to whether one uses multiples or yields (inverted multiples) in calculations, which is convenient and not the case with the simple Z-scores.

standard deviation expensive. Z-scores don't look that extreme in large part because both means, and especially standard deviations of the distributions, were pulled up by the internet (TMT) bubble. The right side of the display, however, makes it clear that on a percentile basis, current P/E 10s are among the most expensive we've seen dating back to 1970. P/E 10s, however, are just one way to view valuations.

Exhibit 4: S&P 500 P/E 10 Multiples Are Stretched

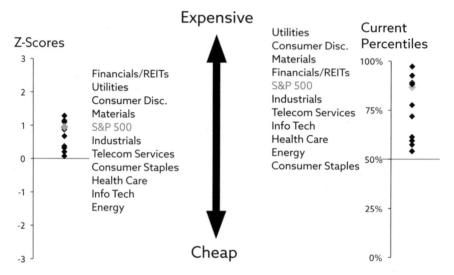

As of 9/30/17. Source: GMO. P/E 10 Z-scores and percentiles based on data back to January 1970.

P/E 10 multiples happen to be one of the more friendly valuation metrics we look at courtesy of the high earnings we've seen over the last decade. When viewed through a sales lens (i.e., Price/Sales, or P/S), today's valuations look even more disturbing. The S&P 500's current 2.1x P/S ratio is 117% overvalued relative to its long-term median and trading just under the peak valuation it reached in March 2000 (see Exhibit 5). Though the dynamic sector approach applied to P/S multiples suggests the S&P 500 warrants a modestly higher P/S multiple due to sector shifts, the S&P 500 would still be 103% overvalued by this measure.

Exhibit 5: Current, Long-term Median, and Dynamic Sector-based Median Price/Sales Multiples

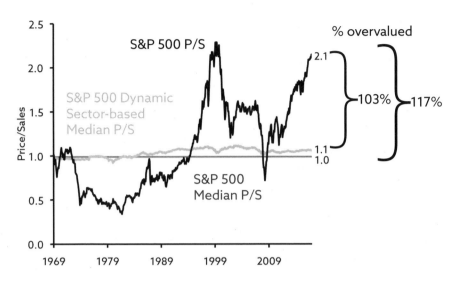

As of 9/30/17. Source: GMO. Median P/S line represents median P/S of the S&P 500 from 1970 through July 2017. Dynamic sector-based median P/S tracks the weighted average of the S&P sector weights times the long-term median sector P/S multiples.

In fairness, many of today's larger capitalization IT companies should trade at higher than historical P/S multiples given their cost structures are significantly more attractive (less traditional cost of goods/higher gross margins) than "old school" technology companies and the broader market. Quite simply, more of a dollar of revenue for these less asset-intensive companies drops down to gross profit and ultimately earnings, the metric that drives equity valuations in the long run. So while these companies typically have higher-than-market P/S multiples, look quite expensive, and pull up the overall market multiple, they do not look as stretched on a Price/Gross Profits (P/GP) basis, which considers revenues net of cost of goods sold. When we look at the P/GP multiple, the S&P 500 looks "only" 64% overvalued adjusting for sector composition (versus 75% expensive without sector adjustments). However you look at it, with valuation discrepancies this high it is still fair to say the S&P 500 is significantly overvalued even after adjusting for sector shifts.

Does EAFE deserve to trade at a lower multiple given its lower weight in IT?

Just as some investors are questioning whether today's S&P 500 is analogous to yesterday's, others are asking if comparing the US to other developed markets is appropriate given the different sector exposures in each geography. Developed ex-US markets as measured by the MSCI EAFE index do look quite different than the US (S&P 500) based on sector weights. At the end of September 2017, 27% of the MSCI EAFE index was in Energy, Materials, and Industrial companies while the S&P 500 had only 19% exposure to those lower-multiple, cyclical sectors (see Exhibit 6). On the other hand, IT and Health Care made up a measly 17% of the MSCI EAFE index while they account for a whopping 38% of the S&P 500. Surely these are disparate assets that should be valued differently. Not so fast.

Exhibit 6: Sector Composition of the S&P 500 and MSCI EAFE

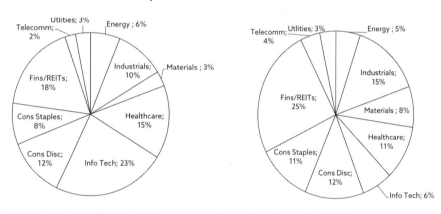

	Median P/E 10 Since 1980	
	S&P 500	**EAFE**
Energy	16.2x	12.5x
Materials	22.0x	21.4x
Industrials	20.8x	26.4x
Financials/REITs	14.3x	25.6x
Info Tech	28.1x	32.8x
Health Care	29.4x	34.1x

As of 9/30/17. Source: GMO.

As Exhibit 7 illustrates, there is a wide gap today between the P/E 10 multiple for the S&P 500 and the MSCI EAFE index at 27.3x and 20.7x, respectively. We would generally expect equities in the US and developed ex-US markets to be priced to deliver similar returns on capital and thus be priced at similar P/E 10 ratios. The chart also plots a line showing the MSCI EAFE sector weights layered on top of S&P 500 sector valuations. Under that approach, the P/E 10 multiple for the S&P 500 falls to 26.1x given lower weights in the more expensive IT and Health Care sectors being applied. However, even after neutralizing the S&P 500 index for sector differences, the index is trading at a significant 26% premium to the MSCI EAFE index.

Exhibit 7: S&P 500 Sector-matched to EAFE and EAFE P/E Ratios

As of 9/30/17. Source: GMO.

The S&P 500's premium, even after adjusting for sector differences, to the MSCI EAFE index is easily explained by looking at the relative valuation levels of the two markets (see Exhibit 8). In eight of ten cases, MSCI EAFE sectors are trading at modest to significant discounts to the S&P 500. Only the IT sector outside the US is trading much above the US level, a sector the MSCI EAFE index is meaningfully underweight relative to the S&P 500.

Exhibit 8: Relative Valuation Levels of S&P 500 and MSCI EAFE Sectors

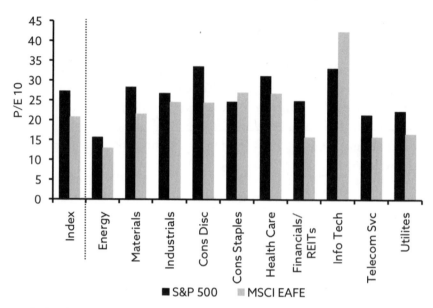

As of 9/30/17. Source: GMO.

Conclusion

Significant sector differences exist across markets and within the same market over time. As economies and markets continue to evolve, so too will shifts in sector composition. Importantly, though, broad equity markets that bear similar levels of risk should deliver similar levels of returns and thus be priced in line with each other. Today's higher S&P 500 weight in the relatively expensive Information Technology sector is cause for some of its expensiveness (both vs. history and other developed markets), but it does not explain away the bulk of its high absolute and relative valuation level. No matter how you cut it, the S&P 500 (and most other markets for that matter) is expensive.

Originally published November 2, 2017; www.advisorperspectives.com/commentaries/2017/11/02/faang-schmaang-dont-blame-the-over-valuation-of-the-s-p-solely-on-information-technology.

ABOUT ANNA CHETOUKHINA AND RICK FRIEDMAN

Anna Chetoukhina is a member of GMO's Asset Allocation team. Prior to joining GMO in 2011, Ms. Chetoukhina was a fixed income quantitative analyst for Wellington Management. Previously, she was a research associate for State Street Associates, LLC. Ms. Chetoukhina earned her B.S. in Economics from Voronezh State University in Russia, her B.A. in Mathematics and Economics from Huntingdon College and her M.S. in Applied Mathematics from Northeastern University. She is a CFA charterholder.

Rick Friedman is a member of GMO's Asset Allocation team. Prior to joining GMO in 2013, he was a senior vice president at AllianceBernstein. Previously, he was a partner at Arrowpath Venture Capital and a principal at Technology Crossover Ventures. Mr. Friedman earned his B.S. in Economics from the University of Pennsylvania and his MBA from Harvard Business School.

Disclaimer: The views expressed are the views of Anna Chetoukhina and Rick Friedman through the period ending October 2017, and are subject to change at any time based on market and other conditions. This is not an offer or solicitation for the purchase or sale of any security and should not be construed as such. References to specific securities and issuers are for illustrative purposes only and are not intended to be, and should not be interpreted as, recommendations to purchase or sell such securities.

Making Private Equity Great Again

DAN RASMUSSEN

From 1990 to 2010, private equity returned 14.4% per year, compared to 8.1% per year for the S&P 500 index. This 6.3% outperformance was net of private equity's "2 and 20" fee structure, meaning that the gross return of private equity over this period was more like 20% per year.

Figure 1: Private Equity vs S&P 500 Total Return (1990–2010)

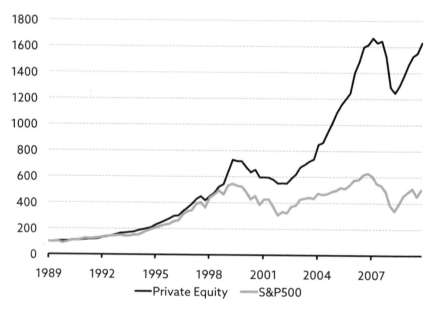

Source: Cambridge Associates, CapitalIQ.

As a result of these two decades of outperformance, the vast majority of institutional limited partners (LPs) believe private equity will continue to outperform the broader market.

Figure 2: Investor Expectations for Private Equity Returns over Public Market Returns

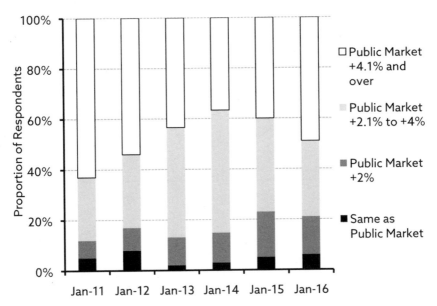

Source: Preqin.

This makes sense theoretically. Private equity firms are leveraging their investments 1:1 and investing in small, illiquid companies, so investors should earn a size and illiquidity premium in addition to getting their leveraged returns. And so investors have poured money into private equity. From 1996 to 2010, private equity firms raised on average $186 billion per year. From 2011 to 2016, private equity firms raised on average $295 billion per year.

The consensus that private equity will outperform public markets is strong. But nobody ever made money agreeing with the consensus, and private equity LPs have missed a tectonic shift in the private equity market. Private equity has, on average, underperformed the public equity market since 2010.

Figure 3: Aggregate Capital Raised by US Private Equity Firms ($B)

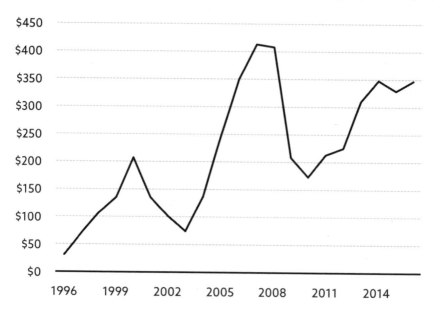

Source: Preqin.

Figure 4: Private Equity vs S&P500 Total Return (2010–2016)

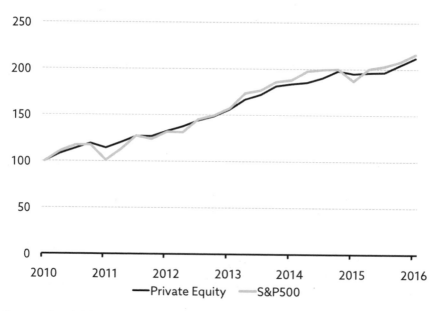

Source: Cambridge Associates, CapitalIQ.

The financial crisis drove a significant shift in the dynamics of the private equity asset class by reminding investors of how painful the volatility of public equity markets could be. The grass looked greener in private markets, where returns had been higher for decades and where reported volatility was much lower. Private equity seemed to solve the two biggest problems for large institutional investors: low yields and highly volatile public markets. And, as a result, private equity became the asset class of choice, a selection cheered on by the investment consultants for whom private funds were a core competency.

But there's no free lunch in markets. The vast influx of new money drove prices up, drove leverage levels into dangerous territory, and diminished the excess return potential of LBO deals.

To fully diagnose what ails private equity, however, we need to understand how private equity traditionally differed from public equity investors and examine what has changed in the post-crisis era.

There are three key differences between private and public equity.

First, private equity deals are significantly smaller than broader public benchmarks. Figure 5 shows the equity capitalization of private equity buyouts compared to the Russell 2000 and S&P500 indices.

Second, private equity deals are significantly more leveraged than the typical public equity. The average net debt to enterprise value ratio at inception for private equity deals is approximately 50%, compared to about 16% for the average small-cap public company (shown in Figure 6).

Thus, private equity deals are much smaller and much more leveraged than public equity investments. These two factors, however, did not change before and after the financial crisis. Private equity deals are roughly the same size and use roughly the same percentage leverage as before the crisis. While these two factors explain what's different about private equity, they do not explain the post 2010 performance drop. This requires examining a third factor.

Figure 5: Size of Private Equity Investments

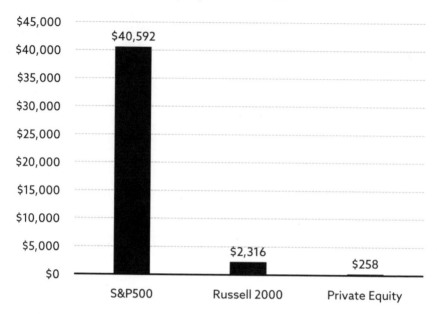

Source: CapitalIQ, Pitchbook.

Figure 6: Net Debt/EV of Private Equity Deals vs Public Markets

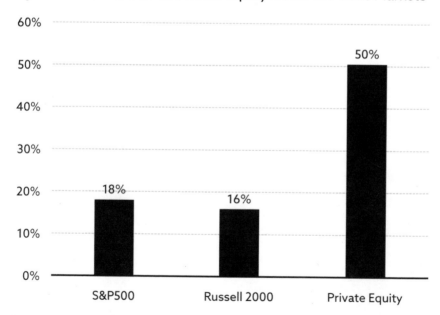

Source: CapitalIQ, Pitchbook.

The third difference between private equity and public equity is that private equity firms have historically bought at a significant discount to public equity markets.

Figure 7: Median EV/EBITDA Multiples of Private Equity vs S&P 500

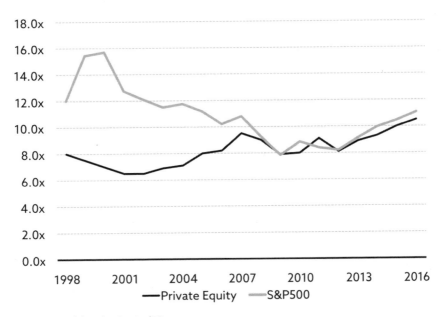

Source: Pitchbook, CapitalIQ.

Here we see a significant shift from before the financial crisis to after. Since the crisis, the flood of money into private equity has driven up purchase prices significantly, eliminating the formerly large gap between private market and public market valuations.

This is more troubling than most market observers understand. Private equity is extremely price sensitive because of the use of debt. Higher prices require more debt, leading to higher interest costs and higher risk of bankruptcy.

The base rate of return on private equity deals done at >10x EBITDA is poor. Historically, over 50% of deals done at >10x EBITDA have lost money. The aggregate multiple of money has been barely 1.0x, and the IRRs have been lower than 5%. In a backtest, a simple "expensive LBO" screen – an equal-weighted portfolio of all liquid public companies trading at >10x EBITDA with >5x Net Debt/EV – underperformed the market with worse drawdowns and higher volatility.

Figure 8: Free Cash Flow Yields vs Purchase Prices at Constant Leverage Ratios

Levered Investment at 5x EBITDA		Levered Investment at 10x EBITDA	
($ in millions)		($ in millions)	
Key Drivers		**Key Drivers**	
Purchase EBITDA Multiple	5.0x	Purchase EBITDA Multiple	10.0x
Leverage as % of TEV	60%	Leverage as % of TEV	60%
Free Cash Flow		**Free Cash Flow**	
EBITDA	$100	EBITDA	$100
(-)CapEx	25	(-)CapEx	25
(-)Interest [8%]	24	(-)Interest [8%]	48
(-)Taxes [35%]	18	(-)Taxes [35%]	9
= Free Cash Flow	$33	= Free Cash Flow	$18
Equity		**Equity**	
EBITDA	$100	EBITDA	$100
(x) Multiple	5.0x	(x) Multiple	10.0x
= Total Enterprise Value (TEV)	$500	= Total Enterprise Value (TEV)	$1000
(-) Net Debt	$300	(-) Net Debt	$600
= Equity	$200	= Equity	$400
Free Cash Flow Yield	17%	**Free Cash Flow Yield**	4%

Source: Verdad.

Private equity deals and public equity investments made with these quantitative parameters are poor, as further evidenced by the lackluster track record of private equity since 2010. These metrics are, of course, foreign to most private equity investors. This is because private equity firms mark their portfolios, rather than relying on a market price. This deceives many investors into thinking that private equity (highly leveraged micro-cap) investments are less volatile than the public markets, which is a statistical illusion. In his paper, "Private Equity's Diversification Illusion," researcher Kyle Welch points out that "private equity returns, based on prior methods of valuation, understate the systematic risk of private equity."[1]

So how can we make private equity great again? What can LPs and general partners (GPs) do to return to the golden era when private equity actually outperformed? The answer is simple: price discipline. Using debt to buy small companies at significant discounts to public equity markets is a well-proven money making strategy. Using debt to buy small companies at double-digit EBITDA multiples is a recipe for failure.

We believe there are three alternatives.

1. Invest in search funds and other micro-cap private equity deals where purchase prices are still low.

2. Invest in private equity firms (like Apollo Global Management) that maintain strict price discipline.

3. Invest in public equities that look quantitatively like the best performing LBOs, trading at <7x EBITDA, with >50% net debt/ EV, and below $1 billion of market capitalization (like the Verdad Leveraged Company Fund).

Figure 9 compares these alternatives to the current state of the private equity market.

Investors shouldn't be fooled by clever marketing about volatility dampening or claims about future returns based on past returns when the asset class was very different. Excess returns in private equity came from buying assets cheap and using debt wisely, not by using debt to pay big prices for trophy assets, all while hiding the underlying volatility of these leveraged microcaps from investors.

We believe the better course is simply to buy cheap, highly leveraged companies in the public markets, replicating the quantitative characteristics of the best performing LBOs. It's a strategy that's served us and our investors well.

---

[1] papers.ssrn.com/sol3/papers.cfm?abstract_id=2379170

Figure 9: Quantitative Characteristics of Alternatives Compared to Broader Private Equity

	Search Funds	Apollo Global Management Fund VIII	Verdad Leveraged Company Fund	Private Equity in the 1990s	Private Equity in 2016
Total Enterprise Value (TEV)	$9.5M	~$1B (estimated)	$2.6B	$250M	$258M
TEV/EBITDA purchase price	5.1x	5.5x	6.7x	6.7x	11.2x
Levarage at acquisition (net debt/ TEV)	70%	~60% (estimated)	50%	50%	48.4%
Historical Return	36.7% IRR gross of fees	13% net IRR as of 12/31/2016	18.5% net IRR since 2012	15.7% average vintage year net IRR	TBD
Source	Stanford Search Fund Primer	Apollo, Verdad Estimates	Verdad	Cambridge Associates, CapitalIQ, Pitchbook	Pitchbook

Originally published May 1, 2017.

ABOUT DAN RASMUSSEN

Dan Rasmussen is the founder of Verdad. Before starting Verdad, Dan worked at Bain Capital and Bridgewater Associates. Dan graduated from Harvard summa cum laude and Phi Beta Kappa and received an MBA from the Stanford Graduate School of Business. He is the *New York Times* bestselling author of *American Uprising: The Untold Story of America's Largest Slave Revolt*. In 2017, he was named in the *Forbes* 30 under 30 list.

@verdadcap

Factors are Not Commodities

CHRIS MEREDITH

"A man with two watches is never sure [what time it is]."

—**Segal's Law excerpt (see below)**

The narrative put forth by "smart beta" products is that factors are becoming an investment commodity. Factors are *not* commodities— rather, they are unique expressions of investment themes. The uniqueness of one Value strategy from another can lead to very different results, and there are many places that factor-based portfolios can diverge. So the difficulty for asset allocators is identifying exactly where and how these factor strategies differ one from another, even when they all claim to use the same themes of Value, Momentum, and Quality.

Over the past couple of years, several multi-factor funds that combine Value, Momentum, and Quality were launched. As these products compete to garner assets, price competition has started among rivals. In December, BlackRock cut fees to its smart beta ETFs[1] to compete with Goldman Sachs, which has staked out a cost leadership position in that market space. Michael Porter, the expert in competitive strategy, wrote in 1980 that there are three generic strategies that can be applied to any business for identifying a competitive advantage: cost leadership, differentiation, or focus.[2] Cost leadership can be an effective strategy,

---

[1]   See bloom.bg/2rO2XHU

[2]   See *Competitive Strategy*, Free Press, New York. The book was voted the 9th most influential management book of the 20th century in a poll of the Fellows of the Academy of Management.

but the key to any price war is for the products to be near-perfect substitutes for one another, just like commodities. This article focuses on how quantitative asset managers can have significant differences—in factor definitions, in combining factors into investment themes, and in portfolio construction techniques—leading to a wide range of investment experiences in multi-factor investment products.

Factor Definition Discrepancies

Value investing through ratios seems to be very straightforward. Price-to-earnings ratios (P/E) are widely accepted as a common metric for gauging the relative cheapness of one stock versus another. Asquith, Mikhail, and Au's "Information Content of Equity Analyst Reports" found that 99% of equity analyst reports use earnings multiples in analyzing a company. P/E ratio is used widely because it's straightforward and makes intuitive sense: as an equity owner you are entitled to the residual earnings of the company after expenses, interest, and taxes. Simply put, P/E tells you how much you're paying for every dollar of earnings.

Getting a P/E ratio is as easy as opening up a web browser and typing in a search. But if you've ever compared P/E ratios from multiple sources, you can get a variety of different numbers for the same company. For example, take a look at Allergan (NYSE: AGN). As of January 12, 2017, Yahoo! Finance gave AGN a P/E of 6.06. But Google Finance gave it 15.84. And if you have access to a Bloomberg terminal, Bloomberg cranked up AGN's P/E to a whopping 734. Meanwhile, FactSet doesn't even have P/E ratios in its database. Given all the latter nuances, you might feel like you're stuck in Segal's Law: "A man with a watch knows what time it is. A man with two watches is never sure."[3]

These discrepancies happen because there are many different ways to put together a P/E ratio. One way could use earnings per share divided by the price of the stock. If so, should "basic" or "diluted" EPS be used? There's a difference if you switch to the LTM Net Income divided by the total Market Cap of the company, as shares can change over a given quarter. But the reason for Allergan's different ratios is that some financial information providers use bottom-line earnings while others

---

[3]　From Arthur Bloch's *Murphy's Law* (2003).

take Income before Extraordinaries and Discontinued Operations. In August 2016, Teva (NYSE: TEVA) acquired Allergan's generics business "Actavis Generics" for $33.4 billion in cash plus 100 million Teva shares, generating earnings of $16 billion from Discontinued Operations. After unwinding this, the company actually lost $1.7 billion in 3Q16—hence no P/E ratio. Depending on whether or not an adjustment is made on this, Allergan would be positioned either as a cheapest percentile stock based on its Earnings Yield (inverse of the P/E ratio) or all the way down into the 94th percentile.

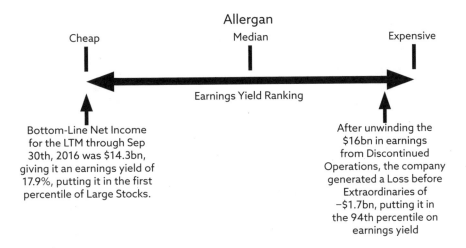

Accounting adjustments for Extraordinaries and Discontinued Operations aren't the only item affecting an earnings ratio. When considering earnings, you really want to measure the available economic surplus that flows to the holder of the common equity. If preferred stock exists, it supersedes the claims of common shareholders. Fannie Mae (OTC: FNMA) is a great example of how preferred dividends can absorb earnings from common shareholders. During the 2008 crisis, Fannie Mae issued a *senior* tranche of preferred stock that is owned by the U.S. Treasury, and is paying a $9.7 billion dividend of the company's $9.8 billion in earnings. There is a *junior* preferred tranche held by investors like Pershing Square and Fairholme Funds—they are currently not receiving dividends and are submitting legal challenges to receive some portion of the earnings. This leaves common shareholders behind a long line of investors with prioritized claims on earnings. But some methodologies' adjusted earnings take preferred dividends after earnings, while others do not, creating a difference in having a P/E of 2.3 (an Earnings Yield of 43%) or a P/E of 185 (Earnings Yield of 0.5%).

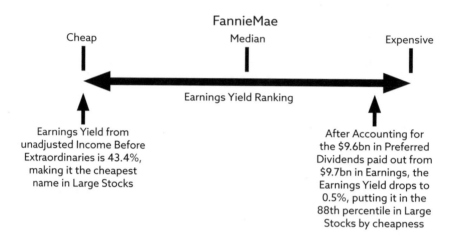

These comments are not about the cheapness of Allergan or Fannie Mae. Instead, it shows the importance of your definition of "earnings" and the adjustments you apply. **If these considerations sound like fundamental investing, it's because they are.** Fundamental analysts consider these adjustments in the analysis of a company. Factor investors work through the same accounting issues as fundamental investors, with the additional burden of trying to make systematic adjustments to create a stronger metric that acknowledges the accounting differences across thousands of companies. Investing results can vary greatly based on these adjustments. In the U.S. Large Stocks Universe,[4] there is a +38bps improvement on the highest decile of Earnings Yield if you adjust for Discontinued Items, Extraordinaries, and Preferred Dividends. To set some comparative scale

---

[4] The universe of Large Stocks consists of all securities with inflation-adjusted market cap greater than the universe average. The stocks are equally-weighted and rebalanced periodically.

using eVestment's peer analysis, the difference between a median manager and a top quartile manager is +60bps a year.

Price-to-Earnings — Cheapest Decile
(Excess Return vs. Large Stocks (1964–2016))

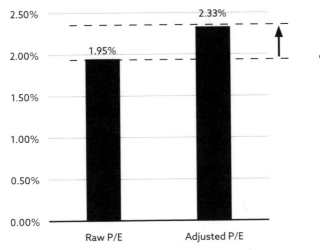

Source: OSAM calculations.

Adjustments to Value signals are not limited to price-to-earnings. Book Value can be adjusted for the accounting of Goodwill and Intangibles. Dividend yield can be calculated using the dividends paid over the trailing 12-months, or annualizing the most recent payment. In 2004, Microsoft paid out $32 billion of its $50 billion in cash in a one-time $3 per share dividend when the stock was trading at around $29. Knowing that future investors won't receive similar dividend streams, should that dividend get included in calculating yield?

Differences in signal construction are not limited to Value factors. Momentum investors know that there are actually three phenomena observed in past price movement: short-term reversals in the first month, medium-term momentum over the next 12 months, and long-term reversals over a three- to five-year period. Put two Momentum investors in a room and they will disagree over whether to delay the momentum signal by one month to avoid reversals, the 12-months minus one-month. Quality investors argue the use of non-current balance sheet items, or the loss of effectiveness in investing on changes in analyst estimates. Volatility can be measured using raw volatility, beta, or idiosyncratic vol, to name just a few methods.

Factors are constructed as "unique expressions of an investment idea" and are not the same for everyone. Small differences can have large impact on which stocks make it into the portfolios. These effects are even more significant when using an optimizer (potentially maximizing errors) or when concentrating portfolios (thereby giving more weight to individual names).

There is **skill** in constructing factors—far beyond simply grabbing a P/E ratio from a Bloomberg data feed.

Alpha Signals

Quantitative managers tend to combine individual factors together into themes like Value, Momentum, and Quality. But there are several ways that managers can combine factors into models for stock selection. And models can get very complicated. In the process of manager selection, allocators have the difficult task of gauging the effectiveness of these models. The common mistake is assuming complexity equals effectiveness.

To demonstrate how complexity can degrade performance, let's take five factors in the Large Stocks space and aggregate them into a Value theme: Price/Sales, Price/Earnings, EBITDA/EV, Free Cash Flow/Enterprise Value, and Shareholder Yield (a combination of dividend and buyback yield).

The most straightforward is an equally-weighted model: give every factor the same weight. This combination of the five factors generates an annual excess return of 4.06 percent in the top decile. An ordinary linear regression increases the weighting of Free Cash Flow-to-Enterprise Value, and lowers the weighting on Price-to-Earnings because it was less effective over that time frame. This increases the apparent effectiveness by +15bps (annualized)—not a lot, but remember this is Large Cap where edge is harder to generate. Other linear regressions, like ridge or lasso, might be used for parameter shrinkage or variable selection and try to enhance these results.

Moving up the complexity scale, non-linear or machine learning models like Neural Networks, Support Vector Machines, or Decision Trees can be used to build the investment signal. There has been a lot of news around Big Data and the increased usage of machine learning algorithms to help predict outcomes. For the example in the following chart, we've built an approach using a Support Vector Regression, a common non-linear machine-learning technique. At first glance, the Support Vector Regression looks very effective, increasing the outperformance of selecting stocks on Value to 4.55 percent, almost a half of a percent annualized return over the equally weighted model.

Highest-Scoring Deciles — Entire Dataset
(Excess Return vs. U.S. Large Stocks (1964–2016))

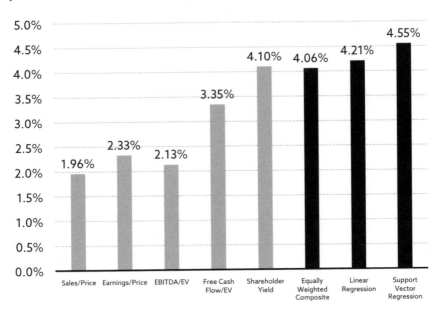

Source: OSAM calculations.

The appeal of a machine-learning approach is strong. Intuitively, the complex process should do better than the simple, and the first pass results look promising. But this apparent edge does not hold up on examination.

This apparent edge is from overfitting a model. Quantitative managers might have different ways of constructing factors, but we are all working with data that does not change as we research ideas: quarterly financial and pricing data back to 1963. As we build models, we can torture that data to create the illusion of increased effectiveness. The linear regression and support vector machines are creating weightings out of the same data used to generate the results, which will always look better.

The statistical method to help guard against overfitting is bootstrapping. The process creates in-sample and out-of-sample tests by taking random subsamples of the dates, as well as subsets of the companies included in the analysis. Regression weightings are generated on an in-sample dataset and tested on an out-of-sample dataset. The process is repeated a hundred times to see how well the weighting process holds up.

In the bootstrapped results, you can see how the unfitted equally-weighted model maintains its effectiveness at about the same level.[5] The in-sample data in the following chart looks just like the first analysis: the linear regression does slightly better and the Support Vector Regression (SVR) does significantly better. When applying the highly-fitted SVR to the out-of-sample data, the effectiveness inverts. Performance degrades at a statistically significant level once you implement on investments that weren't part of your training data.

This doesn't mean that all weighted or machine learning models are broken, rather that complex model construction comes with the risk of overfitting to the data and can dilute the edge of factors. Overfitting is not intentional, but a by-product of having dedicated research resources that are constantly looking for ways to improve upon their process. When evaluating the factor landscape, understand the model used to construct the seemingly similar themes of Value, Momentum or Quality. Complexity in itself is not an edge for performance, and makes the process less transparent to investors creating a "black box" from the density of mathematics. Simple models are more intuitive and likely to hold up in the true out-of-sample dataset, the future.

Various factor products that can generate several hundreds of basis points of difference in a single year are not commoditized and should not be

---

[5] "Bootstrapping" is a statistical resampling technique. It takes 1/3 of the companies for 1/3 of the dates, builds the weighting scheme, and tests the results on the remaining dates.

chosen for investment in because of a few basis points in fees. Cost leadership is the key feature for generic market-capitalization weighted schemes, but product differentiation and focus in the context of fees should be the reasons for investing in multi-factor products.

Cheapest Deciles by Value — Bootstrapped Results (Excess Return vs. U.S. Large Stocks (1964–2016))

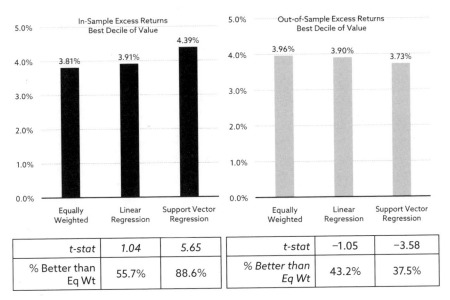

	In-Sample Excess Returns Best Decile of Value	
t-stat	1.04	5.65
% Better than Eq Wt	55.7%	88.6%

	Out-of-Sample Excess Returns Best Decile of Value	
t-stat	−1.05	−3.58
% Better than Eq Wt	43.2%	37.5%

Source: OSAM calculations.

Summary

There is significant edge in how factor signals are constructed. The difficulty is creating transparency around this edge for investors. Complexity of stock selection and construction methodology decreases transparency, almost as much as active quantitative managers that create a "black box" around their stock ranking methodologies. This leaves investors at a disadvantage when trying to differentiate between quantitative products. This inability to differentiate is why price wars are starting between products that have strong differences in features and results.

Investors need education on this differentiation so they're not selecting only on the lowest fees. Sophisticated manager selection focuses on people, philosophy, and process, as well as performance. These things will still matter in understanding a factor portfolio, but now they need to add expertise on understanding factors and portfolio construction. Large institutional and investment consultant manager selection groups will have the difficulty of adding top-tier quantitative investment staff to help with this differentiation. Smaller groups and individual investors will have to advance their own understanding of how quantitative products are constructed. For all of these factor investors, it will help to build trusted partnerships with quantitative asset managers willing to share insights on the factor investing landscape.

Originally published, March 2017; www.osam.com/pdfs/research/_18_Commentary_FactorsAreNotCommodities_Mar-2017.pdf.

ABOUT CHRIS MEREDITH

Christopher Meredith is the Director of Research for O'Shaughnessy Asset Management, an equity asset management group managing $6bn for institutional and individual investors. He is also Visiting Lecturer at the Johnson School of Cornell University where he co-teaches the Cayuga Fund, an asset management program designed to help students start or enrich their career in equity research.

@ChrisMeredith23

Buyback Derangement Syndrome

CLIFFORD ASNESS, TODD HAZELKORN,
AND SCOTT RICHARDSON

People seem to forget some of the very basic lessons of financial economics when it comes to share repurchases. Over the last few years, there has been a lot of press, pundit, and political attention paid to share repurchases, the vast majority unduly critical. A common critique is that each dollar used to buy back a share is a dollar that is not spent on business activities that would otherwise stimulate economic growth. Oh, if only it were that simple.

We do not believe that this harsh narrative appropriately reflects the true impact of share repurchases on the economy as a whole. In fact, the true impact of share repurchases is difficult to estimate, and any estimate requires far more nuanced analysis than has been offered. It is possible, of course, that an individual company's repurchase decision might be in the best interest of shareholders—possibly because of management's pessimistic assessment of investment opportunities, or possibly from reducing the agency costs that can accompany a large cash hoard.[1] In contrast, it is also possible that some repurchase decisions are suboptimally motivated by different agency issues, such as the desire to boost stock prices ahead of anticipated management options exercise.[2]

---

[1] In the academic literature, *agency costs* refer to potential principal–agent problems that can take place when management does not own a firm and thus might pursue negative net present value activities. Some examples include spending money on executive perks and pursuing projects that do not increase shareholder value in the interest of empire building.
[2] See earlier work by Vermaelen [1981] and Brennan and Thakor [1990]. A

403

Note that the preceding arguments are about how share repurchases may help or hurt shareholders. Oddly, some more extreme repurchase critics argue that share repurchases are problematic precisely *because* they maximize current shareholder value. According to this narrative, shareholders act myopically, rewarding share repurchases even though the repurchases ultimately rob them (and the economy as a whole) of future profitable investments. This claim is exceptionally difficult to substantiate, and those proffering it do not make any serious effort to do so. Crucially, this argument also ignores the fact that all of the capital that is distributed via share repurchases must be reinvested somewhere.[3] These sorts of uneconomic blanket claims regarding the collective motivation of aggregate share repurchase activity are particularly concerning but are not our main focus here because addressing unsubstantiated accusations is difficult.

Many of the less extreme criticisms of repurchases seem to arise simply from faulty beliefs and an incomplete presentation of the data. This is where this article comes in. Our goal is to highlight some key myths related to stock repurchase activity for U.S. publicly traded firms.[4] Because so much of the recent criticism of share repurchases relies on these myths, we conclude that this criticism is, to a large extent, unfair.

We are not the first to comment on the relative benefits and costs of share buyback activity. Notably, Edmans [2017] and Fried and Wang [2017] have both recently addressed some of the same criticisms of share

---

recent paper by Manconi, Peyer, and Vermaelen [2015] documents internal evidence that supports previous evidence of short-term and long-term positive excess returns associated with share repurchases in the United States. Dittmar [2000] documented that firms use excess cash to repurchase stock to distribute excess cash, take advantage of undervaluation, and fend off takeovers. The "agency issues" argument is documented by (among others) Almeida, Fos, and Kronlund [2016] and Bens et al. [2003], both of whom show that firms sometimes appear to use share repurchases to manage earnings per share (EPS).

[3]   A set of heroic assumptions is required to support the claim that proceeds from share repurchases are not ultimately invested. One would need to follow the cash received as part of the share repurchases and conclude that it is being held in a safe (or a mattress). Otherwise, the claim is difficult to substantiate.

[4]   Rather than providing formal statistical proof of our claims, we will rely on a set of graphs that visually demonstrate that these claims are unsubstantiated.

repurchases that we address. Our aim is to bring together multiple threads on the topic from both the academic and practitioner communities.

We address four myths related to aggregate share repurchase activity. First, although total dollars spent to repurchase shares is high today relative to history, companies are not self-liquidating, as some claim, because repurchases have largely been financed by debt issuance. Inferences on aggregate repurchase activity are heavily dependent on the source of funds, but this source is often completely ignored. Second, there is no obvious link between aggregate repurchase activity and a decline in aggregate investment activity. Third, aggregate repurchase activity is not, and cannot be, responsible for the strong equity market returns over the last eight years. Therefore, more prosaically, share repurchasers are not "propping up the market." Fourth, aggregate repurchase activity is not associated with mechanical or automatic earnings per share (EPS) growth, as is often claimed. Finally, we share a set of potential pitfalls of share repurchases that merit further consideration because, unlike these four, they might not be mythical.

Myth 1: Companies Are Selfliquidating Using Share Repurchases At A Historically High Rate

Statements about the magnitude of aggregate share repurchase activity need to be placed in context. Yes, the number of dollars spent repurchasing shares is higher today than in the past, but this muddles changes in the scale of the economy and changes in the typical balance sheet of firms through time.

We examine various share repurchase measures for the constituents of the Russell 3000 Index from 1990 through 2017. Exhibit 1 shows the dollar value of gross and net share repurchase activity for these firms.[5] It is true that the dollar value of share repurchases is at elevated levels. However, levels are not as high as they were prior to the financial crisis. More importantly, comparing dollar values through time (as we, following many market analysts, do in Exhibit 1) is misleading if there are substantial

---

[5]   *Gross share repurchases* are total dollars used to repurchase shares, ignoring issuance. *Net issuance* is gross issuance less total dollars raised in share issuance. For more detail on these calculations, see the notes to Exhibit 1.

changes in the aggregate size of firms: Dollar share repurchases can be larger simply because firms are larger. Exhibit 2 shows the same dollar repurchase measures simply scaled by aggregate market capitalization. Here it is clear that current levels of aggregate share repurchase activity are not at all-time highs. On a yield basis (i.e., measured against market capitalization), share repurchases are even lower relative to pre-crisis levels.[6] Furthermore, when properly normalized, the upward trend in share repurchases over the last five years disappears.

Exhibit 1: Gross and Net Share Repurchase Activity

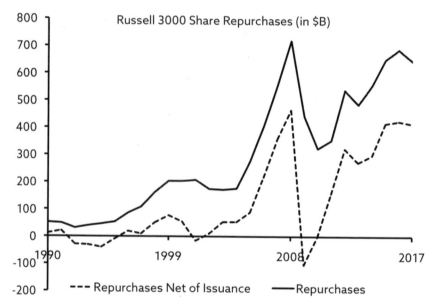

Notes: Repurchases equals the purchase of common and preferred stock, as reported in the financing section of the statement of cash flows for each firm, cumulated over all stocks in the Russell 3000 Index. Repurchases net of issuance equals the purchase of common and preferred stock minus the sale of common and preferred stock, as reported in the financing section of the statement of cash flows, cumulated over all stocks in the Russell 3000 Index. Sources: Compustat and Russell.

---

[6] Some might argue that normalizing by market capitalization is problematic because market capitalization has been pushed upward "artificially" because of share repurchases (we show in Myth 3 that it is unlikely that this effect is large). Share repurchases still seem very normal relative to history if we normalize by the book value of equity or the book value of assets.

Exhibit 2: Gross and Net Share Repurchase Activity Scaled by Aggregate Market Capitalization

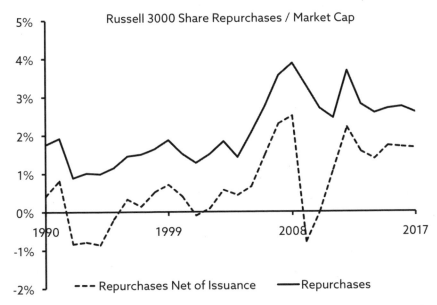

Notes: Repurchases and repurchases net of issuance are as defined in Exhibit 1. Market capitalization is the product of shares outstanding times the price per share, cumulated over all stocks in the Russell 3000 Index. Sources: Compustat, Russell, and MSCI.

Because much of the criticism of repurchases arises from concerns that they come at the expense of investment, it seems reasonable to focus on share repurchases net of issuance, rather than gross repurchases (because *net*, not *gross*, tells us about what is left for investment). Net share repurchases are (by construction) lower than gross share repurchases. However, like gross repurchases, they are high relative to history on an unadjusted basis, but more ordinary relative to history when scaled by market capitalization.

The next question is what is funding these share repurchases. Is it the case that companies are using cash on-hand or liquidating potentially productive assets to fund buybacks? Or are companies using capital raised externally? The answer is, largely, the latter. Although share repurchases have been on the rise since the end of the financial crisis, so has net debt issuance. Exhibit 3 shows aggregate net debt issuance and aggregate net share repurchase activity, both scaled by market capitalization from 1990 to 2017. Exhibit 3 also shows aggregate net capital issued by Russell 3000 companies (net debt issuance minus total net repurchases), also scaled by market capitalization. Aggregate (scaled) capital issuance took a huge hit in the financial crisis, but it has been steadily rising since and is now again above zero. This key fact is usually unmentioned when share repurchase critics link repurchases to diminished corporate investment. Aggregate issuance from firms over the last five years has been *positive*, although not back to pre-crisis levels. Furthermore, it is clear that there is a strong positive correlation between aggregate debt financing and aggregate share repurchase activity. A considerable portion of the recent share repurchase activity has simply been a recapitalization, shifting from equity to debt. Given low real and nominal rates, it is quite possible that corporate treasurers have viewed debt financing as cheaper than equity financing and thus engaged in this swap. This is interesting, but not for reasons that would directly affect investment.

Exhibit 3: Aggregate Net Debt Issuance, Aggregate Net Share Repurchase Activity, and Aggregate Net Capital Issuance, Scaled by Market Capitalization (1990–2017)

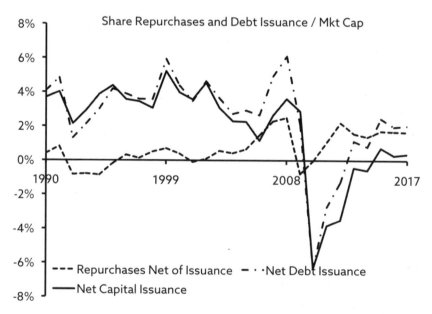

Notes: Repurchases net of issuance equals the purchase of common and preferred stocks minus the sale of common and preferred stocks, as reported in the financing section of the statement of cash flows, cumulated over all stocks in the Russell 3000 Index. Net debt issuance is equal to long-term debt issuance plus short-term debt change minus long-term debt reduction, cumulated over all stocks in the Russell 3000 Index. Net capital issuance is equal to net debt issuance minus repurchases net of issuance. Sources: Compustat, Russell, and MSCI.

Myth 2: Share Repurchases Have Come At The Expense Of Profitable Investment

The claim that share repurchases have come at the expense of profitable investment is not consistent with either finance theory or an empirical examination of the sources and uses of capital among U.S. corporates.

First, empirically, net investment has not declined (we always like it when we can start with "the very thing in question is not happening" and then move on to subtler issues!). We measure aggregate net investment using information from the statement of cash flows for each firm.[7] Exhibit 4 shows that from 1990 to 2017, total investment by Russell 3000 companies has trended steadily upward, other than a precipitous decline and recovery around the financial crisis. Normalized by either total assets or total (debt plus equity) market capitalization, total investment is lower than it was in the 1990s but also increasing since the financial crisis. Most importantly, for present purposes, there is no apparent negative relationship between normalized investment and share repurchase activity. In fact, the two variables have been positively correlated of late, as both investment and share repurchases have increased since the end of the financial crisis.[8]

[7]   We use a cash f low–based measure of investment activity because it allows us to capture both increases (investment, capital expenditures, and acquisitions) and decreases (disposals of property, plant, and equipment) in firm-level investment activity.

[8]   Obviously we are not suggesting any causality.

Exhibit 4: Russell 3000 Investment (1990–2017)

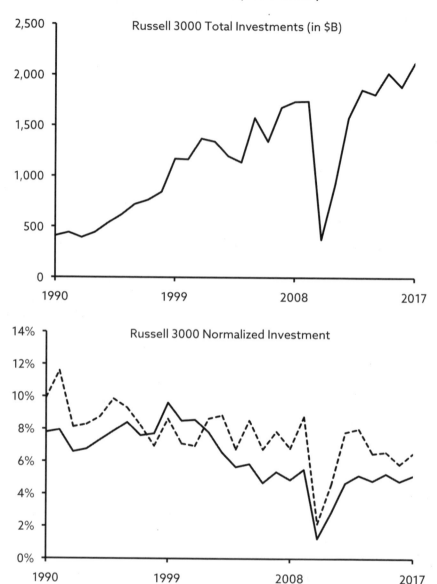

Notes: Investments equals increase in investments minus decrease in investments plus short-term investments plus capital expenditures plus acquisitions plus other investing activities minus sale of property plant and equipment, as reported in the financing section of the statement of cash flows, cumulated over all stocks in the Russell 3000 Index. Total market capitalization is the product of shares outstanding times the price per share plus total long-term debt, cumulated over all stocks in the Russell 3000 Index. Assets equals total assets, cumulated over all stocks in the Russell 3000 Index. Sources: Compustat, Russell, and MSCI.

Second, from a theoretical perspective, the idea that share repurchases prevent profitable investment is causally reversed. In the presence of functioning capital markets, corporations raise capital when they want to invest and pay back capital (in the form of either debt or equity) when they do not have viable (profitable) investment opportunities. Could the claim that companies do have viable investment opportunities and are simply not choosing to pursue them be established empirically by critics? Perhaps, if there existed some well-established measure of investment opportunity and share repurchase critics showed that, controlling for the investment opportunity set, repurchasers underinvest relative to nonrepurchasers. Such a test is implied by many if not all of the recent critiques (that is, they act as if it has been carried out with definite answers damning to repurchasers). Yet, to the best of our knowledge, none of the recent criticisms offer such proof, or even a hint.

Relatedly, investors' proceeds from share repurchases do not simply disappear. Rather, these funds are received by equity investors, who can (and do) allocate the proceeds elsewhere, thereby funding other investments. In fact, the redirection of available capital to the best available investment opportunities is the very purpose of a well-functioning capital market.

Myth 3: The Recent Run-Up In Prices Is The Result Of Share Repurchases

Claims that aggregate share repurchase activity caused the significant run-up in stock indexes over the last decade are heroic at best. These claims are often made ignoring the fact that this issue has been extensively studied.

Academic evidence suggests that the announcement impact on returns of share repurchases is between 1% and 2% on average.[9] Corporate finance theory dictates that share repurchases are greeted positively by investors

---

[9]   Bhattacharya and Jacobsen [2016] and Chemmanur and Li [2014], among others, have looked at returns around share repurchase announcements.

for a few reasons. First, repurchases might signal that management believes that shares are undervalued. Parenthetically, if management sees shares as undervalued—which we believe is the most likely motivator of share repurchases—it seems inconsistent with the idea that management is, at the same time, forgoing abundant attractive growth opportunities.[10] Second, because interest payments are tax deductible, debt-financed repurchases can be viewed as good news because of the resulting lower tax burden.[11] Third, investors may feel as though it is better for management to return excess cash to shareholders, rather than chasing less economic pet projects. This kind of agency cost is often characterized as empire building, and avoiding it has long been viewed as one of the benefits of returning cash to shareholders.

It is very difficult to precisely measure the marginal impact of share repurchases on returns. We compute a (very rough) approximation of cumulative index level returns if returns were driven only by share repurchases. If *every* index constituent repurchased shares in a given year at historically normal sizes, this would account for between 1% and 2% index level price appreciation based on the academic evidence referenced earlier. The recent bull market, whether measured from March 2009 or from January 2013, has been accompanied by annualized returns on the Russell 3000 of more than 15%. The 1% to 2% annual increase from share repurchases is a small percentage of the total run-up of the index, and even this is certainly overstated because far from all firms repurchase shares annually.

---

[10] It is inconsistent that management would engage in a repurchase because it thinks shares are undervalued and simultaneously not care that it could maximize this value further with forgone positive net present value (NPV) projects.

[11] Finance theory posits that there is a trade-off between tax efficiency and bankruptcy costs as leverage increases. If the (competitive and reasonably efficient) market responds positively to share repurchases, then the pre-recapitalization leverage must have been suboptimal.

Myth 4: Companies That Repurchase Shares Do So Only To Increase EPS And Thereby "Price"

Share repurchase critics argue that share repurchases are designed to artificially increase EPS and thereby artificially increase stock prices. We take issue with both claims, but particularly the second claim. The idea is that by repurchasing shares, a company decreases its share count and thus mechanically increases its earnings per share. The problem with this argument is that it ignores the fact that decreased cash means lower earnings, either due to less interest earned on the cash[12] or the loss of returns from other uses of the cash. Only if the cash that is used for share repurchases is truly idle (sitting in the chairman's desk drawer) would we agree that share repurchases increase EPS. Next, the assertion that any increase in EPS leads to a commensurate increase in share price reflects a naive understanding of basic corporate finance (e.g., Modigliani–Miller). The corporate finance argument is that any increase in leverage that increases EPS increases risk at the same time. The net effect is a "wash" on firm equity value. Holding constant P/E ratios and asserting that as earnings rise (due to leverage) price must rise as well misses this obvious point: All else is not equal because risk has gone up commensurately. If increasing share value is this easy, then the question is why do we not see even more share repurchases than we do?

As to the data, this is a harder myth to debunk. A necessary, but not sufficient, condition to support this myth is that firms that engage in repurchase activity should have high levels of EPS growth compared to otherwise similar firms that do not engage in share repurchase activity. However, comparing the EPS growth of firms that do and do not engage in share repurchase activity is not an apples-to-apples comparison.[13]

With the caveat in mind that this comparison is coarse, we compare EPS growth rates for constituents of the Russell 3000 from 1991 through 2016 that do and do not engage in share repurchase activity. Empirically, there is no clear link between repurchases and EPS growth: EPS growth rates

---

[12] Admittedly, this is not as much of an issue at current interest rates.

[13] Although we acknowledge that comparing the EPS growth rates of repurchasing and non-repurchasing firms is problematic, we would have thought that proponents of this myth would at least have evidence that repurchasing firms have *higher* EPS growth rates.

for firms that do not repurchase shares is approximately 1% higher than the EPS growth of repurchasers. We do not find this result surprising, in part because the very fact that firms elected to repurchase stocks quite possibly says something negative about their investment opportunity set and hence future growth. It does, however, throw some water on the myth that share repurchases creates earnings growth.

Finally, more generally, the belief that managers repurchase shares to "juice" EPS and thus stock price is a very strong statement about market inefficiency. It implies markets are very easy to fool in a repeated and obvious way. It also implies that there should be a strong trading strategy taking the other side (buying firms that do not repurchase and shorting firms that do). Any takers? We would caution that the opposite has been true on average for quite a while.[14][15]

Some potentially valid criticisms of share repurchases

It is not all great news. There are ways share repurchases could, at least potentially, be a negative.

Managers of public companies *can* act in a manner that deviates from shareholder value maximization. Again, financial economists refer to the incentives that lead to these deviations as agency problems. For example, the management of a company might choose to repurchase shares ahead of an anticipated managerial options exercise. Senior executives typically have compensation that is directly related to either share price changes or earnings (EPS) levels and growth rates. As discussed in Myth 4, share repurchases should not increase EPS over time. However, a carefully timed share repurchase, just ahead of an earnings announcement, can reduce share count and thus mechanically increase earnings per share

[14] Evidence of positive (negative) returns after share repurchases (issuance) has been given by researchers including Ikenberry, Lakonishok, and Vermaelen [1995]; Loughran and Ritter [1997]; and Bradshaw, Richardson, and Sloan [2006].

[15] The implication of such a trading strategy would be that the market inefficiently processes share repurchase– driven EPS changes. Note that because we are arguing against this particular form of market inefficiency does not imply that we are believers in perfect markets (nobody really believes in perfection).

relative to what it would have been absent the repurchase. Critics of share repurchases offer little evidence, however, that this is the primary driver of share repurchase decisions. If this is an issue, a simple solution would be modification of compensation contracts to adjust EPS growth for repurchase effects, akin to adjustments often made for dividend decisions in the context of employee share options. We would endorse such a change.

It is also possible that management might choose share repurchases in lieu of dividends to protect the value of equity incentives held in the form of stock options (Fenn and Liang [2001]). Usually, management stock options are not protected from the price-decreasing effect of dividend payments. Share repurchases can be used to avoid these price declines. Again, a simple fix to compensation contracts is likely warranted.

A second potentially valid criticism of share repurchases (considered in combination with the concurrent increase in debt), is that (perhaps) firms have taken on too much leverage. If firms issue debt to repurchase shares, balance sheet leverage can, of course, increase. On the other hand, if leverage started out low relative to recent history, then even with an increase due to share repurchases, leverage can remain at a low level. Exhibit 5 shows the evolution of aggregate leverage for Russell 3000 firms from 1990 to 2017. Leverage levels have been increasing recently, as befits a debt-for-equity exchange, but from a level that is low relative to history to a level still low (measured by book value) or relatively normal (measured by market value).

Exhibit 5: Evolution of Aggregate Leverage for Russell 3000 Firms (1990–2017)

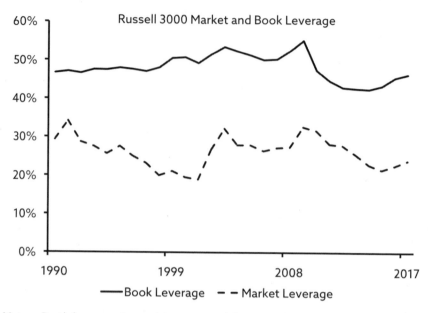

Notes: Book leverage is total long-term debt, cumulated over all stocks in the Russell 3000 Index, divided by the sum of total long-term debt and total common equity, cumulated over all stocks in the Russell 3000. Market leverage is total long-term debt, cumulated over all stocks in the Russell 3000 Index, divided by the sum of total long-term debt, cumulated over all stocks in the Russell 3000 Index, and the product of shares outstanding times the price per share, cumulated over all stocks in the Russell 3000 Index. Sources: Compustat, Russell, and MSCI.

Examining market-level leverage measures conceals some interesting sector-level dynamics. Exhibit 6 shows market and book leverage for financial sector companies and industrial (nonfinancial) sector companies. Since the financial crisis, the financial sector has been steadily deleveraging. At the same time, the leverage of industrials has been edging higher. Market leverage for industrials is close to the historical average, but book leverage for industrials is at a post-1990 high. However, for industrials the range between high and low historical book leverage levels is quite narrow, so current leverage levels still do not appear alarmingly high.

Exhibit 6: Market and Book Leverage for Financial Sector and Industrial Companies

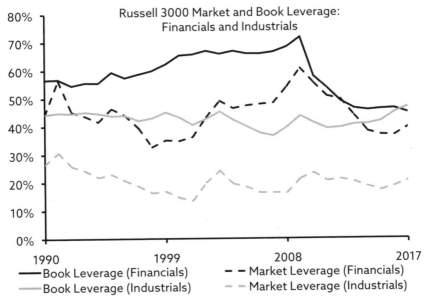

Notes: Book leverage and market leverage are as defined in Exhibit 5. Financials are all companies in the Russell 3000 in the Global Industry Classification Standard (GICS) Sector 40. Industrials are all companies in the Russell 3000 with GICS Sector <>40. Sources: Compustat, Russell, and MSCI.

Conclusion

The popular press is replete with commentary seeking to damn the behavior of corporate managers in handing free cash flow back into the hands of shareholders. Investment professionals have even been heard to comment on the profligate use of free cash f low when it is used to buy back common shares. These criticisms are often, even regularly, without merit (at least merit that can be demonstrated), sometimes glaringly so.

Although there is always the possibility for agency issues to create incentives for corporate managers to engage in suboptimal share repurchase decisions, we feel that in aggregate, share repurchase activity is far less nefarious than the popular press would lead you to believe. In fact, there is at least as much "agency theory" arguing that paying back free cash flow is a positive as there is that it is a negative.

Aggregate share repurchase activity has not been at historical highs when measured properly, and when netted against debt issuance is almost a non-event, it does not mechanically create earnings (EPS) growth, does not stifle aggregate investment activity, and has not been the primary cause for recent stock market strength. These myths should be discarded.

We thank Toby Moskowitz, Antti Ilmanen, Ronen Israel, John Liew, Jacob Boudoukh, Matthew Richardson, Kristoffer Laursen, and Roni Israelov for their helpful comments and suggestions.

References

Almeida, H., V. Fos, and M. Kronlund. "The Real Effects of Share Repurchases." *Journal of Financial Economics*, Vol. 119, No. 1 (2016), pp. 168-185.

Bens, D.A., V. Nagar, D.J. Skinner, and M.H.F. Wong. "Employee Stock Options, EPS Dilution, and Stock Repurchases." *Journal of Accounting & Economics*, Vol. 36, No. 1–3 (2003), pp. 51-90.

Bhattacharya, U., and S. Jacobsen. "The Share Repurchase Announcement Puzzle: Theory and Evidence." *Review of Finance*, Vol. 20, No. 2 (2016), pp. 725–758.

Bradshaw, M.T., S.A. Richardson, and R.G. Sloan. "The Relation between Corporate Financing Activities, Analysts' Forecasts, and Stock Returns." *Journal of Accounting & Economics*, Vol. 42, No. 1–2 (2006), pp. 53–85.

Brennan, M.J., and A.V. Thakor. "Shareholder Preferences and Dividend Policy." *The Journal of Finance*, Vol. 45, No. 4 (1990), pp. 993–1018.

Chemmanur, T., and Y. Li. "The Role of Institutional Investors in Open-Market Share Repurchase Programs." Working paper, 2014.

Dittmar, A.K. "Why Do Firms Repurchase Stock?" *The Journal of Business*, Vol. 73, No. 3 (2000), pp. 331–355.

Edmans, A. "The Case for Stock Buybacks." *Harvard Business Review*, September 15, 2017.

Fenn, G., and N. Liang. "Corporate Payout Policy and Managerial Stock Incentives." *Journal of Financial Economics*, Vol. 60, No. 1 (2001), pp. 45–72.

Fried, J., and C. Wang. "Short-Termism and Capital Flows." Working paper, 2017.

Ikenberry, D.L., J. Lakonishok, and T. Vermaelen. "Market Underreaction to Open Market Share Repurchases." *Journal of Financial Economics*, 39 (1995), pp. 181–208.

Loughran, T., and J.R. Ritter. "The Operating Performance of Firms Conducting Seasoned Equity Offerings." *The Journal of Finance*, 52 (1997), pp. 1823–1850.

Manconi, A., U. Peyer, and T. Vermaelen. "Buybacks around the World." Working paper, 2015.

Vermaelen, T. "Common Stock Repurchases and Market Signalling: An Empirical Study." *Journal of Financial Economics*, Vol. 9, No. 2 (1981), pp. 139-183.

Disclaimer

AQR Capital Management is a global investment management firm and may or may not apply investment techniques or methods of analysis similar to those described herein. The views expressed here are those of the authors and not necessarily those of AQR.

ABOUT CLIFFORD ASNESS, TODD HAZELKORN AND SCOTT RICHARDSON

Clifford Asness is managing principal at AQR Capital Management in Greenwich, CT.

Todd Hazelkorn is managing director at AQR Capital Management in Greenwich, CT.

Scott Richardson is a principal at AQR Capital Management in Greenwich, CT, and a professor at the London Business School in London, U.K.

Reconciliation Principle:
Returns and Forecasts Must Add Up

ED EASTERLING

H ope springs eternal... until it confronts reality.

When it comes to stock market returns, results as well as outlooks are bounded by an axiom that my firm Crestmont Research coined as the Reconciliation Principle. This principle is a tool that can be used in two ways. It can be used in forward mode to develop your own outlook for future returns. In addition, it can be used in reverse to assess the validity of forecasts for stock market returns from analysts and pundits.

Unconventional Wisdom

Conventional wisdom holds that stock market returns are random. That is true over days, weeks, months, and even a few years. But contrary to conventional wisdom, stock market returns are highly predictable over periods that reflect investors' horizons—periods either side of a decade. This predictability occurs because stock market returns are driven by component parts.

First, total return from the stock market consists of capital gains and dividends. Second, capital gains are driven by earnings growth and price-earnings ratio (P/E) expansion or contraction.

Therefore, the Reconciliation Principle states that both past returns and future forecasts must be supported by results or assumptions for (1) earnings growth, (2) dividend yield, and (3) P/E change. Too often, analysts and pundits confidently forecast future returns based upon history or hope, without being able to defend their prognostications with reasonable assumptions for the three components.

Figure 1. Only Three Components of Total Return

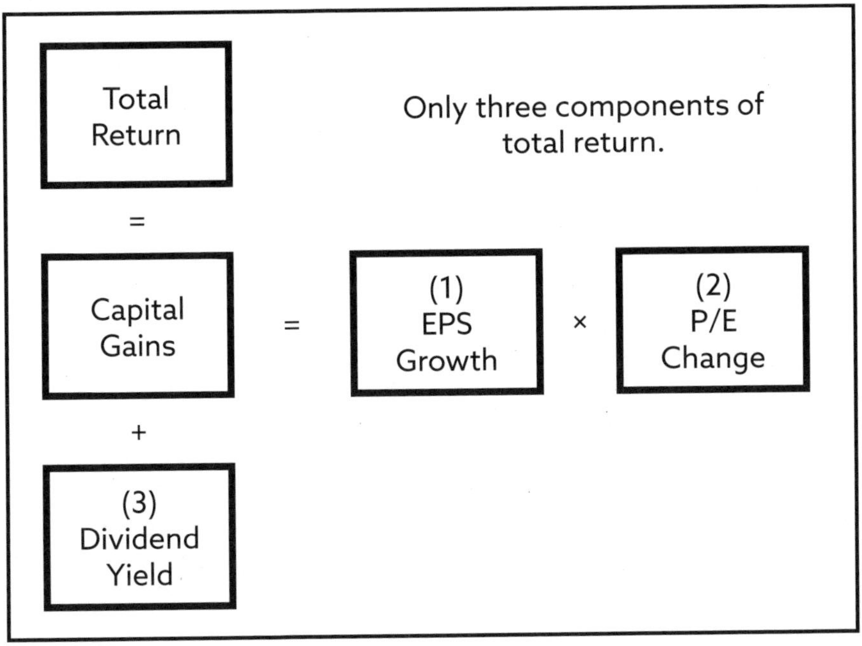

Only three components of total return.

$$\text{Total Return} = \text{Capital Gains} + \text{(3) Dividend Yield}$$

$$\text{Capital Gains} = \text{(1) EPS Growth} \times \text{(2) P/E Change}$$

To illustrate, the *2017 SBBI Yearbook*, by Roger Ibbotson, et al., includes an update to one of the most recognized series of long-term stock market returns. From the start of the series in 1926 to the end of last year (2016), the compounded average annual nominal return was 9.99%.

Ibbotson's *Yearbook* goes further and supports that aggregate average with component values. Earnings growth provided 5.0%, dividend yield added 4.2%, and P/E expansion topped it off with almost 0.8%.

Frequently, 10% is used as a reasonable expectation of return for patient investors. Certainly, the logic goes, an average derived from data spanning more than 90 years should provide a reasonable outlook for investors that are patient enough to allow the long term to deliver that average return.

However, it is most important to note that Ibbotson's 10% is not the average from a collection of long-term returns, but rather it is the average for a specific and unique long-term period (1926–2016).

Thus the 10% return was the result of investing across 91 particular years, starting with P/E at 10.2, receiving a high dividend yield due to a low starting P/E, experiencing average inflation of 2.9%, and ending with P/E having more than doubled.

For an investor today, the starting conditions are quite different. The low rate of inflation has driven normalized P/E into the high 20s. One result of high P/E is low dividend yield. Additionally, low inflation portends lower nominal earnings growth than the historical average (since average inflation was higher).

Principles, Not Randomness

Not only is total return from the stock market driven by the fundamental principle of three components, but also each of the three components is driven by fundamental principles. Not one of the three components is a random element. Each of them has a tangible and definitive driver. This set of relationships further reinforces that stock market returns are not random.

Figure 2. Drivers of the Components

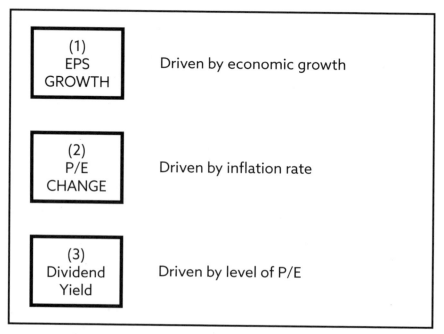

In brief, earnings per share (EPS) growth is driven by economic growth. P/E expansion and contraction are driven by the inflation rate. Dividend yield is driven by the starting level of the P/E ratio. We'll explore each of the components individually.

First, let's look at earnings growth. Figure 3 displays the long-term relationship between economic growth and earnings growth. One line is economic growth, as measured by GDP. The other line is earnings per share for the S&P 500 Index.

The two series have a very consistent relationship over time, *because* they are fundamentally related. GDP is essentially the net sales of all companies in the economy. As noted by the illustration in the lower left of the graph, earnings emanate from sales. The oscillation of EPS above and below the GDP line simply reflects numerous business cycles playing out over time.

Further, earnings are reported in nominal terms. That's the reason that nominal GDP is used in Figure 3. Reporting in nominal terms means that the series includes the effects of the inflation rate. When the inflation rate rises, nominal series tend to increase faster. Likewise, when inflation declines, nominal series tend to have slower growth rates. Then in a deflationary period, nominal series often decline as the effects of deflation more than offset any real growth.

The key takeaway is that earnings growth is driven by economic growth, and over the long term, earnings don't and can't grow faster than nominal GDP. Actually, earnings growth for the larger, public companies listed in the stock market tends to be just slightly slower than economic growth. This difference occurs because economic growth includes faster-growing small companies as well as new start-ups.

Some analysts are quick to respond that the revenues and profits of larger companies, like those in the S&P 500 Index, include a relatively large international component. As a result, those companies can have faster earnings growth than the U.S. economy does as a whole.

That would be true for a single company with lots of emerging-market business, but for the group as a whole, the vast majority of international business occurs in Europe and Japan—both with slower economies than the U.S. Fortunately, those companies also have some business with emerging economies, which does help to increase their earnings growth rate back toward the average U.S. rate.

Finally, when comparing forecasts to historical data, keep in mind that the historical growth rate for real GDP in the U.S. is 3.3%. Current long-term forecasts expect 2.0% to 2.5% real growth for the U.S. (due to demographic changes and other forces).

Figure 3. Earnings & Economic Growth

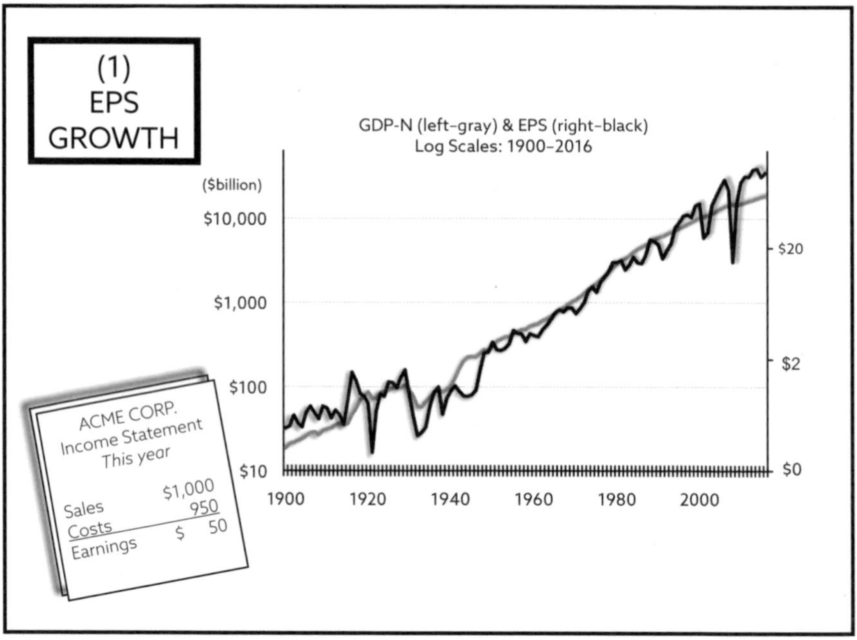

For this article, we'll optimistically assume that real GDP growth returns to its long-term average. That assumption serves two purposes. First, the outlook for stock market returns is sobering enough; a bit of optimism can serve as a spoon full of sugar. Second, it avoids the need to discuss the effect of slower growth on P/E. Slower growth has significant implications. More can be found in my earlier article, "Game Changer."

The next component of total return is dividend yield. Figure 4 displays the very strong relationship between dividend yield and the P/E ratio.

Figure 4. Dividend Yield vs. P/E

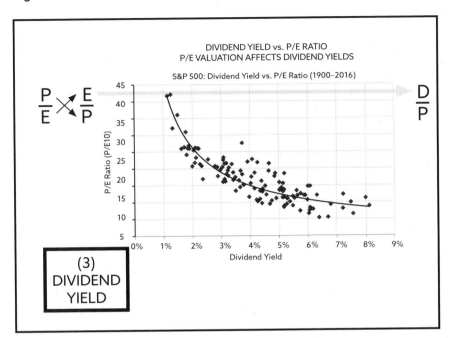

Copyright 2017, Crestmont Research (www.CrestmontResearch.com).

The vertical axis presents a range of values for the P/E ratio. The horizontal axis shows values for dividend yield. Each point on the graph represents the combination of values for each year since 1900.

For years with high P/E, dividend yield tended to be lower. For years with low P/E, dividend yield tended to be higher. This occurs for mathematical reasons.

P/E can be inverted to create the formula for earnings yield. P/E becomes E/P.

Dividend yield is D (dividend) divided by P. Both expressions have P in their denominator, and since dividends are paid from earnings, their relatively tight relationship simply reflects variations in the dividend payout ratio over time.

The key takeaway is that periods starting with high P/Es have low dividend yields. Investors in the market or buying stocks today are baking-in a low dividend yield because their basis will be a relatively-high

P/E. The contribution of dividend yield to total return for a given period, therefore, is necessarily low for periods that start with high valuations.

The final component of stock market total return is P/E change. If the P/E of the market rises over an investor's holding period, the effect of such multiple expansion is an addition to capital gains and total return. A declining P/E takes away from total return.

Figure 5 shows that P/E is not random. It is not simply a factor that is driven by psychology or money flows. On the vertical axis is a range for the inflation rate. On the horizontal axis is a range for P/E. Each dot represents the combination of values for each year since 1900.

Figure 5. P/E & the Inflation Rate

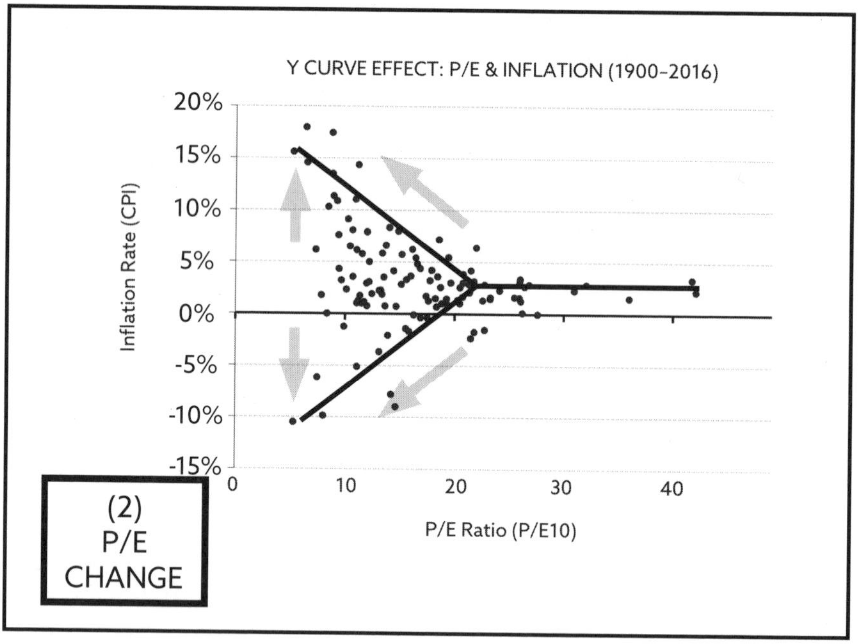

Copyright 2017, Crestmont Research (www.CrestmontResearch.com).

This graph displays the Y-Curve Effect. The stem that extends to the right comprises the late-1990s bubble years. Otherwise, the upper fork shows that P/E declines as the inflation rate rises. The lower fork shows that P/E declines as inflation turns into deflation. The highest sustainable values for P/E occur when the inflation rate is low and stable.

Therefore, today's relatively high P/E is the result of low inflation and low interest rates. Actually, with the current normalized P/E near 30, momentum in the market has P/E about 20% or so higher than the fair-value level associated with low inflation.

The level and trend of P/E is driven by the inflation rate, due to a series of financial tradeoffs. Let's take a moment to explore the underlying driver for P/E. This is the empowering part of our discussion. When we realize that long-term returns from the stock market are principle-driven (rather than random), we become empowered and better able to structure portfolios and align expectations with the market environment. Such understanding can cure an investor's affliction of "market helplessness," which is the anxious feeling that one's portfolio is subject to the arbitrary whims of the market.

Tradeoffs

Would you rather have $20 today or a guaranteed $1 per year for the next 20 years? Of course, you'd rather have the $20 up-front. With $20 today, you can earn a return and have more than $1 per year for 20 years.

But what about $15 up-front instead of $1 for 20 years? ... or maybe $10. How will you decide your point of indifference, the tradeoff price?

Depending upon the environment, there is an amount up-front that delivers $1 of principal and interest for 20 years. That amount will vary depending upon current market returns. When returns are higher, the initial amount needed is generally lower, and vice versa.

This effect is exactly what investors experience with bonds. When the inflation rate and interest rates rise, bond values fall. The point of indifference decreases as rates rise and increases as rates fall.

This happens because investors have tradeoffs between financial instruments and commodity assets. Inflation drives up the prices of commodity assets in nominal terms, and investors often use commodity investments to protect against or to participate in price increases due to inflation.

As a result, investors in financial instruments will seek a return that is competitive with commodities. Since most financial investments can't or don't quickly adjust their cash flows, investors adjust the prices they are willing to pay. Thus, when the inflation rate rises, bond and stock values decline. Since P/E is the price of the market index divided by today's earnings, the effect of inflation-driven valuation change is a change in P/E.

That process holds true until the inflation rate goes negative into deflation. That's the lower-left fork in Figure 5. Worsening deflation leads to lower P/E.

Why does this happen? Consider the example in this graphic. Scenario A reflects slightly rising nominal cash flows. Scenario B is slight deflation. Finally, scenario C is worsening deflation.

Prices in Deflation

A...	$5	$5	$5	$6	$6
B...	$5	$5	$4	$4	$3
C...	$5	$4	$3	$2	$1

Copyright 2017, Crestmont Research (www.CrestmontResearch.com).

Which set of cash flows has the highest value? Of course, A. The second most valuable is B, and C has the lowest value. Since "value" is the P in P/E, we can see that P/E declines into worsening deflation.

In summary, the inflation rate drives P/E over the long term as it moves either toward or away from a low, stable rate.

Over the short run, however, many factors move markets well away from long-term value. These factors include psychology, market momentum, current events, etc.

Quantified & Applied

We started this discussion by refuting the conventional wisdom that long-term stock market returns are random. We acknowledged that short-term returns are highly random, primarily because there are so many noneconomic and nonfinancial factors that affect the markets in the short run.

We then found that the long term is disconnected from the short term specifically because long-term returns are driven by fundamental principles. We saw that stock market returns consist of only three components and that each of the three components is itself driven by a fundamental principle rooted in economic, mathematical, or financial tradeoffs.

The components and their drivers are embodied in the axiom coined as the Reconciliation Principle. That tool is useful not only to forecast returns but also to validate analysts' forecasts. Let's apply the Principle.

We discussed the Ibbotson series of stock market returns earlier. That series is very helpful, because it includes data for each of the three components. Yet that series also has shortfalls when applied to estimating future returns.

The series started when P/E was low, at 10.2 according to Ibbotson. The low starting P/E boosted dividend yields in the series. Further, since P/E has more than doubled since the start of the series, that component is also contributive in ways that are not available from today's lofty P/E level.

Finally, because the inflation rate during the series averaged 2.9%, the third component, earnings growth, also benefited from a tailwind that is not present today. The Ibbotson series threaded the needle of benefits. It was helped by an elevated inflation rate during some years, yet also received the benefit of having the inflation rate decline in later years, thereby increasing P/E.

Looking forward, let's contrast two future outcomes based upon inflation rate scenarios. One assumption is that the inflation rate stays low and stable for the next decade. The second scenario assesses the effect of the inflation rate's increasing to historically average levels.

The first column in Figure 6 shows the values for each component in the 91-year series according to Ibbotson.

The second column reduces the future growth rate for earnings to reflect a low inflation rate.

Rather than the historical 5% average annual growth rate, the scenario in column two assumes 4% (implicitly assuming 1.9% inflation rather instead of the historical 2.9%).

The second column reflects current dividend yields, which are lower due to a P/E that is much higher today than in 1926. Finally, P/E is assumed to remain at current levels.

This is the most optimistic aspect of the column-two scenario. (Almost no one is calling for P/E expansion over the next decade, and many expect that P/E will shift back slightly into the mid-20s. If so, that would shave somewhat more than 1% annually from this scenario's return.)

The most prevalent financial outlook by advisors and investors includes somewhat higher inflation in the near future. The third column shows the effect of the inflation rate rising to its historical average.

Figure 6. Probable Returns Next 10 Years

	Ibbotson (1926–2016)	Low Inflation (2017–2027)	Avg Inflation (2017–2027)
Earnings.......	5.01%	4.01%	5.01%
Dividend......	4.19%	2.00%	2.00%
P/E..............	0.79%	0.00%	–5.50%
	9.99%	6.01%	1.51%

NOTES: (1) In 1926, P/E was 10.2x, (2) inflation rate averaged 2.9%, (3) historical real economic growth 3%+

Copyright 2017, Crestmont Research (www.CrestmontResearch.com).

Under this average-inflation scenario, nominal earnings growth could be expected to be near its average; thus we'll carry over 5% from the past. Since the scenarios in Figure 6 relate to investments in the stock market at today's relatively high valuation, the column-three scenario includes dividend yield at current levels.

Finally, as the inflation rate rises to its historical average, P/E will decline to its own average level. The effect of P/E declining by 40%–50% over a decade is a reduction in returns of near 5%–6%, thus the figure of -5.5% in column three.

Although additional inflation does help each year's nominal earnings growth, the additional inflation also causes P/E to decline. When this trend continues over a period of a decade or so, the valuation change due to P/E decline represents well more than a decade of nominal earnings gains. Only when the investment period nears a century does the effect of inflation on annual earnings gains nearly equal the effect from P/E contraction.

Implications

Just as farmers know to plant watermelon and tomatoes in June and grow winter wheat and onions in cooler seasons, advisors and investors should adjust their investment approach based upon the market environment. During low- and rising-valuation secular bull markets, investors can successfully deploy passive, market-driven strategies. Yet in periods like today's that feature high and potentially falling valuations (i.e., secular bear markets), investors need more active, diversified, and skill-based strategies.

In chapter 10 of my book *Unexpected Returns*, I developed a boatman's analogy to describe this investment philosophy: "Sailing vs. Rowing." During a generally rising secular bull market, investors can open the sail and use the tailwinds of the market to propel portfolio gains. Yet when conditions change into a choppy, volatile, secular bear market, investors need to lower the sail and pull out the oars to row the portfolio forward. Rowing involves a more active and diversified approach to portfolio management, and it requires a broader range of investments.

Here's a key point. Often, investors use the mythical 10% stock market return as a threshold for non-stock investments. They rely on mistaken conventional wisdom to assume that a long-term investor will receive 10% from a portfolio of stocks. Therefore, they reject many other alternatives that often have expected returns of 5% to 7%, or so (e.g., REITs, master limited partnerships, convertible preferred stocks, option strategies, commodities, annuities, active skill strategies, etc.). They mistakenly believe that these alternatives will detract from long-term success.

Conventional wisdom has misled investors to expect 10% to be the norm, especially when patience is amply applied. But no amount of patience will deliver 10% to current investment portfolios. For investments in the market today, or ones that were added during other high-valuation (high-P/E) periods, investors will never achieve long-term average returns near 10%. (See my previous article, "Waiting for Average.")

In reality, the long-term horizon for most investors is a decade or two. Therefore, decade-long periods are most relevant. When we use the laboratory of history and graph the frequency of "average-return decades," we find few of them. Investors far more often confront "summers" and "winters" in the market than some hypothetical annual average of all seasons.

Figure 7 provides the frequency of average returns for decades since 1900 in three categories: below average, average, and above average. Decades start with every year since 1900, thus 1900–1909, 1901–1910, etc. For the average return, since so few of the decades had returns near 10%, the range has been expanded to include all decades with annualized total return between 8% and 12%.

Figure 7. Average Rarely Happens

FREQUENCY OF 10-YEAR RETURNS BY RANGE
Annual Total Returns: S&P 500 (1900-2016)

46%

40%	1902-1911	1935-1944				
	1903-1912	1937-1946				
	1904-1913	1938-1947				
	1905-1914	1961-1970				
	1906-1915	1962-1971				
	1907-1916	1964-1973			33%	
	1908-1917	1965-1974				
30%	1909-1918	1966-1975		1918-1927	1955-1964
	1910-1919	1967-1976		1919-1928	1976-1985
	1911-1920	1968-1977		1920-1929	1977-1986
	1912-1921	1969-1978		1921-1930	1978-1987
	1913-1922	1970-1979		1922-1931	1979-1988
	1914-1923	1971-1980	20%	1942-1951	1980-1989
20%	1915-1924	1972-1981		1943-1952	1981-1990
	1923-1932	1973-1982	1900-1909	1958-1967	1944-1953	1982-1991
	1924-1933	1998-2007	1901-1910	1959-1968	1945-1954	1983-1992
	1925-1934	1999-2008	1916-1925	1960-1969	1946-1955	1984-1993
	1926-1935	2000-2009	1917-1926	1963-1972	1947-1956	1985-1994
	1927-1936	2001-2010	1934-1943	1974-1983	1948-1957	1986-1995
10%	1928-1937	2002-2011	1936-1945	1975-1984	1949-1958	1987-1996
	1929-1938	2003-2012	1939-1945	1993-2002	1950-1959	1988-1997
	1930-1939	2004-2013	1940-1949	1994-2003	1951-1960	1989-1998
	1931-1940	2005-2014	1941-1950	1995-2004	1952-1961	1990-1999
	1932-1941	2006-2015	1956-1965	1996-2005	1953-1962	1991-2000
0%	1933-1942	2007-2016	1957-1966	1997-2006	1954-1963	1992-2001

| <8% | 8% to 12% | >12% |

As you can see in the graph, 80% of decades since 1900 have delivered returns outside this fairly wide range for average. And as you might expect, the periods in the right-hand column generally started with below-average P/E, while the periods in the left-hand column generally started with above-average P/E.

Considering that today's P/E is in the top 5%–10% of highest P/E years, the next decade has virtually no chance of locating in the right-hand zone. Even the middle zone seems beyond hope.

Therefore, based upon the quantitative forecast of 1%–6% annualized returns for the next decade and a reality-check review of empirical history that places the next decade well into the left-hand zone, investors should be prepared to align their expectations appropriately and row their portfolios.

When considering investments for the portfolio, keep in mind that alternatives expected to deliver 5%–7% annualized returns are not only attractive compared to likely near-future stock market returns, but also those alternatives can provide diversification and risk mitigation.

Conclusion

Conventional wisdom holds that long-term returns from the stock market are random. That creates a sense of market helplessness. This affliction is reinforced by the seemingly logical, yet inaccurate, conclusion that short-term randomness is followed by even greater longer-term uncertainty. However, the short term is subject to temporary divergences from principles that are reliably valid in the long term. In recent decades, numerous respected professors and product providers have further engrained conventional wisdom and the acceptance of buy-and-hold as the prudent approach.

Hope springs eternal… until it confronts reality. The past 17 years have led investors to challenge conventional wisdom and to seek a deeper understanding of the stock market. Crestmont's Reconciliation Principle enables advisors and investors to peel back the cloak and see the fundamental principles that drive the market. It's empowering! The Principle enables investors to see that the current high P/E destines the stock market to an extended period of below-average returns, but it also helps them to take the actions necessary to achieve long-run investment success.

Further, the Reconciliation Principle is a powerful tool in discussions with market analysts. When you next talk with one about his or her longer-term outlook, be sure to ask for a breakdown of the component parts of projected market returns. Then, for each of the parts, keep in mind the economic, mathematical, or financial tradeoffs that drive it. Although the components may experience randomness in the short run, they are ultimately driven by financial and economic principles that realign them with natural relationships.

This discussion has been about the value of understanding and assessing the environment over your investment horizon. Just as army generals survey battlefields before advancing, pilots assess the skies before take-off, and farmers plant crops according to the season, successful investors and advisors should assess the market environment in order to develop effective investment strategies. Market weather may be hard to predict, but market climate can be credibly determined.

A confident understanding of the market and its probable outcome will enable much easier and more effective investment decisions. As Albert Einstein once remarked, "If I were given one hour to save the planet, I would spend 59 minutes defining the problem and one minute resolving it."

Originally published July 7, 2017; www.crestmontresearch.com/docs/Stock-Reconciliation-Principle.pdf

ABOUT ED EASTERLING

Ed Easterling is the author of *Probable Outcomes: Secular Stock Market Insights* and the award-winning *Unexpected Returns: Understanding Secular Stock Market Cycles.* He is currently president of Crestmont Research, an investment management and research firm. In addition, he previously served as an adjunct professor and taught the course on alternative investments and hedge funds for MBA students at SMU in Dallas, Texas. Mr. Easterling publishes provocative research and graphical analyses on the financial markets at CrestmontResearch.com.

Stock Size Deciles

—

MEB FABER

Sometimes, powerful investment writing requires few words. Here's one of my favorite charts from Leuthold that says it all. It shows the P/E ratio for stock size deciles in July 2017 vs. Dec 1999. We can see a large valuation disparity across size buckets.

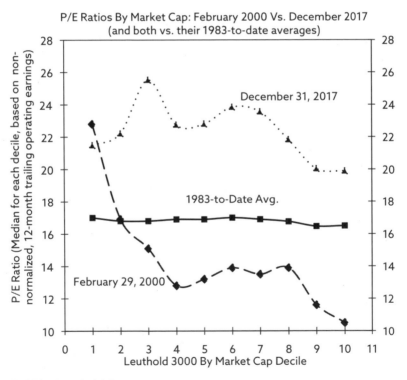

P/E Ratios By Market Cap: February 2000 Vs. December 2017
(and both vs. their 1983-to-date averages)

Originally published July 10, 2017; bit.ly/2wOqmi2

PERSONAL FINANCE, BEHAVIORAL BIASES

BIASES

&

BEYOND

Timely Tale

JONATHAN CLEMENTS

Imagine an idealized chart that summarizes our finances over the course of our lives. What would the chart look like? Picture these five lines:

1. Our nest egg grows, slowly at first and then ever faster, hitting a peak of around 12 times our final salary when we retire.

2. Our portfolio in our 20s stands at perhaps 90% or even 100% stocks. We dial down our allocation in the years that follow, especially during our final decade in the workforce, so upon retirement we have maybe 50% or 60% in stocks.

3. Our debts spike in our 20s and early 30s, as we take on student loans, car loans and a mortgage. But the sum borrowed dwindles from there, allowing us to retire debt-free. At that point, we have clear title to a valuable asset: our home.

4. Our insurance costs rise sharply through our 20s and 30s as we buy cars, purchase homes and have children. That necessitates auto, homeowner's and life insurance, in addition to the disability and health coverage we should already have. But thereafter, the premiums we pay diminish, as our growing wealth allows us to raise the deductibles on our home, health and auto insurance, and possibly drop our life and disability coverage. By the time we retire, we might have just high-deductible auto and home coverage, plus perhaps umbrella-liability insurance, a Medigap policy and long-term-care coverage.

5. Our human capital—a fancy term for our income-earning ability—is at its peak value when we enter the workforce and pull in the first of 40 years' worth of paychecks. But its value fades over time and

eventually goes to zero when we quit the workforce and stop earning money.

While I listed human capital last, it's arguably the thread that connects everything else: It provides the income to service our debts and fund retirement accounts, while freeing us up to invest heavily in stocks. But as our stream of paychecks peters out, and we approach the day when we'll live off savings, we can't afford to invest so aggressively or carry so much debt.

Should everybody's financial lives follow the five trajectories outlined above? Not necessarily. You might chart a somewhat different course, depending on your personal situation.

Save 12 times income

What's the rationale behind this number? Suppose you make $100,000 a year. If your nest egg upon retirement is equal to 12 times that income, or $1.2 million, you could reasonably withdraw $48,000 in the first year of retirement, assuming a 4% portfolio withdrawal rate. That $48,000 would replicate almost half your final salary. Add Social Security benefits, assume all debt is paid off and you'd likely be set for a comfortable retirement.

This presumes Social Security replaces 20% or so of your final salary. But for those on lower incomes, the percentage is often significantly higher. The upshot: Instead of aiming for 12 times income, you might be able to retire comfortably with savings equal to, say, eight times income. At that level, a 4% withdrawal rate would replicate 32% of your final salary. If Social Security replaces another 30% or more, you would likely be in good shape.

This is not to suggest that eight times income is an easy goal. Most retirees don't have anything close to that amount. The National Institute on Retirement Security calculates that 60% of all households headed by someone age 55 to 64 have a net worth equal to less than four times income—with almost 26% of all households at less than one times income.[1] Moreover, the measure of net worth used includes home

---

[1] www.nirsonline.org/reports/the-continuing-retirement-savings-crisis

equity, which can only ever be a partial source of retirement income and only if we're willing to trade down to a smaller home or take out a reverse mortgage.

Buy bonds as we age

While almost everybody should earmark more for bonds as they grow older, the precise allocation will vary depending not only on personal appetite for risk, but also on each investor's individual circumstances. What circumstances? At issue are the bond lookalikes in the rest of our financial lives.

For instance, our paychecks can be viewed as similar to collecting interest from a bond, which then frees us up to invest heavily in stocks. But some workers' paychecks aren't so bond-like—think of folks who work on commission or have poor job security—and they should probably compensate by investing their portfolios more conservatively.

Meanwhile, for others, their holdings of bond lookalikes might go way beyond their paycheck. Let's say you expect to receive not just Social Security retirement benefits, but also a traditional employer pension. With that handsome stream of reliable income to fall back on, you might keep a high percentage in stocks, even after you retire. What are these income streams worth? You can find out by checking what it would cost to buy income annuities that pay comparable amounts of income.

Retire debt-free

As you'll have gathered, there's no firm rule on how much folks need for a comfortable retirement or how much they should allocate to stocks. Debt is different: It rarely makes sense to carry loans into retirement.

Why not? At that juncture, most folks will have substantial sums allocated to bonds and other conservative investments—and the after-tax interest earned on these investments will almost always be less than the after-tax interest charged by their debts. The smart move: Instead of buying bonds, get rid of all debt.

Moreover, by paying off debt before leaving the workforce, we reduce the amount of income we need to generate each year to cover our retirement living expenses. That lower taxable income can, in turn, result in lower Medicare premiums and lower taxes on our Social Security benefit.

And let's not forget the biggest benefit of all: Paying off all debt, especially mortgage debt, can sharply reduce our cost of living, making retirement more affordable. One rule of thumb says that we can retire comfortably on 80% of our final salary because, at that point, we no longer have to pay Social Security and Medicare payroll taxes and, of course, we no longer have to save for retirement.

Shedding all debt can further slash our retirement income needs, to maybe 60% of final salary. Indeed, for many folks, sending off that final mortgage check is the signal that retirement is finally affordable.

Trim insurance over time

As our wealth grows, we can shoulder more financial risk—and hence there's less need for insurance. Suppose you have $1 million or more socked away. You likely need little or no life, disability and long-term-care coverage, and you can also cut your premium costs by raising the deductibles on your health, auto and homeowner's policies.

But not everybody can take so much risk. If you have less than $1 million saved, the financial perils of suffering a disability or needing long-term care will loom large and you'll need to continue carrying substantial insurance, even into retirement. In fact, retirement could involve not only hefty premiums for long-term-care and Medigap insurance, but also significant out-of-pocket medical costs.

Call it quits

Even if we retire from the workforce, we shouldn't ever retire from the pursuit of a fulfilling life. After four decades at the beck and call of others, retirement is our chance to take up activities that we're passionate about and consider important. These activities may bring a newfound sense of purpose to our final decades.

But don't rule out getting that sense of purpose from work itself. Once retired, if we can find enjoyable paid employment that takes up maybe a day or two each week, we won't just make our retirement more fulfilling. We'll also continue to wring some income out of our human capital— and that extra income could make our retirement far less financially stressful.

Originally published December 2, 2017; www.humbledollar.com/2017/12/timely-tale.

ABOUT JONATHAN CLEMENTS

Jonathan Clements is the founder and editor of HumbleDollar.com. He's also the author of a fistful of personal finance books, including *How to Think About Money*, and he sits on the advisory board and investment committee of Creative Planning, one of the country's largest independent financial advisors.

Jonathan spent almost 20 years at the *Wall Street Journal*, where he was the newspaper's personal finance columnist. Between October 1994 and April 2008, he wrote 1,009 columns for the *Journal* and for the *Wall Street Journal Sunday*. He then worked for six years at Citigroup, where he was Director of Financial Education for Citi Personal Wealth Management, before returning to the *Journal* for an additional 15-month stint as a columnist.

An avid bicyclist, Jonathan was born in London, England, and graduated from Cambridge University. He worked for *Euromoney* magazine in London before moving to the New York area in 1986. Prior to joining the *Journal* in January 1990, he covered mutual funds for *Forbes* magazine. Jonathan has written eight personal finance books and contributed to four others.

@ClementsMoney

The Distribution of Pain

JOHN MAULDIN

When you write about economics, you learn very quickly that the economy doesn't care what you say about it. The forces that drive it are beyond any one person's comprehension, much less control.

But at the same time, the economy doesn't work like a law of nature. Unlike gravity, for instance, the economy responds to human choices and preferences. We influence it, even if we don't understand exactly how.

In my "Fragmentation of Society" letter, I wrote about the coming technological changes that will replace many human jobs and disrupt society.[1] Some of the disruption will be good and necessary. Much of it will be painful, too, and the pain won't be evenly distributed.

That is a problem whether you personally feel any pain or not. People don't like pain and will change their behavior to avoid or relieve it. Like the drowning who desperately seek something to hold onto, they will vote for politicians who say they can relieve that pain, regardless of whether they actually can. And if those who suffer see that you don't share their pain, they will wonder why not and seek to gain whatever advantage you possess. And then it gets ugly.

That's not a moral statement but simply a fact-based observation of human nature. Whether we like the facts doesn't really matter: We have to face them. Presently we are not handling them very well.

---

[1] www.mauldineconomics.com/frontlinethoughts/the-fragmentation-of-society

We have engineered society so that we at the upper end of the financial spectrum have little interaction with or knowledge of the people who feel the most pain. I wrote about this chasm between classes last year in my piece "Life on the Edge," as the US elections made the split in our nation harder to ignore.[2]

Peggy Noonan talks about the "Protected" class that makes public policy and the "Unprotected" who must live with those policies. The gulf between those classes continues to widen. The changes I wrote in "Fragmentation of Society" will probably make it worse over the next 10–15 years.

In this piece, I want to delve a little deeper into this widening split and consider where it may take us. As you'll see, the possibilities range from "not so bad" to "very, very bad."

The Two Economies

Ray Dalio is no stranger to my readers. The billionaire founder of top hedge fund Bridgewater Associates got where he is by having keen insight into both human nature and economic trends. Occasionally he shares some of his wisdom publicly. I featured his reflections on the then-forthcoming Trump presidency in *Outside the Box*.[3]

In October 2017 Dalio posted an article, "The Two Economies: The Top 40% and the Bottom 60%."[4] He believes it is a serious mistake to think you can analyze or understand "the" economy because we now have two of them. The wealth and income levels are so skewed between top and bottom that "average" indicators no longer reflect the average person's experience or living conditions.

Dalio explains that the share of US wealth owned by the bottom 90% of the population and the share held by the top 0.1% is now about the same. But the trend has been of the wealthiest 0.1% increasing its share of wealth since the 1980s, while the bottom 90% has been losing ground.

2   www.mauldineconomics.com/frontlinethoughts/life-on-the-edge
3   www.mauldineconomics.com/outsidethebox/dalio-on-trump
4   www.linkedin.com/pulse/our-biggest-economic-social-political-issue-two-economies-ray-dalio

Looking back, we see a similar pattern in the 1920s—which dramatically reversed in the following decade. Then there was an almost 50-year period during which the masses gained wealth and the wealthy lost ground.

(Important note: This doesn't mean the 0.1% ceased being wealthy. It just means they owned a smaller portion of the total wealth. An economy in which 0.1% of the people own 10% of the wealth is still skewed, just less so. But more on that later.)

In the big picture, we see about a half-century when the net wealth gap widened in favor of the bottom 90%, followed by another 30 or so years in which the wealthiest gained ground while most of the population lost it.

It's not a coincidence that populism emerged as a political force in both the 1920s–1930s and the 2010s. In each case, people at the bottom could tell the economy wasn't working in their favor. The best tool they had to do something about it was the vote, so they elected FDR then and Trump now—two very different presidents but both responsive to the most intensely angered voters of their eras.

That previous, roughly ten-year period in which the wealth of the 0.1% was greater than the wealth of the 90% included the Roaring 20s, the 1929 market crash, and the first part of the Great Depression. For the 0.1%'s share of the wealth, 1929 was roughly the high point. Wealth lost in the crash sent their share plummeting. It has not fully recovered to this day, but it's getting close.

Thinking about this situation, I can't help but correlate it to my friend Neil Howe's idea of a historical "Fourth Turning" every 80 years or so. It fits well with Dalio's data. Neil said at my 2016 Strategic Investment Conference (SIC) in Dallas that we are in the middle stages of that Fourth Turning, and he expects conditions to worsen from here. He repeated that warning in 2017 at SIC in Orlando. As he points out, for almost 500 years the last half of Fourth Turning has always encompassed the most tumultuous times in Anglo-Saxon history.

(A Fourth Turning is a time when society's foundational institutions are challenged. The generation who are young adults at that time must face the challenge, and hopefully overcome it. The so-called Greatest Generation did so by persevering through the Great Depression and fighting World War II. It may not be a war, but the Millennial Generation will face a similar test.)

Back to Dalio's article. He goes on to quantify the 60/40 split with some startling numbers. Just a sampling:

- The average household in the top 40% earns four times more than the average household in the bottom 60%.

- Real incomes for the bottom 60% have been either flat or down slightly since 1980.

- In 1980, the average top 40% household had six times more wealth than the average bottom-60% household. Now it is ten times as much.

- Only about a third of the bottom 60% saves any of their income.

Dalio also found some very useful data I had never seen before: household income adjusted to show the impact of taxes, tax credits, and government benefits. This adjustment gets closer to the resources people actually have available for living expenses, savings, and investment.

Splitting that data by the top 40% and bottom 60%, we see a sharply growing difference in the percentage changes since 1980. The top saw its *after-tax* net household income grow almost *three times faster* than household income for the bottom 60%, even including government transfer payments.

And note that there is a significant difference in the income growth of the middle 40–60% segment and the bottom 40%, too, and that difference accelerated during and after the Great Recession. Think about that in the context of recent political trends.

You see the problem here? The bottom 60% know their own experience. Thanks to the internet and social media, the bottom 40% are particularly aware of it and increasingly resentful.

Note also that the lower ranks of the top 40% are not "wealthy" by any stretch. Anyone below the 80th percentile is probably struggling to some degree.

Since the 1980s most of us at the top have believed that a rising tide would lift all boats. We were half-right: It has lifted all the boats but not at the same rate, and a good many boats have sprung holes and are taking on water. We're now near the point where our differences in income and wealth are too great to ignore.

Think back 30 years. None of us would want to go back and live with that same technological base. All of our lives have dramatically improved. From health care to communications to entertainment to transportation and a host of other things, we are all better off.

But the key here is that no matter how much better our lives have become, those in the bottom 20 or 40 or 60 or 80% notice the *relative* differences between where they are and where the top 10% or 1% reside, and they can see those differences growing.

While the majority of those living in Africa, in some parts of Asia, and in the slums in Latin America would see the lives of what we call the poor in America as vastly superior to their own lifestyles, that is not who the bottom 20–40–60% of the income strata in the US are comparing their lives to. It is simply human nature that we compare ourselves to those who have more, and that we want more for ourselves.

Leveraged Stress

The results of the American Psychological Association's "Stress in America" survey of November 2017 show that Americans are not happy campers.

A big majority (59%) think we are now at "the lowest point in our nation's history." To me, that seems a stretch, given that we killed each other in staggering numbers in the Civil War. And the 1820s was not a decade of great civility either. But then, people didn't watch the fighting on their phones. Now we do, and it fills us with anxiety.

I look back on my youth and realize that the late '60s was the first time when the reality of war confronted my generation in our homes, on our TVs and in our newspapers, every day. What we experienced with media coverage of social turmoil in that era was a harbinger of what the internet and social media have created today: instantaneous analysis of almost everything. Now, social media have become a monstrous breeding ground for conspiracy theories of all kinds. It is most disheartening.

The specific issues that worry people are interesting:

What issues are causing Americans stress?

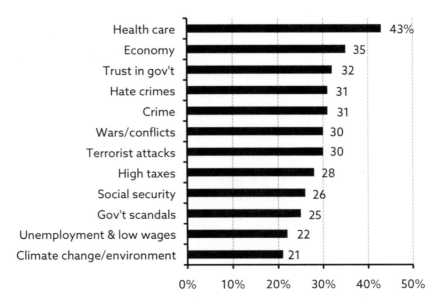

Source: American Psychological Association, Stress in America Survey 2017.

First on the list is health care, by a pretty wide margin. That concern can cover a lot of territory. Maybe you or a family member are seriously ill, or maybe your health is fine but buying insurance causes financial stress.

Just over a third of respondents reported that the economy causes them stress. That seems a little low, but I remind myself that most people don't observe the economy the way I do. "High taxes" are well down the list, at 28%. That's surprising but probably reflects the fact that a small number of people pay most of the income taxes.

"Unemployment and low wages" is also near the bottom with 22% of respondents stressed about it. Maybe that figure reflects today's low unemployment level, or maybe people are just glad to have any sort of job.

One source of considerable stress that isn't on the list but probably should be is household debt. I talk a lot about government debt and pension debt, but for most people the more immediate concern is probably their mortgage, auto, credit-card, and student loan debt. There is a mountain of it.

Deutsche Bank reports that for 1992–2016, leverage more than doubled for the lowest-income 20% and rose significantly for the lower-income 80% of the population. It *dropped* slightly for the 80–89.9th percentiles and even more for the top 10% income group.

Now recall Dalio's data on household income, adjusted for taxes and benefits. The top 20%, whose incomes grew the fastest, managed to reduce their leverage. The lower groups, whose income was up slightly or flat, added large amounts of debt, with the poorest adding the most, percentagewise.

This data doesn't tell us what specific kinds of debt create these leverage ratios. Maybe some of the debt is productive, like mortgages on reasonably valued homes or student debt that helps borrowers eventually raise their incomes. But I'd bet much of the money that was borrowed is simply gone with little or nothing to show for it.

This likely-unrecoverable debt also appears as an asset on some lender's balance sheet. It ends up being sold as asset-backed securities, possibly to a mutual fund or pension fund near you. And it's generally in the high-yield category, with leverage on it.

At the risk of repeating the obvious, debt that can't be repaid won't be. Somebody will eat the loss; the only question is who. Banks managed to socialize much of their losses in the last recession. I'm not sure that plan will work a second time.

I started off talking about pain and how we distribute it. It may not be physical pain. Financial and employment-related pain are very real. Boredom, too, can be painful, as can loneliness or the feeling that no one needs you. We're on the verge of many medical breakthroughs, but we won't cure every disease or heal every kind of wound. People will still suffer, and it's clear we need a lot of societal as well as personal healing.

One Nation, Two Labor Markets

In a column on Bloomberg, Jeanna Smialek and Greg Quinn write:

> Goldman Sachs economists agree with Bridgewater Associates' Ray Dalio: The U.S. economy is running at two speeds.

> Headline joblessness may be at a more than 16-year low, but that bullish trend obscures the fact that the labor market is split into

two "quite different stories," Goldman Sachs economists write. A pool of would-be workers remain on the sidelines, and there are reasons to think they can be pulled back into the game. The share of discouraged workers has shrunk, and people are even coming back into jobs from disability. If the labor market gets as hot as it was back in 1999–2000, the economists think participation could climb by a few tenths of a percentage point.

That conclusion is important. Goldman had been skeptical that a tight labor market could push up participation, so this marks a shift in their thinking. If the Fed concurs, it leaves the central bank with a tough choice: should the rate-setting Federal Open Market Committee run the economy hot to attract disenfranchised workers, even if that risks overshooting on inflation amid low headline unemployment? "The FOMC seems to find this trade-off unappealing and is likely to continue to tighten steadily as a result," the economists write.

While the Goldman analysis focuses on the labor market split, Dalio pointed out that aggregate statistics mask a division in labor, retirement savings, health care and wealth building. The common theme is that uneven outcomes mean the Fed must take underlying details into account when assessing economic progress.

Working Class Versus Service Class

One final thought. We have had this notion of the "working class." These are the people who do not own the businesses and are not professionals in the sense of being doctors or lawyers or accountants.

I have spent a great deal of time thinking about the future of work. It is the single most difficult chapter to write in my upcoming book, partly because I don't like the conclusions I'm coming to. One of the things I am realizing is that there is a distinction between what we have seen as the working class and what I am coming to see as the service class. A working-class person is somebody who has a trade, and because of their skill, they can generally command a decent income.

Then there is the service class—bar and restaurant workers, retail salespeople, general manual laborers, and so on. These jobs are almost plug-and-play. It is not that the greedy restaurant owner doesn't want to pay his staff more; it's that competition generally won't let him do so and still make a profit. So he holds his labor costs down; and he can do so, because in today's market there are typically more people available for jobs than there are jobs.

Health care being number one of the worry list? I think a large part of that is the fact that young people are required to buy ridiculously expensive health insurance packages in order to subsidize a sick elderly population. And if you're making $10–$12 an hour working two part-time jobs, trying to figure out how to hold onto a place to live, eat, have adequate clothing, and a bit for entertainment, you're just not able to spend $400–$600 a month on health care. And then you find out that your taxes are much higher than you thought they would be because now you have to pay the penalty for not having health insurance. Yes, that might stress me out, too.

And yes, I do know young people in exactly that situation. Several of my children literally cannot afford to buy health care, so dad does it for them. But many other friends don't have parents who can buy them what is essentially ridiculously expensive health care, because the parents are struggling with their own healthcare costs.

We are a nation that is increasingly under stress. Dalio talks about it in terms of the bottom 60% versus the top 40%, but he could have made the same case using an 80–20 model or even a 90–10 model. I am reminded of Pareto's 80/20 principle, which states that roughly 80% of effects come from 20% of causes.

Our socioeconomic situation is not going to get better, not for a long time. Let's assume, wildly optimistically, that the US economy and the rest of the developed world grow at a 5% nominal rate for the next 15 years, so that our economies roughly double. Does that mean that the gap between the lower 60% and the upper 40% will be even wider? We will have more than a few people who will be worth more than $100 billion, that's for sure.

Will the lives of those in the lower 60% be significantly better than they are today? Absolutely. They'll have improved health care and health spans (*if* they have access to health care), lower food costs, far more access to services, etc., but the *relative* differences will be even greater between the top and the bottom.

Unless we somehow figure out how to help people deal with their stress and better manage the yawning differences in incomes and outcomes, we're going to see increasing tension and fragmentation in our society.

Originally published November 10, 2017; www.mauldineconomics.com/frontlinethoughts/the-distribution-of-pain.

ABOUT JOHN MAULDIN

John Mauldin is President of Mauldin Solutions, LLC, an investment advisory firm registered with multiple states; and President and a registered principal of Mauldin Securities, LLC, member FINRA-SIPC.

He publishes *Thoughts from the Frontline* through Mauldin Economics, of which he is Chairman. Mauldin Economics publishes a growing number of investing resources, including both free and paid publications aimed at helping investors thrive in today's challenging economy.

John's books have appeared on the *New York Times* best-seller list four times. His current book count is six and includes *Bull's Eye Investing: Targeting Real Returns in a Smoke and Mirrors Market, Endgame: The End of the Debt Supercycle and How It Changes Everything, Code Red: How to Protect Your Savings from the Coming Crisis, A Great Leap Forward?: Making Sense of China's Cooling Credit Boom, Technological Transformation, High Stakes Rebalancing, Geopolitical Rise, & Reserve Currency Dream, Just One Thing: Twelve of the World's Best Investors Reveal the One Strategy You Can't Overlook* and *The Little Book of Bull's Eye Investing: Finding Value, Generating Absolute Returns and Controlling Risk in Turbulent Markets.*

John is a frequent speaker at conferences around the world and is a sought-after contributor to numerous financial publications, as well as a regular guest on TV and radio.

@JohnFMauldin

The Great Financial Forecasting Hoax

Why Stock Market Predictions Are Dangerous To Your Wealth

TODD TRESIDDER

Financial Forecasting Is Meaningless. Learn How To Invest Profitably

Key ideas

1. The critical difference between knowable and unknowable financial advice.

2. How statistics prove you should never put capital at risk on a prediction.

3. Investment strategy that works based on proven facts.

Americans pay millions every year to financial advisors, psychics, fortune tellers, forecasters, and assorted hucksters and gurus claiming to have some insight into the future.

The reason is because the essence of investing is putting capital at risk into an unknowable future so people seek financial forecasters in a desperate attempt to bring certainty to an unknowable future.

They want to believe these soothsayers have enough foreknowledge about financial events to make a meaningful difference.

Unfortunately, they don't, and the facts prove it.

I learned this painful lesson about financial market forecasting the hard way. It literally cost me a small fortune.

The good news is market losses have a mysterious way of helping people sort right from wrong.

You only need to touch the hot stove once to learn it's a bad idea, and investing based on financial forecasts is a bad idea.

That's why, if you walk into my office, you'll notice no financial media. No CNBC, no magazines, no newspapers, or other sources for news-of-the-day "financial porn".

You might also notice my bookcases overstuffed with investment books and the hard drive on my computer filled with academic research papers.

That's because certain types of information help you improve your investing, and other types of information are edu-tainment (or financial porn). Understanding the difference between useful financial advice and useless market forecasting was a lesson hard learned.

Hopefully this chapter will help shorten your learning curve.

What's The Secret To Sorting Good Advice From Useless Financial Forecasting?

The problem today is there's more information than anyone can consume, and much of it's junk.

You must pick and choose what financial advice you spend your limited time and attention on if you want to be financially successful.

But, how do you do that?

The first step is to become crystal clear about the difference between what's "knowable" and what's "unknowable" so that you can stop wasting valuable brain space on unknowable information.

Once you know the difference between unknowable and knowable information, you'll be amazed just how much can safely be ignored.

The reason unknowable information, such as financial forecasting, should be ignored is because it confuses your decision process. It appears credible, causing you to factor it into decisions, but it has no basis in fact.

It's fiction—a figment of the author's imagination. Investment market forecasts are never a rational basis for an investment decision. Therefore, the only solution is to avoid unknowable information altogether so it doesn't muddle your thinking.

That's why I ignore CNBC and don't read most investment periodicals. Most of the information dispensed through these media channels is either unknowable or not usable.

The primary purpose of the content is to entertain because entertainment is how the media business maximizes distribution and ad revenues.

Unfortunately, entertainment isn't what I need to maximize my investment profits—and that's what I care about. How about you?

What Is "Knowable" Financial Advice?

Knowable financial advice is factual, as opposed to conjecture. Market valuations, company statistics (assuming they aren't being misrepresented), economic statistics, and market psychology are examples of current facts that are knowable and can be quantified.

Another type of knowable financial advice is historical research showing how investment markets behaved under specific conditions in the past. The value of historical research is that it provides a meaningful context to current facts.

It converts facts that would otherwise be dry and empty into actionable investment guidelines.

For example, you can know what the historical ten-year returns for stock averages are given certain valuation and economic conditions.

You can also know if you're currently in the upper-end of the valuation range or the lower-end of the valuation range, and what your mathematical expectation for a ten-year holding period would be starting today.

All these facts are knowable based on historical precedent. The problem is that the past may not be indicative of the future. The map isn't the territory.

In other words, you can't know the future because the future is unknowable. Using the above example, financial statistics can help you know the ten-year "expectation" for stocks based on history, but you must be equally clear that you don't know what stocks will do in the next ten years.

You have an indication and a statistical expectation given certain assumptions, but don't think for one minute that you can predict the future. You can't. Nobody can predict the future with statistical accuracy reliable enough to invest on. The future is unknowable.

This may sound like a subtle distinction, but it's not—it's critical. Remember, you must be clear on what's knowable and what's unknowable if you want consistent profitability investing into a future that's unknowable. (Hmmm, that's a mouthful!)

Knowable financial advice isn't based on someone's judgment, opinion, or interpretation—it's rooted in fact. This distinction is black and white, and it has the power to dramatically change your investing when you get it into your bones.

You should never put money at risk based on financial advice that's predicated on the unknowable. The unknowable includes predictions, financial forecasting, opinions, interpretations, stock forecasts, market forecasting, hunches, beliefs, or anything else not rooted in fact.

Why Most Financial Advice Is Really Just Financial Forecasting

Study the headlines, review brokerage analysis reports, and watch the investment media, and you'll quickly realize most of what passes for financial advice is really financial fiction.

It's blatant, unknowable futurism. Below are several examples:

- Ten hot stocks to own for the coming year
- Widget Inc's earnings are forecast to grow at 25% for the next five years
- Overpriced Inc. should trade in the range of $40–$60 per share
- Seven mutual funds to buy for next year
- Stocks will outperform bonds
- Real estate always goes up (an assumed truth prior to 2008)
- Our research indicates the economy will…

Notice that each of these all-too-common statements in financial literature require a crystal ball or direct connection to the Higher Power for there to be any financial relevance.

They might be blindly extrapolating past numbers to create future assumptions or communicating some conjecture about future events, but all of the financial advice above is based on the false premise that the future can be predicted.

And what happens when we invest money based on false premises? Ouch!

You can save a ton of time and money by ignoring all such nonsense. They're all statements about the unknowable because they require an accurate financial forecast to profit.

But My Stock Market Forecasting Is Accurate...

Sure, some financial analysts will make an occasional accurate call here and there, thus appearing to be great prognosticators of future events. But they can also be completely wrong the rest of the time.

The reality is a broken clock is accurate twice a day, but you would never use it to tell time. Why make the same mistake with financial advice that's really forecasting?

Betting on someone's belief about the future when they're wrong will cost you money, and financial advice that forecasts the future is wrong all too frequently.

To understand how financial forecasters rise to stardom, imagine a pool of 5,000 financial experts who toss their hat in the ring declaring themselves capable forecasters.

Let's say they're equally divided between bulls and bears. Next year, half will be right, and half will be wrong. The right ones declare themselves certified geniuses with a "proven track record" and go on to issue their infinite wisdom for next year's forecast and write a book.

Again, half are right and half are wrong, so we now have a pool of 1,250 financial experts with documented track records. Rinse and repeat for a few more years, and a few brilliant geniuses will bubble to the top with undeniably astounding track records and best-selling books.

The only question remaining is whether their track records are truly genius, or merely statistical anomalies?

You can dismiss this oversimplified example as trite, but it's taken from a proven model used by disreputable financial managers to build the trust of naive investors.

They start mailing campaigns sent to massive lists of investors (100,000+) declaring they know the "secret" to the markets.

Each month, they send predictions and continue to follow up only with those who received the accurate predictions. The inaccurate prediction addresses are discarded.

After enough accurate predictions are delivered, they can usually establish sufficient credibility and trust with investors to extract some money.

After all, the huckster just sent you ten accurate predictions in a row. You read them yourself. He clearly knows what he's talking about, right?

Relating this story back to the guru of the day, they usually follow a similar pattern before you hear about them. They usually publish books and newsletters.

In addition, they usually predict the future based on some indicator or theory that just happens to be working perfectly at the time and provides a logical reason for expecting more of the same in the future.

By the time you know about them, they have several books in print with an impressive list of documented predictions. It's hard to deny their brilliance—until you've been burned a few times.

The end result is always the same: the indicator or theory that perfectly accounted for economic behavior in the past suddenly stops working in the future. Their rise to guru status down in flames, and a new guru-of-the-day takes his rightful place on the throne.

Every forecaster faces the exact same fate—they'll eventually be 100% dead wrong—and it will usually occur when they've attracted their greatest following.

If you bet money on their predictions, the damage to your portfolio can be devastating. You must have clearly defined exit strategies and risk control methods to protect your capital when the inevitable occurs.

It's as sure to happen as the sun rising in the morning.

Nobody knows the future with certainty. It's impossible because all predictions are at best probabilistic outcomes.

Eventually those probabilities must come home to roost and bite the forecaster in the backside. It has always been that way, and always will be that way.

It's inherent to the nature of the financial forecasting business.

Statistics Prove Financial Forecasting Is A Waste Of Time And Money

In case you aren't totally clear on the completely invalid premise behind financial advice based on forecasts about the future, or you haven't read the many research studies proving this fact, I'll quote directly from a transcript taken from the infamous Louis Rukeyser's *Wall Street Week* television show where he lays to rest any doubt:

> "Now, before we meet tonight's special guest, let's take one of our periodic looks at why every self-respecting market technician treats the sentiments of his colleagues with contempt, as we track the embarrassing record of market advisors. So come along as we are 'Gonna Take a Sentimental Journey'."

> "Our trip begins with the Dow at 689 on August 2, 1963, the first year Investor's Intelligence conducted the poll of market newsletter writers. With 91.4% of those surveyed bearishly calling for a short or long-term decline, and outright bulls at an all-time low of less than 9%, the Dow then proceeded to rise 250 points in the next 21 months, which represented 38%."

> "Ten years later, in a week when the Dow was moving to new highs, nearly 62% of those polled thought the market would head even higher. And what came to pass? You guessed it. Down 470 points in 23 months. Not surprisingly, by the time the Dow slipped to a 12-year low at 577 on December 13, 1974, the mood was glum again. More than 63% of market advisors surveyed called for further declines, and true to form, the market rose 425 points, more than 70% in 14 months."

"On January 14, 1977, with just 21% of advisers bearish, the crowd missed the mark once more as the Dow derailed with a 235 point loss over a period of 14 months. And with the Dow at 784, the clouds hung heavy over Wall Street in anticipation of further declines, with nearly two thirds of investors feeling bearish."

"The market, in turn, took off with a vengeance, rising more than 1900 points in five years. On August 28, 1987, the week the Dow touched its then all time high at 2722, more than 60% of the advisers were, not to put a fine point to it, full of bull. Seven weeks later, the Dow, you may recall, was more than 900 points lower. On December 2, 1988, though just 21% of those polled were bullish, the lowest total since June, 1982. The Dow, then just under 2100, rallied an impressive 907 points in 31 months."

Has anything changed in the years since Louis Rukeyser did this study on the predictive quality of financial advice for his television show? No.

In David Dreman's 1979 book *Contrarian Investment Strategy*, he analyzed 50 years of forecasts beginning in 1929. His conclusions were as follows:

1. The experts dramatically underperformed the market

2. Their forecasts outperformed only 23% of the time, meaning they were wrong nearly three out of four times

3. As an example, the top ten stock picks from a 1971 "Institutional Investor" magazine poll of more than 150 money managers in 27 states underperformed the market and were down 67% by the end of 1974

4. Another example came from a 1970 conference poll of more than 2,000 institutional investors asked to pick the stock they expected to perform best. The winner was National Student Marketing which promptly declined 95% in value. Two years later, this same group's prediction was airline stocks, which then declined by 50% despite a general market rise.

How's that for forecasting?

The forecasting problem isn't limited to just the stock market, either. It doesn't work in any investment market with enough reliability to risk money on.

For example, James Bianco studied more than 20 years of interest rate predictions made by a panel of prominent economists published in the *Wall Street Journal* every six months.

Amazingly, this group of the "best and brightest" successfully predicted the direction of interest rates just 13 out of 43 times. They were wrong 70% of the time.

These economists are highly trained and highly paid to predict the future of long-term interest rates, and their accuracy is worse than throwing darts or flipping a coin.

If people who spend their whole lives predicting interest rates can't get it right, what's that tell you about the reliability of your mortgage broker, financial planner, newsletter writer, or neighbor down the street?

Did your financial advisor wisely get you out of stocks near the most recent market top? Were your investment magazines filled with bearish prognostications advising you to become cautious? I don't think so.

Did they ring the bell at the last stock market bottom and tell you to back up the truck and load up when opportunities were greatest? Not likely. Who told you to get clear of real estate before the bubble burst? Nobody! Exactly my point.

Sure, there were a handful of financial forecasters who got one or two of these calls right. But is there anyone with a proven track record of keeping you long during each of those multi-year bull markets and deftly stepping aside before the ensuing bear?

I don't know of any forecaster reliable enough to bet money on.

So why listen?

If financial forecasters are wrong when it matters most (and it has always been that way), what makes you think next time will be any different?

Successful Investing Is About Risk Management And Business Analysis – Not Financial Forecasting

If financial forecasting is meaningless, and the bulk of financial advice is forecasting, then how should a smart investor make investment decisions? What can you rely on to create financial security?

Smart investors who want consistent profits over the long-term develop an actuarial investment approach. They recognize that investing is about probabilities, not prediction.

Their decisions are based purely on known facts with the objective of managing risk and maximizing mathematical expectancy, much like insurance companies and many hedge funds manage risk and reward.

Profiting becomes a game of statistical certainty where the odds work for you rather than against you.

Investing in a professional, business-like fashion has nothing to do with picking hot stocks, predicting the future, guessing, taking hot tips, or any of the other typical approaches that pass for financial advice.

Instead, it's about following a disciplined, methodical investment strategy based on a known, positive, mathematical expectancy.

For example, Warren Buffett never knows what the market will do tomorrow and doesn't waste any energy on such nonsense.

He also doesn't know what stocks will outperform their peer groups over the next month or year because that's also unknowable.

What he does know is how to buy solid companies with valuable franchises at a fraction of their inherent value. Eventually, the market realizes the true value, and Buffett makes a fat profit.

Notice there's nothing about this strategy that involves reading a crystal ball. He utilizes past history and proven business principles to understand reasonable standards of valuation while employing present day factual data to determine current mis-pricings in the market.

No prediction necessary—just facts.

The bottom line is successful investing isn't about predicting the future, and any investment philosophy that requires you to predict the future is fundamentally flawed.

I repeat: any investment strategy that requires some prediction of the future is fundamentally flawed and should be avoided.

This one idea will eliminate most investment strategies and financial advice from your life.

I learned this lesson from the school of hard knocks, so please take what I'm saying to heart. I've left millions on the investment table and wasted untold research hours mistakenly pursuing the unknowable.

Learn from my errors and don't make the same mistake. Avoid financial forecasting like the plague and your portfolio will be happier for it.

This Isn't Rocket Science, But It's Very Profitable

If you want to invest with consistent profitability, then you must become clear on what you know, and equally clear on what will forever remain unknowable.

Predicting the future is unknowable. Period!

People seek forecasters because they want to feel some sense of control over the future. It feels gratifying to study the analysts' predictions, take action, and make things happen—even if it's completely wrong. At least you tried and did your best (or at least, that's what you believe).

Humans have an incessant need to control, whether it's spouses, nature, or their finances. To accept the future as unknowable feels out-of-control to the uninitiated, and that's intolerable.

However, when you learn to invest based on mathematical expectation and risk management, much of what passes for financial advice becomes a meaningless waste of bandwidth.

When you learn to accept the future as a probabilistic outcome, you're suddenly free of many burdens the ordinary investor must shoulder.

You don't have to worry about being right or wrong. Instead, just align your portfolio with current probabilities while always managing against the risk of a large outlier loss. It isn't perfect, but it's profitable over time. It reduces risk, increases return, and allows you to sleep at night.

Investing is about making money. It's business.

Predicting the future is about ego gratification for the "genius" forecaster.

Never confuse the two.

Focus your limited time and resources on investment strategies that have statistical validity based on provable facts.

Nothing else is acceptable.

Originally published August 6, 2017: financialmentor.com/investment-advice/investment-strategy-alternative/financial-forecasting-hoax-stock-market-predictions/18251.

ABOUT TODD TRESIDDER

Todd Tresidder holds a B.A. in Economics from University of California at Davis. He is a Member of the Economics Honors Society and Deans List.

Todd has been a serial entrepreneur since childhood, building many businesses before retiring at age 35 from his position as a Hedge Fund Investment Manager responsible for a portfolio in excess of $20 million.

He raised his net worth from less than zero at age 23 to being a self-made millionaire 12 years later by "walking the talk", using the same personal finance and investment strategies as he teaches on his website, financialmentor.com.

Todd was an early pioneer and expert in statistical and mathematical risk management systems for investing. He is still an active investor and earns consistent investment returns in both up and down markets.

You can find more of Todd's investment writing at financialmentor.com.

@Financialmentor

The Evolution of the Four Pillars for Retirement Income Portfolios

MICHAEL KITCES

Executive summary

The research on the optimal strategy to generate retirement income from a portfolio has been evolving for decades.

In the 1950s and 1960s, with the initial rise of a portfolio-based retirement, the leading strategy was simply to buy bonds and spend the interest (by literally "clipping the coupons" from the bearer bonds of the time). Until the inflation of the 1970s ravaged the purchasing power of bond interest.

The harsh consequences of inflation on bond portfolios led to a dramatic shift by the 1980s, as retirees increasingly purchased high-quality dividend-paying stocks instead, counting on the ability of businesses to raise prices and keep pace with inflation... which also helps their dividends to rise and keep pace with inflation as well.

The dividend strategy was popular until eventually retirees realized that owning stocks and focusing on the dividends, while ignoring the capital gains, just leads to large retirement account balances that could have been spent along the way. As a result, by the 1990s, retirement portfolio strategies shifted again, to consider a more holistic "total return" approach that incorporates interest, dividends, *and* capital gains as well.

Unfortunately, though, capital gains may be one of the largest drivers of total return in the long run, but it's also one of the least stable, forcing the retiree to periodically rely on the portfolio principal as well. Of course, in the end, retirement principal that is unspent is arguably a wasted spending opportunity—where the "optimal" retirement portfolio is for the last check to the undertaker to bounce. On the other hand, given the uncertainty of a retiree's time horizon—not knowing when you're going to die—means in practice, the principal can and should be used more dynamically, spending from it in some years but leaving it untouched in others.

Which means ultimately, the modern retirement portfolio will really rely on four pillars for retirement income—interest, dividends, capital gains, and principal. Or stated more accurately, the four pillars of retirement *cash flows*—since the treatment of the pillars as "income" for tax purposes can vary depending on both the pillar itself (interest is taxable and principal liquidations are not), and the varying types of retirement accounts (from pre-tax IRAs to tax-free Roth accounts).

Nonetheless, the fundamental point is simply to recognize that a retirement portfolio has multiple ways to generate the desired cash flows for retirement. And in fact, in a low-yield environment, it can be especially important to diversify across all four pillars—or retirees take on additional risks in stretching for yield, from interest rate and default risk (from longer-term or lower-quality bonds), to the concentration risks of buying just a subset of the highest dividend-paying sectors (which, as the financial crisis showed, can expose the portfolio to severe risk along the way!).

Buy The Bonds, Spend The Coupons

In the early days of bond investing, bonds were issued as "bearer certificates" (or "bearer bonds"), which literally meant that whoever was bearing (i.e., holding) the bond was presumed to be its owner (akin to how cash works today).

In turn, this meant the interest payments that bond issuers would pay to bond owners was paid directly to whoever actually held the bond—redeemed by a paper coupon, attached to the bond, that could be physically cut from the bond and presented for payment. Thus why a bond's interest rate is often called its coupon rate, and why collecting the interest payments from a bond is still often colloquially called "clipping the coupon". (Because in the past, that's literally how it was done.)

With the rise of the 'modern' investing and retirement era after World War II, the strategy of "buying bonds and clipping the coupons" was the leading approach for retirement income from a portfolio, either in lieu of a pension or Social Security (for those who didn't have one or weren't eligible), or to supplement it. The stable coupon payments were an effective substitute for stable pension payments, and were increasingly appealing through the late 1950s and into the 1960s as interest rates drifted higher with economic growth.

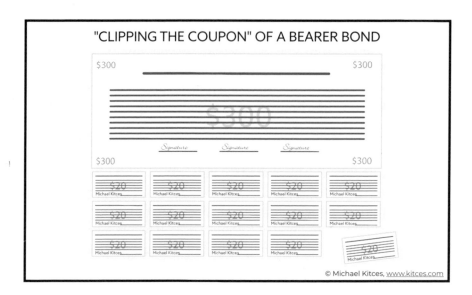

And of course, for those who needed a little more money as well, they could always sell the bonds (or wait for them to mature) for some additional cash flow. In the context of pension funds and institutions that needed to support a large volume of ongoing payments, it was common to "ladder" the maturities of the bonds sequentially, specifically to ensure that the principal value of a maturing bond would be available to supplement cash flows that year. Though for individuals, the liquidation of the bonds themselves was often more ad hoc, given the uncertainty of the retirement time horizon in the first place.

Inflation Triggers A Shift To Dividend-Paying Stocks

One of the key challenges of the "clip the coupons" bond strategy for retirement income is that bonds—particularly the ones issued in decades past—simply paid a "nominal" coupon rate that was always the same, regardless of inflation. Which meant that over time, inflation could and did erode the purchasing power of the bond income. Fortunately, though, inflation rates were modest in the 1950s and 1960s. And most people didn't necessarily plan to live for decades in retirement, which further limited any material long-term danger from inflation.

Then the 1970s struck, and an inflation rate that had averaged only 2.0% in the 1950s and 2.3% in the 1960s jumped to 6.2% in 1973 and then spiked to 11.0% in 1974, severely damaging the purchasing power of bonds purchased in the preceding decades. In fact, from 1973 to 1982 the average annual growth rate of inflation was a whopping 8.7%, which cumulatively cut the purchasing power of bond interest by 57% in a decade. And at the same time, a growing realization was underway that with improving health, "retirement" can actually last a very long time (where the cumulative impact of inflation *really* matters!).

As a result, by the early 1980s, the focus of retirement income planning portfolios had shifted from buying bonds and clipping the coupons, to buying stocks and spending the dividends, instead. The bad news about dividends is that the yields weren't as high—in 1982, the S&P 500 dividend yield was about 5%, while the 10-year Treasury was 12.5%. The good news, however, was that the rising price of goods (from inflation) was lifting up the earnings of the businesses that sold them; of course, the businesses would have to pay employees more in a rising inflationary environment as well, but the net result was still a significant increase in nominal profits.

For instance, if a company used to generate $1,000,000 of revenue with $800,000 of expenses and the remaining $200,000 paid out in dividends, and inflation caused prices to double, then revenue would rise to $2,000,000, expenses would jump to $1,600,000, and the business would pay out $400,000 in dividends. The end result: the business profit margins remain the same, but inflation doubling prices causes the dividends to double along with it, allowing the dividend investor to maintain purchasing power.

And throughout the 1980s, this is exactly what happened. In 1981, the S&P 500 paid out approximately $7 of dividends (when the index was at $133, for a 5.3% yield), and by 1990 it was paying out about $12.5 (when the index was up to $340, for a 3.7% yield). The end result was that the yield actually fell, as stock prices rose, but the retirement spender saw their retirement cash flows rise almost 80% (from $7 to $12.5), easily keeping up with the inflation rates of the decade (which averaged 4.7%, or a cumulative increase of "just" 58%).

Of course, the caveat of the dividend-paying stock strategy for retirement income was that dividends are not guaranteed, and in fact, the stocks themselves have economic risk. Which meant dividend-paying strategies of the day typically focused on the highest quality "blue chip" stocks, that were most likely to stick around and continue to raise their dividend payouts over time.

The Bull Market Stokes Appreciation For Capital Gains

By the 1990s, the leading retirement income strategies began to shift again.

The "challenge" was that while dividends were in fact growing at a more-than-ample rate to keep pace with inflation, the underlying value of the stocks were growing as well, quite significantly. As noted above, not only did dividend payouts rise 80% through the 1980s, but the raw price level of the S&P 500 was up 150% as well. In other words, the retiree's account balance by the end of the decade was more than 2.5 times the account balance at the beginning of the decade, even after spending all those dividends along the way.

This recognition that it's necessary to consider the impact of stock growth and capital gains reformed the thinking on retirement income portfolios once again. The shift was on to view portfolios more holistically, considering the availability of interest, and dividends, *and* capital gains, and spending on the basis of the "total return" portfolio. And the impact was substantial, given the sheer magnitude of the capital appreciation potential. Personal finance publications of the day routinely suggested that 7% to 8% withdrawal rates would be 'reasonable' and sustainable, given total return expectations for markets at the time.

Notably, the inclusion of capital gains as a pillar of retirement income portfolios was also aided greatly by the decline in investment transaction costs since stock trading commissions had been de-regulated on "May Day" of 1975. In the subsequent 20 years, the average cost to complete a stock transaction had fallen by about 90%, which made accessing capital gains (via a sale) "almost" as liquid as just receiving dividend or interest payments.

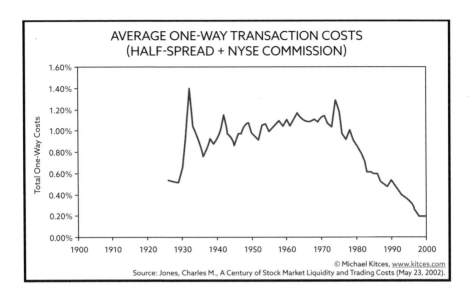

AVERAGE ONE-WAY TRANSACTION COSTS
(HALF-SPREAD + NYSE COMMISSION)

© Michael Kitces, www.kitces.com
Source: Jones, Charles M., A Century of Stock Market Liquidity and Trading Costs (May 23, 2002).

Spending Principal, But Not Too Soon

In the early years of a portfolio-based retirement, it was often used as a supplement to a defined contribution pension plan or Social Security (or other income-producing assets like real estate). However, with the decline of the defined benefit plan and the meteoric rise of the defined contribution plan throughout the 1980s and 1990s, the use of a retirement portfolio shifted from being supplemental to the core of funding retirement itself. Which introduced a new challenge to thinking about retirement planning: what to do with the retirement account balance itself.

In a world of defined benefit pension plans, there was no account balance. The retiree received payments for his/her life, or payments for the joint survivorship of the retiree and his/her spouse, and at death, the payments simply stopped. With a defined contribution plan, though, there was an account balance, which if not fully used, would remain available for heirs.

In some cases, the potential to leave a "legacy" of the remaining retirement account balance was simply a gift to bestow upon family members or charitable entities. But in many cases, the fundamental goal of the retiree was to "use the money" in retirement—which meant not only the growth *on* the retirement account, *but the principal, too.* From this perspective, the retirement account was something to be spent and maximally consumed;

a remaining balance at the end meant wasted opportunities of how the money could have been spent during life. The perfect retirement plan was one where the last check was for the undertaker, and it would bounce.

Of course, the challenge to this approach is that retirees don't necessarily know how long they'll live. Which means planning to bounce the undertaker's check was risky, as if the retiree spent the principal down too soon, and then "failed to die in a timely manner", all the money would be gone. Thus, the use of retirement principal became another part of the balancing act—spending down too soon would lead to disaster, but not spending down at all was a "waste", too.

Coordinating The Four Pillars Of Retirement Cash Flows

Ultimately, these components of interest, dividends, capital gains, and principal form the four pillars of retirement income planning. And as noted earlier, ever-declining transaction costs made it comparable to spend interest and dividends, or reinvest them and liquidate capital gains from some other investment instead, or keep it all invested and spend from principal… in other words, the four pillars of retirement income became increasingly fungible and interchangeable, to be shifted amongst from year to year as necessary to fund the retirement goal.

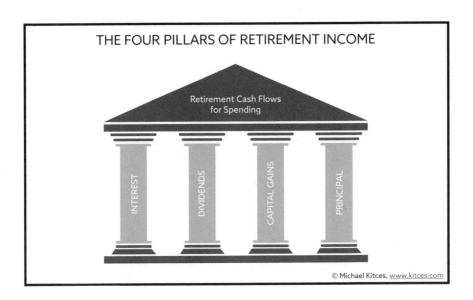

THE FOUR PILLARS OF RETIREMENT INCOME

Retirement Cash Flows for Spending

INTEREST   DIVIDENDS   CAPITAL GAINS   PRINCIPAL

© Michael Kitces, www.kitces.com

In fact, liquidations from the modern retirement portfolio *will* likely shift amongst all four pillars from year to year and decade to decade. In some years, the biggest drivers to total return are from interest and dividends, which can be taken and spent. In other years, a bull market means ample capital gains that can be liquidated for retirement spending instead, especially in times of low yields from interest and dividends. In "bad" years, it may be preferable to tap principal, in order to leave the rest of the portfolio invested for a hopeful future rebound. In fact, diversification across the four pillars of retirement income can be a highly effective way to protect against the potential stressors that can adversely impact a retirement plan.

Notably, it's crucial to recognize that not all retirement "income" is actually *taxable* income. In fact, the process to optimize the tax-efficient liquidation of retirement accounts is entirely separate, including determining when to tap taxable vs pre-tax (IRA) vs tax-free (Roth) accounts, proper asset location of available investment assets across the different types of retirement accounts, as well as ongoing tax-efficiency strategies like the timing of harvesting capital gains and losses and engaging in systematic partial Roth conversions.

In fact, arguably when thinking about a retirement portfolio, it's better to think in terms of "retirement cash flows" than retirement income, as what constitutes "income" for investment purposes (interest and dividends, but not principal) is different than what constitutes "income" for tax purposes (as interest and dividends might be tax-free coming from a Roth, while principal may be fully taxable if withdrawn from a pre-tax retirement account).

In other words, while it's necessary to consider (and possible to optimize) the tax treatment of income, ultimately the purpose of the retirement portfolio is to generate the *cash flows* on a total return basis to satisfy the retiree's spending needs, regardless of whether the Internal Revenue Code calls it "principal", "income", "taxable", or "tax-free".

Risks Of The Traditional "Income" Approach

Notwithstanding the shift in thinking and research about retirement income from portfolios over the years, it's notable that a material segment of retirement investors still focus on a "traditional" income-based approach to retirement, with a focus on investing for interest and dividends.

As noted earlier, the first challenge of this approach is that it completely ignores the other two pillars of capital gains and principal. While some might simply argue that leaving the principal untouched and letting capital gains be a bonus is simple conservatism, the sheer magnitude of their potential introduces a risk that the retiree *drastically* underspends relative to the lifestyle that the portfolio could afford. As is, even a total return approach already leaves a high likelihood of not touching principal until the last decade of retirement.

However, the situation is clearly further complicated in today's environment due to the low absolute level of yields, including both dividend yields and bond interest rates. In turn, this can lead retirees to "stretch for yield", which typically entails an increase in risk, as bond investors must either buy longer-term bonds (increasing interest-rate risk) or lower quality bonds (increasing default risk) to get more yield. Similarly, stock investors looking for better yields by focusing on the highest-dividend-paying stocks typically end up concentrating the portfolio into narrow sectors, which introduces new risks as well; after all, financials were the highest dividend-paying sector of the mid-2000s (right up until they weren't, when the financial crisis unfolded in 2008!), and in today's environment, the top-paying dividend sectors also include utilities and basic materials (energy), both of which are now attracting warnings as valuations move to historically dangerous levels. In the meantime, as investors have stretched for yield in bonds and dividend-paying stocks, the S&P 500 is up over 200% from the market bottom in 2009.

But again, that's actually the whole point of relying on (all) four pillars of retirement income. You don't necessarily know which one will produce the desired results from year to year, but diversification gives you the best shot to get it from somewhere, without taking on excessive risk or portfolio concentration in stretching for yield along the way.

Originally published March 22, 2017; www.kitces.com/blog/four-pillars-retirement-income-portfolios-interest-dividends-capital-gains-principal.

ABOUT MICHAEL KITCES

Michael E. Kitces, MSFS, MTAX, CFP®, CLU, ChFC, RHU, REBC, CASL, is a partner and the Director of Wealth Management for Pinnacle Advisory Group, a private wealth management firm located in Columbia, Maryland that oversees approximately $1.8 billion of client assets. In addition, he is the co-founder of the XY Planning Network, AdvicePay, and New Planner Recruiting, the former practitioner editor of the *Journal of Financial Planning*, the host of the *Financial Advisor Success* podcast, and the publisher of the e-newsletter The Kitces Report and the popular financial planning industry blog Nerd's Eye View through his website www.Kitces.com.

Beyond his website, Michael is an active writer and editor across the industry and has been featured in numerous print, radio, and television appearances. In addition, Michael has co-authored several books, including *The Annuity Advisor* with John Olsen (now in 3rd edition), the first balanced and objective book on annuities written for attorneys, accountants, and financial planners, and *Tools & Techniques of Retirement Income Planning* with Steve Leimberg and others.

Michael is one of the 2010 recipients of the Financial Planning Association's 'Heart of Financial Planning' awards for his dedication to advancing the financial planning profession. In addition, he has variously been recognized as financial planning's 'Deep Thinker', a 'Legacy Builder', an 'Influencer', a 'Mover & Shaker', part of the 'Power 20', and a 'Rising Star in Wealth Management' by industry publications.

Michael is also a co-founder of NexGen, a community of the next generation of financial planners that aims to ensure the transference of wisdom, tradition, and integrity, from the pioneers of financial planning to the next generation of the profession.

@MichaelKitces

Why Selling a Big Position of Puts the Day Before the Crash of '87 was a Great Trade

JIM O'SHAUGHNESSY

Tada Viskanta saw a series of tweets I did when reading about the new book, *A First Class Catastrophe* by Diana B. Henriques which chronicles the 1987 crash, the largest one-day crash in U.S. Market history and he urged me to write up my experience at the time. While I have not yet read the book, in my tweets I reminisced about what it felt like to me. I was 27 years old and had been investing—or more properly—speculating in the market since age 21.

At the time, I was using a much different methodology for determining buys and sells then I do now, and I had, for several weeks before the crash, been accumulating a large put position on the OEX, which represented the S&P 100. The OEX and XMI where popular with options traders of that era and had the greatest liquidity for the options tied to them. Going into the crash, I had a larger position in puts than at any other point in my nascent career. I was sweating bullets, as many of them were deeply out of the money and my worry was they would all expire worthless, leaving me with a huge loss.

When I was 27, I already believed in a series of indicators that were mostly accurate, but I also paid great attention to the news and what people were saying about the future direction of the market. I watched as the markets roiled on Friday, October 16th, with the Dow losing more than 4.6% of its value.

I then made what at the time looked like the biggest mistake of my trading career—about a half an hour before the market close on Friday,

476

reacting to assertions that the market's drop was way overdone and that we would see a huge snapback on Monday, I sold my entire put position.

Just so it really sinks in, I repeat, on the day before the biggest crash in history, I let my emotional reactions to what I was reading and hearing drive my behavior, and I sold every single put option that I had carefully accumulated over the previous several weeks.

Had I held, I would have made a not so small fortune. But I didn't. Indeed, I barely broke even on the entire trade. But as I reflected and wrote about this in my trading journal, I think that turned out to be the greatest trade in my life.

For that trade sent me down the road that led to where I am today—I concluded that my emotions were my worst enemy in the market and that listening to predictions from gurus and other prominent market forecasters was worse than useless, it was destructive. It also opened my eyes to how early reactions by the media to such momentous events are almost always spectacularly wrong. I still have many of the newspapers and Barron's from that time, as well as news magazines, etc. Re-reading them now shows how any early reaction is also primarily based upon emotions and utterly fails to put anything in correct context.

It was the best wakeup call I could have received. I resolved to begin searching for empirically supported investment strategies that withstood the test of time. It got me to understand that if I were to succeed over the long term, I had to match my investment strategy to my time horizon. If I had 30 or more years to go to achieve my goals, I thought I should find out which strategies performed the best over much longer periods of time and which had the highest base rates of success against their benchmarks.

Most importantly, it cemented in me that while in many areas of life emotions were great, in the world of investing they were your worst enemy. And that only an unwavering discipline, devoid of any emotional override, would win in the end. Over the 30 years since the crash, I have witnessed time and again some of the smartest people in the world undone by making emotional investment decisions based on very short-term events. This will never, ever change. Lest you think that rules-based, quantitative investing can solve this, think again. An analyst from a major Wall Street bank was visiting OSAM after the financial crisis and he noted that over 60% of quants overrode their models during the crisis.

Remaining unemotional in my time as a portfolio manager has been one of the hardest things I have done, and yet, well worth it over the longer term. Oddly, it took the agony I felt selling my huge put position the day before the crash to teach me that agony, let alone any other emotion, has no place in implementing a successful investing career.

Originally published September 19, 2017; jimoshaughnessy.tumblr.com/post/165518683994/why-selling-a-big-position-of-puts-the-day-before.

ABOUT JIM O'SHAUGHNESSY

Jim O'Shaughnessy is the Chairman and CEO of O'Shaughnessy Asset Management (OSAM). Also serving as the Chief Investment Officer of the firm, Jim is ultimately responsible for OSAM's investment strategies. He directs the Senior Portfolio Manager, Director of Research, and the Portfolio Management Team and helps to set the agenda for the team. He is also responsible for the development of OSAM's existing strategies and directs the team on idea generation and specific initiatives to improve the models and develop new factors and products.

Prior to founding OSAM, Jim was the Director of Systematic Equity at Bear Stearns Asset Management and a Senior Managing Director of the firm. Prior to Bear Stearns, he was the CEO and Chairman of O'Shaughnessy Capital Management (Netfolio).

Long recognized as one of America's leading financial experts and a pioneer in quantitative equity analysis, he has been called a "world beater" and a "statistical guru" by *Barron's*. In February 2009, Forbes.com included Jim in a series on "Legendary Investors" along with Benjamin Graham, Warren Buffett, and Peter Lynch.

Jim is the author of four books on investing: *Invest Like the Best*; *What Works on Wall Street*; *How to Retire Rich*; and *Predicting the Markets of Tomorrow*.

Jim has a B.A. in Economics from the University of Minnesota. He is married with three children and lives in Greenwich, Connecticut.

@jposhaughnessy